KARAC

LAURENT GAYER

Karachi

Ordered Disorder and the Struggle for the City

HURST & COMPANY, LONDON

First published in the United Kingdom in 2014 by
C. Hurst & Co. (Publishers) Ltd.,
41 Great Russell Street, London, WC1B 3PL

A Cataloguing-in-Publication data record for this book is available from the British Library.

ISBN: 978-1-84904-311-3

www.hurstpublishers.com

This book is printed on paper from registered sustainable and managed sources.

To the memory of Perween Rahman (1957–2013)

Let nothing be called natural in an age of bloody confusion, ordered disorder, planned caprice, and dehumanised humanity, lest all things be held unalterable!

Bertolt Brecht, *The Exception and the Rule* (1937).

CONTENTS

List of Figures, Tables and Maps xi
List of Images xiii
Acknowledgements xv
Note on Transliteration xix
Frequently Used Abbreviations xxi
Select Glossary of Urdu Terms xxiii

Introduction 1
The Enigma of Karachi's 'Ordered Disorder' 9
Scope, Sources and Structure of the Book 14

1. A Contested City 17
A City Up for Grabs 21
An Arena for National Conflicts 30
The Normalisation of the Unofficial 33
The Burden of Geography 41
A Palimpsest of Sovereignties 49
Conclusion 51

2. From Student Brawls to Campus Wars 53
Discontent Central: The Student Movement and Political Change in West Pakistan (1947–1979) 54
The Facilitating Factors of Political Violence 60
Predictable but Contingent: The First 'Political' Killing at Karachi University 66
Conclusion 76

3. 'The Mohajirs Have Arrived!' 79
The Unremarkable Beginnings of Mohajir Nationalism 81

The MQM, Between Party and Movement 90
The MQM's Challenged Predominance 100
Conclusion 119

4. The Bandits Who Would Be Kings 123
Lyari and Its *Dacoits* 127
The Volatility of Politico-Criminal Configurations 134
Rehman Dakait's Failed Transition from Crime to Politics 138
Bis Repetita? The PAC 2.0 and Rehman's Legacy 150
Conclusion 158

5. Jihad Comes to Town 163
A Secular City? 165
Sectarian Turf Wars 171
Towards the 'Talibanisation' of Karachi? 183
Conclusion 201

6. A City on the Edge 205
The Institutional Fabric of Karachi's Armed Conflicts 206
The Limits of Control 221
Conclusion 236

7. Geographies of Fear 239
City of Fear 241
Everyday Geographies of Fear 250
The Architecture of Safety 255
Conclusion 272

Conclusion 275

Notes 285
Selective Bibliography 325
Index 333

LIST OF FIGURES, TABLES AND MAPS

Figures

Fig. 1: Killings in Karachi by year (1994–2012) 10
Fig. 2: Mother tongue of the residents of Karachi (1981–2025) 25
Fig. 3: Pragmatic demands and ideological goals of the APMSO and MQM over the years 98
Fig. 4: Two generations of *dacoit*s in Lyari (1960s–2000s) 135
Fig. 5: Distribution of land ownership rights in Karachi 262

Tables

Table 1: Karachi's demographic growth (1729–2011) 26
Table 2: Share of migrants born outside Karachi in the city's total population (1921–1998) 27
Table 3: Vote share of major political parties in Karachi (Sindh Provincial Assembly elections) (1988–2013) 103

Maps

Map 1: Karachi map xxvi
Map 2: Karachi administrative map xxvii
Map 3: Spatial distribution of killings in Karachi (1995) 6
Map 4: Spatial distribution of killings in Karachi (2011) 8
Map 5: The main clusters of violence in Karachi (2011) 9
Map 6: Gang turfs and ethnic groups in Lyari (2008) 141
Map 7: Taliban influence in Karachi 191

LIST OF IMAGES

(Between pages 162–163)

Image 1: MacLeod Road (I.I. Chundrigar Road) in the early 1950s (Courtesy *Dawn*).

Image 2: MacLeod Road (I.I. Chundrigar Road) today.

Image 3: Paramilitary Rangers in front of the gates and wall constructed by the MQM in its stronghold of Azizabad, June 1992 (Courtesy *Dawn*).

Image 4: Army soldiers in Karachi after the launch of Operation Cleanup (June 1992) (Courtesy *Dawn*).

Image 5: An alleged torture cell of the MQM unearthed by the army in the course of Operation Clean-up (Courtesy *Dawn*).

Image 6: Afaq Ahmad and Amir Khan, the leaders of the MQM (Haqiqi), return to Karachi in June 1992 (Courtesy *Dawn*).

Image 7: Cover of a calendar issued by the MQM in 2001, with Altaf Hussain guiding the 'Mohajir Nation'. The slogan in Urdu reads: 'Rise! Gather your forces and be the arm of the leader.'

Image 8: Poster celebrating the 30th anniversary of the APMSO. The slogan in Urdu is a verse: 'In every circumstance, we have protected the garden [the nation].'

Image 9: A cover of the magazine edited by the APMSO, *Naqīb* (The Scout).

Image 10: Poster of the Sunni Tehrik celebrating the 'holy warrior of the nation' Mumtaz Hussein Qadri, the murderer of former Governor of Punjab Salman Taseer. Lines Area, 2011.

Image 11: Jihadist mural. Lyari, 2012.

Image 12: Demonstration organised by the Ahl-e-Sunnat wal Jama'at (formerly Sipah-e-Sahaba Pakistan). Saddar, 2011.

Image 13: Poster of the Peoples' Aman Committee (PAC), with the late Rehman 'Dakait' (left) and his successor at the head of the PAC, Uzair Baloch (right). The graffiti on the wall abuses the Sindh police, following an operation that targeted the leadership of the PAC. Lyari, 2012.

Image 14: Poster of the PAC, with the late Rehman 'Dakait' (right) and his successor at the head of the PAC, Uzair Baloch (left). Lyari, 2012.

Image 15: Poster issued by the PAC on the occasion of Independence Day 2012. Uzair Baloch (right) presents his respects to the army and the Rangers. At the bottom, the poster is 'signed' by notorious gangsters active in the locality of Khadda Market: Shiraz 'Comrade', Suni Bhai and Hafiz Kutchi. Lyari, 2012.

Image 16: Uzair Baloch hearing the plight of an elderly resident of his neighbourhood. Lyari, 2012.

Image 17: Uzair Baloch receiving Baloch elders in his palatial mansion. Lyari, 2012.

Image 18: Graffiti abusing the former MNA from Lyari: 'We cannot accept Nabeel [Gabol] the dog. Nabeel is a dog.' Lyari, 2012.

Image 19: 'Wall-chalking' by the Sunni Tehrik: 'We are all soldiers of the Sunni Tehrik.' Clifton, 2011.

Image 20: Entrance to a colony contested by the Sindhi nationalists of Jiye Sindh Qaumi Mahaz (JSQM) and the MQM. The banner above the gate proclaims that the neighbourhood is 'Altaf [Hussain]'s Fort'. Gulistan-e-Jauhar, 2011.

Image 21: Qasba Colony and Orangi seen from the hills of Kati Pahari, 2011.

Image 22: The 'border' between Urdu-speaking and Pashto-speaking localities in Kati Pahari/Qasba Colony. Notice the bullet holes riddling the walls, which are revealing of the intensity of the clashes that took place here during the summer of 2011, a few months before this picture was taken.

Image 23: Protective wall or *morcha* (shooting post)? Kati Pahari, 2011.

Image 24: Kati Pahari seen from the Qasba Colony side, 2010.

ACKNOWLEDGEMENTS

Drawing upon oral, textual and visual material collected during more than a decade of quasi-yearly fieldtrips to Karachi (2001–2013), this book is a testimony to the innumerable debts that I have accumulated over the years, starting with my long-time *ham qadam sathi* Christophe Jaffrelot, who was the first to suggest that I focus my attention, as a PhD candidate, on the ethnic and political fault lines of Karachi. My publisher, Michael Dwyer, was the driving force behind this book, inviting me to refocus my attention on Karachi at a time when I was drifting towards another domain of research. The successive consuls généraux of France in Karachi, Pierre Seillan and Christian Ramage, honoured me with their trust and occasionally with their hospitality, while sharing with me their intimate knowledge of the city and its politics. I am also grateful to Pierre Seillan for having introduced me to someone who rapidly became my *ustad* (mentor) in Karachi, Hidayat Hussain, who initiated me into Urdu poetry while being a constant source of knowledge and inspiration on all the topics that caught my attention over the years.

Asif Farrukhi also helped me pursue my interest in Urdu poetry and introduced me to the 'family' of Urdu scholars and lecturers who make the Bedil Library of Shareefabad such a unique literary institution. Its chief librarian, Muhammad Zubair, lived up to his reputation as a benevolent and immensely resourceful head of this small community. Publisher Ajmal Kamal was also a source of inspiration and one of the few persons I know who lived up to his dreams no matter what. Architect and urban planner Arif Hasan, for his part, made me benefit from his unrivalled knowledge of the city's history and sociology, forged by decades of research and activism. His former colleague at the Orangi Pilot Project (OPP), the late Perween Rahman, helped me understand better the changing realities of land supply in Karachi, and more generally the articulation between the 'official' and the 'unofficial' economy in the city—a distinction that I borrow from her. Her brutal death, in March 2013, came as a terrible shock and this book is dedicated to her memory.

Within the journalistic fraternity of Karachi, Ashraf Khan accompanied me on several difficult interviews, during which he always displayed an ironclad coolness, even when our interviewees came under fire, as was the case during our visit to the Markaz Ahl-e-Sunnat. Documentary film-maker Aziz Sanghur introduced me to Lyari and other Baloch settlements of Karachi, helping me widen the scope of my research by making me more aware of the 'indigenous', non-Mohajir Karachi, of its struggles for survival and distinctive cultural make-up. Ahmed Wali Mujeeb and Zia ur Rehman never ceased to impress me with their knowledge of Karachi's Pashtun communities, while Mahim Maher helped me get acquainted with the Pashtun residents and political workers of Kati Pahari, no matter how bumpy the road to the 'cut mountain' proved to be. Nadeem F. Paracha, for his part, was a wonderful guide in my exploration of Karachi's student politics and popular culture in the 1960s and 1970s. I am also grateful to Zaffar Abbas, the Editor of *Dawn*, for allowing me to reproduce some photographs published over the years in the newspaper.

Among my researcher colleagues, Farhan Hanif Siddiqi regularly updated me on student politics at the University of Karachi and kindly shared some of his research material with me. Nida Kirmani accompanied me during most of my visits to Lyari in August 2012 and helped me revise some of my initial assumptions in the face of empirical evidence. Her sister and brother-in-law, Najia and Aasim Siddiqi, as well as their brilliant children, Samaa, Kiran and Rayan, were incomparable hosts and, along with Aarij and Tasneem Kirmani, made Eid-ul-Fitr 2012 one of my most pleasant and gastronomically fulfilling experiences ever in Pakistan. My geographer colleagues at the Centre de Sciences Humaines (CSH), Rémy Delage and Olivier Telle, helped me in the preparation of graphs and pie charts, while Bertrand Lefebvre designed the maps of the book, displaying admirable patience in the face of my repeated hesitations. Gilles Favarel-Garrigues, at the Centre d'études et de recherches internationales (CERI), as well as Karen Barkey at Columbia University, provided me with valuable comments on the sections dealing with Lyari's bandits, while Mariam Abou Zahab, at CERI, was a constant source of encouragement and an unparalleled fount of knowledge on Islamist networks in Karachi and Pakistan at large. Nichola Khan, at the University of Sussex, taught me that Mohajir militancy was also a labour of love, and her contacts in Karachi proved to be immensely beneficial to this study. Last but not least, I owe a great deal to the three referees who commented upon the first draft of the manuscript. Mastering the art of maieutics, these inspiring readers helped me bring forth arguments that were only latent in the earlier draft.

During my stay in Delhi, between 2010 and 2013, Maulana Waris Mazhari assisted me in the translation and exploitation of the oral and printed Urdu material used throughout the book. Besides his erudition, his warmth and humour made our long working sessions truly exhilarating moments. At CERI, Irina Vauday and Miriam Perier helped me finalise the revised version of the manuscript, patiently searching for the devil in the details.

My earliest visits in Karachi benefited from the support of the French Ministry of Education and Research and the Fondation nationale des sciences politiques, where I was *allocataire* during the first three years of my PhD research (1998–2001). The Centre de Sciences Humaines, under its successive directors, Véronique Dupont and Basudeb Chaudhuri, was the major financial support behind my following field trips, besides the Agence nationale de la recherche (ANR), under the research group Conflits Turquie-Iran-Pakistan (Conflits-TIP), coordinated by Gilles Dorronsoro.

Most of all, my gratitude goes to my wife Mayuka and our daughter Anju for their joie de vivre and for being the most critical readers of them all, never hesitating to speak their mind, sometimes even in polychromy, all across the pages of my successive manuscripts.

NOTE ON TRANSLITERATION

For matters of clarity and since this text does not only target specialists of Pakistan, I have followed a simplified system of transliteration of Urdu words, which omits to signal long vowels as well as retroflex consonants in the main text. The letter xe (خ) was transcribed as 'kh', the letter ğain (غ) as 'gh', the letter šīn (ش) as 'sh' and the letter ' ain (ع) as ‘. Diacritical marks (*hamza*) are omitted and *izafas* are transliterated as '–e–'.

I have retained a more academic system of transliteration, signalling long vowels, for the titles of referenced Urdu texts only.

آ	ā	ط	t
ب	b	ظ	z
پ	p	ع	‘
ت	t	غ	gh
ٹ	t	ف	f
ث	s	ق	q
ج	j	ک	k
چ	ch	گ	g
ح	h	ل	l
خ	kh	م	m
د	d	ن	n
ڈ	d	و	v, w, o or ū
ذ	z	ہ. ـہ	ah
ر	r	ھ	h
ڑ	r	ی	ī, y
ز	z	ے	e
ژ	s	س	s
ش	sh	ص	s
ض	z		

FREQUENTLY USED ABBREVIATIONS

ANP	Awami National Party (National Popular Party)
APMSO	All Pakistan Mohajir Students Organisation
ASWJ	Ahl-e-Sunnat wal Jama'at (The Organisation of the Followers of the Tradition)
BSO	Baloch Students Organisation
CDGK	City District Government of Karachi
CJP	Chief Justice of Pakistan
CML	Convention Muslim League
COAS	Chief of Army Staff
CPP	Communist Party of Pakistan
DSF	Democratic Students Federation
FIR	First Information Report
IGP	Inspector General of Police
IJI	Islami Jamhoori Ittehad (Islamic Democratic Alliance)
IJT	Islami Jamiat-e-Tulaba (The Organisation of Islamic Students)
JeM	Jaish-e-Muhammad (The Army of Muhammad)
JI	Jama'at-e-Islami (The Islamic Organisation)
JSM	Jiye Sindh Mahaz (Front for the Protection of Sindh)
JSQM	Jiye Sindh Qaumi Mahaz (National Front for the Protection of Sindh)
JuD	Jam'at-ud-Dawa (Organisation for the Predication [of Islam])
JUI	Jamiat-e-Ulama-e-Islam (Society of the Islamic Ulama)
JUP	Jamiat-e-Ulama Pakistan (Society of the Ulama of Pakistan)
KDA	Karachi Development Authority
KESC	Karachi Electric Supply Corporation

KKF	Khidmat-e-Khalq Foundation (Foundation for the Welfare of the People)
KMC	Karachi Municipal Corporation
KRC	Kutchi Rabita Committee (Kutchi Coordination Committee)
KU	Karachi University
LJ	Lashkar-e-Jhangvi (Jhangvi's Army)
MDM	Muttahida Deeni Mahaz (United Islamic Movement)
MIT	Mohajir Ittehad Tehrik (United Mohajir Movement)
MMA	Muttahida Majlis-e-Amal (United Action Council)
MNA	Member of National Assembly
MPA	Member of Provincial Assembly
MQM	Mohajir Qaumi Movement (Mohajir National Movement; until 1997)/Muttahida Qaumi Movement (United National Movement; since 1997)
NAP	National Awami Party (National Popular Party)
NSF	National Students Federation
OPP	Orangi Pilot Project
PAC	Peoples Aman Committee (Peoples Peace Committee)
PkSF	Pakhtun Students Federation
PML	Pakistan Muslim League
PML-(N)	Pakistan Muslim League (Nawaz)
PPP	Pakistan Peoples Party
PSF	Peoples Student Federation
PTI	Pakistan Tehrik-e-Insaf (Pakistani Movement for Justice)
SITE	Sindh Industrial Trading Estate
SLGO	Sindh Local Government Ordinance
SSP	Sipah-e-Sahaba Pakistan (The Army of the Companions of the Prophet—Pakistan)
ST	Sunni Tehrik (The Sunni Movement)
TTP	Tehrik-e-Taliban Pakistan (Movement of the Pakistani Taliban)
USM	United Students Movement

SELECT GLOSSARY OF URDU TERMS

aam admi	common man
akhlaq	ethics/social etiquette
alim; pl. *ulama*	Islamic scholar(s)
aman	peace
amir	leader of a religious group
badmash	rogue
banya	member of Hindu trading castes
baqa	survival
bara admi	big man
basti	unofficial neighbourhood
bhatta	protection money
biraderi	lit. 'fraternity'; patrilineal descent group in the Punjab
bori band lash	corpse wrapped up in a body bag
chapati	unleavened flat bread
dacoit	bandit
dahshatgard	terrorist
dallal	middleman/pimp
dhandli	forgery
fatwa	religious edict
faza	environment
fitra	Islamic tax payed at the end of the fast of Ramadan
gali	lane
ghazal	classical poetic form expressing the pain of loss or unrequited love
ghunda	hoodlum
goth	urban village
halat	situation

hangama	riot
hartal	strike
iftar	meal following the rupture of the fast during Ramzan
imambargah	Shia place of worship
jama'ati	JI activist
jang	war
janissar	bodyguard
jannat	paradise
jhuggi	hut
jirga	tribal assembly among the Pashtuns and the Baloch
jiyala	PPP activist
julus	religious procession
kafir	unbeliever
karachiwala	Karachiite
karkun	activist
katchi abadi	residential area unofficially developed on state land
klashni	Kalashnikov
laqab	honourific title for political leaders
lashkar	tribal militia
lassi	yogurt-based drink
londe, *lipare*	backstreet boys
madrasa	Quranic school
mahdi	the prophesised redeemer of Islam who will rule the world before the Day of Judgment
markaz	headquarters
maslak	school of Islamic jurisprudence
mazlum	oppressed
Mohajir(s)	ethnic group mainly composed of Urdu-speakers and to a lesser extent of Gujarati-speaking trading communities (Memons, in particular), which came into being during the 1980s around the MQM
mohalla	neighbourhood
morcha	shooting post
muhajir pl. *muhajirin*	'the migrants'; first-generation refugees from India
musha'ira	recital of poetry
namaz	prayer
naib nazim	deputy mayor

nazim	mayor
parda	lit. 'curtain'; fig. seclusion/veiling
pir	Sufi religious figure of authority
qabila	tribe
qaum	nation/ethnic group/religious community
qaumiyat	nationality
qazi	Islamic judge
quaid	leader
quaid-e-azam	the great leader (Muhammad Ali Jinnah's *laqab*)
quaid-e-tehrik	leader of the movement (Altaf Hussain's *laqab* within the MQM)
qabza	lit. capture; fig. land grabbing
qurbani	sacrifice
riyasat	the state
roti	Punjabi variant of *chapati*s
sardar	Baloch tribal leader
shahid	martyr
sharif; pl. *ashraf*	noble(s)
sifarish	recommendation
suba	province
tabqa	social class
*takfiri*s	radical Islamists accusing secular regimes and large sections of society of apostasy
talib; pl. *tulaba*	student(s)
tehrik	movement
thana	police station
urf	alias; nom de guerre
zakat	alms-giving; one of the pillars of Islam
zulm	tyranny

Map 1: Karachi map

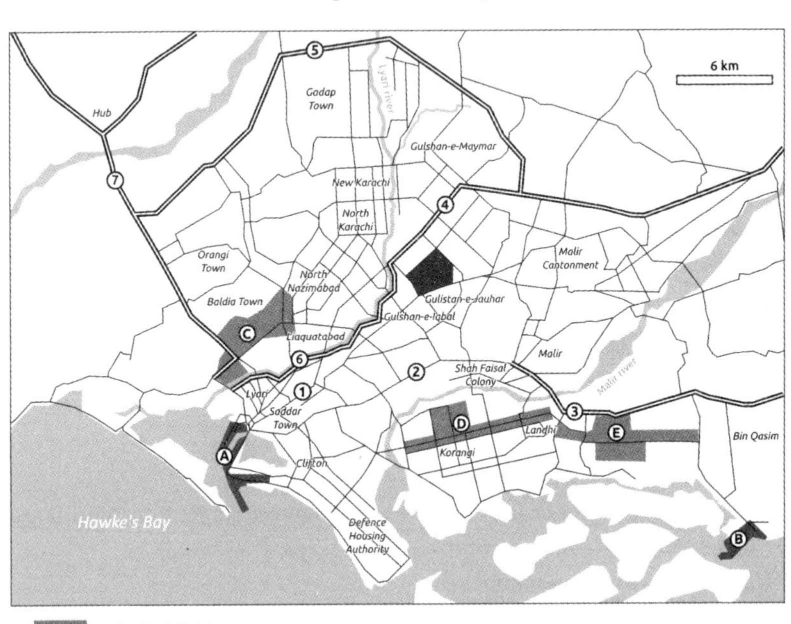

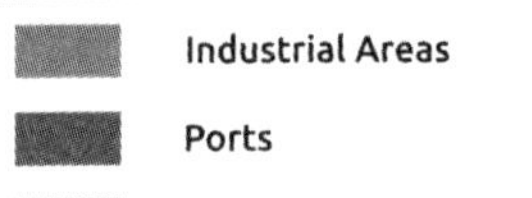

Main Roads — Highways

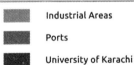

Sites
A: Karachi Port
B: Bin Qasim Port
C: SITE Industrial Area
D: Korangi Industrial Area
E: Landhi Industrial Area

Roads
1: M.A. Jinnah Road
2: Sharah-e-Faisal
3: National Highway
4: Super Highway
5: Northern Bypass
6: Lyari Expressway
7: RCD Highway

Sources: openstreemap.org

Map 2: Karachi administrative map

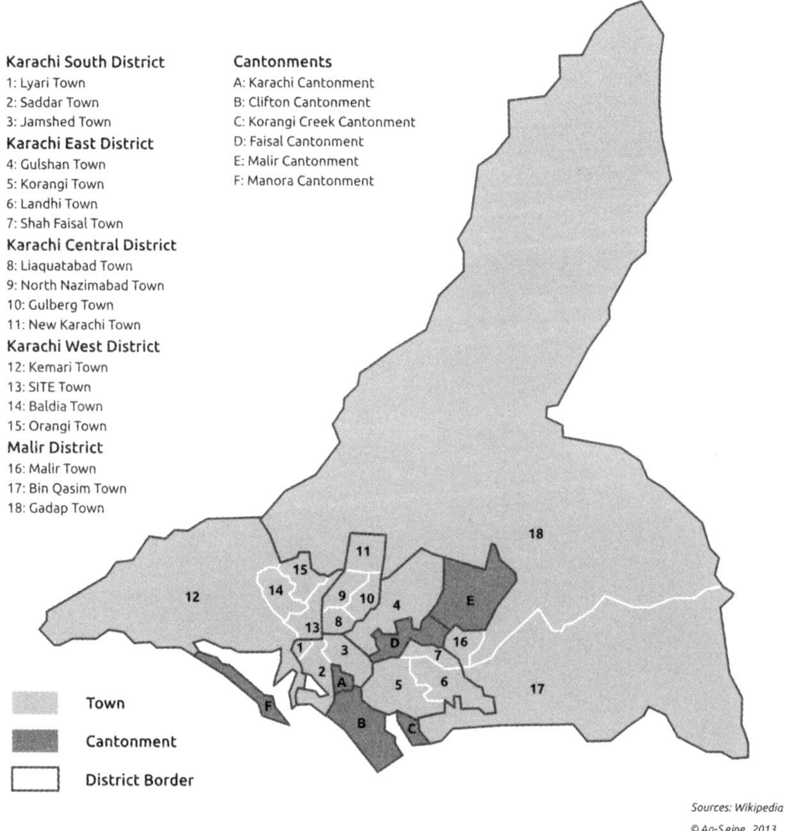

N.B. The five districts of the Karachi Division were merged into a single Karachi District by the Sindh Local Government Ordinance (SLGO) 2001. However, they were restored by the Sindh government in July 2011.

INTRODUCTION

Har roz shehr mein
Idhar, udhar jate hue

Sab ko dar lagta hai
Kahin koi ati hui goli
Hamen na mar de
Jinhen golian lagti hain
Voh mar jate hain ya zakhmi hokar

Aspatal mein apni bari ka intezar karte hain
Har roz maut ki khabren
Har roz jali hui garion ke dher

Akhbar
Phuljhari ki tarah
Subhe se sham tak
Hamare hathon mein chutta rahta hai
Marne wallon marta dekhkar
Ab hamari ankhon se pani nahin bahta
Hamare dilon mein dard ke bajae
Dhuvan bhar gaya hai […]

Everyone in the city,
while attending to business
everyday,
is afraid
of getting hit
by a stray bullet.
Those who get hit,
either they die or, laying
wounded,
wait for their turn in hospitals.
Every day, death in the news.
Every day, piles of charred car
wrecks.
The newspaper,
in the manner of a firecracker,
from dawn till dusk,
blows in our hands.
Now, when we look at the dead,
tears no longer come to our eyes.
Instead of pain, our hearts
are filled with smoke […]

Zeeshan Sahil, 'Ek Dīn' (One Day) (1995).[1]

Every city has its back pages: its trivialities, so banal that newsreaders don't pay heed to them, and yet so scented with local aromas, be it the reek of the gutter or the stench of the morgue. The French refer to these columns made up of filler items as the *rubrique des chiens écrasés* (lit. 'the column of ran over dogs'). In Karachi, Pakistan's turbulent metropolis and one of the largest cities in the world, with a population estimated at 21.2 million in 2011,[2] ran over dogs have been replaced by bullet-riddled bodies stashed in gunny bags (*bori band lash*), a trademark of the city's three-decade-old armed conflicts, whose daily numbers are widely acknowledged as Karachi's most reliable political barometer. Probably the most iconic artefact to have emerged from Karachi's killing fields, the *bori band lash* also became a source of inspiration for painters[3] and writers reflecting upon their city's predicament. As the body count kept on rising, from the mid-1980s onwards, Karachi's poets, in particular, started mulling over the false sense of normalcy—the 'apparent normality of the abnormal'[4]—that went along this embedding of death and disorder in the Karachiites' everyday life. Since the creation of the country in the tumult of the 1947 Partition, poetry occupies an important place in everyday life and state-citizens interactions in Pakistan. This is particularly true in Karachi, which in the years following Partition became a predominantly Urdu-speaking city, with the arrival of hundreds of thousands of Muslim 'refugees' from India (the *muhajirin*, a Quranic term institutionalised by the 1951 Census,[5] which was appropriated by the descendants of these migrants in the course of the 1980s, a period during which this population reinvented itself as the 'Mohajirs').[6] As Ralph Russell, the dean of Urdu studies, underlines, the traditions of Urdu poetry, and in particular of the *ghazal*, 'are part and parcel of the whole outlook of the Urdu-speaking community'.[7] In postcolonial Karachi, it became a key element in the cultural make-up of this migrant population, but also a channel of communication with the nascent state as well as a powerful tool of mobilisation. In the context of the housing crisis that affected the city after Partition, for instance, some of these refugees applying for 'evacuee properties' tried to give more weight to their request by including a few Urdu verses (by the late Mughal poet Mirza Ghalib, in particular) to their letter of application.[8] In the following decades, poets provided successive generations of protesters with catchy, ironic or dramatic rhymes, challenging authority in various registers. And when Karachi was engulfed in a spiral of ethnic and political strife, from the mid-1980s onwards, Urdu poets were among the most prolific and incisive chroniclers of the city's plight, as exemplified by Zeeshan Sahil's verses reproduced above.

Zeeshan Sahil (1961–2008) was an avant-garde poet born in Hyderabad (Sindh) in a family of post-Partition Urdu-speaking migrants from

India, who spent most of his adult life in Karachi. The poems gathered in *Karāchī aur Dūsrī Nazmen* (*Karachi and Other Poems*) were written between May and August 1995, a year when political violence reached an unprecedented level in Karachi, with 1,742 killings, many of them politically motivated.[9] Combining, in the words of one of their translators, 'the child's fairy-tale wonder and the adult's hardened cynicism',[10] these poems convey the sense of fear that gripped the inhabitants of a city turned into a battleground for rival armed groups competing for votes, land, jobs and *bhatta* (protection money). Every morning, *Karachi-wala*s would wake up to macabre news of more *bori band lash*—a practice that was apparently borrowed from the police by the henchmen of the political parties competing for control of the city.[11] Sahil's simple, straight-to-the-point verses also suggest how, as in other chronically violent cities such as those of Colombia in the 1980s and 1990s,[12] violence came to be routinised within a 'chronic state of emergency'.[13] By the mid-1990s, violence—even extreme violence, including massacres of civilians, acts of torture and mutilations—no longer belonged to the realm of the extraordinary for the residents of Karachi, but rather to that of the uncanny. Still strange and fearful, yet awfully familiar, violence was brought home—sometimes literally, for parents worrying at their sons' political activities or at the possibility that relatives be caught up inadvertently in banal and yet potentially deadly incidents of rioting (*hangama*).[14]

One illustration of this routinisation of violence was the ironical renaming of the violence-torn locality of Gulbahar (lit. spring flowers) as Golimar (lit. gunfire) by its residents. This act of renaming goes back to the colonial period, when the British opened a firing range in the locality.[15] Today, most residents of Karachi are unaware of this, though. To them, 'Golimar' evokes the armed clashes that erupted here on an almost daily basis in the mid-1990s between the police and the militants of the Muttahida Qaumi Movement[16] (formerly Mohajir Qaumi Movement—MQM), Karachi's dominant party since the late 1980s, which claims to represent Urdu-speaking Mohajirs (who were thought to constitute around 44 per cent of the city's total population in 2011; cf. Fig 2). As this act of renaming suggests, the residents of Karachi, especially in the most violence-prone localities, gradually became accustomed to violence. The *savoir faire* that they developed in the process was an instrument of social navigation in a dangerous environment, as exemplified by the use of codes by local entrepreneurs to carry on working in the city's war zones. Knowing where to horn, turn the headlights on or flash the beam—signals used to distinguish friend from foe by neighbourhood militants—would make the difference between those living through the day and those ending up in a gunny bag.[17] It should be noted, however, that such chronically violent social configurations retain a part of uncertainty and a fluidity that prevent routines for the management of violence from evolving into a full-blown habitus.[18] And while Karachi's multifarious violence resembles that of some Colombian cities such as Medellin, in the latter case violence receded from 2002 onwards after the paramilitaries agreed to demobilise (out of fear of being prosecuted locally or extradited to the United States for their involvement in the drug trade).[19] On the contrary, there seems to be no end in sight to Karachi's conflicts. After a few years lull, political violence escalated once again from 2007 onwards and 'target killings' continue to make hundreds of victims every year, while 'riots'—a somewhat misleading term that tends to depoliticise these short-lived but deadly forms of collective action[20]—shut down the city on a regular basis, every six months or so, each time claiming dozens of lives.

For the residents of Karachi, including the barricaded city elites, violence has become part of the order of things. This is not to say that violence has become acceptable to *Karachiwala*s, but simply that they cannot imagine a future without it. This is for instance what Asif,*[21] a middle-aged Urdu-speaking resident of Orangi Town (one of Asia's largest unofficial settlements and the epicentre of political and criminal violence in Karachi since the mid-1980s), replied after I asked him if he saw some end in sight to the violence affecting his locality: 'No, I don't see peace coming in the future... it will be very difficult... because most people don't have any affection for each other [*koi ek dusre ko pasand karte hi nahin, zyadatar*]... so tensions will remain and the next generation will have to live with that.'[22]

The lasting contribution of 'political' and 'criminal' violence—two categories that cannot be taken for granted—to the fabric of Karachi has earned the city the reputation of a 'South Asian Beirut',[23] drifting towards chaos. As the memory of the Lebanese civil war faded away among audiences, this analogy was dropped in favour of a more global construction. Karachi earned the title of 'the world's most dangerous city',[24] attracting in the process a new blend of maverick journalists searching for a thrill and, if possible, a gunfight.[25] This title was won in the most unfair way, as Karachi is only the most violent of the *largest* cities in the world, with a murder rate of 12.3 per 100,000 habitants in 2011 (still well behind smaller cities with a 100+ murder rate, such as Caracas and Guatemala City).[26] Nevertheless, this reputation now sticks to the city and Karachiites themselves sustain it by deploring the great 'commotion' (*inteshar*), the 'chaos' (*khalfashar*) or the 'lawlessness' (*laqanuniyat*) that prevails in their city.

And yet, despite this chronic state of violence, Karachi remains the jewel in the Pakistani crown: the first source of tax revenue in the country (it accounts for 54 per cent of central government tax revenues and 70 per cent of national income tax revenue, which means that it generates $21 million in daily tax revenues),[27] it contributes around 25 per cent of Pakistan's gross domestic product (GDP), handles 95 per cent of the country's international trade, contributes 30 per cent to its manufacturing sector, and holds 50 per cent of its bank deposits.[28] This enduring centrality of Karachi in Pakistan's economy suggests that its chronic state of disorder has attained some degree of sustainability. Against media reports describing Karachi as chaotic and ungovernable,[29] I argue that there is indeed order of a kind—patterns of domination, rituals of interaction, forms of arbitration—in Karachi's 'continuous civil war'.[30] Far from being entropic, Karachi's polity is predicated upon routines of organisation, interpretation and action that have made violence manageable, both at the level of the city at large and at the micro-level of its populations.[31] Whether this state of 'ordered disorder' will remain sustainable on the long run remains to be seen, but for now Karachi works *despite* and sometimes *through* violence.

Karachi's predicament stands out from the situations of chaos affecting war-torn societies where social change is too rapid for domination to become sustainable, thus precluding the institutionalisation of politics and society in a context of chronic uncertainty. In such contexts, such as that of Guinea Bissau studied by Henrik Vigh, 'the players are constantly changing (both affiliations and configurations), and the demarcated space for the game is constantly in flux'.[32] This is not the case in Karachi, where the players and the terrains of their confrontation have shown a significant level of continuity since the mid-1980s. Among the ten most violent towns in 2011 (cf. Map 4), four were already major sites of violence in 1995 (Orangi in the west; New Karachi in the north; Korangi in the south-east; Garden/Lines Area in the city centre; cf. Map 3). This conti-

Map 3: Spatial distribution of killings in Karachi (1995)

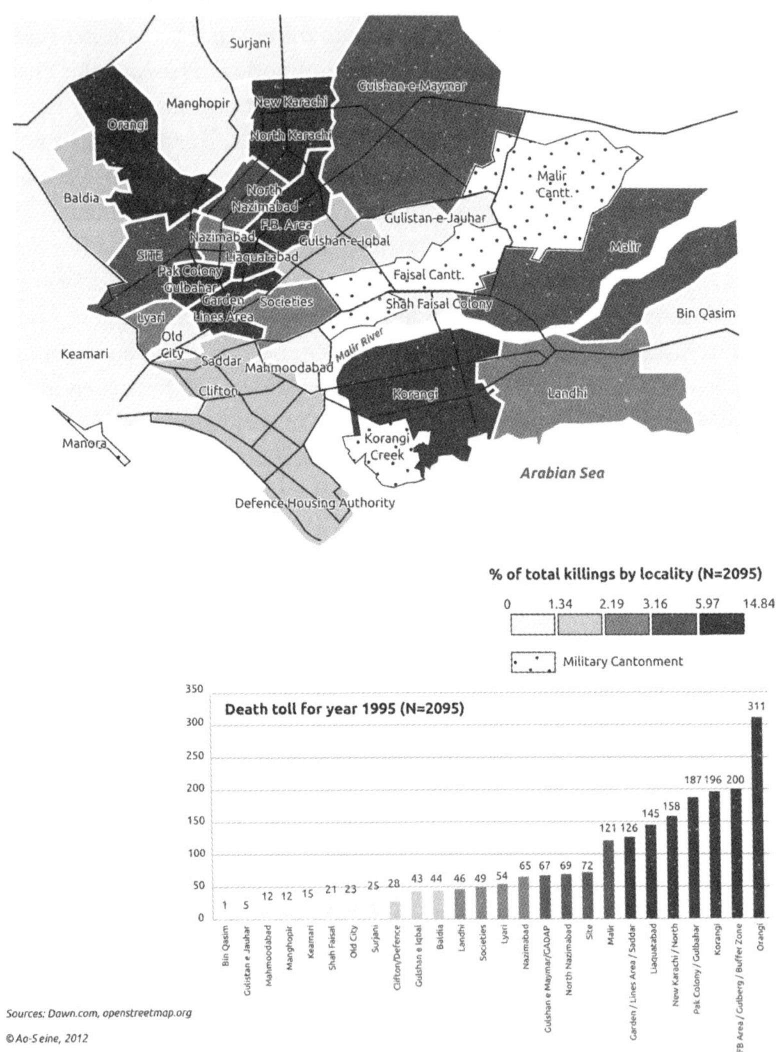

N.B. The death toll for 1995 gathered from *The Herald* is slightly higher than the more conservative estimates of the CPLC used for Fig. 1.

nuity goes back further than 1995. The most dangerous part of the city in 2011–2012 was the zone covered by the Pirabad police station in SITE Town. It includes localities such as Banaras Chowk, Aligarh Colony and Qasba Colony, which were on the frontline of Karachi's first major 'ethnic riots' in 1985–1986. Between 1 January 2011 and 31 August 2012, this particular police station registered more political killings (140) than the entire city of London registered general murder cases during the same period.[33] True, important variations must be factored in when considering these two peaks of violence. In 1995, besides Orangi, violence was concentrated on Mohajir-dominated localities disputed by the two factions of the MQM (Malir, Korangi, Federal B Area, Liaquatabad, Gulbahar,...), whereas the spatial distribution of violence in 2011 was revealing of the emergence of new protagonists in Karachi's battles: Sunni sectarian groups fighting among themselves (in New Karachi/North Karachi) and Baloch criminals with political ambitions, challenging the hegemony of the MQM (in Lyari and the Old City). Some regular patterns emerge nonetheless, such as the centrality of the MQM in these battles for the city and, despite its clustering around certain areas, the geographic dispersion of violence. If Orangi, the largest unofficial settlement in Karachi, with a high level of ethnic mixity, remains Karachi's most volatile area since the mid-1980s, the homicidal violence plaguing the city is irreducible to slum wars and has also affected middle-class areas (Federal B Area, parts of Gulshan-e-Iqbal,...), while upper-class neighbourhoods were not completely immunised (the Darakshan police station, which covers the residential area of Clifton, registered ten political killings between 1 January 2011 and 31 August 2012).[34] This violence is semi-peripheral: out of the seven major clusters of violence in 2011, six were located in a 7–20 km. radius from the city centre, drawing a 'ring of fire' around the city (cf. Map 5). In 2011, these major clusters of violence accounted for 47 per cent of the murders registered across the city while accounting for 3.5 per cent of the total urban area of Karachi and 8.4 per cent of its total population only.[35] However, the former colonial centre (Saddar, Garden, Lines Area) and the Old City (Kharadar, Mithadar) were not spared either. Whereas Lines Area was a major site of intra-Mohajir violence throughout the 1990s, Kharadar and Lyari bore the brunt of the conflict between the MQM and the Peoples Aman Committee (PAC, the politico-military organisation set up in 2008 by Lyari's most famous Baloch 'bandit') in recent years. These enduring socio-spatial patterns of homi-

Map 4: Spatial distribution of killing in Karachi (2011)

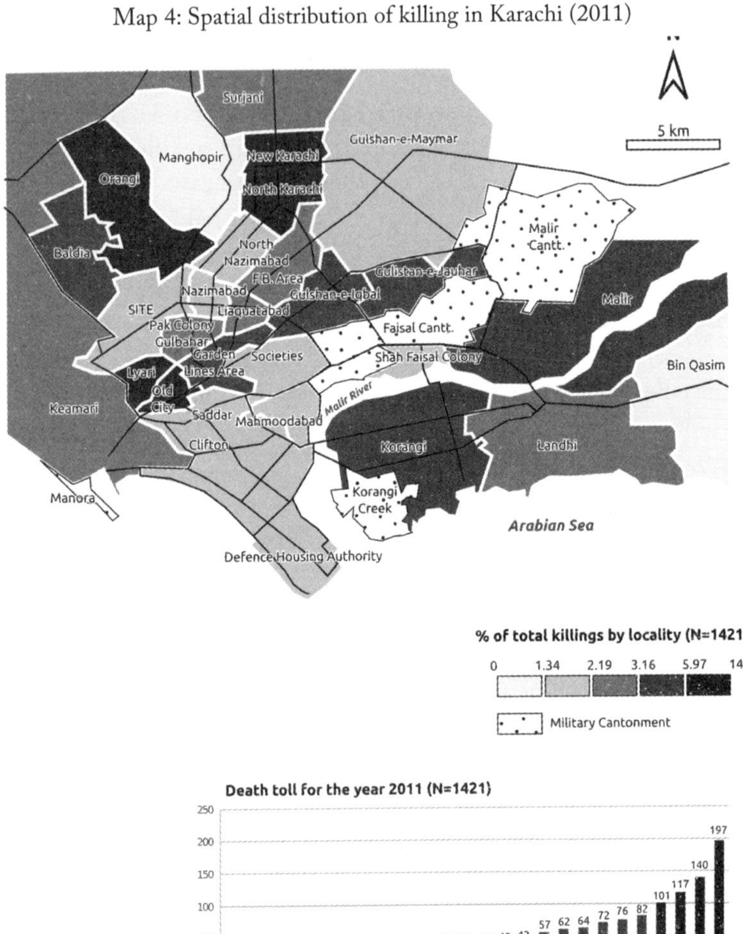

N.B. The death toll given here covers the period from 1 January to 31 August 2011, as the spatial distribution of the ninety-nine murders registered during the last four months of 2011 (CPLC estimate) could not be obtained from the CPLC despite repeated requests. The margin of error (6.5 per cent) is, however, acceptable.

Map 5: The main clusters of violence in Karachi (2011)

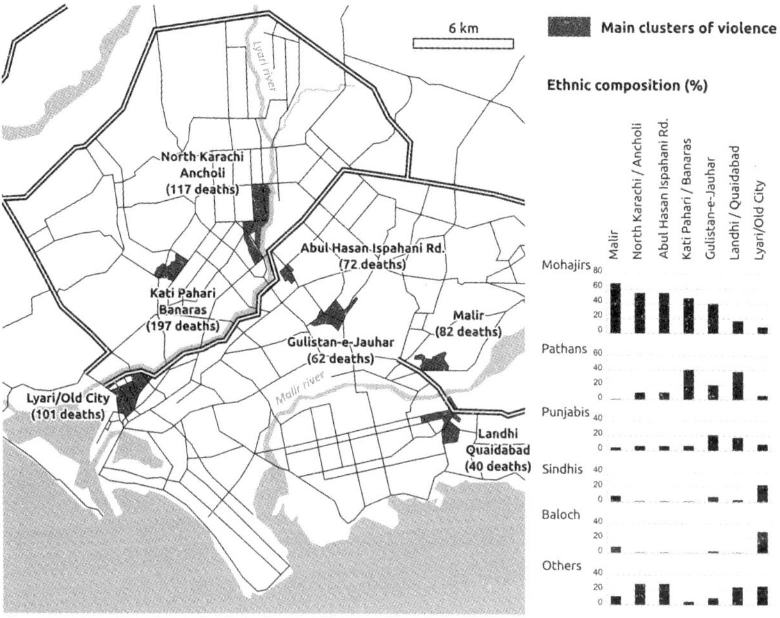

Sources: OpenStreetMap.org, The Herald, September 2011, Demographic figures based on 1998 census projection

© Ao-Seine, 2013

N.B. The death toll given here covers the period from 1 January to 31 August 2011, as the spatial distribution of the ninety-nine murders registered during the last four months of 2011 (CPLC estimate) could not be obtained from the CPLC despite repeated requests. The margin of error (6.5 per cent) is, however, acceptable.

cidal violence are a preliminary indication that there is more to Karachi's apparent state of chaos than meets the eye. The following pages are an attempt to pierce this veil of disorder. By distinguishing analytically between 'orderly' and 'ordered' social configurations, this book is also an experiment in deprovincialising our conceptualisations of social organisation in the face of Karachi's intriguing trajectory.

The Enigma of Karachi's 'Ordered Disorder'

Karachi's story of civil strife challenges conventional dichotomies between war and peace. Rather than a continuous process of violent escalation, it involves successive violent upsurges interrupted by periods of de-escalation and (uneasy) peace (cf. Fig. 1), an uneven trajectory that assimilates it to the 'no peace, no war' situations brought to light by Paul Richards.[36] Although the escalation of homicidal violence witnessed since 2007 is unprecedented in its intensity and duration, the episodes of collective violence that brought the city to a halt during this period never lasted more than three to four days and remained highly localised, without escalating into a general conflagration. The multiplication of 'target killings' since 2007 also bears testimony to the self-restraint of Karachi's belligerents, whose propensity to turn to violence to settle the score is only equalled by their ability to resume politics as usual as soon as the guns fall silent.

Karachi's armed conflicts rarely amount to a radical form of closure. More often than not, these conflicts do not pit ontological 'enemies' against each other, but past or even present 'friends': violent entrepreneurs and/or political parties which have been, remain or could become again coalition partners. However, the banality and self-restrained nature

Fig. 1: Killings in Karachi by year (1994–2012)

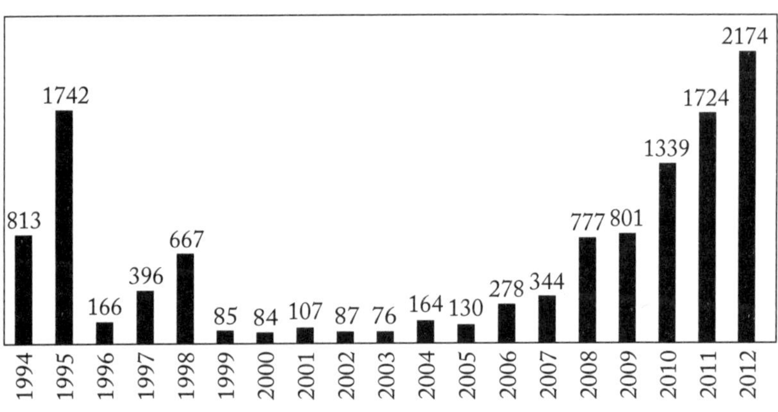

Source: Citizens-Police Liaison Committee (CPLC). The CPLC is a semi-official body launched in 1993 to monitor crime and register complaints from the public in Karachi, regarding kidnappings in particular. Its data are based on First Information Reports (FIRs) filed by the police and do not identify politically motivated killings specifically, although it is widely acknowledged that political and general violence are closely related.

of this 'friendly' violence (at least in quantitative terms) goes along the systematic recourse to atrocities against rivals. Both the political parties and the criminal groups involved in these turf wars have their own 'torture cells', where their henchmen detain, maim and kill opponents, 'traitors' and dissidents, before mutilating the bodies and dumping them in the streets of the city. Karachi's enigma of violence could thus be summarised as that of a megacity confronted with endemic forms of collective and targeted violence that remain contained within certain bounds (in time and space, as well as in terms of casualties) and, thus, do not preclude the existence of a democratic order and a thriving economy; and do not rely upon a 'Schmittian' ontology of conflict[37] informed by visceral hatreds between arch-enemies but involve violent performances without any parallel elsewhere in Pakistan, in terms of cruelty and 'creativity' in their macabre designs.[38]

It is this enigma that the present book aims at confronting, if not at elucidating. Drawing upon the sociology of Norbert Elias, I retrace the formation of a violent 'order sui generis'[39] in Karachi from the 1980s onwards, in a context of escalating student conflicts and fast-ethnicising urban struggles that paved the way for the rise of the MQM at the helm of city politics. In the following years, the predominance of the MQM brought some stability and predictability to a city otherwise characterised by its fragmentation and volatility. However, the resistance faced by the dominant party within and without the freshly imagined Mohajir community continued to feed violent conflicts that did not only compromise the attempts of the MQM to normalise itself but also contributed to the emergence of new politico-military forces contesting to the MQM and the state the monopoly over the use of coercion, representation and revenue collection. It is this peculiar social formation that I define here as 'ordered disorder', a formulation which, after anthropologist Michael Taussig, I borrow from Bertolt Brecht.[40] My understanding of this notion and its theoretical elaboration in the course of the book is slightly different from Taussig's, though. Building his argument upon an ethnography of state, guerrilla and paramilitary terror in Colombia in the 1980s, Taussig aimed to reflect upon the routinisation of terror in the context of a permanent state of exception.[41] Although Karachi's trajectory presents some striking similarities with the Colombian context studied by Taussig, as far as this normalisation of exception is concerned, my understanding of Karachi's ordered disorder is more expansive and refers to the complex ecology of violence co-produced by the city's belligerents in the course of their interactions.

This book moves away from a long tradition, whether in sociology or political science, equating social order with the control of violence and its gradual monopolisation by the state.[42] Instead, I understand the notion of 'order' more neutrally as the underlying principles (the rules of the game) of a historical *figuration*,[43] in Elias' sense of a 'game structure' organised around interdependent actors and reproducing itself through a 'fluctuating, tensile equilibrium',[44] which may accommodate a significant level of competition over the means of coercion. Even in situations of apparent chaos, social life acquires a 'very particular social form',[45] irreducible to the intentions of individuals and to the mere sum of their interactions. Against dominant theories of social organisation (especially Parsons' answer to the 'Hobbesian problem of order'),[46] Elias argued that every form of social order is by definition unplanned and emerges incrementally from human interdependence.[47] Drawing inspiration from this pioneering work, I regard Karachi's ordered disorder as the particular social form (the gestalt, in the sense of Elias) of a city subjected to the violent confrontation of competing aspirants to sovereign power, that is, of social and political forces contesting to each other the right to 'kill, discipline and punish with impunity'.[48] My approach converges, here, with recent works on 'emergent orders' in sub-Saharan Africa, which point at the (re-)structuring effects of protracted crises for the dispensation of authority, the allocation of resources or the shaping of the public sphere.[49] This conviction that war and civil strife are 'inescapably sociological'[50]—that they are components of social processes and that they are a matter and a factor of organisation—has important methodological repercussions. It pleads in favour of a study of conflict *in motion*, as it transforms its social environment and feeds on these societal changes, rather than *in intention*, through the fetishisation of root causes, background explanations and individual motivations. At the most, the latter may be conditions of possibility for violence and its escalation. But as the conflict intensifies, new variables come into play, disrupting or at least updating initial motivations, constraints and opportunities.[51] This 'metamorphosis of effect into cause',[52] key to the endogenous reproduction and escalation of collective violence, pleads against self-professed causal explanations in favour of more processual approaches attentive to its contingent and self-generative nature.

Disentangling the notion of order from the containment of violence opens rich analytical venues for the study of Karachi's transformations over the past three decades, challenging dominant interpretations of these transformations and of Pakistan's evolutions at large as a descent into chaos and anomie. However, since in this neutral acceptation at least, order does not equate with the containment of violence, the story of Karachi's tryst with ordered disorder only provides the context for a larger, and more complex question: how has a city subjected to successive cycles of violent escalation and polarisation over the past three decades somehow avoided a fully fledged explosion? This book does not claim to bring a definitive answer to this question. I share Michael Taussig's unease with the tendency of many social scientists working on conflict zones to search for an 'essential core to the dread',[53] in order to reintroduce coherence where 'actors' only see confusion ('Your disorder, my order', as Taussig puts it).[54] My account of Karachi's history of violent conflict tries to embrace this complexity and the ever increasing sense of insecurity of local populations. At the same time, it is possible—and necessary—to move beyond a purely ethnographic account of this regime of uncertainty in order to bring to light the regulatory mechanisms that, until now, have prevented Karachi's violent conflicts from escalating further into a general conflagration—what Paul Richards refers to as the 'institutional fabric to keep armed conflict within bounds over the long term'.[55] As we will see, four mutually reinforcing phenomena have been sustaining political strife in the city over the years while moderating it, setting the conditions for a fragile equilibrium:

1) The inability of any actor to totally dominate and establish a monopoly of violence *and* the ability of one actor (the MQM) to introduce a disequilibrium in interdependencies, which makes it less dependent on others than others towards it;
2) The propensity of this predominant party to 'rule on the edge', that is, to demonstrate and actualise its power through disruptive performances that draw their efficacy from their potential to run out of control. At the same time, the MQM's 'power over disorder' relies upon its capacity to restore order at short notice;
3) The advent of coalition politics that amount to a violent form of consociationalism, with political parties representing distinct ethnic groups forming coalition governments that are both a check on their

latent conflicts and a factor of confrontation, as these coalition partners compete for the control of the state and its resources; and
4) The repeated instances of state intervention (using the stick of repression or the carrot of patronage) to establish new, if inherently unstable, compromises between public and private aspirants to sovereignty.

Scope, Sources and Structure of the Book

Several fine-grained ethnographies of 'life on turf' in Karachi have been published over the past few years.[56] While engaging in a dialogue with this emerging body of work—and more generally with the anthropology of conflict and violence—this book departs from it by adopting a synoptic perspective which puts the city at large at the centre of its investigation. If some neighbourhoods of Karachi, such as Lyari, have received more attention than others in the following pages, it is not in a monographic perspective; rather, these particular towns were selected because, while presenting important singularities, they were the terrain of battles larger than them. The central argument of this book is precisely that Karachiites at large live under an architecture of conflictuality both patterned and disorderly, which does not exclude important neighbourhood effects deriving from the populating history of these localities and from their specific insertion into the city. And because social structures do not float into thin air, this book makes an attempt to map the impact of this social configuration of ordered disorder on the everyday struggles of Karachi's residents.

In this exploration of the patterns and routines of ordered disorder in Karachi, I primarily build upon a relative large corpus of semi-directive interviews (circa 200) conducted during nine field trips (totalling eight months of fieldwork) spread over a period of twelve years (2001–2013). These interviews were generally conducted in Urdu and, less frequently, in English, and although the bulk of them involved political activists (both political representatives and rank-and-file party workers), I also recorded a number of more independent voices from all social and ethnic backgrounds—with a predilection for social workers active in the most volatile areas of the city and confronted daily with the combined pressure of criminal elements and political parties. These oral sources were complemented by a study of party literature for internal consumption, both in prose and verse, by autobiographical accounts of party leaders and more ordinary (though generally middle-class) citizens, by Urdu poetic compositions concerned with Karachi's violent politics, and finally by an analysis of the local press since the mid-1980s (with a focus on two news magazines, *Newsline* and *The Herald*).

The book opens with an introductory chapter framing the structural conditions of Karachi's unending conflicts by locating these conflicts and their continuous transformation into five major developments in the city's postcolonial history: 1) the economic, cultural and political vacuum left by the departure of the city's non-Muslim elites after Partition; 2) the insertion of Karachi's conflicts into the battles for political supremacy in Pakistan at large; 3) the spectacular development of the unofficial economy and the resulting informalisation of the state in the face of successive waves of mass migration, whose disruptive effects were amplified by the absence of planification schemes addressing rapid demographic growth in a sound and socially cohesive way; 4) the dramatic transformations of the city's society and economy following the revival of its role as the antechamber of Afghan conflicts; and 5) the militarisation of its political arena and the emergence of de facto sovereign powers contesting to the state and to each other the monopoly over the use of force, over the representation of the city's populations and over revenue collection.

The four following chapters unfold Karachi's postcolonial history of violence and violent transformation, starting with the escalation of student conflicts at Karachi University (Chapter 2). The spectacular success of the MQM, in a context of escalating ethnic conflicts, redefined the rules of the political game in Karachi and gave birth to a system of domination best characterised as 'challenged predominance' (Chapter 3). Chapters 4 and 5 consider two of the major challenges that emerged in recent years to the MQM's predominance, in the shape of the Baloch political bandits of Lyari (Chapter 4) and the radical Islamist groups that have taken roots in the city, particularly in its Pashtun settlements (Chapter 5). Chapter 6 builds upon the evidence examined in the preceding chapters to address the burning question raised in the opening section of this introduction: after almost three decades of violent conflict and repeated sequences of escalation, how was Karachi spared a full-blown, free-for-all conflagration? Finally, Chapter 7 aims to map out the impact of this configuration of ordered disorder on Karachi's increasingly insecure populations.

1

A CONTESTED CITY

Jahan hamesha garbar rahti hai
[This city] where disorder is permanent.
Fahmida Riaz, *Karāchī* (1996).[1]

Karachi was not always synonymous with charred buses and mutilated bodies wrapped in gunny bags. The 'Guide to Karachi' distributed to American soldiers posted in the city during the Second World War described it as the 'Paris of the East' and the 'cleanest city in the whole of India', while praising its 'sea beach and bathing places'.[2] Many Karachi-ites who grew up in the 1950s and 1960s also remember the city as pleasant and secure—a safe haven where children would spend most of their time playing outside, where doors would be left unlocked and where women could go to see films and relish the latest Indian hits without chaperones. With its abundant fruit-bearing trees and ubiquitous butterflies, Karachi seemed like an idyllic place to live, as journalist Zinat Hisam recalls in her childhood memoirs.[3] Moreover, for the candidates to rapid upward social mobility, Karachi was brimming with opportunities. As Anwar Ehsan Siddiqi—another *muhajir*, who arrived in the city in the early 1950s as a teenager—writes in his own memoirs, Karachi was 'the city of free hard work' (*azad mehnat ka shehr*), where bonded labour was unknown of (unlike in interior Sindh) and where old tribal and *biraderi* bonds no longer dominated social interactions (unlike in the Frontier and the Punjab). Here was a city that belonged to 'the workers and the middle classes', where even women could have 'their first opportunity to breathe freely'.[4]

While these middle- and upper-class refugees remember those days as an 'era of serenity' (*pur sakun dor*),[5] Karachi also earned the reputation of a city that never slept. In the 1960s and early 1970s, it was known as the 'City of Lights', after Mehdi Hasan's hit song, '*Aye Roshnion ke Shehr Bata*' (Tell me, O City of Lights!), from a Pakistani film released in 1964, *Chingari*. This song describes the liveliness of Karachi's nightlife—although on a critical mode, to denounce its vulgarity—at a time when the city's colonial centre, Saddar, was famous for its restaurants, bars and nightclubs rather than as a high-security zone under constant threat from terrorist groups. This was a time when names such as 'Tony Casino'[6] had precedence over 'Nadeem Commando'[7] and the like. And even if these libations and distractions only concerned a tiny elite, they remain an important element in the imaginings of the city, for its older residents but also for city officials who obstinately continue to project Karachi as the 'City of Lights'[8]—even though this nickname has recently taken an ironical resonance, by alluding to the massive electricity shortfall of the city, resulting in frequent and prolonged episodes of 'load-shedding' that are increasingly accompanied by 'power riots'.

These nostalgic recollections of Karachi have in common their elitism, as they tend to occult the social conflicts that were brewing under the alleged serenity of the times. To a large extent, this serenity is a myth propelled by Karachi's Urdu-speaking elites, which does not find any historical validation.[9] Indeed, far from being as peaceful as these nostalgic elites claim, the 1950s saw the emergence of labour and student movements that only amplified in the following decade, despite state repression (the 1 March 1963 strike organised by SITE workers, for instance, was severely repressed and forty-two workers lost their life in police firing, according to labour leaders).[10] This restlessness of Karachi's working classes and students made the city a dreadful place for Pakistan's authoritarian elites, a reputation epitomised in another surname: the 'unsubdued city' (*shehr-e-shorida sar*).[11]

Karachi's 'lights' started waning in the late 1970s, when Zulfikar Ali Bhutto aimed at rallying conservative elements to his project of 'Islamic socialism' by enforcing a ban on all 'immoral' activities in Karachi, thus signing the death warrant of the bars and cabarets that had made Saddar's sulphurous reputation. Bhutto also severely repressed the labour movement in Karachi, a repression which culminated in an incident of police firing on 7 June 1972, which was followed by another similar incident the next day, during the funerals of one of the deceased workers. Ten people were killed on that day, which marked 'the beginning of the end of one of the most protracted labour struggles in Pakistan's history'.[12] A few months later, Karachi was engulfed by its second major episode of ethnic violence since Partition,[13] after Urdu-speaking and Sindhi-speaking students clashed with each other following the adoption of a bill promoting the use of Sindhi in the education system and the provincial administration.

Then came the Afghan Jihad, during which Karachi became—once again, a century and a half after the British ill-fated campaign in Afghanistan—the entry point for arms and ammunition destined to the *mujahidin*. A large part of these arms consignments were lost in transit and, in Karachi, ended up in the hands of drug traffickers, slumlords and student activists. First introduced on Karachi's campuses by the Thunder Squad, the armed wing of the Islami Jamiat-e-Tulaba (IJT, the student branch of the Jama'at-e-Islami [JI], Pakistan's largest Islamist party, which at the time benefited from the patronage of the Zia-ul-Haq regime), firearms became an essential tool of the trade for student activists in the early 1980s. As a result, the student strife of the preceding decade, which pitted 'progressive' students against Islamists, evolved into a full-blown campus war.

In the opposite direction, Karachi became one of the major exit points of Afghan heroin—the 'white gold' that transformed the city's formal and shadow economies, as well as the rules of coexistence of ethnic communities in the city. It is in this context of criminal rivalries, ethnic consolidation and unchecked demographic growth that the MQM emerged as the muscular spokesman of the Mohajirs, who by then were in a majority in the city. But far from pacifying Karachi, the spectacular rise of the MQM at the helm of city politics, from the streets of its *basti*s (unofficial settlements) to the town hall, fed on and nurtured increasingly violent conflicts.

Rather than a historical sketch of Karachi's spectacular demographic and economic growth, or of its turbulent politics, this introductory chapter aims to provide a framework for hanging the various threads of the narrative unfolding in the following chapters. My main concern, here, is not merely how violent conflict came to Karachi, but how it became a permanent, structuring feature of city life and politics. As the following chapters will argue in more detail, demography, geography, Pakistan's political economy as well as national and international politics joined their forces to make Karachi the volatile city that it is today and that it will probably remain in the years to come. To make a complex story short, five cumulative processes deserve to be brought to the fore:

1) The postcolonial history of Karachi was over-determined by the conditions of its decolonisation, and more specifically by the economic, cultural and political vacuum left by the departure of the city's non-Muslim elites in the months following Partition;
2) As the first capital of Pakistan, Karachi became an arena of conflict for the social and political forces competing for the control of the nascent state and economy of Pakistan. Although the city lost its centrality in national politics after the transfer of the capital to the Punjab in 1959, its control remained critical for political elites at the centre, if only for the city's unrivalled contribution to the state exchequer and the national economy;
3) A modern city that expanded on the pattern of the colonial 'dual city', Karachi lacked an integrated planning model until the 1950s, which left the development of the poorest parts of the city to the unofficial sector. Although Pakistan's first military government and its sucessors tried to correct this deficiency by commissioning foreign planners and architects, postcolonial masterplans often did more harm than good to the city and, far from regularising its development, ended up reinforcing its informalisation. This normalisation of the unofficial exposed the poorest sections of Karachi's population to the reign of uncertainty, while providing unofficial entrepreneurs and public officials acting unofficially with lucrative opportunities of brokerage and protection, which turned increasingly violent as Karachi was flooded with arms and drugs in the wake of the Afghan Jihad;
4) Since its foundation, Karachi bears the burden of its geography. Its natural port, located at the crossroads of the Persian Gulf, East Africa, Central Asia, and India, made its fortunes but also sealed its fate. Since the nineteenth century, it has turned Karachi into an antechamber of Afghan conflicts, exposing its populations to external shocks of high magnitude. The escalation of collective violence witnessed in Karachi in the 1980s was precipitated by one such external shock—the Afghan Jihad. This local, regional and international conflict had important spill-over effects for the politics and economy of Karachi,

by democratising the access to firearms and by giving birth to new criminal markets (the heroin trade, in particular) that disrupted the city's official and unofficial economies. In the process, political conflicts militarised and the relations between ethnic groups became increasingly strained, two developments that go a long way to explain the spectacular rise of the MQM in the second half of the 1980s, as well as its peculiar political culture; and

5) The militarisation of Karachi's unofficial economy and politics, in the wake of the Afghan Jihad, reinforced pre-existing trends towards the dispersion of power and gave rise to myriad unofficial authorities, transforming the city into a zone of contested sovereignties.

A City Up for Grabs

A few years before her premature death in a car accident, the poetess Parveen Shakir (1952–1994) published a 'tribute' to her natal Karachi. Far from celebrating the city, though, these verses are saturated with anger, comparing Karachi with a worn-out prostitute used and abused by all those she gives herself to:

Karachi
Ek aisi biswa hai
Jis ke sath
Paharon, maidanon aur saharaon se ane walah
Har saiz ke batwe ka admi
Rat guzarta hai
Aur subhe uthte hi
Uske dahne rukhsar par
Ek thappar rasid karta hai
Aur dusre gal ki tawaqoh karte hue
Kam par nikal jata hai
Agli rat ke nashe mein sarshar

Karachi
is a whore,
with whom every eligible man,
descending from the mountains
or emerging from the plains and deserts,
with wallets of different sizes,
spends the night.
In the morning,
slapping her on one cheek,
he expects the other one,
and leaves for work,
drunk in anticipation of the night to come.[14]

Parveen Shakir's sexualisation of Karachi and its comparison with a prostitute was not an isolated act of provocation in South Asia's literary world. It can be likened, for instance, to the famous verses of the Dalit poet Namdeo Dhasal on his 'dearest slut' (*priya rande*), Bombay: 'Bombay, Bombay / O my dearest slut / I may say a good-bye / But not before

/ I take you / In multiple ways / Not before / I will pin you down / Here and how / Thus and thus.'[15] The analogy between Shakir's and Dhasal's verses speaks volumes on the affinities between Bombay and Karachi—two megacities that had to cope with the crisis of their 'cosmopolitan ideal' in the last decades of the twentieth century.[16] And yet, in spite of this resemblance, Parveen Shakir's verses belong to another social world and literary tradition. Lament for the city has a long history in Urdu poetry and even constitutes a specific genre, the *shehr-e-ashob* or *ashobia shairi*, a genre in which poets such as Shafiq Aurangabadi, Mir Taqi Mir and Mirza Rafi Sauda excelled and which 'encapsulates the socio-cultural turbulence of cities in the late Mughal period'.[17] The *shehr-e-ashob*, whose influence over Karachi's poets is sometimes made explicit—such as in Mohsin Bhopali's *Shehr-e-ashob*, which denounces the army's intervention in the city in 1992[18]—was originally the swan song of decaying Muslim elites whose lament for the city was inseparable from their resentment at witnessing the rise of the lower classes. The city lamented by these poets was a world upside down, where the rulers of yore had become destitute and beggars, where poor carpet weavers wore expensive shawls and shavers of pubic hair composed poetry.[19] Though Parveen Shakir's verses lament the fate of a city lacking as ancient and prestigious a history as the centres of Islamicate power and culture sung by classical Urdu poets and in this sense as well, closer to Bombay, they can be related to this literary corpus, especially in their indictment of migrant workers from the Punjab, interior Sindh and the Pashtun Belt, who have been attracted in large numbers to the city since the 1960s. Following Gyan Prakash, one can read Namdeo Dhasal's verses as an invitation to look critically at Bombay's iconic status—that of an 'emblem of cosmopolitan modernity'—and uncover the 'account of oppression and exploitation' lodged in this fable.[20] On the contrary, Parveen Shakir's rage and her own metaphor of the city-as-prostitute are not directed at the city herself but at her residents. Whereas Dhasal accuses Bombay to be a slut—'one that enchants only to deceive'[21]—Shakir empathises with Karachi, against her 'clients'. At first sight, her indignation seems less related to the mere presence of these migrants in Karachi than to their reluctance to return the favours to their whore of a city. This appears to be neither a class nor an ethnic problem, but one of urban citizenship: reversing Henri Lefebvre's proposal of a 'right to the city',[22] these verses can be read as a reminder of the Karachiites' duties towards their city of election, a disillusioned yearning at an elusive social contract between the city and its ungrateful residents. These verses cannot be read in abstraction from the city's conflictive identity politics, though. They are also consonant with a common critique among members of the Urdu-speaking middle-class towards the migrant workers who settled in Karachi after Partition, seen as insufficiently attached to the city because of their persisting bond with their villages of origin. 'They eat the city, but they don't feed it', an official of the Karachi Development Authority (KDA) thus told anthropologist Oskar Verkaaik.[23] Being herself an Urdu-speaking Mohajir born and raised in Karachi, Parveen Shakir expresses in these verses a similar longing for the 'clean' Karachi of the early 1950s, a golden age when one could still feel at home in the city at large. Even if implicitly, Shakir's poem pertains to this urban myth of origins, 'structured by stories that describe a conveniently arranged city that [...] emerged out of the very beginnings of the Pakistani nation'.[24] Although contradicted by historical evidence—post-Partition Karachi was certainly not the neat, peaceful and manageable city imagined by nostalgic Mohajirs—this myth has endured and was reinvigorated by the more exclusivist conceptions of home that emerged in the city in the past decades.

In their multivocality, these verses remain one of the most powerful evocations of Karachi's recent history and of the role of migration, internal as well as transnational, in it. From its origins, Karachi has been a city of migrants. It was developed in the early eighteenth century by Hindu merchants (*banya*s) from the Sindhi hinterland, before attracting large numbers of traders, entrepreneurs and workers from Kutch, Gujarat, Bombay and Balochistan, so much so that by 1921 the number of residents born outside of Karachi amounted to almost half of the total population of the city (cf. Table 2). The Partition of India and the exodus of hundreds of thousands of *muhajirin* to the city (cf. Table 2) put it under severe demographic pressure, with the population of Karachi increasing by 369 per cent between 1941 and 1961, possibly the fastest rate of growth ever registered for a city of that size in world history.[25] By 1951, according to the first Census of Pakistan, the composition of Karachi's population had drastically changed. In 1941, 51 per cent of the city's inhabitants were Hindu and only 42 per cent Muslim. Ten years later, 96 per cent of the city's total population was Muslim, and only 2 per cent Hindu. According to the Census, refugees from India now accounted for 55 per cent of the total population of the city,[26] which had almost tripled between 1941 and 1951.

By then, only 27 per cent of the residents of Karachi were born in the city (see Table 2). Whereas, in 1941, Sindhi was the mother tongue of 61 per cent of the city's residents, ten years later 51 per cent of the population returned Urdu as their mother tongue, as against 8.5 per cent for Sindhi.[27] The bulk of these refugees hailed from Delhi and the United Provinces, whose Muslim minority population spearheaded the movement for Pakistan. Until the introduction of a passport system by India and Pakistan in 1952, 100,000 *muhajirin* continued to arrive yearly in the city.[28] Two years later, there were still 5,000 to 6,000 reaching Karachi every month,[29] most of these latecomers reaching the city through East Pakistan.

By 1961, migrants, that is, Pakistanis born outside Karachi, amounted to 56 per cent of the total population of the city. In the following years, Karachi continued to attract outsiders in large numbers. These newcomers were mostly Punjabi and Pashtun labourers, who were attracted to the city by its vibrant industrial sector. The share of migrants in the city's total population has been declining steadily since the 1960s, although Karachi became a haven for nearly a million Afghans during the 1980s (there were still, at the very least, half a million residents of Afghan origin in the city in 2004,[30] but these numbers remain unverified and could actually be much higher).[31] Most of these Afghan refugees were of Pashtun stock but Karachi also became home to smaller contingents of Uzbeks (30,000 to 40,000 according to some estimates) and Hazaras and Tajiks (20,000 each). Officially, 474,162 Afghan residents of Sindh (most of them non-Pashtun residents of Karachi) opted for voluntary repatriation to their country of origin between March 2002 and October 2004.[32] At present, the exact number of Afghans still present in Karachi remains uncertain.

Karachi is also home to large numbers of illegal immigrants—mostly Bangladeshis but also Burmese, Sri Lankans, Filipinos, Thais, Iranians, Iraqis and even Ethiopians, who add to the cosmopolitan character of the city.[33] It is estimated that this population of illegal 'aliens' (including Afghans) has grown from 511,835 in 1989 to 1,455,460 in 1993[34] and 2.5 million in 2011.[35] These illegal aliens would be spread over twenty-two localities in the city, using twenty-nine government schools and nine hospitals, while running forty-four out of the city's 869 religious seminaries (as of 2003).[36] In the 1998 Census (to date, the Census 2011 has been limited to a House Listing Operation, failing to produce any data on the ethnic break-up of Karachi's population), 49 per cent of Karachi's residents returned Urdu as their mother tongue, 16 per cent Punjabi/Seraiki, 11 per cent Pashto, 7 per cent Sindhi and 4 per cent Balochi (cf. Fig. 2), while the number of residents of foreign origin was estimated at 600,000 (probably a gross underestimation).[37]

In recent years, the migration of over 300,000 Pashtuns from the north-west,[38] displaced by the combat between the army and the Taliban or by the 2010 floods, has altered this ethnic equilibrium to the detriment of Mohajirs. However, Karachi's exact demographic profile remains a matter of controversy in the absence of reliable census data. This uncertainty has been making the fortune of ethnic leaders, who have been allowed

Fig. 2: Mother tongue of the residents of Karachi

Census results (1981, 1998) and projections (2011, 2025) in per cent

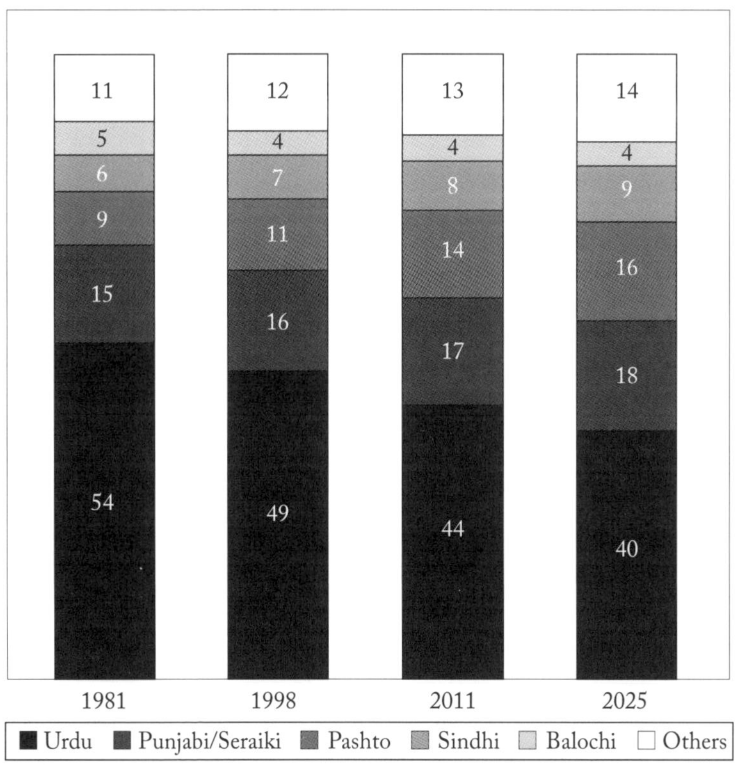

Source: Gazdar, Haris, 'Karachi: violence, duality and negotation', SPO Discussion Paper Series No. 10, 2011, p. 8.

to freely deploy their numeral imagination and instill in their followers a sense of power in numbers. This is how the leader of the Awami National Party (ANP) in Karachi, Shahi Syed, has been able to claim that the number of Pashtuns in the city approaches four million, which would amount to almost 20 per cent of Karachi's total population.[39] Some estimates put Karachi's Pashtun population even higher, somewhere around 25 per cent of the city's total population, which would make it the second largest ethnic group in the city.[40]

Space constraints do not permit me to go into the details of these migrations and their impact on Karachi's social fabric and cityscape,

Table 1: Karachi's demographic growth (1729–2011)

Year	*Population*	*Variation over the previous survey*	*% Increase / Decrease*
1729	250	–	–
1838	14,000	13,750	5500
1842	15,000	1000	71
1850	16,773	1773	12
1856	22,227	5454	32
1861	56,859	34,632	156
1881	73,560	16,701	29
1890	98,000	24,440	33
1901	136,297	38,297	39
1911	186,771	50,474	37
1921	244,162	57,391	30
1931	300,779	56,617	23
1941	435,887	135,108	45
1951	1,137,667	701,780	161
1961	2,044,044	906,377	80
1972	3,606,746	1,562,702	76
1981	5,437,984	1,831,238	51
1986	7,443,663	2,005,679	37
1998	9,802,134	2,358,471	32
2011	21,200,000	11,343,470	115

Source: adapted from Siddiqi, Ahmad Hussein, *Karāchī. Gohar-e-Buhīrah 'Arb* (Urdu) (Karachi. The Pearl of the Arabian Sea), Karachi: Fazli Sons, 1995, p. 62 and Table 1, in Zaidi, Akbar S., 'Politics, institutions, poverty: the case of Karachi', *Economic & Political Weekly*, 32, 51 (1997), p. 3283.

Table 2: Share of migrants born outside Karachi in the city's total population (1921–1998)

	1921	*1951*	*1961*	*1981*	*1998*
Total population of Karachi	244,162	1,137,667	2,044,044	5,437,984	9,802,134
Total population of migrants	101,000	830,667	1,154,000	1,700,000	2,155,500
Share of migrants in total population (%)	41	73	56	31	22

Source: *Census of Pakistan, 1951*, map no. 5.1, p. 89; Hasan, Arif, *The Scale and Causes of Urban Change in Pakistan*, Karachi: Ushba, 2006, Table 8.2, p. 117.

which in any case have already been well documented.[41] For the purpose of the present argument, I merely want to emphasise three crucial points. First of all, the role of post-Partition migrations from India over the postcolonial politics of Karachi cannot be overemphasised. These migrations transformed the demographic composition and cultural outlook of the city virtually overnight, while setting the basis for Karachi's perennial housing crisis. Moreover, with the departure of the wealthy Hindu and Parsi business communities that had made the fortune of Karachi during the colonial era,[42] the very 'ownership' of Karachi, legally and metaphorically, was up for grabs. If the social, economic and political history of Karachi presents striking similarities with that of Bombay, it singularises itself in this regard. In Bombay, postcolonial claims to the city had to contend with the enduring dominance, in the city's economy and institutions, of the forces that had shaped it during the colonial era.[43] In Karachi, on the contrary, the departure of the non-Muslim elites that had developed the city until Partition left an economic, cultural and political vacuum that was never fully filled by the *muhajirin* and that is still being fought over between their descendants and other communities claiming their own right to the city. Conflicts over the status of Karachi—and thus over its rightful 'owners' and rulers—started right after Partition. The decision passed by the Constituent Assembly on 22 May 1948 to make Karachi the capital of Pakistan and detach it administratively from Sindh to make it a federally administered territory alienated Sindhi elites, as it implied a significant loss in revenue and shattered the ambitions of these elites to take the place of Hindu businessmen in Karachi.[44] After the enforcement of the One Unit system[45] in 1955, Karachi remained under the direct authority of the central government, and it was only reunited with Sindh in 1970, with the abolition of the One Unit system by Ayub's successor, General Yahya Khan. By then, Karachi was no longer the capital of Pakistan. Ayub Khan, Pakistan's first military ruler, claimed that the physical proximity of politicians, bureaucrats and economic elites created a deleterious environment, although his profound distaste for Karachi was primarily related to the restlessness of its highly politicised students and working classes. Indeed, since the 1950s, Karachi was the centre of social and political movements leaning to the left, which challenged the authoritarian drift of the Pakistani state. In June 1959, Ayub Khan approved a project of delocalisation of Pakistan's capital in the Punjab. On 24 February 1960, Zulfikar Ali Bhutto, then Information Minister in Ayub's Cabinet, announced that this new capital would be named Islamabad, the 'City of Islam'. In the process, Karachi lost its Federal Capital Area status and was retrograded to a Federal Territory, before being reunited with Sindh in 1970. This reintegration reactivated the conflict between Sindhi and Urdu-speaking elites over the status of Karachi and its relation to the Sindhi hinterland. From the 1950s onwards, some members of the Urdu-speaking elite demanded that Karachi be made a province in its own right. This movement for the Karachi *suba* remained marginal but fuelled the tensions between Sindhis and Urdu-speakers, which culminated in the 'language riots' of 1971–1972 (see Chapter 3).

Second, it should be emphasised that the ethnic diversity resulting from these successive waves of migration did not translate into a full-blown cosmopolitanism, that is, into an ethical programme of coexistence between strangers.[46] The tendency of the city's diverse populations to regroup themselves around ethnic clusters endured after Partition, with Urdu-speaking refugees from India regrouping themselves on the basis of language, sect, region and sometimes city of origins, while Pashtun labourers relied upon village-based networks to find work and accommodation. These phenomena of ethnic clustering did not preclude peaceful inter-ethnic encounters—especially in the city's *basti*s—but limited their scope and set the basis for an ethnic partitioning of urban space that would only harden following the episodes of 'ethnic' violence of the mid-1980s (see Chapter 7). Last but not least, it should be noted that large sections of these migrant populations were composed of refugees who came to Karachi with a heavy background, having witnessed episodes of mass violence at close range, be it the *muhajirin* (many of whom, though not all, having been witness to the massacres of Partition), the Biharis (who were deeply affected by the 1971 civil war that led to the secession of East Pakistan) or the post-1979 Pashtun refugees and internally displaced persons (IDPs) from Afghanistan and north-west Pakistan. This pre-exposition to violence was not, per se, a factor of violent mobilisation in Karachi. However, it did provide a pool of battle-hardened recruits to the various militias that emerged in the city from the mid-1980s onwards, while sustaining the sense of entitlement to Karachi of some of these migrant communities (such as the Mohajirs), as a well-deserved compensation for their past sacrifices—what Vazira Zamindar refers to as the 'trope of sacrifice' of the Mohajir community.[47] The Mohajirs' claim of a special entitlement to Karachi has been contested by later migrants, Pashtuns in particular, whose political representatives also claim that their community built postcolonial Karachi, but this time literally (most construction works in Karachi since Partition were contracted to Pashtun and to a lesser extent Punjabi labourers). As the leader of the ANP in Karachi, Shahi Syed, told me in 2007, 'The Pashtuns have built Karachi. They have made a lot of sacrifices for this city. But these sacrifices have gone unrecognised.'[48] The MQM's claim of ownership over Karachi also alienated its 'indigenous' populations: descendants of the earliest settlers of the precolonial and colonial period, such as the Baloch, Sindhi and Kutchi populations of Lyari. The rise of the PAC at the helm of Lyari's politics in recent years, which will be examined in details in Chapter 4, is not only a sign of the weakening of the Pakistan Peoples Party's (PPP) hold over Karachi's inner city, to the benefit of local 'gangsters'. It also signals the emergence of an armed politics of autochthony in Karachi's oldest working-class neighbourhood, reclaiming the city for its original inhabitants and reimagining it as a non-Mohajir city in the process. In the words of Zafar Baloch, the second in command of the PAC,

When Karachi did not exist, when Pakistan did not exist, there was only Lyari. [...] Before Partition, Nazimabad, Liaquatabad [currently Mohajir-dominated localities of District Central] used to be rural areas. Lalu, Nazim, they were all

Baloch. They were cultivators living on the bank of the [Lyari] river. The area known as Liaquatabad today used to be called Lalukhet ['Lalu's field'] but they [Mohajirs] could not tolerate that name so they changed it to Liaquatabad as a reference to Liaquat Ali Khan [Pakistan's first prime minister and a major patron of the *muhajirin*, who was murdered in 1951]. [...] Sohrab Goth ['Sohrab's village'; a Pashtun/Afghan settlement in the north of the city] is in fact 'the village of Sohrab Khan Gabol', this land belongs to the Gabols [a prominent Baloch family of landowners which became one of Lyari's most influential political family after Partition]. Today the people think of it as a Pashtun area, but it wasn't always like that. The Pashtuns only started migrating to Karachi in the 1960s.[49]

These competitive claims over the ownership of the city are at the heart of its increasingly complex conflicts, where the battle for votes overlaps with a contest for economic rents (land, water, electricity, jobs, development funds, *bhatta*...). For the smaller stakeholders, such as the PPP, the ANP and the PAC, ownership entails the exclusive control of the populations and economic rents of their respective turf. The MQM remains more ambitious. Although its militants are involved in small-scale turf wars against political rivals or criminal groups, the MQM is not merely fighting for a turf in Karachi, but for control over the local state and its different organs—the city government, the police, the courts, universities and colleges, hospitals, and so on.

An Arena for National Conflicts

Karachi has also been an important arena of conflict for political forces competing for the control of the Pakistani state at large. Until the 1980s, it shared with Lahore the status of 'political pulse of the country':[50] local protest movements were often preliminaries to larger social and political struggles across Pakistan, and every aspirant to power at the national level had to prove himself in the city. The ethnicisation of Karachi's political scene, following the rise of the MQM, estranged it from the national mainstream. Prominent political trends in the city no longer had a national scope, as the MQM failed to expand its activities, and stakes, outside urban Sindh. Nevertheless, Karachi was not completely 'cut off' from national politics. With the notable exception of the years 1993–1996 (following its boycott of the National Assembly election and the clear victory of the PPP in the provincial election, which made it possible for Benazir Bhutto to govern alone in Sindh and at the centre), the

MQM was an important protagonist of the coalition politics that emerged after the death of Zia (1988) and the restoration of democracy. This did not prevent violence from escalating in the city, dragging national governments into local battles for supremacy and on three occasions (1990, 1993 and 1996) contributing to their fall.

The destabilisation of successive civilian governments over the issue of Karachi was the outcome of the coalition politics specific to these governments, and in particular of their difficulty to bring and keep on board the MQM. Since it first entered into an alliance with Benazir Bhutto's PPP in 1988, the MQM has been an erratic partner, both kingmaker and kingbreaker, simultaneously assuming the role of a pragmatic, mainstream political party and that of a disruptive social movement (see Chapter 3). In 1989, a year after the signature of the 'Karachi Accord' between the PPP and the MQM, the latter supported the no-confidence motion moved by the Islami Jamhoori Ittehad (Islamic Democratic Alliance [IJI]) led by Nawaz Sharif, arguing that the PPP had failed to keep its promises. The motion failed but the following year, Benazir Bhutto's first government was dissolved by Ghulam Ishaq Khan, who justified this dismissal by the worsening law and order situation in Karachi and Hyderabad. The MQM then entered into a new alliance with Nawaz Sharif's Pakistan Muslim League (Nawaz) [PML-(N)]), which came out victorious in the general elections. In June 1991, the MQM attracted the wrath of the Sindh Corps Commander, Asif Nawaz Janjua, after its workers abducted an intelligence officer, Major Kalim, as well as three of his subordinates, while they were conducting a fact-finding mission in Landhi. The four men were taken to a building known as the 'White House', where they were subjected to severe torture, including electric shocks.[51] In 1992, the same Asif Nawaz, by now Chief of Army Staff (COAS), sent the army—apparently without Nawaz Sharif's knowledge, let alone approval—to crack down on the MQM. The following year, Nawaz Sharif was in turn dismissed, partly over the worsening law and order situation in Karachi. This time, the PPP was reluctant to enter into an alliance with the MQM and its clear victory in Sindh as well as the latter's boycott of the National Assembly election made it easier to sideline it and unleash 'legitimate' violence against it. Following the withdrawal of the army from Karachi in December 1994, violence escalated and 1995 entered the annals as the most violent year in Karachi's postcolonial history (that is, until 2012). The same year, Benazir Bhutto's Home Minister, General (retd.) Naseerullah Babar, launched another, even more ruthless crackdown against the MQM. This operation brought down the number of violent deaths in Karachi (at least at the hands of MQM militants, since it went along with a large number of extrajudicial killings), but this improvement in the 'law and order situation' was short-lived and the number of killings shot up once again in 1997 and 1998. On 20 September 1996, Benazir's brother and rival, Murtaza, was murdered in front of his Karachi residence by the Sindh police. A rumour that refuses to go away attributes Murtaza's murder to those close to Benazir, who had no love lost for her hotheaded brother-in-law. Among other things (revelations on her acquisition of a sumptuous villa in Surrey, political manipulations in the Punjab, etc.), the possible involvement of Benazir's entourage in the murder of Murtaza, as well as the dramatic increase in extrajudicial killings by the police and the Rangers in Karachi, provided President Farooq Leghari with strong arguments to dismiss her government and dissolve Parliament on 5 November 1996. The PML-(N) was brought back to power in the following elections and enteredinto an alliance with the MQM. Yet again, this alliance proved to be fragile. After failing to obtain satisfaction in its demands, the MQM withdrew from the provincial government in Sindh although it continued to support it from outside. In September 1998, the party was apparently on the verge of re-entering the provincial government when Hakim Said, a popular medical practitioner and former Governor of Sindh, was assassinated—allegedly by MQM militants. Nawaz Sharif ordered the MQM leadership to deliver Said's killers and following the MQM's decision to withdraw its support to the government, the prime minister dissolved the assembly and proclaimed a state of emergency (the Governor's rule) in Sindh.

The alliance (2002–2008) between the MQM and the military regime of Pervez Musharraf (himself an Urdu-speaking *muhajir* from Delhi) proved to be more enduring, although the relations between the MQM and the civilian protégés of the general-president were fraught with tensions. For the second time since Karachi was engulfed in a spiral of political, ethnic and sectarian strife in the mid-1980s, violence receded. But whereas the 1996 lull, which followed Naseerullah Babar's crackdown, proved to be short-lived, this time peace seemed to have returned to Karachi for good. By 2000, the 'law and order situation' had sufficiently improved for the *Herald* magazine to publish a cover story on Karachi, the 'city of life'.[52] The last years of Pervez Musharraf's rule were however marked by a revival of Karachi's turf wars, this time pitting the MQM against the ANP. Following its victory in the 2008 elections, the PPP once again turned to the MQM for support in Sindh and in Islamabad. And as usual, the MQM proved to be a volatile partner, withdrawing thrice its support to the coalition government (December 2010, June 2011, February 2013) and threatening to do so on several other occasions. In the meantime, political violence escalated and has continued to do so over the past few years, with 2012 becoming the most violent year ever in the history of the city (with 2,174 killings, according to CPLC data).[53]

The Normalisation of the Unofficial

A modern city born of the proto-global sea trade of the early eighteenth century, Karachi was never the object of the meticulous planification that came to characterise earlier, more prestigious cities of the subcontinent, where the topography of the city visualised the social order while setting the basis for a functional economy.[54] Spatial segregation in Karachi emerged incrementally along socio-professional lines, an economic partitioning of urban space that overlapped with cultural divisions (whether ethnic, linguistic or religious). One of the first initiatives of the Hindu *banyas* who founded modern Karachi at the beginning of the eighteenth century was to protect the settlement—and more prosaically their shipments—against incursions from pirates. Seth Bhojoomal, the founder of modern Karachi and himself a prosperous merchant from the interior of Sindh, proceeded to fortify the city. The surrounding mangrove trees were cut down, and foreign workers were recruited to assist local labourers in the construction of mud and wood ramparts, while six cannons were brought from Masqat, according to Bhojoomal's great grandson, Seth Naomul Hotchand.[55] The entire population of Karachi found refuge behind these walls, which on one side opened on the sea (through the *Khara Darwaza*, the 'salt-water gate') and on the other on the Lyari river (through the *Mitha Darwaza*, the 'sweet water gate'). The pirates never showed up (although the Vaghers of Gomti and Beyt, in Kathiawar, 'began to infest the seas and capture and plunder any vessel they could lay their hands upon' around 1793–1795, according to Seth Naomul Hotchand),[56] but the ramparts proved useful during the three successive sieges of the Amir of Sindh, at the end of the eighteenth century. In the following decades, however, the poorest sections of the city's population, such as Muslim fishermen and craftsmen, started gathering in suburbs outside the city walls. In 1848, the British brought down these ramparts and the city's expansion only accelerated after the colonisers started modernising Karachi's port while extending its railway connections to the Punjab in the 1860s. Karachi would remain an 'open city'[57] from then on, with a large part of its urbanisation being left to the unofficial sector.

Under the British, the city was divided—for social, political as well as health reasons[58]—between the Old Town and the New Town, with the latter being reserved the privilege of modern town planning. The New Town consisted of the Cantonment (Karachi was initially conceived by the British as a garrison town where troops and ammunition were to be stationed and despatched to Afghanistan), the Civil Lines (where colonial officials and their families, as well as some indigenous elites, resided) and the Saddar Bazaar (which concentrated modern shopping facilities). This New Town was the site of numerous architectural experimentations, which in this regard as well liken Karachi to Bombay. The landscape of Saddar, which would become the centre of intellectual and leisurely activities in the decades following Partition, was dotted with neo-classical buildings, ranging in style from the Indo-Gothic (Frere Hall, Empress Market, Saint Patrick's Cathedral) to the Mock-Tudor (the Karachi Gymkhana, the Boat Club, etc.) and the Neo-Renaissance or 'Italianate' style (Saint Joseph's Convent, the Sindh Club, D.J. Science College). In the late nineteenth century, some indigenous families, who often hailed from affluent mercantile groups, emulated this trend and financed the construction of impressive buildings (the Hindu Gymkhana, Mohatta Palace,...) in the Indo-Saracenic or Anglo-Mughal architectural style then in vogue.

In the meantime, the 'black' parts of the Old City, where the bulk of the indigenous population resided, remained largely unplanned, developing in a haphazard away around the port and the often polluting factories dotting the area. Whereas residential and workplaces were separated in the New City, on the model of British industrial cities, no such division was implemented in the black parts of town. And while the residential areas of the New City were carefully planned, dotted with elegant bungalows facing each other across wide and green alleys, the Old City became a maze of densely populated *mohalla*s roughly organised on ethnic and religious lines, without any access to water, electricity and sewage lines. Some improvements were however registered under the leadership of Seth Harchandrai Vishandas (1862–1928), a wealthy Hindu businessman who was the president of the Karachi Municipal Corporation (KMC) between 1911 and 1921.[59] Under his chairmanship, major public works were completed, such as the construction of a series of roads (MacLeod Road, Elphinstone Road, Clifton Road and especially Bandar Road, which became M.A. Jinnah Road and remains one of the city's main arteries to this day), which contributed to the decongestion of the city centre. During the same period, the Lyari river was diverted in order to protect against floods the small settlements of lower-income populations (many of them of Baloch origins) who had recently sprung up on the riverbanks.

These small steps towards an integrated and socially inclusive conception of urban planning for Karachi were compromised by the demographic upheaval brought by Partition. In the absence of any resettlement plan, the poorest refugees thronged public places, while the more fortunate ones squatted in religious and residential buildings formerly occupied by non-Muslims. Even the upper sections of the *muhajirin* faced difficulties to find accommodation. Rais Amrohvi's *qatat* (four-line poems, which this popular *muhajir* poet from Amroha started publishing regularly in the Urdu daily *Jang* from June 1947 onwards) echoed these 'upper caste' (*ashraf*) anxieties, for instance in the following poem, 'Pagrī' (Honour), published in *Jang* on 9 May 1948:

Is shehr mein ashian hai 'anqa	There is no shelter in this city [Karachi].
Dil sakht yahan uljh raha hai	The heart is in great turmoil.
Pagri ki taleb hai ghar ke badle	When our immediate concern is to preserve our dignity,
Pagri mein makan uljh raha hai	how will we manage to find a new home?[60]

In 1953, 250,000 of these refugees were still homeless[61] and this number only increased in the following years: a survey conducted in 1959 concluded that 527,535 persons were without proper shelter in the city.[62] During this period, some localities of the city centre—Burns Road, Frere Road, Kharadar—became *muhajir* clusters. Along with these informal concentrations of refugees, the early 1950s saw the emergence of a movement of co-operative societies that catered to the needs of wealthier refugees and led to the development of new residential areas such as the Central Pakistan Government Employees' Co-operative Housing Society (PECHS). Some of these 'colonies' (Hyderabad Colony, Delhi Colony, Aligarh Colony, Kutch Colony, C.P. and Berar Society, Bangalore Town, etc.) explicitly targeted refugees from certain regions of India and applicants were sometimes asked to prove their connection with the region in question.[63] Whereas these refugee colonies were often located in the north-west of the city, wealthier *muhajirin*, including public servants, were allocated prime housing in downtown localities around Saddar (Fort Mansion, Ilaco House, Garden East and West,...) or relocated in new residential colonies in the East (PECHS, Muhammad Ali Society, Muslimabad,...).

In 1949, a major housing scheme was launched, which specifically targeted refugees: 60,000 of them were to be resettled on the north bank of the Lyari River, in a locality that would come to be known as Nazimabad. An even larger resettlement colony was developed to the east of Nazimabad a few years later. By 1956, Lalukhet—later on renamed Liaquatabad, in memory of the first prime minister of Pakistan, assassinated in 1951—could boast of 100,000 residents. Ayub Khan's coup, in 1958, gave a new impetus to these initiatives, as the resettlement of refugees was an integral part of the clean-up campaign of Pakistan's first military regime. In Baldia, west of Karachi, 50,000 refugees were to be resettled within five years, whereas in Malir, in the East, already existing accommodation was to be immediately attributed to homeless refugees. A more ambitious project, which was supposed to provide accommodation to hundreds of thousands of refugees, was inaugurated by Ayub Khan himself in Korangi, in south-east Karachi, on 1 August 1959. A part of the Greater Karachi Resettlement Plan (GKRP), which included the development of another satellite town in the north of the city (New Karachi), this initiative was supervised by a Greek planning firm, Doxiadis, and constituted 'the major "symbolic" achievement of the regime as far as rehabilitation was concerned'.[64] For Pakistan's first military ruler, these initiatives did not merely aim to bring a permanent solution to the refugee issue. Ayub Khan was determined to tame what he perceived as Karachi's turbulent plebs. In his conception—which contrasted with that of Constantinos A. Doxiadis[65]—the GKRP was a disciplinary project, which aimed to sanitise and secure the city centre by sending away the poorer, working-class segments of the refugee population to the periphery. The development of industrial estates in the vicinity of these satellite towns was expected to 'fix' the residents of these colonies of exile, turning them into 'stationary state subjects'.[66] In the short term at least, this project was a failure: the populations which were forcibly displaced there were reluctant to make their lease payments or re-sold their plots on the black market, basic amenities (water, sanitation and, until the end of the project, electricity) were lacking, while industrialisation turned out to be slower than expected, even though it did pick up in the course of time. The project was shelved in 1964 but had important repercussions on Karachi's cityscape and social fabric nonetheless, as emphasised by architect Arif Hasan:

> Inner city refugees and squatter settlements were bulldozed. It became impossible to build new squatter settlements within the metropolitan area. But then, there was an unmet demand for housing. This resulted in the creation of squatter settlements on the roads that connected the city with Landhi-Korangi and New Karachi. These settlements were created along the dry natural drainage channels and were developed by middlemen who in later years were to become the city's main suppliers of land for housing the poor and a powerful interest group. The plan also caused Karachi's perennial transport problem and converted a high density multi-class city to a low density urban sprawl with the poor living far away from the city centre and the rich in its immediate vicinity. Much of Karachi's 'ethnic' problems are directly related to this aspect of the GKRP.[67]

The shifting of the university (1959), the moralisation policy of Z.A. Bhutto (which signed the death warrant of Saddar's cultural life), the development of wholesale markets as well as the clogging and environmental degradation of the city centre, which started being used as a transit area by private transporters, also deprived the city centre of Saddar of the socially integrative role it had played during the first decades of independence. During the 1960s, the periurbanisation of Karachi accelerated with the development of middle-class co-operative societies in the outskirts of the city, which was supplemented by the development of lower-income settlements on land reclaimed from the Sindhi/Baloch *goths* (urban villages). Besides these official dynamics of periurbanisation, this period saw the spectacular growth of *katchi abadis* formed through the invasion or illegal subdivision of public land along the roads leading to the newly developed satellite towns. A poverty belt formed around Karachi, from Malir in the east to Orangi in the west, while the inner-city working-class neighbourhoods (such as Lyari) became increasingly congested. Both in peripheral refugee/migrant settlements and in inner-city 'slums', *jhuggi*s gradually ceded the way to single- or double-storey houses made of stone or unplastered concrete blocks with tin roofs, which in the course of time were sometimes upgraded by their owners (Lyari's landscape, for instance, started changing with the construction of five- to seven-storey apartment blocks from the 1970s onwards). With the support of unofficial land suppliers, slumlords, politicians and bureaucrats, transient housing became more permanent, while retaining a 'spectral' dimension consubstantial to its unofficial character, which places 'the ghostly, the speculative, the fantastic' at the heart of Karachi's real estate politics, another point of comparison with Bombay/Mumbai.[68]

This reign of the unofficial sector remains particularly blatant in housing for the poor, as only 35 per cent of the 75,500 new housing units required every year are provided by the formal private and public sector. However, it does not stop there: 42 per cent of the water supply would be in the hands of the so-called 'tanker mafia',[69] 45 per cent of the electricity consumed in the city is procured illegally through *kunda* installations siphoning off current from regular electric cables[70] and in 2002 it was estimated that 75 per cent of the population was employed in the informal economy (against 48 per cent in 1974).[71] This prevalence and tolerance of the informal provides political and violent entrepreneurs with numerous opportunities of brokerage between the state (the bureaucracy, the judiciary and the police) and the populations the most exposed to informality and uncertainty (the residents of squatter settlements). As we will see in detail in the course of the book, the state has not receded in Karachi; it remains an essential source of patronage and its alleged *qabza* (capture) by certain groups is a hugely controversial matter, structuring political discourses and fuelling ethnic conflicts. The resilience of the state—both as a social reality and an act of imagination—does not mean that it has risen above the melee, walking away unscathed from the development of the informal economy. On the contrary, public officials themselves have been major contributors to the informalisation of the state. Whereas the lower echelons of the local state often work on the sides for the informal sector (Karachi's municipal staff would devote at least a third of its official working time to the informal recycling industry, for instance),[72] intermediate and upper echelons of the bureaucracy have been renting their protection to informal entrepreneurs, providing some security to these entrepreneurs and their clients (the protection of land suppliers alone generated yearly revenues estimated at $10 million in 2002).[73]

The formal/informal dichotomy may not be the most appropriate to capture what is at stake in the often illegal yet licit interactions between public officials and private entrepreneurs. As Perween Rahman, the late director of Karachi's most influential postcolonial NGO—the Orangi Pilot Project (OPP)[74]—used to emphasise, a more heuristic distinction is between actors operating in their official and unofficial capacities. This semantic shift from the informal to the unofficial underlines that the proper line of cleavage, here, is not between state and society or between the public and the private. First of all, '[even] the official is illegal', Rahman used to say, as those buying plots from the so-called 'formal sector' have to pay bribes to public officials involved in these transactions.[75] Second, the survival of the unofficial sector has always been premised upon the involvement of public officials acting in an unofficial capacity—that is, without any official sanction and sometimes in violation of the law. By distinguishing between the capacities under which economic and political entrepreneurs operate (i.e. their mandate or the lack thereof), rather than between the social identities of these actors (i.e. their public or private 'nature'), it becomes possible to factor in one of the major criticisms voiced against the dichotomy between 'formal' and 'informal' economies, namely that these two sectors of activity do not operate in opposition to each other but, rather, pertain to a single system of exchange.[76] Not only do public officials act unofficially and thereby contribute to the informalisation of the state, a preliminary step towards the emergence of what Achille Mbembe, in the context of sub-Saharan Africa, refers to as 'indirect private government'.[77] In the opposite direction, the trajectory of some archetypal figures of Karachi's unofficial economy, from the Baloch *dacoits* of Lyari (see Chapter 4) to the Pashtun land suppliers of Baldia Town (see Chapter 7), demonstrate that these actors have not retreated from the state to find solace in the shadowy world of the 'informal' economy. Violent entrepreneurs, that is, economic agents converting their access to certain means of coercion into power, influence and wealth,[78] are constantly interacting with public officials, when they have not claimed an official mandate themselves. This is not to say that the relations between public officials and unofficial entrepreneurs are not fraught with tensions, though. On the contrary, the latter may primarily engage with the state in order to neutralise it from within, and these collusive arrangements are never strong enough to dissipate mutual mistrust, leaving room open for turnovers, betrayals and open conflicts.

The second reason for relinquishing the formal/informal dichotomy has to do with its normativity, as if the 'informal' was intrinsically of a lesser quality than the 'formal'. This assumption is made explicit in the vernacular terms used in Karachi since the 1970s to distinguish between officially and unofficially developed areas: *pakka* and *katchi abadi*s. In the Hindu imagination, which has made a deep imprint on Muslim societies of the Indian subcontinent, the distinction between *katcha* and *pakka* is related to that between the raw and the cooked, the highborn and the lower castes, the pure and the impure. *Katchi abadi*s, therefore, do not only refer to 'slums' made of huts (*jhuggi*s), but, pejoratively, to all lower-income settlements that developed without any official sanction—which is not to say without official protections. This rather loose and deeply condescending labelling equating the unofficial with the lowly and uncouth does not do justice to the diversity of living conditions within these unofficial settlements, some of which were the result of better planification than many official colonies, which gave them better access to water, electricity, sewerage or public transport (see the case of Muhammad Khan Colony in Chapter 7). The labelling of these settlements as 'unofficial' does not pass any judgement on their infrastructure, which may present significant variations from one case to another. However, by underlining their unsettled status, on the verge of legality—the legalisation of these settlements implies their 'regularisation', a much debated issue in Karachi since the 1970s[79]—this terminology highlights the uncertainty in which their residents live, as well as their dependency towards various kinds of middlemen (*dallal*s,[80] *thalewala*s,[81] etc.), the police and local politicians who navigate the murky waters between the official and the unofficial economy.

As the evolutions of the housing sector in the postcolonial period demonstrate, the unofficial has become the norm for the majority of Karachiites. Neither the state-sponsored housing projects of the 1960s nor the construction boom of the 1970s and 1980s (during which almost 50 per cent of the remittances sent back by Pakistanis working in the Gulf were thought to be reinvested in real estate in Karachi)[82] could alleviate Karachi's endemic housing problem and slow down its urban sprawl. As Karachi went increasingly vertical—the cityscape started changing drastically in the 1970s, with the construction of multi-storey apartment buildings that gave birth to a new 'flat culture'[83]—it continued to expand horizontally along the so-called eastern corridor (Landhi, Korangi and Malir), as well as along the northern corridor (Nazimabad, Liaquatabad, New Karachi). And far from receding, the contribution of the unofficial sector to this urban sprawl never ceased to increase. Thus, unofficial settlements have been catering to the housing needs of an ever increasing number of Karachiites: from 50 per cent of the population in 1998 to 61 per cent in 2001.[84]

Far from being reserved for the urban poor and freshly settled migrants, the *katchi abadi*s have also been catering to the housing needs of the Urdu-speaking lower-middle-class (skilled workers, clerks, government employees, teachers, etc.). And while these *basti*s, as they were affectionately called in the first decades of independence, were initially the terrain of dense but non-exclusive cultural solidarities, they were turned into more inward-looking and more ethnically homogenous citadels by the political parties and criminal groups that emerged in the city in the wake of the Afghan Jihad.[85] While continuing to attract hundreds of thousands of migrants and refugees every year, the city became increasingly fragmented from a social, spatial and political perspective, thus undergoing a far-reaching process of 'decosmopolitanising'.[86] The role of the Afghan war in this reconfiguration of the cityscape and in the emergence of its violent politics cannot be overemphasised, and it is to these externalities of Karachi's urban sprawl and ethnic fault lines that I turn now.

The Burden of Geography

The history of Karachi has been shaped by its geography, and in particular by the strategic location of its port, at the crossroads of important trade and military routes between the Persian Gulf, East Africa, Central Asia and India. During the medieval period, its natural port was known to navigators sailing from the Persian Gulf to India. Thus, the small fishermen's settlement which would become the site of modern Karachi was known as Dirbo (from *darb*, Arabic for 'entry'), an indication that the port of Karachi was known to Arab navigators of the medieval age as the gate of Hind.[87] The modern city of Karachi was itself developed by a group of Hindu traders who relocated there after the neighbouring port of Kharakbandar was choked with sand. Given its importance in regional seaborne trade and its connections with Sindh's hinterland and further, with Central Asia, Karachi also attracted the attention of the East India

Company early on. The first Anglo-Afghan War (1839–1842) was the precipitating factor of Karachi's occupation and subsequently of Sindh's conquest. Writing in the last decade of the nineteenth century, Alexander Baillie argued that, 'our occupation of Kurrachee resulted from the military operations in connexion with the Afghan War of 1838'.[88] Forty years later, Sir Montagu de P. Webb converged with Baillie in his preface to the annual edition of the *Karachi Residents Directory*, which opens with the following lines:

> Karachi is no longer a village of 'mud houses' sheltering between 10,000 and 12,000 traders as it was when Russian designs on Asia forced the British government to take up a position in Sind, that would enable a more effective defence of north-west India from outside aggression to be made.[89]

Determined to counter Russian influences in Central Asia, the British sent troops to Afghanistan to establish a friendly regime in Kabul. Following the refusal of the ruler of Punjab, Maharaja Ranjit Singh, to see British troops traverse the Punjab, the 9,500 men of the Bengal Army mobilised in this operation were constrained to take a different route, through Bahawalpur and Sindh. At the same time, 5,600 men of the Bombay Army, under the command of Sir John Keane, got stranded at the mouth of the Indus after the Talpur rulers of Sindh objected to their passage through Sindh. As a result, Keane called for some reinforcements, which occupied Karachi on 2 February 1839. Under the terms of the treaty signed with the Talpurs following this occupation, Karachi became a military depot, where military supplies for the troops deployed in Afghanistan could be stored, and where 3,000 soldiers could be stationed on a permanent basis. Karachi retained a strategic role for allied forces during the two world wars. During the First World War, it became an important military base, for its proximity to the Suez Canal and because it provided a gateway to Afghanistan and Central Asia, through which transited the supplies to the White armies fighting the Bolsheviks in Central Asia. During the Second World War, Karachi played an even more important logistical role in the conflict, as supplies to allied forces fighting on the eastern front were channelled through the port city.[90]

Karachi's role as the antechamber of Afghan conflicts was revived during the jihad of the 1980s. Its port became the major point of arrival of arms and ammunition destined to the Afghan *mujahidin*, while in the other direction the city was flooded with refugees—and drugs. In the process, Karachi's demographic profile, as well as its economy and politics, underwent dramatic transformations, fuelling social conflicts that gradually ethnicised and paved the way for the spectacular rise of the MQM in the second half of the 1980s.

The Democratisation of the Access to Arms

Arms supplies to the Afghan *mujahidin* increased massively between 1983 and 1987—a staggering 600 per cent increase was registered during this period.[91] The bulk of these weapons arrived by sea in Karachi and were then transported by road or rail to Peshawar. Even under such a repressive regime as that of Zia-ul-Haq, it was common knowledge that a large number of these weapons would never reach their destination. A report published in *Newsline* magazine in August 1987 thus suggested that, '20–25 per cent of the arms supplied are pilfered at different levels'.[92] A large part of this pilferage took place in Karachi itself, when weapons shipments were disembarked at the port, with the complicity of customs officials and under the supervision of operatives of the Bank of Commerce and Credit International (BCCI), who gradually took control of Karachi port.[93] At the end of the 1980s, the rules of gun running started changing in Karachi and Sindh at large. In 1989, a report by Mohammad Hanif in *Newsline* suggested that, 'in the last year, the business has been taken over by a new breed of independent underground entrepreneurs—students and political activists patronised by political parties who maintain what one student terms the "minimum safety distance". These boys have not only taken over the local distribution network, but also bring in their own supplies through regular visits to the tribal areas. They travel in small groups, always by train, and return to Karachi with their bags brimming with metal.'[94] Between 1986 and 1989, the price of guns went down by 40 to 50 per cent in Karachi. The TT-pistol (the favourite weapon of MQM militants) sold for 5,500 rupees in 1987. In 1989, it was priced at 3,000 rupees.[95] In the Frontier, the price of an AK-47 went down from 40,000 rupees in 1980 to 16,000 rupees in 1989.[96] During ethnic clashes in Karachi and Hyderabad, 'a rise in the prices of weapons was noticed because supplies were reportedly being rushed from the NWFP',[97] but the large influx of arms in Karachi in the following years stabilised the price of weapons and eventually led to their decrease.

This sudden influx of firearms contributed to the rapid escalation of political conflicts that, until then, had remained relatively benign. This was the case, in particular, of the student conflicts that pitted 'progressive' students against Islamist activists, which will be the focus of the next chapter. It is in this fast militarising student milieu that the founders of the MQM had their first taste of politics and that they developed a martial conception of the political struggle, which would become the trademark of the MQM. The militarisation of the MQM was reinforced by the 'ethnic riots' of the mid-1980s, which underlined the vulnerability of Urdu-speaking populations in the face of heavily armed criminal gangs dominated by Pashtuns from the north-west.

Drugs, Slums and 'Yellow Devils'

As the prime seaport of Pakistan, Karachi became a major export centre of Afghan heroin and, in the process, saw the emergence of powerful crime syndicates dominated by the Pashtuns. These crime syndicates controlled the production, transport and, to a lesser extent, the export of heroin from Karachi.[98] With the support of Afghan refugees who acquired a significant share of overland cargo services from Afghanistan and within Pakistan around the same time, Pashtun drug barons tightened their grip over this lucrative trade—by the mid-1980s, the export of heroin from Karachi was thought to generate billions of dollars every year.[99] As Arif Hasan pointed out in the midst of Karachi's first major 'ethnic riots' of the 1980s, 'certain Pashtun settlements in Karachi have become centres of mafia operation. Most of these settlements grew out of the transport trade and as such are strategically placed on the entry points to various areas of the city. In recent years the mafia [...] has created Sohrab Goth [...] at the entrance to Karachi and become a major slumlord in Quaidabad, thus controlling [Karachi's other exit] as well.'[100]

As these drug-barons reinvested their huge profits in the transport sector and in real estate, the rules of coexistence between Karachi's ethnic groups were brutally uprooted. By the early 1980s, the Pashtuns were already firmly entrenched in Karachi's transport sector: most bus routes permits were allocated to Pashtun transporters in the aftermath of the 1965 election by Ayub Khan as a reward for the support of his ethnic brethren in the presidential race. However, important changes started occurring in Karachi's transport sector in the late 1970s/early 1980s, with the influx of drug money. Initially, the owners of minibuses (which appeared in the city in the early 1970s) used to hire drivers to operate their own vehicles. In later years, this system ceded the way to new operating patterns: permit holders no longer operated minibuses themselves but financed their acquisition by prospective owners who had to refund the loan—with high interests—in monthly installments. This system encouraged minibus operators to drive recklessly and resort to overcrowding to pay off their debt, with their minibuses earning the nickname of 'yellow devils' as a result. In 1984 and 1985, road accidents claimed two lives daily in a city where the number of vehicles had more than tripled in ten years,[101] with 5,000 new minibuses being put into circulation between 1978 and 1986.[102] It was one of these accidents that prompted the 'ethnic riots' of April 1985. On the morning of 15 April 1985, a minibus driver,[103] while racing with a competitor, hit a group of students of Sir Syed Girls College, in Nazimabad, killing one of them. In the hours that followed the death of Bushra Zaidi, angry students organised a protest demonstration that was brutally repressed by the police. The attitude of the police, who were accused of molesting young female students, fuelled the anger of Mohajirs and Punjabis alike and in the following days violence spread across the city, from Liaquatabad to Orangi. Far from being unorganised, these rioting incidents often involved young Mohajir and Punjabi activists of the IJT. The young *jama'ati*s set buses on fire, which met with harsh responses from the police (many of these buses were [co-]owned by policemen). In the afternoon of 16 April, the army was deployed in Liaquatabad and Nazimabad, the Mohajir-dominated lower-middle-class areas where violence had erupted after Bushra Zaidi's death. But while the army was trying to defuse tensions in those two localities, a new incident set Orangi ablaze. A bus carrying Mohajir students to Bushra Zaidi's funeral was attacked by a band of armed Pashtuns in Banaras Chowk, a strategic location at the 'interface' between Pashtun- and Mohajir-dominated localities. In the words of Allen Feldman, the 'interface' is 'the topographic ideological boundary sector that physically and symbolically demarcates ethnic communities', where rioting functions as 'a traditional mechanism for setting and even extending territorial boundaries'.[104] In Karachi, Banaras Chowk was the main point of contact of Bihari and Pashtun residents: it was an informal bus terminal linking the lower-income neighbourhoods of SITE Town and Orangi to the rest of Karachi and it remains, to this day, a centre for activities related to transport and its ancillary needs. On 16 April 1985, it became a battlefield after Pashtun gangs attacked Mohajir students, before invading adjacent Abdullah Girls College, where they molested female students and damaged costly laboratory equipment. The 1985 riots thus erupted in 'a context of general public grievances, which included the transport problem',[105] as well as the new politics of real estate that emerged in the city following the development of the heroin trade.

The 'riots' of April 1985 and December 1986—which were only the deadliest and most reported incidents in a long series of disturbances[106]—were intimately linked with land conflicts, and more specifically with the changing dynamics of real estate development in the city's *katchi abadi*s. If the April 1985 'riots' started as a student-led protest against Pashtun transporters in the Urdu-speaking lower middle-class localities of Nazimabad and Liaquatabad, they escalated into a much deadlier battle for real estate after spreading to the unofficial settlements of Orangi, where they pitted Bihari slum-dwellers vs. Pashtun and Afghan gunmen recruited by land suppliers with links to the drug trade. After having taken control of the new *katchi abadi*s developing in the city, these real estate entrepreneurs were trying to lay their hands on older settlements situated at the margins of their new turf, whose residents were reluctant to sell their properties despite being offered three to four times their market value.[107] In Orangi, the main battlefield was situated between Banaras Chowk and the Metro Cinema, an area at the border of new Pashtun strongholds. During the December 1986 riots, Pashtun gunmen also attacked *mohalla*s adjacent to their zones of influence, such as Aligarh and Qasba colonies, where they singled out the shops and homes of Bihari residents while sparing those of the Pashtuns. Although the call to arms given by the imam of the adjacent Pirabad mosque played on the Pashtuns' sense of honour and masculinity,[108] these attacks were far from being spontaneous. Their level of organisation left little doubt about their premeditation. The assailants were provided cover and a way out by Pashtun residents who had recently been settled at the exit points and on the strategic lanes of these neighbourhoods.[109] When the signal for the assault was given, armed men with kerosene tanks set houses on fire and slaughtered their residents while gunmen positioned on the hills covered them with machine-gun fire.[110] Even if these attacks might have been a response to a recent anti-narcotic operation in Sohrab Goth,[111] the meticulous planning recalled above attests of their premeditation and of their irreducibility to a spontaneous response from the 'drug mafia' to this operation. Once again, this episode of violence provided land suppliers linked to the drug trade with an opportunity to expand their turf. It was also a warning to the MQM, which was widely perceived as the instigator of the Sohrab Goth operation. Far from capitulating, though, the MQM retaliated by sending its militants to extol revenge on Pashtun bystanders in the hours following the Qasba and Aligarh Colony massacres.[112]

Whereas the 1985 'ethnic riots', which officially cost fifty lives, remained cantoned to lower-income localities—whether *katchi abadi*s or lower-middle-class Mohajir-dominated localities—the incidents of December 1986 signalled an escalation as well as a geographical expansion of these fast-ethnicising urban conflicts. Officially, 200 people died in these 'riots', although the actual figure might have been much higher. The literary critic Asif Farrukhi, a medical practitioner by training, who used to provide medical support to lower-income residents of Orangi, has left a gripping account of these events. It is worth quoting at length for its first-hand report on the events of Aligarh Colony, which unequivocally points at the role of police and military officers in abetting if not inciting violence against Urdu-speakers:

> [Violent incidents] had become a common utterance in Orangi. But this time, geysers of blood sprayed from heads [*mauj-i-khun sar se guzar gai*; lit. 'waves of blood flowed from the heads'; this is a quotation of a famous verse by late-Mughal poet Mirza Ghalib]. We were informed that in the dark of the night, unidentified men had broken into Aligarh Colony, which was located near our centre, where they looted houses, attacked people and killed so many of them. This was the only information we had, because Orangi was cut off from the rest of the city. Then, finally, one of our workers managed to phone us with great difficulty, and told us, 'we [Aligarh Colony residents] are so isolated [*jaise kuen mein band baithe hain*; lit. 'sitting in a well'], there is a shortage of food, water and electricity, and the children, being deprived of milk, are continuously crying'. With the help of some top officials we managed to obtain a special permission [to go to Orangi] and we set off in an ambulance loaded with medical and food supplies. [...] A bit after Banaras Chowk, soldiers were blocking the road. They took such a long time to check our identity and the reason of our visit that people started gathering around us. 'If we get a chance, we'll teach them a lesson' [*unko maza chakha den*; lit. 'we'll give them a taste (of Hell)], said their officer while pointing at the bystanders. Burnt houses, looted belongings... A burqa-clad woman who was crying continuously insisted to show us her house. Something was pasted on the grillage of the window of her destroyed house. 'They dragged my son to kill him, so he grabbed the grillage,' said the woman. 'So they cut his hand. These are his fingers.'

Everyone was eagerly waiting for this day. There would be so much glamour [*ronq*] at Farnaz's wedding. [...] It had been decided that the festivities of the *mehndi ki raat*[113] would go on all night long. Wasim had told his friends that he would organise the singing party. Wasim was a respected officer but all day long, he prepared himself for an imitation of Madhuri Dixit [a famous Bollywood actress of the time], during which he would interpret '*Channe ke khet mein*' [this is an anachronism: the song is from the movie *Anjaam*, which was released eight years later]. There was a fear that the strike and the riots would rob the function of its glamour [*rang mein bhang na par jae*; lit. that bhang—a cannabis-based intoxicant—would not fall into the colours; this is a reference to the Hindu Spring festival of Holi]. But everything went according to plan. The function was going to last all night long so I decided to go home as I had to travel to Islamabad in the morning. My younger brother Tariq told me that when the call for Fajr [dawn] prayers resonated, the music stopped and the speakers were disconnected. He was on his way home when the whole street resonated with gunfire. He backtracked. This peaceful morning resonated with the noise of flying bullets. The noise was coming from nearby. It seemed that the bullets were flying over their heads, that cross fire would happen and the whole place would become a battlefield. The noise frightened everyone and led some of the last guests to take shelter in a locked room. Small children were told to lie under the beds and sofas. The noise was becoming more intense and a woman started screaming. Those who were on the upper floor could not come down but they could see what was happening. A police car drove by, while shooting. Then a white car appeared, looking like an ambulance. Two youths were pulled out from it. They had been blindfolded and their hands were tied behind their back. They were aligned against the wall and bullets were pumped into them, spraying fountains of blood and tearing their organs to shreds. Leaving the dead bodies behind, the assailants left in the white car. Then the police car came back, still firing. Later, I saw on TV that the police claimed to have killed two terrorists in an encounter in this locality. There were no details either in the newspaper but those who were still on the scene as the function was coming to an end will probably never forget how 'colourful' it was.[114]

This autobiographical text is not a transparent testimony and does not lend itself easily to historiographic use. It was obviously written several years after the events, as the anachronism around the Madhuri Dixit's song at the *mehndi ki raat* suggests, and it is heavily influenced by poetic tropes that sometimes obscure the subjective experience of the author, or what he personally saw and heard at the time. These problems, inherent to any vernacular history, do not deprive this account from its value, though. Despite the anachronisms, beyond the poetic quotes and with the temporal distance validating this interpretation of the events, Farrukhi shows that the Qasba and Aligarh colonies massacres for the first time brought ethnic violence home to middle-class families like his, who still believed that they could be insulated from it. The absence of any transition between the scenes of horror witnessed by the author in Aligarh Colony and the glamorous marriage festivities depicted in the following paragraph underlines that, until then, middle-class life remained largely insulated from incidents of 'ethnic violence'. The dramatic epilogue of this wedding night, in the early hours of 15 December 1986, shattered this sense of security and exposed the vulnerability of affluent Karachiites who thought they were shielded from what they perceived as the violence of the poor.

A Palimpsest of Sovereignties[115]

The trajectory of the Pakistani state does not fit well with the normative models of the modern state, be it—in classical Weberian fashion—an association claiming a monopoly over the legitimate use of force in a given territory, or—in Joel Migdal's more recent conceptualisation—a legal framework ensuring the enforcement of 'a rule of law in which the rules are the same from border to border'.[116] For all its discrepancies with these classical models of state-building, the history of state formation in Pakistan deserves better than pathological accounts in terms of 'failure', 'collapse' or even 'weakness'.[117] Not only do state agencies—within the security and judicial apparatus, in particular—retain a capacity to govern, that is, to structure the field of the possible for others.[118] More importantly, in Pakistan as in other seemingly 'weak' states, the dynamics of state formation deserve to be thought on their own terms, by paying attention to the everyday exercise and negotiation of public authority. As Marielle Debos suggests in her recent study of state formation in Chad, the most pressing issue for social scientists is not where the state begins and ends, but how to capture its continuous (trans)formation through the procedures and performances of those giving it flesh and blood, within and without state institutions.[119]

The political changes witnessed in Karachi over the past three decades provide ample ground to advance in this direction. The militarisation of the city's politics and unofficial economy did not only challenge the monopoly of the state over the means of coercion—a monopoly that, in any case, the Pakistani military had already trampled on by outsourcing its illegitimate violence in Kashmir and Afghanistan to non-state actors (tribal militias and later on jihadi organisations). More largely, the changes in the technologies of warfare and the transformation of Karachi's official and unofficial economy brought by the Afghan Jihad reinforced pre-existing trends towards the dispersion of power and the informalisation of the state, leading to the proliferation of what Christian Lund, in contemporary African contexts, refers to as 'twilight institutions': de facto public authorities attempting to define and enforce collectively binding decisions and rules.[120] In his study of the overlapping repertoires of authority in postcolonial India, Thomas Blom Hansen goes one step further and proposes to look at these actors as 'de facto sovereigns'.[121] This fragmentation of public authority went even further in Pakistan than in India. In Pakistan, state power never permeated society as deep and far as in India, as the dissemination of highly technological forms of violence within society and the inability of state authorities to enforce a national system of taxation exemplify—two developments that have no parallel in neighbouring India. The evolutions of Karachi's society over the past four decades bear testimony to this. The proliferation and ever-increasing power of these non-state sovereigns, claiming for themselves the right to discipline and punish but also to protect, tax and represent local populations, has turned the city into a 'zone of unsettled sovereignties and loyalties',[122] where the access to arms has become the privileged if not the sole venue towards power and wealth. Once again, it should be emphasised that this development was at least partially encouraged by the state itself. As the Inspector General of Police (IGP) Sindh informed the Supreme Court in 2011, 500,000 licences for arms and ammunitition of prohibited bore were issued by the Home Department of Sindh province for the past ten to fifteen years.[123]

The predominance of the MQM in city politics since the mid-1980s could not prevent the ever-increasing dispersion of power within society. As the party armed itself to provide 'support, defence, and retaliation' to Urdu-speaking populations against the Pashtun 'drug mafia',[124] it reinforced ethnic polarisations while contributing to the militarisation of political conflicts that had begun a few years earlier on Karachi's campuses. The violent mobilisation of the Mohajir community conducted by the party during this period, which was the product of dangerous and frightening times, was later on supplemented by an attempt to supersede formal power structures. The MQM's 'secondary state'[125] was less a parallel government than an unofficial power apparatus colonising the official state (through the seizure of public institutions—hospitals, schools, universities, public companies, the bureaucracy,...) while extending well beyond (through the meshing of the territory by the party's grid, through the taxation of the population and through the provision of various services duplicating, often with greater efficiency, those of the state, from the health sector to legal counselling). At the peak of its power, between 1990 and 1992, the MQM did not only exert a power of life and death over the residents of Karachi: according to some medical sources, it also took charge of the bureaucratic management of the dead by issuing medicolegal certificates (MLCs) for its own victims.[126]

This unofficial power structure was uprooted by a ruthless military operation between 1992 and 1994 but it was reactivated in later years and greatly benefited, in terms of funds and human resources, from the control of the local state after 2005. However functional it may be, though, this 'twilight institution' operating at the juncture of state and society could never re-monopolise the means of coercion, taxation and representation. As already indicated, the army broke the backbone of this unofficial structure of governance in the early 1990s. Moreover, despite its efforts to widen its audience by relinquishing its original ethnic discourse—as indicated by its renaming (from *Mohajir* to *Muttahida* [United] Qaumi Movement, in 1997)—the MQM failed to extend its domination beyond the Mohajir community. The breaches in its hegemony have only grown wider in recent years, as the demographic balance of the city was shifting in favour of non-Mohajirs (cf. Fig. 2). Last but not least, the MQM's hegemonic ambitions have been challenged in recent years by a new generation of organic sovereigns, who have drawn inspiration from the MQM's combined use of legal and extra-legal resources to carve their own dominions across the city.

Conclusion

Karachi never fully recovered from the shock of Partition, which set the basis for a perennial housing crisis while igniting unending battles over its 'ownership', legally and figuratively. The economic, social and political vacuum left by the departure of the non-Muslim population of the city was never fully filled by the Urdu-speaking immigrants who flooded the city in the years following Partition. Their sense of entitlement to Karachi became a major bone of contention with Sindhi elites, who expected to take the place of the departing Hindus and Parsis. Far from fading away in the course of time, this ontological battle for Karachi—which focuses on the city's identity and rightful 'owners'—was reactivated by the rise of the MQM at the helm of city politics, and more recently by the emergence of a Pashtun middle-class claiming its own right to the city, by the armed politics of autochthony of Karachi's 'indigenous' Baloch population as well as by the spectacular spread of jihadi movements challenging the reputation of Karachi as Pakistan's 'secular centre'. This enduring ontological battle for Karachi has been supplemented by increasingly fierce struggles over its human and economic resources, which brutally escalated in the context of the Afghan Jihad. The spectacular transformation of the city's unofficial economy during this period challenged the rules of coexistence between populations that were reinvented as rival 'ethnic groups' in the course of their violent confrontation. This confrontation initially had little to do with ethnicity and was primarily related to the investment of the huge profits of the heroin trade into the transport sector and the unofficial real estate market. As intercultural frictions and economic rivalries escalated into armed confrontations, they were reframed by violent and political entrepreneurs as 'ethnic' conflicts, a label that would remain the major frame of interpretation of Karachi's fault lines for the years to come. The role of the MQM, which met with its first electoral successes shortly after the 'ethnic riots' of 1985–1986, was decisive in this regard, as it mobilised its fearful Urdu-speaking constituents under the banner of Mohajir nationalism, a political project that had emerged in the course of the 1970s but that had failed to find a large audience until then. The MQM has remained Karachi's dominant political force ever since, but its hegemonic ambitions were resisted within and without the Mohajir community it had so successfully imagined. The battle for Karachi has taken several twists and turns in the process. It is these struggles which constitute the focus of this book: struggles over Karachi's territories, but also over its economies (both official and unofficial), and as local journalists like to put it, over its 'soul'—what the founding father of urban sociology, Robert Park, would have referred to as the 'moral order' of the city.[127]

2

FROM STUDENT BRAWLS TO CAMPUS WARS

Jab shabab par akar
Khet lahlhata hai

When the youths turn up,
the wind starts blowing over the fields.

Habib Jalib, 'Jamhurīyat' (Democracy) (1968).[1]

The previous chapter meant to bind together the successive chapters of Karachi's already long story of civil strife by singling out a series of historical processes that did not merely set the context for fierce social, economic and political struggles but that, each in its own way, transformed the city itself as an object of desire and contention. With this larger picture in mind, it is now time to start unfolding the story of these battles for the city. The present chapter makes a first step in this direction by retracing the chain of events and interactions that ignited and fuelled Karachi's first major armed conflict: the campus wars of the early 1980s, during which political violence did not only escalate but also took an organised and permanent character that set these student conflicts apart from previous outbursts of violence, such as the language 'riots' of 1971 and 1972.

My principal concern here is with one of the most understudied of conflict dynamics: violent escalation. What are the mechanisms at play in the shift from one sequence of a conflict to another? What are the technological and organisational contexts in which they operate? How are they related to changes in the social identities of the protagonists and in the manoeuvres of the state? These are some of the questions that will be addressed here through an exploration of student violence at Karachi University, between 1979 and 1989. During this decade there was a spectacular rise in student violence in this university, from fistfights to gunfights (in 1979), to murders (from 1981 onwards), to a massacre (in 1989). On one occasion, this violence spilled over from the campus and acquired an international dimension (when a PIA aeroplane was hijacked by Salamullah Tipu in March 1981). During the second half of the 1980s, it also spread through the city of Karachi, fuelling larger social and political conflicts. This case study will therefore consider two different aspects of the dynamics of conflict escalation: that of *intensification* (which concerns the *magnitude* of the violence in terms of casualties) and that of *expansion* (which concerns the *amplitude* of the violence in spatial terms).

Discontent Central: The Student Movement and Political Change in West Pakistan (1947–1979)

The Rise of Pakistan Leftist Student Organisations

In the years that followed the creation of Pakistan in 1947, the student wing of the Pakistan Muslim League, the Muslim Students Federation (MSF),[2] reigned supreme over Pakistani student politics. But this hegemony did not last long. In the early 1950s, the MSF imploded along factious lines and was overrun by a new student body, the Democratic Students Federation (DSF), which was launched in Rawalpindi in 1948 and extended to Karachi in 1950. Initially, the DSF concentrated on student matters (admission procedures and fees, improvement of the teaching environment...) but it gradually politicised under the influence of Marxist student leaders.[3] Although the JI launched its student branch, the IJT, in the months following Partition, it took several years before the organisation could stand on its own feet (its constitution was ratified in 1952 only and the organisation's structure and strategy were formalised between 1952 and 1955 with the help of a Muslim Brotherhood member based in Karachi, Said Ramazan).[4] Moreover, in its early years, the IJT showed less concern for student politics than for religious work. Although it took part in students' union elections at Karachi's Urdu College in the 1950s, it remained a marginal actor in these elections until the following decade. Candidates sympathetic to the IJT won the students' union election at Karachi University in 1963, before its own candidates won the following election. However, until the 1970s, student politics in Karachi and in Pakistan at large remained dominated by left groups, whose activists were confident that they could 'turn' Islamist activists. Munawar Hassan, the current *amir* of the JI and a former *nazim-e-ala* (supreme leader) of the IJT (from 1964 to 1967), was himself involved with the left during his early student years. As a student at the Central Government College in Karachi in the 1960s, he claims to have turned three activists of the IJT before being in turn 'converted' to political Islam after reading Maududi's *Dawat-e-Islami aur Uske Mutalibat* (The Call to Islam and its Demands).[5]

Left activists imprinted a strong international outlook on the student movement, at least in West Pakistan.[6] Under their leadership, students protested against the rapprochement between Pakistan and the United States, as well as against the policies of the Western block across the Third World (the 1956 Suez crisis was, for instance, the occasion of an intense mobilisation). This agitation was severely repressed. On 8 January 1953, a demonstration organised by the DSF and the Inter-Collegiate Body (ICB, which consisted of the vice-presidents and general secretaries of all students' unions) turned violent, and seven students were killed in police firing. The news of these killings rapidly spread across the city and the high-handedness of the police alienated even those students who were not present at the demonstration. 'A firestorm was unleashed in my heart and mind when I heard the news of this incident,' thus writes poet Anwar Ehsan Siddiqi, a *muhajir* from Fategarh (U.P.), who at the time was preparing for his matriculation examination and had no political affiliation. Enraged by the address of the prime minister the next day—which started with the words, 'Your benevolent father is talking to you'—Siddiqi wrote a protest poem at once, which was published by several children's magazines and which included the following verses: 'While shooting at us in the chest, you project yourself as a benevolent father/ Have a look at your feet soaked in blood.'[7] This event was widely relayed and protested across the two wings of Pakistan, and more established poets also addressed tributes to the martyred students. The biggest 'hit', among students, was Ibn-e-Insha's '8 Janwarī 1953', in which this poet better known for his satirical streak lambasted a government murdering its own children. In the following years, these events would become a rallying point for the student movement. Each year, on the 8 January, college and university students celebrated 'Martyrs of January Day' (*yom-e-shuhada-e-janwari*) by boycotting their classes. In Karachi, a rally was organised at D.J. College, during which student leaders paid tributes to their fallen comrades.[8]

In 1954, students' unions, as well as the Communist Party of Pakistan (CPP), were officially banned. So was the DSF and the new platform of student organisations that had emerged the previous year, the All Pakistan Students Organisation (APSO), which was suspected of subversive activities.[9] In an attempt to regain control over the student movement, which had become a rallying point for all those disappointed by the drift of Pakistan towards authoritarianism and social conservatism,[10] the government supported the creation of a new student body, the National Students Federation (NSF), in 1955. However, left-wing activists managed to take over the organisation after infiltrating it, under the guidance of underground activists of the CPP and possibly with the financial support of Moscow. In 1958, martial law was proclaimed and a few weeks later General Ayub Khan staged a successful coup. The NSF was banned and the ICB was revived. Once again, this organisation was infiltrated by leftist activists, who tried to stage a mass protest against the visit of President Eisenhower in 1959. But the plan was leaked to the authorities and most leaders of the Left were arrested. Some died in detention (such as Hasan Nasir, the Secretary General of the CPP) while others were freed in the early 1960s and turned to agitation once again.

One of the major figures of this agitation, in Karachi, was Mairaj Muhammad Khan. This Afridi Pashtun was born in 1938 in a family which traced its roots to the Tirah Valley but which had resettled in Qaimganj (in what is now the Indian state of Uttar Pradesh). After enrolling at the (anti-Pakistan) Jamia Millia of Delhi, Mairaj migrated to Pakistan in 1949, at the insistence of his father, a *hakim* (traditional physician) of repute, who had settled in Quetta before Partition. In order to gain autonomy from this strict and austere father, he moved to Karachi and gained admission at Sindh Muslim Arts College. In 1959, he was sentenced to a year in jail for taking part in the aforementioned demonstration against the visit of President Eisenhower. Shortly after his liberation, he was elected president of the college's students' union and in the following years, he imposed himself as one of the prominent leaders of the NSF and of the student uprising against Ayub Khan (1968–1969). In

1961, Mairaj and other left-leaning students organised a procession in Karachi following the death of Patrice Lumumba in the Congo (Lumumba was celebrated by progressive students as a martyr of freedom and poems dedicated to him were recited during recitals of poetry, or *musha'iras*),[11] before taking part in the mass demonstration that rocked the city following the Jabalpur communal riots in India. In the repression that followed, hundreds of students were arrested and twelve of them were put under trial in military courts. This decision provoked the ire of the students and thousands of them demonstrated in support of their comrades, at the sound of the lead song of a recent Indian film, *Shahid* (The Martyr), celebrating the memory of India's first revolutionary martyr, Bhagat Singh.[12] Following this intense mobilisation, most student leaders were freed but chose to go underground, out of fear of being rearrested. In 1963, the ban on the NSF was lifted and in the following years, the student agitation against Ayub's regime amplified and received the support of the working class, the Urdu-speaking and Gujarati business community, some major poets (such as Habib Jalib) and even a section of Ayub's entourage. Mairaj remembers that, a day after setting on fire the headquarters of the Convention Muslim League (CML, the faction of the Pakistan Muslim League loyal to Ayub Khan) in Karachi, he approached the leader of the local chapter of the party, Khalid Jamil, and requested his financial support. Against all odds, the infuriated politician answered favourably to his request, out of tribal solidarity (both were Afridi Pashtuns) but also out of pragmatism: Ayub's regime was getting shaky and members of his entourage were eager to ensure their political survival in these uncertain times.[13]

A Weapon of Mass Disruption: Bhutto and the Student Movement

In the second half of the 1960s, the student leadership engaged in a rapprochement with a former protégé of Ayub Khan, Zulfikar Ali Bhutto, who had become a popular figure among left students for his anti-India stance after the 1965 war and his apparent socialist inclinations. Bhutto, for his part, saw in the student movement a tool of destabilisation of Ayub's regime, particularly in the Punjab. The second most populated province of the country after East Bengal, the Punjab was also the major recruitment centre of the army. As such, it was—and remains—the backbone of the Pakistani state and the key to any project of regime change.

The student movement was thus Bhutto's weapon of mass disruption. The anti-Ayub uprising of 1968–1969 was spearheaded by students and overseen by Bhutto himself. On 7 November 1968, while Bhutto was sitting at the Intercontinental Hotel in Lahore, students confronted the police on the Rawalpindi-Peshawar Road. According to Mairaj Muhammad Khan, they deliberately provoked the security forces by throwing stones at them, expecting an armed response that would radicalise the movement and delegitimise further Ayub's regime. The plan 'succeeded': a student was killed in police firing and Bhutto was immediately informed of this expected development.[14] The following year, Ayub Khan was replaced by another general, Yahya Khan, who organised the first free elections in the country's history, in December 1970. During the election campaign, Bhutto received the support of student leaders and in return some of them got PPP tickets (Mairaj Muhammad Khan, for instance, was the party's candidate in Lalukhet [Liaquatabad] but had to return the ticket under the pressure of the leadership of the CPP).[15] Despite the victory of the Awami League (which won 162 seats in the National Assembly against 88 for the PPP), the army and West Pakistan's political class refused to allow its leader, Mujibur Rehman, to become the country's prime minister, and Pakistan plunged into civil war. In 1971, East Pakistan proclaimed its independence, becoming Bangladesh. In the meantime, in former West Pakistan, Bhutto became president and committed himself to a profound reform of the state apparatus and its relationship to society. Initially, Bhutto attempted to enroll student leaders to his cause. With the support of the underground leadership of the CPP, Mairaj Muhammad Khan became a member of the PPP and joined Bhutto's cabinet, where he became a minister without portfolio. However, the relations between these young Marxists and the leader of the PPP quickly went sour. Mairaj and other left activists denounced the authoritarian drift of the regime and the repression of the labour movement, which started in 1972. Under pressure from the CPP, though, Mairaj did not immediately quit the government and it is only in 1973 that he broke up with Bhutto, who announced his sacking through a memo to the other members of government, where he accused Mairaj of 'weakening the government'.[16] In 1975, Mairaj was arrested and sentenced to four years imprisonment in a case which would be remembered as the 'Hyderabad Conspiracy Case'.[17] Adding insult to injury, Bhutto might also have provided cover support to the IJT during this period,[18] which saw him relinquish his socialist leanings while trying to appease the most conservative sections of Pakistani society. In 1977, this tainted democratic experience came to a brutal end with Bhutto's overthrow by General Zia-ul-Haq. Once again, the country came under martial law and the channels of democratic expression of student discontent shrunk, paving the way for more violent forms of mobilisation.

KU: A Young and Turbulent University

The University of Karachi was established in 1951 and was originally situated at the heart of the city, on Baba-e-Urdu Road, in a former private Hindu Trust-run middle school for girls.[19] The congested and polluted atmosphere of the area was not conducive to studies, though, and in order to appease student agitators, Prime Minister Muhammad Ali Bogra promised them to shift the university to a more appropriate location, twelve kilometres east of the city centre. This decision was seen, at the time, as a victory for the DSF, which had been campaigning for a better studying environment.[20] However, the relocation of the university away from the legislative and administrative centre (1959) also suited Pakistan's first military ruler, who aimed to contain student agitation by shifting the university to an area of relatively low-density population.[21]

Opened as an examination centre for college students, the university started offering courses from 1953 onwards at its two faculties of arts and sciences. Karachi University (KU) grew rapidly in the following years, to become the country's largest public university (it presently enrolls 24,000 students in eight faculties). In the early 1950s, KU was a marginal actor in the city's student politics. With an initial batch of only fifty students, the university was a light weight on the local educational scene, which was dominated by better-endowed colleges. The major hotbeds of student agitation were Dow Medical College, D.J. Science College and the Sindh Muslim Arts College, and it is only from the 1960s onwards that KU students started contributing in a major way to the student movement. In 1957, the NSF swept over students' union elections in Karachi and it consolidated its hold over the city's educational institutions, including KU, over the next few years. In 1960, the ban on students' union elections was partially lifted and the NSF confirmed its supremacy over the local student scene, although in the early years of the decade, the IJT started making its presence felt on Karachi's campuses.

In 1962, Fatehyab Ali Khan, a *muhajir* from Hyderabad (Deccan) and one of the major figures of the student movement, became the first president of KU's students' union. Two years later, another leader of the NSF, Hussain Naqi (a *muhajir* from Lucknow), shortly became the president of the union, before being expelled from the university for his political activities.

The 1962 Sino-Soviet split took its toll on the left movement, as it led to a fissure of the NSF along pro-Moscow/pro-Beijing lines. This factionalisation of the NSF benefited the IJT, which won students' union elections at KU between 1969 and 1974. By then, the NSF had imploded into two major factions (the pro-China NSF-Mairaj and the pro-Moscow NSF-Kazmi)[22] and Karachi student politics were getting increasingly polarised around the struggle between leftist and Islamist activists. In 1973, independent progressive students formed the Liberal Student Organisation (LSO), which took the lead of an anti-IJT alliance including factions of the NSF as well as the PPP's student wing, the Peoples Student Federation (PSF), which was formed in 1972. This coalition of progressive groups formed an electoral alliance (the Progressive Students Alliance) and managed to defeat the IJT at KU's students' union elections in 1975–1976. However, the IJT managed to regain control over KU's students' union the following year. In this rise to power, the IJT relied upon the support of science students, a trend which is not specific to Pakistan (among students, most recruits of Middle-Eastern or South-East Asian Islamist groups have come from science, engineering, law and medicine).[23] Progressive and left organisations, for their part, found their strongest support in the Faculty of Arts, which would later on fall into the orbit of the APMSO.

The Facilitating Factors of Political Violence

Until the late 1970s, the occasional brawls between left-wing and Islamist student activists at KU remained relatively benign and mainly involved fistfights or incidents of egg tossing (a favourite modus operandi of the IJT).[24] Fahim Khan, a former progressive student activist, who would later on become the mayor of Karachi, remembers that at the end of the 1970s, 'when someone pulled out a knife, it was really a big deal'.[25] Occasionally, student activists would also fight with sticks. The activists of the IJT stored their own stock in a campus mosque, whereas left-wing activists of the NSF would break into classrooms and tear apart furniture to craft their weapons.[26] The first significant clash at KU opposed the IJT to the NSF in 1968. Violence gradually escalated in the following years, particularly after the rise of the IJT's militia, the Thunder Squad, which started making its presence felt at KU from 1972 onwards,[27] although it was formed several years earlier in Punjab. This low-intensity conflict culminated in March 1978, after a gathering of the IJT was disrupted by left activists. When the guest of honour, education minister Muhammad Ali Hoti, stood up at the podium to deliver a speech, left students erupted, unfolded banners and shouted anti-Zia slogans. Expecting trouble, they had brought sharp logs and a melee ensued. Although women students did not take part in the fight, they were part of the planning of the operation and had smuggled the banners in.[28] This would remain one of the rare incidents of violence that involved women students on the campus. The escalation of student violence at KU, from the late 1970s onwards, alienated female student activists, who deserted en masse from student politics. Young men were left to themselves and to their politics of 'musculinity',[29] in what gradually evolved into a full-blown campus war.

This escalation of violence at KU was not a sudden, unpredictable development. It was made possible by changes in the infrastructure of the conflict (with a sudden access to large quantities of firearms), in the manoeuvres of the state and in small groups' dynamics within student organisations. However, these developments should not be mistaken for causal factors: they facilitated the recourse to lethal violence, but in no way did they trigger it.

Changes in the Technologies of Student Warfare

The patterns of student violence started changing with the inflow of firearms to Karachi campuses. Modern weaponry (Sten-guns and revolvers, and later on Kalashnikovs) was introduced onto the campus by the militants of the Thunder Squad, the armed wing of the IJT. These firearms were possibly acquired in the weapons markets of Khyber Agency, or from some *mujahidin* factions (such as Gulbuddin Hekmatyar's Hizb-e-Islami, which received a delegation of IJT members in Peshawar as early as 1975). It is also possible, as the arms raid related below suggests, that these weapons were directly delivered to the IJT in Karachi by its patrons (the JI leadership but also, at that time, the army). This sophisticated weaponry was put to use for the first time on the occasion of the oath-taking ceremony of the Karachi University Students' Union (KUSU) on 12 August 1979. When a group of progressive students organised a protest against the ceremony (the Union, by then, was dominated by the IJT), militants of the Thunder Squad fired at them with Sten guns, injuring eighteen of them (including two women).[30]

Leftist and pro-PPP student organisations initially had greater difficulty obtaining weapons. In its initial years, the United Student Movement (USM), a platform of progressive and nationalist student groups,[31] turned to Baloch toughs to ensure its security and used the Baloch Students Organisation's (BSO) connections to procure its first weapons. Among the IJT's rivals, the PSF was the first organisation to acquire firepower. In 1979, a group of PSF students managed to get hold of a delivery of weapons intended for the IJT. As recalled by one of the participants to this arms raid, PSF activist Akram Qaim Khani:

> I was going on a motorbike with a friend of mine in my area [Shah Faisal Colony] and suddenly we saw a university students' union van. At that time, the union was run by the Jama'at-e-Islami [IJT]. It was very surprising because the *jama'atis* never dared to enter our area. Then I saw one *badmash* [rogue] called Sayyid in the van. So I told my friend: 'Maybe they are planning to do something to us, to attack us. There must be something wrong, we must follow them.' So we followed them in the colony and they parked the van in front of a house and Sayyid and another *badmash* came out of the car and they had two large *boris* [gunny bags] that looked very heavy. Then they dumped these two bags in that house. [...] I decided that we should check on them in the morning. I gathered all our friends, maybe 20, 30, in my house, and in the early morning, we surrounded their house. At eight o'clock, Sayyid came back with the van and they started uploading the bags. When they were about to upload the second one, Tipu [the most well known PSF militant] came and, you know, he had no patience in him. I had told everyone, 'Let them complete their job and then we'll do something.' But after the first batch [was uploaded in the van], Tipu shouted 'O, Sayyid!' He was carrying a gun—we only had one gun, with maybe 20 bullets—and he started firing at Sayyid. Sayyid ran away and the other man ran away and we captured all those bags. They were full of pistols, Sten guns, knives... Hundreds of them... That is the day we became rich in Karachi, when we realised that we could conquer all Karachi. Jama'at was vanished from Karachi University for a month. Not a single of them went outside because they knew that we had guns now. It was the first time that we saw so many guns. Then the thinkers, the political people [like him] realised that something is happening. How

come they have that much and are bringing that many revolvers in Karachi University? [Nearly] 500 revolvers and Sten guns? What is happening? Everybody realised that things in Karachi were about to change.[32]

As this testimony suggests, changes in student warfare technology, against the backdrop of the Afghan Jihad, transformed the ontology of the conflict in the eyes of its protagonists. Until then, the power and influence of student organisations was primarily measured by their results in student union elections. But with the militarisation of student organisations (by 1982, the IJT, PSF, PkSF, BSO and USM all had a weapons stash in the hostels under their control, including AK-47s), their actual power became conditional upon their military strength. The stakes of the conflict also became higher, with student organisations now detaining the ambitions of 'conquering' the city campuses by 'vanishing' their rivals, to use Akram Qaim Khani's words. This representation of the conflict as a fight to the finish, based upon a new way of perceiving the adversary, represented a clear departure from past ways of conceiving of student strife. Until the arrival of weapons and the first gunshot incidents, the distinction between friends and enemies remained blurred by mutual benevolence, if not mutual respect, as suggested by Akram Qaim Khani:

We might have had differences but we had respect for each others, like 'I am in politics, he is also in politics'. [...] After the NSF broke with Bhutto and I had to go underground, I was given shelter by a local *nazim* of the IJT in my neighbourhood [Shah Faisal Colony]. So we fought but also respected each other.[33]

Although this testimony might be informed by nostalgia for a supposedly golden age of student politics ('respect' is a big word indeed for rivals who regularly clashed and denigrated each other with highly derogatory language, including frequent sexual connotations), it should not be entirely dismissed as an idealised reconstruction of the past. It suggests that, at least at the level of representations, something changed in Karachi's student politics at the turn of the 1970s, with the ontology of the conflict taking on a more 'Schmittian' dimension in the eyes of its protagonists.[34] The changes that occurred in the technologies and practices of student warfare transformed its representations, rather than the other way round. Technological and behavioural changes came first, and attitudes adjusted later.

The Role of the State (I)

This weapons procurement spree was tolerated, if not encouraged, by the regime of General Zia-ul-Haq, which sought to reduce the influence of left-wing and pro-PPP forces on the campuses. The participation of the JI in Zia's government guaranteed Islamist student activists political protection when they flouted the law, which encouraged the IJT to deploy strong arms tactics on the campuses, against students but also against the liberal teaching staff (some teachers' societies had a record of resisting government interference in academic affairs).[35] Zia himself once congratulated the IJT for the 'splendid job of maintaining peace on campus and the safety of Islam'.[36]

By facilitating the militarisation of its IJT protégés, the Zia regime helped 'mak[e] violence conceivable; so that it was thinkable and deemed ordinary and inevitable'.[37] Yet this state-centric explanation of the increase in student violence on Pakistan's campuses does not provide the full picture. It tends to neglect the forces at play within student organisations, and the new dynamics within student activism arising from internal power shifts. The Zia regime certainly facilitated the militarisation of student politics, hoping that the militarisation of the IJT would silence left-wing and pro-PPP troublemakers. Yet it is far less clear whether the state played a role in making violence ordinary, at both the practical and the psychological level. Some Pakistani authors see the Zia regime as the agent to blame not only for the rise of the rightists but also for the brutalisation of students by 'encroaching upon the cognitive and social constructs of the polity's educated inhabitants'. The same authors argue that, 'convictions were instilled that made violence possible in the social, political and religious spheres'.[38] In other words, the escalation of violence on the country's campuses is said to have been the outcome of a culture of violence patronised by the military regime of Zia-ul-Haq. But cultural or cognitive explanations of political violence tend to reify their object, obliterating the social identities of the actors (who are always party to a plurality of social worlds and value systems) and intra-group dynamics (which may be far more effective in constraining individuals than exogenous ideas and vague sentiments).

Changes in the Small Group Dynamics of Student Organisations

The arrival of weapons on the campus was a source of bewilderment for political activists of the time. According to the former General Secretary of the USM, Fahim Khan, 'we never decided to become militants, it just happened'.[39] This narrative of bewilderment is also one of disempowerment, as it expresses the frustration of these political workers at having gradually lost the initiative to the supposedly more unpredictable militants. Thus, whilst political workers such as Fahim Khan claim that, 'we never wanted violence to replace politics', they concede that they had to rely on armed militants for their survival: 'when we came under threat [from the IJT], we needed someone to fire back. Lives were at stake.' The relationship between activists and militants was not strictly functional though, and unfolded in a complex emotional context. Militants inspired fear, but also awe, and their impulsivity was not always considered a liability but was also seen as a political virtue infusing the group with energy. This was particularly true as regards the PSF. Under Bhutto's leadership, the PPP had been encouraging the recruitment of party workers from the lower-middle-class, known for their enthusiasm and loyalty to the Bhutto family. These hotheaded party workers were known as *jiyala*s, and were seen by the party leadership as one of its major assets. Thus the unpredictable and impulsive behaviour of militants such as Tipu was as much praised by their comrades as it was feared. When recollecting the role played by Tipu in the aforementioned 1979 arms raid, Akram Qaim Khani does not blame him for having compromised his well thought out plan and having put the lives of his comrades at risk. Tipu's forward rush might have compromised the group's strategy, but it was also the sign of his courage, enthusiasm and sense of initiative in a tough call. As Randall Collins emphasises, every belligerent group has its 'violent few': experienced and self-confident fighters who tend to take the initiative during violent confrontations. These specialists of violence usually deal with danger by seeking it out instead of avoiding it. The most actively violent are not necessarily the most competently violent, though, especially if we understand such 'competence' as a capacity of 'interactional dominance' enabling this military elite to perform its duties cooly and effectively while interacting with others who are not—what Collins refers to as 'being cool in the midst of other people's hot emotions'.[40] Tipu, on the contrary, was a maverick action-seeker, who overcame the tension/fear characteristic of potentially violent situations such as the arms raid recalled above through 'frenzied hot participation',[41] with complete disregard for his personal safety or that of his companions. However, what could have passed for a personal weakness and a collective liability was elevated to a political virtue by his more middle-class comrades, who were as fascinated with violence as they were unfamiliar with it.

These militants were generally petty criminals (*badmash*s) recruited from outside the campus to provide muscle to student organisations. The most notorious Thunder Squad militant, Raja Javed, was apparently the son of a police officer from Punjab, and he was already involved in petty crime when he joined the IJT. He worked in tandem with another petty criminal, Noshah, and both were later hanged for their involvement in a series of (non-political) murders in the early 1980s. Although leftist and pro-PPP students' unions were initially hostile to the involvement of outsiders in student conflicts, they promptly emulated this trend. Thus according to Akram Qaim Khani:

> We managed to get these people admitted to the university and colleges, so that we at least had some protection. There was a very famous *badmash*, Shabir. After that he joined MQM. I got him admitted to Jamia Millia. Then the first day he cut the face of a famous *jama'ati badmash*, Mehbub Chishti, who also joined MQM later on. Then we were free to come and go as we liked.[42]

The involvement of these outsiders with a criminal background and familiarity with weapons rapidly contributed to the escalation of violence on the campus. As we saw, the first firing incident occurred in 1979, at the initiative of notorious Thunder Squad militants Raja Javed and Noshah, who opened fire with Sten guns on a group of progressive students. This was a major breach in the informal code of conduct of student organisations. Yet the escalation of violence was not a mechanical process, and despite what is suggested by some of the testimonies quoted above, there was nothing mechanical about the increasing number of killings on the campus, which took student conflicts to a whole new level.

Predictable but Contingent: The First 'Political' Killing at Karachi University

On 25 February 1981, a group of left-wing students from the NSF and PSF was gathered at the Arts Faculty lobby of KU for a demonstration in downtown Karachi when they heard that a military jeep was parked in front of the Administration building. An army major had come to help his daughter get admitted to the university and though he was there for personal reasons, the students were enraged—this was Zia's Pakistan, a country under military rule, where the left was living its twilight but remained a force to be reckoned with on the campuses, particularly in Karachi. As the organiser of the demonstration, Akram Qaim Khani, recalls, 'it was a surprise. It was a challenge to us. I was a student leader and the army was in my university…'. At Khani's instigation, the fifty-odd crowd set off for the Administration building, collected petrol from parked cars, filled a Coca-Cola bottle with it and tried to set fire to the jeep. Khani claims that he saved the driver ('he ran away, anyway…'), so no one was hurt in the incident, but while the students—unsuccessfully—tried to set the jeep on fire, a group of Thunder Squad militants arrived on the scene and assaulted the agitators. Khani (who contracted polio in his childhood and thus suffered from limited mobility) had been spared from physical assault in the past ('even the big *badmash* thought "we cannot touch Akram, otherwise his friends will kill us"'), but this time he was roughed up by Thunder Squad *badmash*s Farooq and Zarar Khan, and he was eventually captured, detained, and delivered to the army, which arrested him. As Khani suspected, his friends decided to retaliate and the next day an enraged PSF militant came to the university to exact revenge. Salamullah Tipu was the PSF's own 'big *badmash*'. He hailed from a lower-middle-class Pashtun but Urdu-speaking family which had migrated to Pakistan from present day Uttar Pradesh. Tipu planned to embrace a military career but was kicked out of the prestigious Kakul Military Academy, in Abbottabad, after it was discovered that he had a criminal record (while in college, he had committed numerous car thefts).[43] When he returned to Karachi, he initially flirted with religious conservatives, before drifting towards the left. According to some sources, he was in charge of the formation of the street fighting units of the NSF before leaving it to join the PSF in 1975.[44] Following the 1977 coup, he went underground and only returned to Karachi after the August 1979 firing incident at KU. In November 1980, he briefly left for Afghanistan, where he joined the two sons of Zulfikar Ali Bhutto, Murtaza and Shahnawaz, who were trying to launch an armed resistance movement against the Zia regime. According to Raja Anwar, a former adviser of Bhutto and founding member of al-Zulfikar (the terrorist group set up by Murtaza and Shahnawaz in Kabul), Tipu earned Murtaza's confidence and was entrusted with a grand project: the hijacking of a PIA plane from Karachi to Damascus.[45] He returned to Pakistan in January 1981 and was hiding in Karachi when he heard the news of

Akram Qaim Khani's arrest. Despite his mission, he decided to avenge his friend's ill-treatment at the hand of the IJT. When he arrived on the campus, the day after Khani's arrest, he went looking for IJT militants and as soon as he came across a group of them, opened fire with a Sten gun and threw a couple of grenades in their direction. When the assault was over, a senior IJT activist, Hafiz Aslam, lay dead. Tipu, who was known for his impulsivity, probably fired haphazardly at the IJT group and Aslam might have been killed by a stray bullet (this hypothesis tends to be confirmed by the fact that some bystanders, including several Iranian students, were also hurt in the attack). In any case, the use of such firepower by a left-wing militant was unprecedented and baffled the entire student community, including Tipu's comrades ('We were surprised… We did not even know where he had got these grenades from,' Akram Qaim Khani told me). Khani was brutally tortured over the following weeks, until Tipu managed to obtain his liberation (and that of fifty-four other political prisoners) by fulfilling his mission to hijack a PIA flight from Karachi to Damascus (via Kabul) the next month (March 1981). In organising this hijacking, Tipu was also trying to ensure his own survival, since he was facing the wrath of the JI (at the time part of the government) for his involvement in Hafiz Aslam's murder.

However predictable it may have been, in the increasingly militarised context of student politics at KU, the chain of events recalled above underlines that Hafiz Aslam's murder was also strongly contigent: it was *indeterminate* (things could have turned out differently, if that officer had not stepped onto the campus or if Khani had not been physically challenged), *conditional* (to the affective bonds between Khani and Tipu but also to the latter's easy access to firearms) and *uncertain* (Tipu had to improvise his response to an event he had no control over).[46] As such, this first killing at KU suggests that political violence is not merely the outcome of social, economic and political changes predating the conflict; it also takes unanticipated courses and tends to reproduce itself by generating its own causalities in the course of violent interactions. This is as true at the individual as at the collective level: new costs or incentives to participate generated in the course of the conflict lead individuals to join in or defect at different stages, while social polarisation and violence may be endogenous to the conflict itself,[47] and for some belligerents warfare can become a prerequisite for their social reproduction and political survival.[48]

With the February 1981 incident explored above, a banal (and unsuccessful) arson attempt set in motion a chain of events that ended up with a homicide and an act of international terrorism,[49] which was the opening act of a transnational armed struggle led by the terrorist organisation set up by Murtaza Bhutto, al-Zulfikar. The consequences for KU student politics were no less remarkable. Tipu did not only commit a murder: even if it had not been his intention, he redefined the rules of student strife and elevated it to the level of warfare. Now that guns had spoken, no one seemed able, or even willing, to silence them. In December 1981, a former IJT activist who had defected to join the progressive USM, Shaukat Cheema, was shot at by IJT militants while passing in front of a mosque controlled by the Islamists. Severely injured, he died three days later in hospital. A week later, a leader of the Thunder Squad, Danish Ghani, was killed by USM militants led by the BSO's strongman, Boro, and by a PSF militant, Shirin Khan. A few months later, on 1 July 1982, it was the turn of a progressive activist, Qadir Abid, to fall to the bullets of the IJT during an attack on a USM stand. Again, it is not clear if this murder was intentional or if, as some of Qadir's friends claim, he was hit by a stray bullet during the gun fight.[50] What was clear was that the patterns of violence had changed in the matter of a few months. Gun battles and targeted killings were now taking place on a regular basis and most student activists had started sporting guns, for security purposes but also to conform with their comrades. Lethal violence was no longer extraordinary. It had become routine due to everyday procedures, language and attitudes, to such an extent that for student activists the involvement in violent groups and actions was now seen as a natural process occurring independently of agency, as the following quote from a former PSF activist suggests:

> I was with the PSF and I ended up carrying a gun. What was the reason for that? I don't know. The reason given was always security. Otherwise you become an easy target. There was also the politics of numbers [after the ban on students' unions in 1984, the power of each student organisation was principally measured in terms of military strength]. [...] There was a lot of show as well.[51]

What is striking in this account, apart from the reflexive abilities of the speaker (presently a well-known columnist for a major daily newspaper), is his complete denial of agency in the description of his becoming a 'militant'. In the same way as Fahim Khan recalls the militarisation of his own group, this former student activist suggests that he was acted upon by political routines. The striking image of the gun that simply 'ended up' in his hands exemplifies the process by which violence—or at least its possibility—may become a routine incorporated into everyday life. Hafiz Aslam's murder had set in motion a process of violent escalation and systematisation, which was made possible and accelerated by the changes set out above in student warfare technology, in the positioning of the state and in small group dynamics within student organisations. None of these variables was, in itself, a causal factor for increased violence. Yet, after Hafiz Aslam's murder they all worked together to escalate the conflict, with the militants asserting their authority and conception of politics within student organisations, thanks to their modern weaponry and, at least in the case of the IJT, the covert support of the state.

The Role of the State (II)

In the second half of the 1980s, student violence at KU entered a new phase, which proved even bloodier than the preceding ones. Once again the role of the state was undeniable. The ban on students' unions accelerated the militarisation of student politics, while the rumours of a covert support of the tail-end Zia regime to the MQM changed power equations at KU and in Karachi at large. Whatever truth there might have been behind these rumours, the MQM never was the creature of the military establishment. It pursued its own agenda and was a product of the violent world of student politics that took shape at KU at the turn of the 1970s, as acknowledged by the founders of the MQM themselves in their autobiographical accounts of the early days of the Mohajir movement (see the next chapter). In this new phase of the conflict, the escalation of violence was largely a by-product of the conflict itself, as it sustained new political polarisations, new routines of belligerence and new thresholds of acceptable violence, where transgression could only lead to capitulation or retaliation on the part of the aggrieved party. After Hafiz Aslam's murder, such a transgression of the informal code of conduct of the belligerents occurred for a second time in 1989, when a group of PSF militants was executed in cold blood by their APMSO rivals in the gymnasium of KU. Contrary to the violent outbursts that ignited KU's campus wars in the early 1980s, which bore testimony to the rise of hotheaded militants within the ranks of student organisations, this time the escalation of violence resulted from the spillover of inter-party conflicts. What was now at stake was no longer the control of the campuses but that of the city at large.

In 1984, General Zia-ul-Haq banned students' unions across Pakistan, justifying this decision on the basis of student violence, even though his motives were probably more political (he feared a student uprising similar to the one that uprooted Ayub Khan's regime in the late 1960s). In the short term this ban contributed to a rapprochement between the IJT and its rivals, with the IJT defying its mother party (which had approved the ban) to take part in protest marches alongside progressive and left-wing students in Karachi. For two months, IJT, PSF and NSF activists confronted the police across the city and burnt dozens of vehicles. Violence seemed to be spilling out of the campuses and threatened to engulf the city. The situation might have got out of control for the military regime had the IJT not ended up complying with the JI's directive. But after a few months of agitation IJT activists returned to the fold, after having been given assurances that their organisation would be authorised to maintain a presence on campuses. This betrayal and the threat of being evicted from KU led progressive and left-wing student activists to launch a pre-emptive strike. They took over the hostels formerly under IJT control and stored weapons in them to deter the Islamists from counter-attacking. Fearing an armed uprising, the police launched an operation against these progressive and left-wing militants at the end of the year. But they met with stiff resistance and a siege ensued, which lasted for more than ten hours. Police fire was returned by well armed USM students and reinforcements had to be called in to evacuate the buildings where these embattled students had entrenched themselves. Miraculously, there was no fatality on either side, although dozens were injured in the fighting.

Far from containing violence on the campuses, the ban accelerated the militarisation of student politics. Students' union elections used to provide a platform to student organisations to present their grievances but also acted as a check on their potential violence, since organisations resorting to violence were bound to be sanctioned come election time. Moreover, only those students who attended courses and who did not fail any of them were eligible for candidature, which prevented outsiders or 'undesirable elements' from taking over. The 1984 ban did not put a halt to these elections but made their organisation the sole prerogative of the administrations of colleges and universities (whereas they had become official, government-funded events after the enforcement of the 1974 Student Union Ordinance).[52] In a context of escalating student violence, these administrations were reluctant to organise such elections in the following years. And although some educational institutions in Karachi (such as the elite Saint Patrick's College) did continue to organise students' union elections despite the ban, they remained the proverbial few. As the element of accountability provided by these elections withered away, the relative weight of student organisations started being measured exclusively in terms of military capability. Student organisations were thus encouraged to acquire more weapons, and more sophisticated ones. The IJT's main rival, the USM, built up a veritable arsenal via the same Peshawar-based arms dealers that had provided the IJT with modern weaponry in the early 1980s. Whereas the IJT had benefited from the JI's financial support to acquire arms, the USM had greater difficulty raising funds for the same purpose. PPP leaders were asked to contribute and, out of fear of reprisals, generally obliged. Several Pashtun and Baloch politicians also contributed to this war effort.[53] If the exact impact of the 1984 ban on these developments remains contested, students' unions were put into extended stand-by in the following years. This only reinforced the hold of political organisations over student life, with the disappearance of unions making them the sole representatives of students, while the suppression of extracurricular activities previously organised by unions made students more available for recruitment.

Unlike in the late 1970s and early 1980s, when weapons were stored in safe houses outside the campus, the increasing militarisation of the conflict led student activists to store their arsenal in student hostels, either at KU or at the adjacent NED Engineering University. Within these hostels, entire rooms were used to stash guns, ammunition and drugs. Snipers took position on the roofs of these student residences and frequently engaged in gun fights with rivals occupying adjacent buildings. These incidents were particularly frequent between the IJT militants occupying the largest hostel of NED Engineering University and the USM militants who controlled the KU hostels, a few hundred metres north. By now student organisations had taken on the attributes of student militias, and the conflict had turned into a war of position, which cost the lives of sixty students between 1984 and 1988 (as against twenty for the period 1981–1983). If student militias were active in other parts of Pakistan (particularly in the Punjab, where the IJT's Thunder Squad was very active as well), the intensity of this violence was specific to Karachi, which accounted for 91 per cent of campus deaths across the country in the four years following the 1984 ban.[54]

The Geographical Expansion of 'Student' Violence

The second half of the 1980s was marked by the rise of a new party to the conflict, which aimed to represent and defend the interests of Mohajirs. This political force grew out of a student organisation to become the city's most powerful political party. The APMSO was launched on 11 June 1978. Forcefully expelled from KU by the IJT in 1981, its cadres launched the MQM three years later, which met with its first electoral victory in the 1987 municipal election. This victory came as a direct challenge to the dominant position of the JI in Karachi, which tried to resist the rise of the MQM by expanding the campus war between the IJT and the APMSO to Urdu-speaking localities across the city, leading to violent clashes between the two student organisations in February and August 1988.

The military build-up of the MQM and the APMSO, in the second half of the 1980s (see the next chapter), coincided with the expansion of student violence across the city. Whereas previously the violence had been confined to the campuses, with the exception of a few cases of rioting (when rival organisations rioted together), the tussle between the APMSO and the IJT brought the conflict to the streets of the city. Rival militants were abducted or targeted in their neighbourhood and gun fights erupted in the streets. In August 1988, the death of an IJT activist, Aameer Saeed, led to armed encounters between IJT and APMSO militants across the city, in which more than fifty people were injured. The intensity of the violence led the authorities to close down KU, NED University and Sindh Medical College for several months.[55]

One explanation for this expansion of the geographical scope of student violence resides in the resumption of democratic forms of expression in the last years of the Zia regime. The MQM's rise to power, following its successes in the 1987 municipal election and even more so in the 1988 general elections, came as a direct challenge to the political hegemony of the JI, the parent body of the IJT, which had a strong support base among Mohajirs since the 1950s. Thus, the conflict was no longer primarily between student organisations defending their campus turf but between political parties competing for the control of the city and its electorate. With Pakistan's reversion to democracy the stakes of the conflict became higher and the democratic transition, instead of containing it, actually amplified it. Rather than a mere continuity of the campus war, this new sequence of political violence inaugurated a larger and deadlier conflict. This does not mean to say however that there was no continuity between these sequences: on the contrary, student activists turned party leaders recycled their experiences of the 'campus wars' into this new conflict. Former student activists had learned to think in military terms[56] and had become familiar with modern technologies of warfare on the campuses. As Altaf Hussain and his companions acknowledge in their autobiographic writings, war was not so much the continuity of politics by other means as a precondition for ensuring their political survival (see the next chapter). Had the APMSO been allowed to pursue its activities on the KU campus in the early 1980s, this might not have occurred. But the IJT ban on the APMSO led its officials to expand their activities, holding street-corner meetings as they no longer had any office space.[57] The transformation of student violence, in the second half of the 1980s, was therefore doubly paradoxical, at least from the point of view of the 'democratic peace' thesis: it was its shrinking structure of political opportunities that led the APMSO to shift to party politics, whereas the opening of new channels of democratic expression a few years later precipitated its militarisation.

By expanding across the city, violence originating in the campuses changed form and intensified to reach an unprecedented level of brutality. In the opposite direction, campus violence escalated further after replicating patterns of inter-party violence. Once again, the impact of the democratisation process, and in particular the resumption of elections, is evident. In 1989, Prime Minister Benazir Bhutto lifted the ban on students' unions, and elections were held the same year. In the Punjab, the IJT paid the price for its collaboration with the Zia regime and was defeated by its rivals. Students' union elections were not held in KU this year but the APMSO, followed by the PSF, won elections in several colleges. With the IJT withering away, APMSO and PSF activists started flexing their muscles and competing for complete supremacy over the campuses. Clashes soon erupted between the two groups at KU as well as in other major academic institutions (NED University, Dow Medical College, Sindh Medical College, etc.). The most serious of these incidents occurred in late 1989 when a group of PSF militants clashed with their APMSO rivals at NED University. A gun fight ensued and PSF militants managed to push their rivals back into the KU campus. They seemed to be gaining the upper hand when they ran out of ammunition. Although they tried to obtain reinforcements from their comrades at

Sindh Medical College (a thirty-minute drive from NED University), the PSF boys were soon overpowered by their rivals, who erupted in the NED hostel where they had taken shelter. The disarmed militants (around six of them were captured, while four others managed to escape) were taken to the KU gymnasium where they were all shot dead by APMSO militants.[58] Even if Karachiites, by then, had become accustomed to extreme forms of political violence, this incident sent a shockwave across the city. Violence erupted on all the major campuses, claiming dozens of lives on both sides, including that of the leader of the PSF, Najeeb Ahmad, who was ambushed by a group of APMSO militants. These clashes placed severe strain on the co-operation between the PPP and the MQM (who were then coalition partners in Islamabad and in Sindh) and precipitated their break up. In 1991–1992 the conflict between PSF/PPP and APMSO/MQM reached its climax, with Mohajir militants being used by the chief minister of the time, Jam Sadiq Ali, to crush the PPP. By now, the MQM and its student wing were running Karachi as a personal fiefdom, going as far as assaulting outsiders who dared enter their bastions. It was one of these incidents—the abduction and torturing of Major Kalim and his subordinates in Landhi (see Chapter 1)—that prompted the army to react. In June 1992 the COAS ordered his troops to enter Karachi to teach the MQM a lesson. This military operation (codenamed Operation Clean-up), which ran until 1994, brought the MQM to heel but did not break it. And when the army finally left the city, the party celebrated its 'victory'. An uneasy calm prevailed on the campuses, with paramilitary forces deployed at strategic points all across the KU campus. This show of force succeeded in curbing the violence, but did not entirely eradicate it. More importantly, the Rangers' primary concern was with incidents of lethal violence, and they did not interfere in student politics as such. Given the situation, the APMSO has managed to retain its hold over the campus, though the IJT has made a successful comeback in recent years. At present, a precarious balance of power prevails at KU, and although deadly clashes erupted in 2007 and 2008, students and teachers alike consider the situation to be 'manageable'.[59] In fact, this perception has less to do with the receding of student violence, which is yet to materialise, than with mechanisms developed over the years by the teaching staff to contain student conflicts at tolerable levels. Thirty years after the first gunshot incident at the University of Karachi, violence is perceived by its students and personnel as an integral part of student politics, if not of student life.

Conclusion

The escalation of violence at the University of Karachi was not the handiwork of violent entrepreneurs with a political or economic agenda. It was not a deliberate attempt to escalate a conflict which, for two decades, had been relatively benign. Neither was it a matter of ethnicity. Ideological affiliations initially transcended ethno-linguistic identifications, which would only come to play a role at a later stage in the conflict. The intensification of this conflict, at the end of the 1970s, was precipitated by the political strategies of the military elites governing the country at the time, and by a sudden change in the technologies of student warfare. In the wake of the Afghan Jihad, student organisations found it easier to obtain weapons, which started flooding the campus. In the process, new protagonists arrived on the scene of student politics. These outsiders with a background in petty criminality introduced new patterns of violence and upset the internal dynamics of student organisations by challenging the hold political activists had over these organisations. A further outcome of these student conflicts was the rise of the MQM/APMSO in the second half of the 1980s and the subsequent intensification of political violence at KU and beyond. It brought to the fore a new type of political activist, whose militarised way of apprehending and practicing politics traced its roots back to KU's campus wars. Moreover, once it had strengthened its military capacities and met with its first electoral victories, the MQM/APMSO started attracting former *jama'ati* and left-wing *badmash*s, who placed their expertise in violence at the service of the Mohajir movement.

Rather than by the initial motivations of the belligerents, the escalation of violence at KU is far better explained by changes occurring in the structure of political opportunities for student movements (which, as we have seen, may have paradoxical effects),[60] and even more importantly by transformations in the technologies of warfare, in the profile of the belligerents and in the nature of their interconnections in relation to a changing local, national and international environment. This case study demonstrates that escalation in violence is not overdetermined by its alleged root causes or by the strategies of the belligerents. Instead, it seems to be precipitated by externalities (both institutional and material) that operate as facilitating factors of violent escalation, although their activation always retains a strong part of contingency. Violent escalation then creates new opportunities and new constraints for the belligerents, structuring new representations and repertoires of collective action on which the endogenous reproduction of the conflict will be premised. Thus, Karachi's ordered disorder, of which the escalation and systematisation of political violence at KU set the basis, was less the outcome of structural factors or individual cognitions predating the conflicts of the 1980s than of new polarisations, new chains of interdependence (between activists and militants, in particular) and new routines of violent mobilisation born out of these conflicts.

3

'THE MOHAJIRS HAVE ARRIVED!'

[...] *hub-ul-watani ke sale mein... sarzamin-e-pak se mohabbat-o-aqidat ke sale mein... abao ajdad ki jan-o-mal ki qurbanion ke sale mein... tawil-o-kathan... pur dard hijraton ke sale mein... mila kya is qaum... muhajir qaum ko...* [...]

[...] in reward for its patriotism... in reward for its love and devotion for the land of the pure... in reward for the lives and wealth sacrificed by our forefathers... in reward for the long and difficult... for the extremely painful migrations... what did this Mohajir nation get?.[...]

Extract from a text in prose celebrating the sacrifices of Mohajirs, published in the mouthpiece of the APMSO, *Naqīb*, in 2000.[1]

As we saw in the previous chapter, Karachi's predominant political force since the late 1980s, the MQM, is the offspring of a student organisation, the APMSO, which was launched at the University of Karachi in June 1978. With a few notable exceptions,[2] these early years of the Mohajir nationalist movement have been neglected by analysts of the MQM, an omission that leads to naturalise the party's electoral successes in the mid-1980s, while losing sight of the impact of this student milieu over the political culture of the MQM and its leadership. The following pages, however, do not intend to locate a hypothetical point of origin of the MQM or to reduce it to a surprisingly successful brand of campus nationalism. Instead, the present chapter aims to retrieve the pluralism and indeterminacy of the early years of Mohajir nationalism, as well as the enduring legacy of these 'street fighting years'.[3] The grand narrative of the MQM's success tends to obliterate that, throughout the 1970s—the decade when Mohajir nationalism emerged as a public discourse and vehicle for political mobilisation—several organisations competed for the imagination, defence and mobilisation of the 'fifth nationality' of a newly truncated Pakistan. And whereas the MQM would rapidly inspire fear and awe from its friends and foes alike, the APMSO and its leadership remained a source of mockery until the mid-1980s. Thus, the better armed and politically more organised activists of the IJT, who competed with progressive activists for the control of Karachi universities and colleges, used to ridicule Altaf Hussain and his companions when they assembled on campus lawns to preach their message of ethnic mobilisation and social revolution: 'He has arrived, he has arrived… The Mohajir has arrived…' (*Aya, aya, mohajir aya*), these Islamist students used to shout ironically at their still insignificant rivals.[4] By 1981, the challenges encountered by the APMSO had become so daring that its leader, Altaf Hussain,[5] seems to have considered putting his political career on hold. The years 1982–1984 remain the least documented in Altaf's life and he simply skips them in his autobiography. In 1981, he visited Saudi Arabia and, according to one of his former colleagues at KU, contemplated settling in Jeddah, where he started exploring job opportunities.[6] However, this plan did not materialise and Altaf went back to Pakistan, before setting off to the United States. He settled down in Chicago, where he worked as a taxi driver (officially to finance his studies while contributing to the functioning of the APMSO, although MQM sources never mention where he would have completed his medical studies in the United States).[7] Possibly after having received some positive signals from Pakistan's intelligence agencies, Altaf Hussain returned to Karachi on 4 November 1985. Therefore, he was not present at the launch of the MQM on 18 March 1984. However, he quickly reasserted his authority over the party.

Instead of presenting a teleological account of the MQM's rise as an irresistible process, the first section of this chapter consists in an exploration of the Mohajir movement's stammering, internal divisions and original weaknesses. This examination of the APMSO's rough beginnings tends to underline the remarkable success of the MQM in the following decade, but it is also a reminder that there was nothing mechanical in the success of Mohajir nationalism, a political project which originally failed to find its public despite an apparently favourable socio-economic context, characterised by the relative but steady decline of the Mohajirs since the 1960s and even more so since the 1970s.[8] The second section examines the transformation of the APMSO into a political party that has retained its original duality even after joining the political mainstream. The third and last section of the chapter focuses on the consolidation of the MQM's domination over Karachi's electoral and armed politics, while pointing at the challenges to this domination, which have only increased over the years.

The Unremarkable Beginnings of Mohajir Nationalism

The emergence of Mohajir nationalism, at the end of the 1970s, offers a paradigmatic example of stigma reversal. The term *muhajir* was initially positively connoted in the context of post-Partition Pakistan, as it referred to the glorious example of the Prophet's *hijrat* from Mecca to Medina. This historical analogy was sometimes resented by Sindhi elites, who saw in it a manifestation of the *muhajirin*'s sense of cultural superiority and reluctance to assimilate to their host society.[9] With the passage of time, however, the term *muhajir* became largely depreciative, stigmatising these 'migrants' along with other derogatory terms such as *hindustani* (Urdu for 'Indian'), *makar* (Sindhi for 'locust') or *talir* (Sindhi for 'sparrow'). In turn, the second generation of Urdu-speakers born in Sindh proceeded to a normative inversion of the term, turning the stigma into a source of pride and giving shape to the 'Mohajir nation' (*mohajir qaum*) in the process. One of the first pamphlets circulated by the APMSO shortly after its creation in June 1978 is particularly explicit in this regard:

Listen to my voice

Who am I? ... What am I?
I am the echo... of the 1857 war of independence.
I am the conscience... of Sir Syed Ahmed Khan.
I am the movement... of Syed Ahmad Shahid.
I am the courage... of Muhammad Ali Jauhar.
I am the looted caravans... of 1947's Pakistan.
I am the frozen blood... of 1971's East Pakistan
... and...
... those patriotic Pakistanis... who died on dark paths...
... However...
... I am nowhere in Pakistan... because...
... we were deprived... we became objects of hatred...

... Then...
... people asked me... 'Where are your mother and father from?'
... and I was told that... 'you are not a son of the soil [*farzand-e-zamin*]'
... Then...
I was deprived of admission [at university]... the job market was closed to me...
I said... 'I am a fervent patriot'.
The hatred directed towards me... 'You are a Mohajir'... 'are a Mohajir'... 'You are a Mohajir'...
I listened... I waited patiently... with great forbearance...
... But then other voices started being heard...
... 'You are a locust [*makar*]'... 'You are a sparrow [*talir*]'... 'You are a refugee [*panahgir*]'
... My patience reached its limits...
... I lost my patience...
... and I became a Mohajir...
... and now I take pride in the fact that I am a Mohajir...
... I am a powerful and positive force [*mazbut aur musibat quwat*]...
... in the shape of the All Pakistan Mohajir Students Organisation...
[...][10]

This partisan literature as well as the autobiographical accounts of the founders of the APMSO converge in projecting Mohajir identity politics as a reactive nationalism, forced upon 'patriotic' Urdu-speakers who would rather have identified as Pakistanis if only the country's other four nationalities had let them do so. The return of the stigma here proceeds through a double movement of historical re-appropriation (by reclaiming the legacy of the leading Muslim reformists of colonial North India, across the political spectrum) and victimisation (through a 'trope of sacrifice' invoking the human and material cost of the *hijrat* and claiming a special entitlement to the Pakistani state in return).[11] This discourse of ethnic pride is also manifest in Altaf Hussain's autobiography (first published in Urdu in 1988), where the MQM leader claims that Urdu-speaking refugees from India brought a 'cultural revolution' (*tehzibi inquelab*) and 'intellectual awakening' (*zehni bedari*) to Pakistan—an assertion implying that the indigenous populations of Pakistan, and particularly of Sindh, came from an uncultured stock.[12] This discourse of Mohajir pride was not simply a matter of recognition or, as Rubina Saigol recently suggested, 'a claim to rights based on loss'.[13] It was, first and foremost, a discourse of revolt. This is exemplified by the following verses, taken from one of the first poems circulated by the APMSO:

[...] *Uthao parcham baghawaton ke mita do asar ghasbon ke Bisat-e-ishrat pe kab tak akhir yeh wad 'ashrat diya karenge?*

[...] Raise the banner of rebellion and wipe out all traces of the grabbers. How long will they keep on making merry?[14]

Besides this discourse of ethnic pride and rebellion, the MQM would inherit from the APMSO its obsession with secrecy. Saleem Shahzad, who would become one of the top leaders of the MQM,[15] joined the APMSO shortly after its creation, in 1978, while studying at the Federal Urdu Science College. He remembers how he was officially made a member of the APMSO after giving the following oath in a small park located near KU:

I am a Mohajir and I will keep on fighting for the Mohajirs to get their rights. I will remain loyal [*wafadar*] to the organisation and I will not share any secret [*raz*] of the organisation with any outsider.[16]

A few years later, the MQM recuperated and radicalised this rhetoric of exclusive loyalty, characteristic of those 'greedy institutions' striving for the undivided commitment of their members.[17] The loyalty oath marking the entry of a new member into the MQM was an elaboration of the earlier APMSO oath, extending to family members the status of outsiders, while personifying the object of this loyalty:

I,... believing that Allah is here and watching over me, swearing by His book and my mother, take oath that I shall remain loyal to the MQM and Altaf Hussain for my whole life [...] I swear by my mother that if any conspiracy against MQM or Altaf Hussain or any act harmful to them come into my knowledge, I shall immediately inform Altaf Hussain or other main leaders, even if the conspirator be my brother, sister, mother, father, any relative or friend. [...] I swear that I will keep every secret of my party and regard it more precious than my life.[18]

However influential the early years of the APMSO may have been for later developments of Mohajir nationalism, one should remember that at the end of the 1970s, Altaf Hussain and his companions were neither the first nor even the most vocal proponents of Mohajir identity politics. The first promoters of this new ethnicity were left-wing Urdu-speaking intellectuals. At the end of the 1960s, Amir Haider Kazmi, head of the pro-Moscow faction of the NSF, supported the movement launched by a businessman from Aligarh, M.A. Bashir, for the creation of a separate province of Karachi.[19] The echo of this movement remained limited, though, as Sindh's Urdu-speakers remained attached to unitary Pakistani nationalism. Around the same time, Nawab Muzaffar Khan organised the Muhajir-Pashtun-Punjabi Muttahida Mahaz (Mohajir-Pashtun-Punjabi United Front—MPPM), with Hyderabad as its stronghold and Sindhis as its main adversaries (Punjabis and Pashtuns only had a token representation in the movement). In 1970, Nawab Muzaffar Khan was elected at the Provincial Assembly and in January 1971 the MPPM took an active role in anti-Sindhi protests, following the decision of Hyderabad's Board of Intermediate and Secondary Education to have Urdu-speaking candidates examined in Sindhi in the Secondary School Certificate examination. This mobilisation prompted a counter-reaction by Sindhi students and clashes erupted across the province, leading the army to deploy itself in Hyderabad while parts of Karachi were placed under curfew. In Karachi, violence erupted after a student group, the Qaumi Muttahida Tulaba Mahaz (United National Students Front), encouraged car owners to change their English number plates to Urdu ones. Urdu-speaking and Sindhi students then went on the rampage, forcibly removing 'enemy' plates and signboards across the city.[20]

The events of January 1971 were followed by an even deadlier round of 'language riots' in July 1972, following the formation of a PPP government in Sindh and in Islamabad, which promoted the use of Sindhi in the education system and the administration. In Karachi, Sindhi settlements were attacked by Urdu-speakers, shops and vehicles were set on fire in the Urdu-speaking localities of Liaquatabad, Paposhnagar and Gulbahar, among others, while the Department of Sindhi at KU was torched by activists of the JI. In the three days following the passage of the Language Bill by the Sindh Provincial Assembly on 7 July 1972, which among other controversial provisions made Sindhi (as well as Urdu) a compulsory subject from class IV to class XII, twenty-two persons were killed in the city. From Karachi, the violence spread 'from city to city and village to village as a prairie fire', to quote a report published at the time, with the initial incidents of violence being amplified by certain media leaning towards the JI. One need not agree with the conspiracy theory put forward in the same report—which suggests, in typical progressive fashion, that these riots were hatched by Karachi-based business families to weaken the workers' movement[21]—to see that these language riots had a polarising effect on Sindhi society and reinforced the ethnic and rural/urban divide between Sindhis and Urdu-speakers.

According to linguist and historian Tariq Rahman, these riots played a major role in making Mohajirs, 'a firmly non-assimilationist collectivity who saw Urdu as their identity-marker'.[22] It is in this context that the projection of Mohajirs as a 'nationality' (*qaumiyat*) in its own right gained currency. In July 1972, a few days after the language riots, Mahmud-ul-Haq Usmani, a *muhajir* left-wing political personality (he was, at the time, General Secretary of the leftist National Awami Party [NAP]), launched the Urdu Qaumi Council (National Council for Urdu), which for the first time declared the Mohajirs as the 'fifth nationality' (*panchwin qaumiyat*) of Pakistan. The Council included several members of the Urdu-speaking progressive intelligentsia, with a strong presence of Shias (Akhtar Rizvi, Kavish Rizvi, as well as the Amrohvi brothers, Rais Amrohvi and Syed Muhammad Taqi). Its charter of demands did not fundamentally differ from the agenda of the NAP, its only notable innovation consisting in the introduction of the concept of 'fifth nationality',[23] which Rais Amrohvi (whose verses in the defence of Urdu, originally published in 1952, had galvanised Urdu-speaking demonstrators in July 1972) would continue to promote in later years in his writings. In his columns and poems in *Jang* (which at the time was edited by his brother, Syed Muhammad Taqi), Amrohvi defended the recognition of the 'Pak-Indians' as the 'fifth nationality of Pakistan' and demanded the creation of a separate homeland for the 'inheritors of the immortal Indo-Islamic culture'.[24]

Throughout the 1970s, small groups with a limited, local outreach, continued to mobilise Urdu-speakers on the basis of language and ethnicity. After the Urdu Qaumi Council failed to rally support to its cause, Rais Amrohvi, Syed Muhammad Taqi and a few others joined the Tehrik-e-Istiqlal (Movement for Independence). The same year (1973), a group of Urdu-speaking lawyers launched the Tehrik-e-Shehri Hukumat (Movement for the City Government), which defended the right of self-determination for the residents of Karachi. The leader of the movement, Mirza Jawwad Baig, was arrested in November 1974, charged with secession of Karachi from Pakistan and curtailment of sovereignty of Pakistan over Karachi, and subsequently sentenced to twelve years imprisonment and a fine of 7,000 rupees.[25]

Urdu-speaking students, who were at the forefront of the 'language riots' of 1971 and 1972, were not immune to this emergence of Mohajir nationalism. In May 1978, Salim Haider launched the Mohajir Medicos Association at Sindh Medical College. A month later, Haider was one of the founding members of the APMSO but he soon developed differences with Altaf Hussain, after the latter engaged into a rapprochement with the Sindhi nationalist leader G.M. Syed. On 13 March 1984, Haider launched the first Mohajir political party, the Mohajir Ittehad Tehrik (United Mohajir Movement—MIT), which managed to carve a place for itself in the small towns of Sindh, through its virulent opposition to Sindhi nationalist groups. The MIT's influence culminated in 1986–1987, at a time when the MQM was pursuing a rapprochement with Sindhi nationalist organisations such as the Jiye Sindh Mahaz (Front for the Protection of Sindh—JSM), and in February 1987 it organised in Sukkur one of the largest Mohajir rallies ever hosted in the province. The MIT, however, lost much of its political clout at the end of the 1980s, following the deterioration of the relations between the MQM and Sindhi nationalists and the subsequent *reconquista* of Sindh's small urban centres by the MQM, which by then was no match for a smaller organisation such as the MIT.[26] More anecdotal was the competition of the Mohajir Students Organisation (MSO) at KU. According to Altaf Hussain, this organisation was launched shortly after the creation of the APMSO and received the support of 'some political personalities' who were eager to discredit the former by suggesting that Mohajirs were unable to sit on a common platform.[27]

This competition over the representation of the freshly imagined 'Mohajir nation' did not stop with the creation of the MQM in 1984, with the most significant challenges coming from the Mohajir elders gathered in the Mohajir Rabita Council (MRC, founded in 1988), and even more seriously from the MQM-Haqiqi (MQM-H, formed in 1991). This fissure of the MQM, which would trigger one of the most brutal conflicts ever witnessed in Karachi, was rooted in power conflicts between ethnic factions in the entourage of Altaf Hussain. Afaq Ahmad and Amir Khan, the founders of the MQM-H, were non-Biharis who protested the influence of Bihari leaders such as Imran Farooq and Saleem Shahzad on Altaf.[28] After being expelled from the party on charges of corruption and conspiracy to murder Altaf Hussain, Afaq Ahmad and Amir Khan briefly took shelter in the United States, before returning to Karachi in the army's trucks the following year.

The academic neglect of the foundation years of Mohajir nationalism is all the more surprising that MQM leaders themselves devote long developments to their initial erring, which have become an integral part of the party's mythology. For Altaf Hussain and Saleem Shahzad, whose autobiographies I draw most of the following material from,[29] these humble beginnings serve to emphasise the low social extraction of the party's founders, their relentless dedication to the cause of Mohajir nationalism and more originally their personal *merit* in committing so much of their time and meagre resources to take on the establishment without the social and economic capital of more conventional Pakistani politicians. If the APMSO had such rough beginnings, these two texts argue, it is primarily because its founders did not hail from the 'exploitative classes' (*istehsali tabqe*) but from the 'middle classes' (*mutawassit tabqe*). Lacking the funds necessary for the expansion of their activities beyond KU,[30] as well as to the production and circulation of their literature, these 'small house-dwellers' (*chote gharon mein rahne wale*) turned to Urdu-speaking shopkeepers and entrepreneurs to finance their activities. But their request for help was systematically turned down for they were seen as a bunch of hoodlums, not even powerful enough to be cultivated for their muscle power. Both Saleem Shahzad and Altaf Hussain insist upon the initial reactions of contempt they faced from the community they aimed to represent, particularly as far as its economic elites are concerned. And far from denying their label as 'backstreet boys' (*londe, lipare*) by these elites, both Shahzad and Hussain endorse this plebeian identity, making it a sign of political distinction and a promise of another kind of politics. Recalling the reactions of Mohajir shopkeepers to their request of donations, S. Shahzad writes:

> Wherever we went to collect donations, we were told, 'Brother, forgive me [for not giving you anything]'. Then, as soon as we left, we heard them whispering in our back, 'Look at that: these boys really know how to have a fling; these hoodlums and backstreet boys, as soon as they'll be out of here, they'll go and make merry ['*aya shayan karenge*].' Hearing this caused us great sorrow, because instead of giving us donations they made allegations against us and scolded us contemptuously [*hiqarat se jhatak dete hain*].[31]

Following the blatant failure of this 'donation campaign' (*chanda mohim*), Altaf Hussain was convinced by his companions to turn to Mohajir entrepreneurs and 'big men', but to no avail:

> Some of our companions advised us to pay a visit to Mohajir capitalists [*sarmaydar*]. I told these friends that it was useless, that they would not extend any

help. But these friends insisted by suggesting that we could not go on asking for donations in bazaars and lanes for ever. I replied to them that this would go on as long as every member of our nation would not be awakened [*basha'ur*] and would not start loving the Mohajir nationality. At the same time, I wanted to avoid any friction with my friends so I told them 'Alright, let's pay them a visit at least once, and I will let you draw a list of names.' However, I challenged them to find even one of these wealthy [*khate, pite*], capitalist Mohajirs, who would be ready to extend some help to the APMSO. We knocked on every door, we went to the office or to the house of every big man, but all we got was some advice and lip service. Some people told us 'Alright, you Mohajir students have taken this organisation this far. Now, if you follow our advice, we will finance you. But you will have to do all the work.' My friends and I flatly refused [...]. In this way, we turned down every conditional offer of financial help.[32]

The resentment showing through these pages does not merely target Mohajir 'capitalists' but the Mohajir elders (*akabarin*) and elite (*nami garami log*) at large, who preferred to donate money to mainstream political parties than to a committed student organisation from their own community. Always ready to administer lessons of politics to the youths, these elders were less inclined to raise the banner of Mohajir nationalism themselves. Using a common idiomatic expression, Saleem Shahzad expresses his lassitude at hearing these elders declaim 'their philosophy and Hippocrates' (i.e. boast), without accomplishing anything tangible.[33] These autobiographical accounts therefore posit the APMSO as the voice of the Mohajir youth challenging the oppression and exploitation of the Mohajirs by other, dominant 'nationalities', but also questioning the moral authority and political acumen of Mohajir elites themselves. By insisting upon the initial amateurism, lack of resources and hostile reception of their authors—to such an extent that the latter appear more grotesque than exemplary—these two narratives serve another political end. They emphasise the personal merit of these pioneers of Mohajir nationalism, by translating to the political field the ideology of achievement that these authors initially developed in their considerations on education.[34] 'We could only rely on ourselves to take this movement forward,' thus writes Saleem Shahzad.[35] This ideology of achievement, drawing the contours of a meritocratic ethos, may well be a defining attribute of middle classes across time and space. In 1970s Pakistan, however, this discourse was highly original, as attested to by the absence of a vernacular term for 'merit' (to date, the English term remains in use in Urdu). Original, but also oppositional: in the Pakistani context, the meritocratic ethos came as a direct challenge to the entrenchment of landed elites—locally decried, in particular by the MQM, as 'feudals'—in the politics of the country. It is precisely at this juncture that the pragmatic politics of interest pursued by the APMSO and the MQM (centered on the Mohajirs' better access to educational, political and economic positions/resources) meets a discourse of revolt with apocalyptic overtones, carrying the opposite vision of politics as a fight to the finish and a battle for 'survival' (*baqa*), an issue explored in greater detail further.

While they faced incomprehension if not outward hostility from Mohajir shopkeepers and entrepreneurs, it is on the campuses of Karachi that Altaf Hussain and his companions faced the most serious opposition. The IJT objected to the use of the term 'Mohajir' as an ethnic marker and systematically tore down the banners and posters of the APMSO. Altaf and his entourage even had to change the title of their first journal from *al-Muhajir* (The Mohajir) to *al-Adab* (Literature), after the IJT objected to this title.[36] The IJT also controlled the allocation of rooms in student hostels and prevented the APMSO from getting a foothold at KU by restricting its access to these rooms. This armed opposition to the APMSO became even more intense after the latter started making its presence felt in the students' union elections: whereas the APMSO only garnered 95 votes in the 1979 election, this number shot up to 900 the following year (by that time, KU had 10,000 registered students).[37] A few months later, Mohajir student activists were expelled from the KU campus by the IJT's strongmen.

The success of this deterrence relied upon the unparalleled fire power of the IJT and its strong arms tactics. For Saleem Shahzad, the firepower (*aslahah taqat*) of the IJT could not be matched by the APMSO, making the 'policy of violence' (*tashadud ki polici*) an unrealistic option for the latter. It carried the risk of having the APMSO expelled from educational institutions by the better armed IJT, whose activists occupied the main mosque at KU and used it to store their weapons. Altaf Hussain also insists that APMSO workers could not compete with better armed organisations as they had no weapons at their disposal—only passion and emotions (*jazbe*). This left Mohajir activists at the mercy of Thunder Squad militants, who occasionally ransacked APMSO stalls and roughed up its activists.[38] Altaf Hussain himself was a favourite target of the *jama'ati*s and both he and Saleem Shahzad claim that the IJT's 'goons' (*ghundas*) made two attempts on his life, in June 1979 and February 1981.[39] This opposition of the IJT culminated on 3 February 1981, when Thunder Squad militants assaulted APMSO activists during a convention for newcomers at KU. Following this incident, the IJT effectively denied entry to APMSO activists at KU. The situation had become so critical that, the next day, Altaf Hussain gathered his companions at a private residence in the Mohajir-dominated locality of Federal B Area and announced the suspension of all the activities of the APMSO on Karachi's campuses. Male and female activists were then dispatched to Landhi, Korangi, Malir, Azizabad and Nazimabad—all neighbourhoods with a large Mohajir presence—to publicise the 'Mohajir cause'.[40] The armed opposition of the IJT had prepared the ground for the transformation of the APMSO into a political party, although a party projecting itself as a movement.

The MQM, Between Party and Movement

In a section of his autobiography where he vehemently criticises Mohajir elders for not siding with the APMSO in its early years, Saleem Shahzad reproaches them to 'sit in their drawing rooms and practice the politics of interest [*mafad parasti ki siyasat*]'.[41] Against this 'politics of interest', the founders of the APMSO/MQM claim to have articulated a different kind of politics, in the shape of a 'movement' (*tehrik*). Although the MQM endorsed electoral politics early on, this dualism has endured in the projections and self-representations of the party's leadership and it resurfaced after the latter tried to de-ethnicise the MQM and transform it into a 'catch-all party' at the end of the 1990s.[42] It is to this tension between party and movement at the heart of MQM politics that I turn now: what kind of 'movement' do these political entrepreneurs refer to, and how does it articulate with the more pragmatic politics practiced by the MQM as a party?

Blind Faith, Unity and Discipline: The MQM as Movement

To date, the most elaborate formulation of the grammar of authority of the MQM can be found in a small essay written by the former Secretary General of the MQM, Dr. Imran Farooq,[43] which was originally published in 1986. *Nazm-o-Zābat ke Taqāze* (The Requirements of Discipline) begins with a typology of social movements in world history. According to Farooq, two different kinds of movement must be distinguished, on the basis of their structures (rather than ideologies). He refers to the first kind as 'natural movements' (*qudrati tehriken*), comparing them to 'plants that grow on their own in the forest' for their lack of structures, centralised leadership and planning. On the contrary, 'organised movements' (*muntazam tehriken*) rely upon strict 'rules and regulations' (*nazm-o-zabat*), 'planning' (*mansubabandi*) and 'consensual leadership' (*mutafiqah qayadat*), which makes them more 'powerful' (*taqatwar*) and eventually more successful than the former. This last point is crucial to the demonstration: unity, discipline and 'blind faith in the consensual leader and leadership' (*mutafiqah quaid ya qayadat par andha etemad*) are not worth defending for their own sake but for their greater efficiency in the face of adversity. According to Farooq, 'organised' movements are prone to achieve their goals more rapidly than 'natural' ones because when dissensions emerge within their ranks, the uncontested leader is able to subsume these divergences and lead the movement forward towards victory. Political expediency therefore requires placing the leader above the institution, particularly in those critical situations which Farooq refers to as 'complex, fast-paced and unusual' (*pechidah, tez raftar aur ghair m'amuli*) and which are best exemplified by the 'state of war' (*halat-e-jang*). For Farooq, this state of war is the norm for revolutionary movements such as the MQM, for 'war situations happen in every era and every movement finds itself at war with adverse powers all along its course'. As a result, 'every revolutionary movement spends most of its time in a state of war'. In the face of such a predicament, the growth of these movements as well as their mere 'survival' (*baqa*) are conditional to their structuring around a 'central axis' (*mehur markaz*) in the shape of a 'consensual leader'. This personalisation of authority is the only guarantee of a system of decision-making fast enough to accommodate the specific requirements of troubled times, while providing a rampart against factionalism. This 'consensual leader' is particularly 'greedy' in the sense of Lewis Coser:[44] he does not merely demand loyalty but 'devotion' (*aqidat*), superseding all social relations and personal desires. Farooq here makes use of organicist metaphors by suggesting that 'with the development of the collectivity, all participants to the movement, though they live in different bodies, fuse into a single body'. The organisational model that Farooq defends here comes with its moral obligations for party workers, namely 'altruism' (*isar*), which

Farooq equates with the 'sacrifice of the ego' (*zati ana ki qurbani*) on the altar of the movement's interests and objectives.[45]

Under the garb of a comparative historical sociology of social movements, this text is essentially a rationalisation of Altaf Hussain's charismatic leadership, and thus of the MQM's process of institutionalisation. Following Francesco Alberoni, one can see in the personalisation of authority characteristic of charismatic organisations an attempt to overcome the tensions inherent to their institutionalisation, that is, of their transition from the 'nascent state', in which 'the possible was experienced as something imminent and realisable', to the less exhilarating realm of everyday life and petty politics. Alberoni here reverses Weber's famous thesis on the routinisation of charisma, by suggesting that institutionalisation does not amount to the dissolution of charismatic leadership but that, on the contrary, the concentration of power is one possible path among others towards institutionalisation. The charismatic leader addresses these tensions by bearing witness to the continuity of the 'nascent state' in the present, while indicating the venue towards the realisation of the state of perfection in the future. Like any other path towards institutionalisation, the consolidation of a charismatic leadership involves 'extinguishing the nascent state and ensuring its continuity *in another way*', most notably by ensuring that the institution becomes 'the heir to and custodian of the hope of the movement'.[46] This transition is irreducible to a complete fusion into everyday life, as the institution 'repeats the promise of the nascent state even though scaled down and impoverished because it is incarnate in the world'.[47] This process is fraught with tensions: just like the nascent state was 'haunted by betrayal',[48] since everyone is potentially a traitor to the high (impossible?) ideal of the nascent state, the transition to everyday life is a struggle, an ordeal even, where the total surrender of the individual to the movement (or, now, to the institution) is put to the test.[49] While the concentration of power in the leader constitutes a tentative answer to the dilemmas raised by such a transition from movement to institution, the mobilisation for war can operate as a substitutive institution, 'like a festival' suggests Alberoni.[50] The state of permanent warfare referred to by Imran Farooq seems to serve this purpose, while legitimating Altaf Hussain's charismatic authority as the most *rational* option in troubled times (i.e. not a value in itself but a means to an end). This classic of MQM party literature is proof that the cult of personality around Altaf Hussain—which developed *after* the creation of the MQM—is merely the emerging part of a grammar of consent and authority that regulates, through constant internal and external crises, the tensions inherent to the institutionalisation of a party born as an oppositional movement. It also displaces the centre of attention from the leader himself to the charismatic entrepreneurs who systematised the MQM's anti-institutional path towards institutionalisation.

Nazm-o-Zābt ke Taqāze was reprinted in 1998, a year after the MQM changed its name from *Mohajir* Qaumi Movement (Mohajir National Movement) to *Muttahida* Qaumi Movement (United National Movement). As Noman Baig shows in a recent study, this transformation was the outcome of a gradual evolution of the MQM from an ethnic-based to a 'catch-all' party. Baig also shows that the attempt made by MQM leaders at the end of the 1990s to join Pakistan's political mainstream was accompanied by programmes of political 'reeducation' for its party workers. Thousands of pamphlets, leaflets, books and posters were published around that time (mostly in Urdu), stressing the importance of discipline within the party and 'decent' behaviour outside it. This political and moral (re)education of party workers also proceeded through training programmes of two kinds: general training sessions (*tarbiyati nishist*) and lectures by Altaf Hussain on varied subjects, from education to party discipline, piety or loyalty (*fikri nishist*, lit. 'intellectual sessions').[51] The impact of these training sessions on party workers was mitigated, as they were generally perceived to be an excruciating experience. Thus, according to a party worker based in a lower-middle-class, Mohajir-dominated colony:

> When attending *tarbiyati nishist*, you had to wear a white *kurta* [long white shirt without collar associated with Mohajirs]. Then you had to listen to very long speeches, which often lasted for several hours, and no one was allowed to leave the room during that time, even to go for a drink or a pee! It was really bullshit! It was also the proof that MQM workers were still uneducated. In my colony, for instance, out of 200 members, maybe three or four would be graduates. The standard of education was very low.

Although this emphasis on social etiquette/ethics (*akhlaq*) was quite new for the MQM and expressed a concern for a better policing of the public behaviour of its party workers, this literature also shows preoccupations with discipline, loyalty and secrecy which, as we have seen, were already present in the APMSO and in the MQM of early years—although the exclusive loyalty demanded from party members was transferred from the movement to the party and even more importantly to the leader after the creation of the MQM. In the process, the threat posed by 'outsiders' became more expansive and started to include friends and family members. The MQM's increasing 'greediness' went in par with its institutionalisation and constituted an answer to the uncertainties inherent to this process. Thus, another pamphlet published at the end of the 1990s on the 'guiding principles' of the party, later on translated into English and circulated by the units of the party in the United States, invites party workers to avoid discussing controversial party matters with outsiders, while keeping away from friendships both within and without the movement, as 'the relationship of friendship may prove lethal and poisonous [...] by creating disruption in the structure of the party'.[52]

If this literature attests of the increasing 'greediness' of the MQM, as well as of the increasingly personalised nature of its leadership over the years, it is also, and more specifically, reminiscent of the 'self-expressionist' movements that emerged within the Urdu-speaking middle classes of North India in the 1920s and 1930s. As Markus Daechsel recently showed, these movements were loosely inspired by European fascism, with which they shared their cult of physical strength, their paramilitary poses, their exaltation of discipline and obedience, their propensity towards rhetorical excess or their belief in the redemptive nature of nationalism, both at the individual and collective level.[53] This 'middle-class politics of the marginalised'[54] relied upon a conception of politics as a war without end, a conception which as we have seen was reactualised by MQM ideologues. Within the Urdu-speaking Muslim communities of North India from where the Mohajirs originated, this 'politics of self-expression' was best exemplified by the Khaksar movement of Inayatullah Khan Mashriqi (1888–1963). This paramilitary movement presents striking analogies with the MQM, in terms of social base (Urdu-speaking, urban-based Muslim middle classes), leadership (with an intense personality cult around its leader) and discourse (marked by an aestheticisation of rhetorical excess and an intense use of poetry). Significantly, the leadership of the MQM is not only familiar with the history of this movement—despite the fact that it remained marginal, even in North India—but has also drawn inspiration from it. This legacy is made explicit, for instance, in *Nazm-o-Zābat ke Taqāze*. In the concluding remarks of his essay, Imran Farooq refers to the exemplary behaviour of a famous Khaksar activist, Muhammad Bahadur Khan (aka Bahadur Yar Jung, 1905–1944), who was born into an aristocratic family of Hyderabad but did not frown at being sanctioned like every other worker when he went astray. Farooq here refers to an episode during which this important figure of South Indian Muslim politics (he became the president of the Majlis-e-Ittehad-ul-Muslimeen in 1938) was sentenced by the party leadership to run around a parade ground and promptly complied despite his social rank. The importance given to this figure of exemplarity by Farooq can be gauged by the fact that Bahadur Khan stands alone besides Sir Syed Ahmed Khan, the great modernist Muslim educationist of the early twentieth century, among the South Asian personalities elevated by Farooq to the rank of role models as far as discipline and ego-sacrificing are concerned.[55]

If critics of the MQM in Pakistan have regularly pointed at its 'fascist' tendencies, these critiques miss their target by losing sight of the historical process of vernacularisation of fascism within the Urdu-speaking middle classes of early twentieth century North India, so vividly described by Daechsel. Sixty years later, when Altaf Hussain and his companions set off on their political journey, self-expressionist ideas, poses and aesthetic tropes had become an integral part of the moral and political landscape of the Urdu-speaking middle classes of Pakistan, who inherited this political legacy from their migrant parents. The 'politics of self-expression' have undoubtedly exerted a strong influence on the MQM's leadership, as evidenced by the party's political iconography, which mixes Maoist influences with aesthetic tropes more evocative of European fascist movements of the 1930s (see photographs in Appendix). The resonance of the MQM's poetic discourse with the 'politics of self-expression' of the Urdu middle-class milieu of the 1930s and 1940s is even more striking. The poems published over the years by MQM leaders, cadres and workers in the party's publications celebrate in the same way the triumph of passion over reason, while intoxicating themselves with fantasies of apocalyptic showdowns and the power of words themselves.[56] This is the case, for instance, of a poem written by a controversial party cadre from Landhi, Javed Kazmi,[57] which was published in 2006 in *Naqīb* (The Scout), the magazine of the APMSO, and which includes the following verse: 'Such a great upheaval will take place that the whole universe will tremble' (*Ek hashr uthega aisa ki phir kaun-o-makan bhi larzenge*). The term 'upheaval' does not fully translate what is at stake here: although the phrase *hashr uthana* can be translated as 'wreaking havoc', the term *hashr* refers to the Day of Judgement, when the dead will resuscitate in a great tumult, at the sound of the trumpet of the angel Israfil (Raphael). With this eschatological background in mind, Kazmi invites Mohajirs to let themselves be carried away in an ecstasy of violence. The opening verse of his poem makes a call to arms to the *ahl-e-junun*, a concept which figuratively means 'the brave' but which literally refers to 'the ecstatic ones' (in Sufism, *junun* is the mystical experience of fusion with God). Further in the poem, Kazmi suggests that 'all hell will be let loose', the literal meaning of the Urdu terms being 'madness and savagery will be unleashed in the manner of a wave' (*Ek mauj ki manind bikhrengi phir pagal wahshi zanjiren*).[58] The eschatological resonance of these verses should not be read too literally, though. It is an aesthetic trope rather than an attempt to define the MQM as a millenarist movement executing God's own plans through its violence. It is precisely for its hyperbolic nature, for its natural inclination towards symbolic excess *as excess*, that poetry is so attractive to the cadres of an existential movement such as the MQM, and before them to the 'self-expressionist' activists who emerged within the Urdu middle-class of India in the 1930s. The MQM could not be further, here, from the politics of interest which its leadership has otherwise actively pursued, by searching for the patronage of the military or civilian rulers of the time. One may even hypothesise that, at least for its editors, this existential poetry serves to counterbalance the pragmatism guiding the party's politics. This is not to say that poetry is merely a discursive placebo, compensating for the normalisation of the party in the eyes of its most uncompromising fringes. In a more complex way, it points at the MQM's simultaneous practice of two seemingly opposite forms of politics, one existential, devoted to the salvation of the Mohajir nation through an endless fight of epic proportions against tyranny, and one more earthly, centered on the restoration of the Mohajirs' 'rights' (*huquq*). The poetry discussed here is therefore irreducible to political imagery, or to the radical alibi of an otherwise opportunistic party: it is, instead, a form of politics by itself, where the intoxicating power of words meets the equally mesmerising beauty of war.

The MQM's Strategic Dualism

This existential nationalism has been coexisting with its apparent antonym—the 'politics of interest'—within the Mohajir movement/party.

Despite Saleem Shahzad's claim to the contrary, this 'politics of interest' has been another defining feature of the MQM, which has been counterbalancing its maximalist postures with a resolutely pragmatic approach towards politics. From its earliest days, Mohajir nationalism has been concerned with the control and allocation of public resources, starting with admissions to the universities and colleges of Sindh. Altaf Hussain's first struggle was about his admission in the Pharmacy faculty of KU and the first major campaign of the APMSO was a two month long 'Mission for admission' (*dakhla mohim*) opposing forged admissions (*dhandli*) at the same university. A strong element of pragmatism, centered on the privileged access to—if not the capture of—public resources and state institutions by the Mohajirs and their representatives has been infusing Mohajir nationalism since its infancy as a student movement. The transformation of this movement into a political party during the mid-1980s has only reinforced this trend, although the party never completely broke away from its movement past. Noman Baig's claim that the MQM shifted from 'making choices based on ideology to a strategy-based politics', at the end of the 1990s,[59] should therefore be nuanced. Though the name, the rhetoric and the charter of demands of the party were amended to accommodate other ethnic communities (cf. Fig. 3), the 'politics of interest' was not unknown to the APMSO while the *Muttahida* Qaumi Movement retained much of the confrontational posturing of the *Mohajir* Qaumi Movement after 1997, the year when this change of name was made official. In fact, as Noman Baig himself underlines, the attempt of the MQM's leadership to join the political mainstream following years of confrontation with the army (1992–1994) and a relatively poor performance in the 1997 general elections (during which the party lost three National Assembly seats) was accompanied by a 'new' revolutionary posturing. The party no longer claimed to defend the rights of the Mohajirs exclusively—who were relabelled as 'Urdu-speaking Sindhis'—but of all the 'oppressed' (*mazlum*) populations of Pakistan. This revolutionary posturing was not completely new for the Mohajir leadership, and we have seen how the early literature produced by the APMSO was already infused with a language of rebellion drawn from the progressives. After the MQM tried to widen its social base beyond the Urdu-speaking population of urban Sindh, this revolutionary rhetoric was simply reconfigured into a universalist discourse of social and political change, whereas it had participated in the ethno-militant posturing of the party in its first

Fig. 3: Pragmatic demands and ideological goals of the APMSO and MQM over the years

APMSO (1978–1984)	*Mohajir Qaumi Movement (1984–1997)*	*Muttahida Qaumi Movement (1997–)*
Pragmatic demands	**Pragmatic demands**	**Pragmatic demands**
– Bring an end to 'forged' admissions in Sindh's universities and colleges; – Promote admissions based solely on 'merit' and giving precedence to local applicants over candidates from other cities/provinces; – Promote Urdu in educational institutions; – Bring down student bus fares.	– Restrict the issuance of domicile certificates to permanent residents of Sindh; – Replace non-local police officers by locals; – Facilitate the issuing of arms licences to Mohajirs and Sindhis; – Relocate Afghan refugees near the Afghan border; – Stop in-migration to Sindh; – Criminalise land grabbing; – Modernise the transport system in the cities of Sindh; – Give precedence to locals for recruitment in the public and private sector; – Revise the quota system in force in educational institutions and administrations;	– Stop the construction of the Kalabagh Dam (after 1998); – Better share of water and revenue between provinces; – Devolution of power to local governments; – Transform Karachi into a 'worldclass city' (from the 2000s onwards).

- Repatriate 'stranded Pakistanis' from Bangladesh;
- Open the Khokrapar route to facilitate travel and trade between India and Pakistan.

Ideological goals	**Ideological goals**	**Ideological goals**
– 'Awaken' Mohajirs; – Free Pakistan from the 'grabbers'; – Promote a culture of 'merit' in Pakistan.	– Restore the 'rights' of the Mohajirs; – Free Pakistan from 'feudals' and 'capitalists'; – Unite with the 'oppressed classes' of other 'nationalities' against the former.	– Follow the politics of 'realism and practicalism'; – Free Pakistan from 'feudals' and 'capitalists'; – Promote federalism; – Promote 'secularism' and gender equality.

Sources: Hussain, Altaf and Khalid Athar, *Safar-e-Zindagī*, op. cit; Shahzad, Saleem, *Sha'ur kā Safar*, op. cit. and press reports (*Dawn*, *The Daily Times*, *The Express Tribune*).

decade of existence. Even then, the MQM appealed to the 'exploited classes' and 'the poor' of other provinces, Altaf Hussain's autobiography being replete with such appeals to 'all the oppressed classes of this country'.[60] However, in this early stage, the ethnic agenda of the party took precedence over its commitment to social and political change at the national level, with Altaf Hussain calling 'poor' and 'oppressed' Punjabis, Pashtuns, Sindhis and Baloch to form organisations 'similar to the MQM'. Despite its commitment to support such groups against 'exploitative forces', the MQM did not yet have the ambition to represent these populations on its own.[61]

This coexistence of pragmatism and idealism within the MQM, since its earliest days as a student movement, has made it a difficult coalition partner: while putting forward quite down-to-earth demands, the leadership of the party has also cultivated an oppositional style of politics that does not sit well with the exigencies of a coalition. The MQM's strategic dualism, which amounts to a form of political bipolarism, makes it easy to co-opt, but difficult to accommodate in the long run, particularly when the party has a substantial number of representatives at the Provincial Assembly of Sindh and at the National Assembly, which gives it some leverage over its coalition partners (a pattern which was only disrupted after the MQM decided to boycott the 1993 National Assembly election, a decision which the party later on acknowledged as a massive blunder since it deprived it of much of its bargaining power over the ruling PPP, which between 1993 and 1996 was in open conflict with Mohajirs and their political representatives).

The MQM's Challenged Predominance

Since its first electoral victories of 1987–1988, the MQM remains Karachi's predominant political force. If its vote share declined significantly in Karachi between 1990 and 2002, and again between 2008 and 2013, this did not prevent the party from playing an important role in most governments of the period (except between 1993 and 1996, when the PPP governed alone in Sindh and in Islamabad) and to retain its control over large parts of Karachi (District Central, in particular). This predominance did not solely rely upon official institutions, though. It also relied upon an unofficial power apparatus both overlapping with and circumventing the official state, as well as on formidable military capacities. The party was gradually militarised in the second half of the 1980s, through the recruitment and training of 'violent specialists'[62] as well as through the acquisition of an arsenal that has been constantly upgraded over the years. This conjunction of electoral successes, unofficial power networks and military strength did not prevent the party from facing significant resistance within and without the Mohajir community, though. Since 2007, these challenges to its hegemony have even gained in intensity, threatening Karachi's tensile political equilibrium.

A Party of Government

For all its reputation as a violent and disruptive political force, the MQM primarily owes its longevity to official power structures. The repeated successes of the MQM in local, provincial and national elections did not only help the party sustain its domination over its constituents, but provided it with some bargaining power over its allies of the time in Sindh and in Islamabad. If the party's vote share declined steadily between 1990 and 2002, the 2008 elections marked a reversal of this trend. Moreover, even in 2002, when the vote share of the party in provincial elections reached an all time low, it remained above 40 per cent (cf. Table 1). This resilience of the MQM in Karachi is even more pronounced in District Central, where Urdu-speaking populations are concentrated. Between 1988 and 2008, the vote share of the party in Central in provincial elections remained above 80 per cent, with only one exception in 2002, when the coalition of religious parties of the MMA managed to erode the vote bank of the MQM in the aftermath of the events of 11 September (even then, the party's vote share in Central constituencies remained above 60 per cent, for an overall vote share of 42 per cent in Karachi). In the next election, however, the MQM managed to reassert itself in District Central and to repeat its record score of 1990, with more than 90 per cent of the votes.[63]

Between 2008 and 2013, the MQM's vote share in provincial elections went down by almost ten percentage points (cf. Table 3). The main factor in this sharp decline was the arrival of the Pakistan Tehrik-e-Insaf (PTI) on Karachi's electoral scene. With an overall vote share of 15 per cent in the provincial election and 18 per cent in the National Assembly election, the PTI proved that it could become a credible threat to the MQM's hegemonic ambitions. This is all the more true when the party made a dent in the traditional vote bank of Karachi's aspiring hegemon. Thus, the PTI fared relatively well in a number of constituencies that until now were considered impregnable fiefdoms of the MQM. This was the case, for instance, of NA-245 (National Assembly constituency covering North Nazimabad), where it registered 54,937 votes against 115,776 for the MQM. This was also the case—and even more remarkably, considering that this is the 'home' constituency of the MQM—in NA-246 (Azizabad), where Amir Sharjeel registered 31,875 votes against Nabeel Gabol (who won with 137,874 votes).

If the PTI won the same number of seats as the PPP (one National Assembly seat and three Provincial Assembly seats) in 2013, it registered more than twice its number of votes in the National Assembly election and 230,000 more votes in the Provincial Assembly election. The MQM has reasons to worry: not only did the PTI become Karachi's second party in terms of vote share (and a party which, adding insult to injury, garnered a significant number of votes from MQM traditional constituencies, unlike the PPP), but its candidates polled in second position in twenty-two provincial constituencies (out of forty-two) and fifteen (out of twenty) national constituencies.

While no one can rob the PTI of its symbolic victory, concluding an imminent electoral demise of the MQM would be preposterous. The gap between the MQM and the PTI remains relatively large, especially in the constituencies of District Central, where the MQM registered a much larger number of votes than during its previous 'defeat' of 2002 for instance. With more than 70 per cent of the votes in the national and provincial constituencies of Karachi Central, the MQM continued to 'over-perform' in its traditional bastion, to use the terms of Haris Gazdar:[64] even if it were to lose a significantly larger number of votes to the PTI in the next elections, it would still retain all seats there by virtue of the first-past-the-post system. Of course, an MQM cantoned to this handful of constituencies would no longer be the kingmaker (and kingbreaker) that has been presiding over the destiny of Karachi for the past three decades. But it would remain an important stakeholder in the management of the city nonetheless.

This resistance to incumbency is all the more remarkable in that the MQM has been the target of massive repression during the 1990s and that its leader, Altaf Hussain, has sat in exile in London since 1992. Moreover, the MQM has been facing a major vilification campaign since its early days, being regularly accused by its adversaries as well as by the media to be a 'fascist' and 'terrorist' organisation, conspiring to break up the country with the support of India. Whatever truth may lie behind these accusations and whatever malpractices may have been registered during recent elections in Karachi,[65] it is undeniable that the party has retained a strong vote bank over the years. In other words, the enduring domination of the MQM over Karachi is irreducible to coercion. And if electoral results may not reflect the state of public opinion faithfully (if only because of the large number of unregistered voters), they are an important source of legitimacy and power nonetheless, especially as they give access to state resources (jobs but also land, in a city where a large part of un-built terrains remain the property of local, national and federal state agencies—cf. Fig. 5, Chapter 7).

Table 3: Vote share of major political parties in Karachi (Sindh Provincial Assembly elections), 1988–2013

	MQM	*PPP*	*PML*	*ANP*	*MMA/JUI*	*PTI*
1988	63	20	6	2	0	0
1990	71	16	7	2	0	0
1993	65	19	4	1	0	0
1997	56	10	22	1	0	0
2002	42	13	4	1	26	0
2008	68	22	4	2	1	0
2013	59	8	5	1	1 (JUI–F) 3 (JI)	15

Source: Gazdar, Haris, 'Karachi's violence', art. quoted, p. 5 for 1988–2008 and Election Commission of Pakistan for 2013.

The MQM's grip over Karachi politics culminated under the provincial government of Jam Sadiq Ali (1990–1992) and under the regime of Pervez Musharraf (2002–2008), two periods during which the party was given a free reign to rule over Karachi in exchange for its loyalty and contribution to the containment of opposition forces. Jam Sadiq Ali used the MQM to wage war against the PPP and allegedly issued tens of thousands of arms licences to its party workers for this purpose.[66] Fifteen years later, Pervez Musharraf used the MQM's street power to contain the spread of the lawyers' movement, which threatened his regime after the dismissal of the Chief Justice of Pakistan (CJP) Iftikhar Muhammad Chaudhry, in 2007. In exchange for its loyalty, the MQM was rewarded with unrestrained authority over local affairs and with considerable power as far as job allocations in the local bureaucracy were concerned. These moments of unchallenged supremacy were short-lived, though. Not only were they conditional to the rule of controversial political personalities (a patronage which, in the case of Jam Sadiq Ali, ended with the latter's death in office in 1992 and in the case of Pervez Musharraf with his resignation in the face of mass popular discontent in 2008). They also nurtured excessive confidence among party cadres and workers, by convincing some of them that they could rule Karachi as their personal fiefdom. This over-confidence was epitomised by the abduction and torturing of Major Kalim, which precipitated the party's downfall in 1992 by inciting the army to launch a crackdown that lasted until 1994. The MQM's attempt to 'capture' the local state after 2005, in the terms of its opponents, for its part aroused a military backlash from 2007 onwards (with the ANP, the PAC and more recently the TTP trying to regain some terrain from the aspiring hegemon). Last but not least, as MQM sources themselves acknowledge while referring to the party's collaboration with Jam Sadiq Ali's government, 'with power came dissent and indiscipline'.[67] This led to the 1991 fissure, which ignited a fratricidal war that only ended around 2003 after the Musharraf regime cracked down on the MQM (Haqiqi) and provided the Altaf faction with the opportunity to reassert its authority over the former 'no-go areas' of Landhi and Korangi. In other words, the rare moments of full supremacy experienced by the party created the conditions for its subsequent downsizing. And if the party managed to check its spiral of decline following Pervez Musharraf's 1999 coup by allying itself with the new ruler of the day, its capacity to bounce back in the near future appears uncertain, as the new aspirants to power in Karachi are simply too numerous and too powerful, each in its own right, for the MQM to regain the terrain lost over the past few years—a crucial development that will be explored in detail in the following chapters.

The MQM's 'Secondary State'

Like the Shiv Sena in Mumbai, the MQM owes its predominance to its ability to operate 'both within the framework of state institutions as well as outside',[68] through a parastatal power structure. This political structure duplicating the regular state while partially overlapping with it aims to remedy the gradual socio-economic marginalisation of the Mohajirs as well as their lack of patronage networks along clanic, tribal or feudal lines (such as the *biraderi* for the Punjabis or the *qabila* for the Pashtuns and the Baloch).[69] As such, this apparatus plays the role of an employment and real estate agency, a welfare organisation, a dispute settlement body, a tax collector, a money-lender, etc. But it also assumes a more militant role and shelters a secret martial society that runs a well-trained and well-equipped private army, a highly efficient surveillance network, as well as its own torture cells and execution chambers. To summarise, the MQM's 'secondary state'[70] is the fusion of a formidable redistributive machine capable of giving unsparingly with a disciplinary institution that has systematised the recourse to third-degree torture as a form of social control. As we will see in the next chapter, this dialectic of terror and benevolence was replicated with some success by the MQM's rivals, the PAC in particular. This should not come as a surprise: far from being an exotic oddity, this duality is at the roots of sovereign power,[71] which is precisely what organisations like the MQM and the PAC are craving for.

The basic structure of this secondary state is the party's organisational grid, which covers the city in twenty-six 'sectors', each of them overseeing fifteen to twenty 'units'. The activities of these units and sectors are overseen by an Organisational Committee (Tanzeemi Committee). The Coordination Committee, for its part, is essentially the public face of the party, devoid of any real decisional power. The units-in-charge and sectors-in-charge supervise the party's everyday activities at the *mohalla* and constituency level respectively and they are selected by Altaf Hussain himself among long-time party workers with an unblemished record of loyalty towards the party. These grassroots leaders, who remain unknown to the general public, have 'a great deal more power than the MQM politicians'.[72] Their authority reigns supreme over party workers, who can be assigned a task by their unit-in-charge at any time of the day or night, as I could discover for myself with some of my respondents, who would sometimes abruptly put an end to a late-night dinner to comply with a directive of their immediate superior. The units-in-charge, who were described to me by a party worker as 'very powerful and autonomous, like the SHO [Station House Officer] of a police station', are theoretically answerable to the sectors-in-charge. However, the MQM has a long history of compartmentalisation of its 'dirty work'. In the early 1990s, for instance, the elite corps in charge of torturing and murdering 'traitors' (which was rumoured to be headed by Imran Farooq), operated under the direct authority of the Markaz (the party's headquarters), without the knowledge of sectors-in-charge.[73] Today, most of the party's tougher assignments seem to be divided between the incarcerated leaders of the MQM's militant wing (such as Saulat Mirza, who has been sitting on death row since 1999 but continues to operate from his jail)[74] and the units-in-charge. Thus, according to the aforementioned party worker, 'in most cases they [the units-in-charge] bypass the sectors-in-charge and hide the criminal activities of the *karkun*s [party workers] deliberately'. When I asked my interviewee the reason for this occultation, he explained that 'the criminals of MQM are useful and rare these days', suggesting that units-in-charge shelter them to increase their autonomy of action and possibly to build up their reputation within the party. If some of the dirty work overseen by these units-in-charge might evade the control of their immediate superiors, their activities are tightly monitored by 'London', where the centre of command of the party (its International Secretariat) was relocated in 1992, following the exile of Altaf Hussain shortly before Operation Clean-up. The tightness of this transnational control is striking, especially after such a prolonged period of physical estrangement between the top command of the party and its cadres in Pakistan. I was once interrupted during an interview with a unit-in-charge of the party in Landhi by a phone call from London. After hanging up, the unit-in-charge told me that the interview was over as he had just received a request from his bosses in Britain: a party worker had recently lost a relative and he was asked to present his condolences to the grieving family. Although the incident had taken place in the vicinity (this family lived barely 200 metres away from the unit office), the news of this death had not yet spread in the neighbourhood. But it had already reached London, which had informed the unit-in-charge at once.

If a political ethnography of these local functionaries of the MQM remains to be written, it is most certainly at their level that the de facto sovereignty of the MQM is the most visible. While these men are merely small-time cadres of a political party, without any official mandate, they are entrusted with considerable disciplinary, extractive and regulatory powers. The public authority of the MQM at the local level largely rests on their shoulders, as they are assigned critical tasks such as the surveillance of party workers, the identification of 'unpleasant individuals' (*napasandida afrad*),[75] the collection of revenue from residents and shopkeepers (in the form of *bhatta* or, on the occasion of Eid-ul-Adha, of animal hides, which are sold to the tannery industry) or the adjudication of interpersonal disputes. Their political clout is reinforced by their power of recommendation (*sifarish*) for job positions in the public sector, while their intervention can prove decisive in having access to water, electricity, education, health facilities and even legal counselling. The provision of these services is facilitated by the myriad branches of the party, which runs an ambulance service as well as some hospitals through its welfare branch (the Khidmat-e-Khalq Foundation [KKF], which was established the same year as the APMSO, in 1978, on the patterns of the philanthropic branch of the JI), while maintaining a Legal Aid Committee as well as a Labour Division. The MQM even runs its own traffic police, the City Wardens, which is mainly composed of party workers and sympathisers and which was attributed an 8 million rupees budget in April 2011 by the Administrator of the City, Fazlur Rehman (who succeeded the City Nazim, Mustafa Kamal, in 2010). During the month of Ramzan 2012, the 1,500 traffic wardens (who have access to twenty police cars) were called in to assist the police in the regulation of traffic at 111 different spots across the city.[76] The creation of this unarmed but uniform-clad force widely perceived—and thus regularly targeted—as 'the MQM's police' has naturally been contested by the rivals of the dominant party, and in particular by the JI. In January 2010, the Sindh JI Chief, Asadullah Bhutto, accused the wardens of illegally occupying a football ground in Gulshan-e-Iqbal, where they planned to construct their headquarters. Bhutto also expressed his doubts about the legality of the wardens, as the local government law contained no provision about 'parallel policing'.[77]

Despite what its opponents have been repeating since the early 1990s, however, the MQM's enduring predominance in Karachi is not the outcome of a 'parallel government' or a 'state within a state'. True, the MQM has sometimes been tempted to circumvent and duplicate the state in its citadels, for instance by erecting concrete walls and digging trenches around its strongholds, or by building iron gates and setting up checkpoints guarded by young armed men at their entrance—all practices that were discontinued after the launch of Operation Clean-up, as one of the first initiatives of the army was precisely to bring down the ramparts of these Mohajir citadels. But even when it flirted with separatism, the MQM remained a party of government, which drew most of its public authority from official (re)sources. Which is not to say that this authority is essentially formal: on the contrary, the MQM largely benefited from the informalisation of the state and from the politics of patronage of ruling elites. This is what the militarisation of the party under Jam Sadiq Ali already suggested. Under Pervez Musharraf, the MQM has also used its control of the local state (see Chapter 6 for further details) to consolidate its hold over its constituents and, more originally, over its party workers. These favours to dedicated party workers and sympathisers are an integral part of the MQM's 'performative politics', that is, of its capacity to 'deal with everyday problems rapidly, visibly, and though rarely aimed at transforming institutions or practices, with some immediate effect'.[78] By increasing the presence of MQM-affiliated workers within public institutions, they also contribute to strengthen the party's grip over the local state. Finally, the intermingling of political and professional careers, through the *sifarish* of the sectors-in-charge and units-in-charge, increases the dependence of individual workers on their party for the management of their lives. Favours come with obligations on the part of the benefactor and the allocation of a position in a public office can come along with solicitations of greater involvement in the party's affairs, including its dirty work. This is exemplified by the trajectory of Faisal Mehmood, one of the co-accused in the murder case of journalist Wali Khan Babar in 2011. According to the interrogation report prepared by the Special Investigative Unit (SIU) of the city police, of which I was shown a copy, Mehmood is a 'Madrasi', or Tamil Muslim. Between 1998 and 2001, he managed a small roadside restaurant in Kharadar, in the Old City. In 2003, he and his family moved to Orangi Town. The following year, he obtained a job in the City District Government of Karachi (CDGK) on the recommendation of his unit in-charge. But instead of settling down (he was now forty-one, married, with four daughters), Mehmood was allegedly involved in a case of kidnapping-cum-murder (of a Pashtun ice-cream seller) and in a murder attempt on a PPP cadre (who managed to escape) the very same year. The chances of a court of law validating his confession were extremely thin. Nonetheless, the credence given to such police reports by the judges of the Supreme Court (see Chapter 7) has granted them some veracity in the eyes of the media and the public, thus reactivating the debate around the MQM's involvement in violence. And against all odds, an anti-terrorism court (which, significantly, was located in the interior of Sindh rather than in Karachi, and could thus operate more freely) handed death and life sentences to six of the accused on 1 March 2014. Faisal Mehmood himself was sentenced to life imprisonment, in a verdict that confirmed his double life—clerk for the city by day, killer for his party by night.

The Military Component of the MQM's Public Authority

The military build-up of the MQM, which provided the party with a significant advantage over its rivals, at least until recently, must be contextualised. As we already saw in detail, the founders of the MQM had their first taste of politics in an increasingly violent student milieu, and they drew lessons from their expulsion of KU by the better armed IJT. It should also be remembered that the MQM emerged a few years later in a context of escalating 'ethnic' violence, which saw Urdu-speaking populations grow increasingly insecure under the threat of the Pashtun 'arms and drug mafia'. In this context, the turn to arms of the MQM leadership, in the mid-1980s, expressed an existential fear as far as the survival of the party but also of the Mohajir community at large was concerned. In a famous speech made in Liaquatabad in 1987, Altaf Hussain thus declared, 'Mohajirs will have no good use for their VCRs, colour televisions and other luxuries, because these things cannot defend us. They will have to arrange for their own security.'[79] Twenty years later, in a context of renewed confrontation with the Pashtuns, the *quaid-e-tehrik* (leader of the movement, Altaf Hussain's *laqab* within the MQM) would renew his call to arms and extend it to women: 'Women should learn how to shoot and even they should take karate classes. After all, self-defence is the key to survival in today's violent world.'[80]

Searching for security—for its leaders and activists as much as for its constituents—the MQM started stocking its own arsenal from 1984 onwards. After having obtained their first revolvers and Sten guns from progressive students, the leaders of the party started looking for Kalashnikovs. MQM officials first encountered the *klashni* at Sindh University, in Hyderabad, in January 1986, when Altaf Hussain was invited to attend G.M. Syed's birthday.[81] JSM militants introduced MQM workers to the handling of modern weaponry, including AK-47s. After their return to Karachi, the participants went looking for their own *klashni* and it was not long before one of Altaf's 'bodyguards', Javed Langra, came back with one.[82] In the following years, the MQM and the APMSO managed to build up a formidable arsenal and they attracted a number of the *badmash*s previously affiliated with the IJT or with the progressives. These military capacities were initially built up with the help of the progressive and left-wing groups (NSF, PSF and USM) with which the APMSO remained allied until 1988. In the late 1980s, the MQM also traded cars for guns with the PPP.[83] More surprisingly, militants of the IJT also sold weapons to the APMSO around the same time.[84] Finally, around 1987–1988, the MQM/APMSO bought its first shipment of AK-47s from the Sindhi nationalists of the JSM, which would soon become arch rivals of the party and its student wing. These weapons provided the APMSO with a tactical advantage over the IJT, which started losing its hold over KU and other campuses in the city at the end of the 1980s.[85]

The formation of the MQM's elite corps

The militarisation of the MQM did not merely serve defensive purposes, deriving from the existential fears mentioned above. In its early years, the MQM's leadership adopted a resolutely militant posturing, which aimed at toughening up the (self-)image of the Mohajir community. Indeed, ethnic stereotypes which remain prevalent to this day—especially among Punjabis—project Mohajirs as a meek and effeminate community, if only for its favourite diet of tea and *chapati*s, pitted against the richer—and supposedly sexually empowering—diet of *lassi* and *roti*s dear to Punjabis. Altaf Hussain himself suffered from this stigmatisation of Urdu-speakers as 'tea drinkers' (*chai pine wale*) during his military training as a cadet in 1971—an experience that, according to him, was crucial in his ethnic awakening.[86] Militancy was therefore an integral part of the imagination of the Mohajir *qaum*. The fear of the Pashtuns was tainted with a fascination for their supposedly more 'martial' culture—a gross oversimplification of Pashtun history[87] but a performative belief nonetheless. Thus, when the MQM's leadership decided to upgrade the military capacities of its first 'bodyguards', in 1987, these young men were sent to Afghanistan, where they stayed with a Pashtun tribal leader who helped them improve their military skills. On their return, these newly trained 'bodyguards' would transmit their freshly acquired knowledge to other recruits.[88]

In the late 1980s, the members of this elite corps were regrouped under the MQM's Security Wing, which initially comprised two cells of seven militants each. Each of these cells corresponded to a 'zone' covering half of Karachi. The activities and personalities of one of these two cells (that of Zone C, based in Liaquatabad and covering Central Karachi) have recently been brought to light by Nichola Khan.[89] Combining detailed ethnographic observation with interview-generated life-histories, Khan managed to approach these elusive characters at close range. On the basis of this prolonged fieldwork, Khan suggests that for the MQM's killer elite, extreme violence provided access to and affirmation of a form of 'hypermasculinity', as well as a source of status enhancement. In their testimonies, these militants suggest that the identity of their victims and the way they were killed was left to the initiative of their 'leaders'. In some cases, these leaders are even said to have suggested using the most gruesome forms of violence to terrify the 'enemies of the MQM'. However, it is difficult to distinguish between fact and fiction here. These former militants may be tempted to attribute moral responsibility for these atrocities to their leaders, in order to live in peace with their painful memories. In the process, they downplay the role of peer pressure in their acts of extreme violence. Yet, following Christopher Browning's seminal study of the 101 reserve battalion of the German police during the Second World War,[90] it is hard to believe that the increasing brutality of these killers (involving cases of bone drilling, mutilations, decapitations, etc.) was simply an expression of the ever-more bloody tactics of their leaders. I am more inclined to think that intense dynamics of peer pressure prevailed within these micro-groups, which encouraged each of their members (who often lived together and 'worked' in the same premises) to emulate if not outsmart his peers by the number of his victims and the sheer 'creativity' of his macabre designs. 'Excesses' would then have occurred at the confluence of party discipline and horizontal interactions presenting affinities with a professional competition.[91] This finds confirmation in the testimonies of some MQM militants, who talk of 'unending competition' within the party's killer elite.[92]

The MQM's intermittent combatants

All the young men who were recruited into the MQM along the years for militant activities were not full-time fighters. Many of these armed fighters were intermittent combatants, who were only occasionally sent to the 'frontline'. Iqbal* is one of these Sunday fighters, otherwise a regular MQM party worker in one of the party's contested turfs. In recent years, he has been sent to the 'frontline' on several occasions; and while he insists that most temp-warriors like him turn out to make poor combatants, he also points to the professionalisation of Karachi's turf wars, whether in terms of tactics or armament. Iqbal's self-restrained militant career also demonstrates that unlike what dominant approaches in conflict studies suggest, one does not always need to be 'motivated' to take parts in acts of collective violence with lethal consequences, such as war, terrorism or 'ethnic riots'.[93] His trajectory points at alternative paths towards violent mobilisation, which neither proceed from full adhesion nor coercion. His gradual enrolment into the turf war between the MQM and Pashtun 'criminals' of a neighbouring locality is best described as a form of reluctant mobilisation, where he let himself be mobilised for violent operations while keeping some details of his past life hidden to his party leaders, out of fear that they could use it to make him a full-time killer rather than an episodic Sunday fighter. This life-story does not claim any form of representativity. On the contrary, its heuristic value lies in its questioning of many commonly held assumptions about the profile, aspirations and violent behaviour of the MQM's foot soldiers. Moreover, Iqbal's rather atypical career offers a valuable addition to the existing literature on MQM workers and militants, which until now has been primarily concerned with the first or second wave of MQM militants, recruited during the 1980s and 1990s. Iqbal, who joined the MQM in the mid-2000s, belongs to the next generation of MQM workers, who joined a party that had already lost much of its 'fun'[94] and was getting increasingly involved in practices of economic accumulation. These practices might have scorned the image of the party but they also attracted to it some disgruntled youths in search of rapid upward social mobility—a quest which for many of them, such as Iqbal, would remain unfulfilled.

Nothing predisposed Iqbal to become a party worker of the MQM. His ethnicity alone should have worked as a powerful deterrent against his joining the party. Though he was born in Karachi, Iqbal is not a Mohajir. His parents migrated from another province (I have deliberately withheld some information, which could have compromised the anonymity that I guaranteed him) but he grew up in a Mohajir-dominated *katchi abadi*, and rapidly became as fluent in Urdu as in his native tongue. His father was relatively well-off (he had earned some money as a migrant worker in the Gulf) and Iqbal, who was the second youngest of four brothers and four sisters, could pursue an education up to university level. He was a rather bright student and joined a pre-engineering college after his matriculation. After successfully completing the first year of a three-year course, he failed his exams the second year. On his own admission, he had lost his concentration in the deeply politicised atmosphere of the college. One incident, in particular, deeply affected him. Sometime around 1995 or 1996, he witnessed a fight between activists of the IJT and of a student union which claimed to represent students of his own community. The latter were badly hurt and fell to the ground. When their rivals jumped on their motorbikes, seemingly to run over the wounded, Iqbal spontaneously ran towards them, hoping to save them from a certain death. His initiative was emulated by other students and the boys of the IJT ran away. Iqbal's courageous reaction probably saved the boys' lives. But it also exposed him to reprisals from the IJT, whose activists threatened him with dire consequences if he dared interfere again in their affairs. Iqbal took these threats seriously, but it is his mother's reaction which prompted him to give up his studies. When he reached his place, wearing a blood-stained white shirt, his mother was horrified and asked him to leave the college at once, as she feared for his life. 'This time, it is someone else's blood on your shirt. Next time, it will be yours,' his mother told him. He abided by her advice, which he considers 'wise' retrospectively, and never returned to college after this incident.

After dropping out of college, Iqbal tried his luck in the army. He soon realised, though, that the prospects of rapid upward social mobility in the military were pretty grim, and he did not renew his contract after its term. He returned to Karachi, doomed to 'timepass' while waiting for an opportunity to present itself to him. Then, one day, as he was taking part in a demonstration, around 1996, he was arrested by the police and sent to jail. There, he was threatened by some inmates but was spared a serious trashing due to the timely intervention of some prisoners affiliated with the MQM. Following this incident, Iqbal developed, in his own words, a 'soft corner' for the MQM: 'They did what they said. They were actually protecting us. That was the motivation factor.' However, this motivation was not sufficient to translate into actual engagement. At that time, Iqbal was learning Japanese and dreamt of finding a job in Japan. It was only after the implementation of the Sindh Local Government Ordinance (SLGO) 2001, which gave birth to a three-tier local government system (see Chapter 6), that Iqbal 'decided' to join the MQM. Far from being personal, this choice was primarily a response to familial pressure, as his father was encouraging him to join the party and contest local elections, taking advantage of the new career opportunities that were opening to lower-middle-class but educated youths like him under the devolution plan.

Shortly after officially joining the party, Iqbal was elected a local councillor. He was soon involved in a case of corruption—he candidly admits that he had been taking bribes 'from builders, contractors, everyone', but justifies his act by relating it to the 'ethics of illegality' allegedly prevailing in his milieu, which enables him to deem his act illegal and yet licit:[95] 'taking bribes is common and not considered a crime'. He was apparently denounced to the party by a relative, following a dispute with the latter, and was suspended for six months. After this probation time, he resumed his functions and was noticed by a party cadre who took him under his protection. However, a few years later, Iqbal's patron was murdered by a rival group and he considered for a while leaving the party, where he felt discriminated against for his ethnicity. His exit plan did not materialise and, instead, Iqbal started getting increasingly involved in the militant activities of the party in his locality. In 2010 and 2011, he took part in several clashes with gunmen of a rival group, which he identifies as the Pashtun 'drug mafia', supported by militants of the ANP and officers of a 'law and order agency'.

If Iqbal let himself be recruited for martial activities, with his activism becoming increasingly risky in the process, he consistently refused to become a full-time killer for the party. This reluctance led him to withhold some details of his past life to his party. Thus, he avoided mentioning his past experience in the army out of fear of being pressurised to take part in even more brutal activities (targeted killings, acts of torture,…). This withholding of information which he could have used to his advantage, had he been 'motivated' to join the elite corps of the MQM's 'shooters' and 'bodyguards', points at his reluctance to be mobilised for violent activities, at least beyond a certain point that he himself determined. This did not deter him from capitalising silently on his 'controversial' past, though. During armed clashes, Iqbal generally tries to get hold of weapons he became familiar with while in the army, which provide him with a greater sense of control and safety. He is also aware that his military past makes him a more experienced foot soldier than other temp-warriors like him, a sense of confidence that can be grasped in the following extract of one of my conversations with him, during which he related an episode of fighting (the third he was involved in) in his locality during the month of Ramzan 2011:

- They [the MQM unit-in-charge for his locality] called me and I went there [to the place where the fighting was about to start]. It was 12 am and I started my duty—it's eight hours. At 2 am, they told me that I had to accompany two senior *karkun*s. They were *supposed* to be senior, because they were Urdu-speaking and I was non-Urdu speaking. Then I accompanied them. Both of them were carrying guns. Only I was empty-handed. Then we reached the [firing] post. It was a sensitive post. The distance between our post and the enemy post was like... 200 metres... [...] When we reached there, it was all dark. You could not even light a matchstick, otherwise it would have revealed our position to the enemy. There, one of the so-called senior *karkun*s handed me over his rifle, and he went back, 20, 30 m. away from the frontline, he picked up his cell-phone and started talking to his girlfriend... I stood there, in the bunker, pointing my rifle at the enemy post...
- What do you mean by 'bunker'?
- It was just a *desi* [South Asian] type of bunker, made of temporary brick walls... So anyway, I was standing there, pointing my rifle at the enemy's post, chamber unlocked, ready to fire... During night time, we generally keep the chamber unlocked and loaded with bullets, because it's a crucial time. All that time, I kept my eyes wide open, looking at the enemy post. Then, at 3 am, the second *karkun* handed over his Kalashnikov to me and left. I stayed there alone, with the Kalashnikov in my back and the other rifle in my hand. Then around 5, 5.30, another *karkun* arrived and said 'Oh, you are alone!' I said 'Yes...' So he replied, 'Ok, I'll stay with you.' Until 8 in the morning he was with me. That day, I ended up staying until 8 pm. It's ok... Sometimes, when you are a *karkun* or work for MQM, you have to be that dedicated... The fighting with the drug mafia there lasted for several days. The drug mafia was helped by ANP people... Some agencies were also helping them... The crucial time was during *iftari* or *sehri* [meals served after the rupture of the fast, respectively at nightfall and at the crack of dawn] and during the *azhan* [prayer call]... Two or three times, the fighting started at *iftari*...
- Did you see some fighting that day?
- No, not that day. I returned home and the fighting started the next day. By that time I was back there. I don't do *roza* [fasting], that's why they called me there: the timing of *iftari* and *sehri* are crucial [as most party workers leave their post to break the fast], so they needed someone there at that time. Then three or four shots were fired by the enemies and I replicated. Then the oth-

ers turned up once they heard the gunshots and many rounds were fired at the enemies. Then after 40 to 50 minutes of fighting, the agencies came—law enforcement agencies [the Rangers]—and told us we had to back off from that area. It happened three or four times. Then, after three, four hours, the Rangers went back to their position and we went back to the frontline. At one point, I was caught by the Rangers but they did not recognise me because I spoke in my mother tongue and they didn't pay attention to me. Because they know that normally only Urdu-speakers are allowed to carry guns [in the MQM] and allowed to fight. Normally, non-Urdu speakers don't have access to the merchandise [guns].

- Were any of your companions killed during these clashes?
- No, one of them was injured in the leg but no one was killed. During those five days of fighting, people said that bullets worth 20 million rupees were fired… That was a rumour… I think it was closer to 2 million… When they [MQM] captured the area, they fired with automatic weapons continuously…
- How do you 'capture' an area?
- There were special teams, equipped with special weapons. Those were new. Those who handled them were unknown to us, they came from some other area. They were well-trained. They knew their job. We had some strategic planners, who knew the maps. We had some military-standard binoculars, sniper rifles with telescopes. Anybody knows the Dragonov is expensive, right? But the snipers had some with them. There were three to four of them, and they did the real damage, not the light machineguns… The thing that was surprising was that the law enforcement agencies… they provided the drug mafia with weapons…
- What makes you say that?
- Our touts were in the area… our spies, you could say. They informed us that government vehicles were being used to deploy weapons… to distribute weapons among those people.

Iqbal's past military experience makes him a valuable witness here. It enables him to appreciate, from a 'professional' point of view, the fighting skills of his companions and the military-grade planning and equipment put at their disposal. Iqbal is thus pointing at the amateurism of most temp-warriors episodically sent to the battlefield, a critique infused with his own sense of being discriminated against for his ethnicity, a discrimination that he found all the more unfair that his fighting skills were well above those of the 'so-called senior *karkun*s' and that this very ethnicity provided his party with a tactical advantage during armed clashes, as it made him less suspicious in the eyes of law enforcement agencies. He also insists on the formidable war-machine built by the MQM in recent years, whether in terms of personnel, strategic planning or military equipment. Finally, his first-hand account of some of the worst episodes of fighting witnessed in Karachi since the mid-1990s points at the ambiguous role of 'law enforcement agencies'—some of which apparently sided with the belligerents while others (the Rangers) adopted a more neutral approach, though without seriously interfering with the combats.

When I recorded this conversation, in December 2011, Iqbal was once again considering leaving the party. He was well aware that his life was becoming increasingly dangerous and he was considering moving abroad, or at least to another city in Pakistan. He was dreaming of opening a photo studio and forgetting politics altogether, before it was too late. His family were encouraging him to do so: his two parents had passed away and although his brothers and sisters remained unaware of the exact nature of his activities for the party, they feared for his life. One cannot fail to perceive multiple dynamics of (self-)occultation, as well as the profession of a deeply idiosyncrasic ethic of violence, here. So as to avoid being (even) more involved in acts of violence, some of which he considers reprehensible, Iqbal has been consistently hiding parts of his past to his party, dissimulating valuable biographical resources in the process. On the other hand, he has been trying to maintain a veil of ignorance over the exact nature of his activities in the MQM within his household. Living in fear (of his 'enemies' but also of his own party) and denial, Iqbal also lives in chronic uncertainty. He remains uncertain about his future, but for now has nowhere else to go. The next time we met, in August 2012, he was once again considering leaving to go abroad, and was busy gathering documents and funds to move to the United States, where one of his brothers was staying. Iqbal wanted to hear my opinion on this emigration project and I could only encourage him to put some distance between himself and the increasingly dangerous world of Karachi politics. This would cost me a precious informant but I remembered vividly his request, a year earlier, to treat him as 'a friend, not a source', and this seemed to be the day of reckoning.

The Challenges to the MQM's Domination

Despite its political clout and military power, the MQM has had to cope with an ever increasing number of competitors, from dissidents (the Haqiqis) to mainstream political parties (the PPP, and more recently the ANP) to sectarian groups (the Sunni Tehrik, the Sipah-e-Sahaba Pakistan), to jihadis (the Tehrik-e-Taliban Pakistan), to more recent organisations with links to the underworld (the PAC). As we will see in detail in the next two chapters, these challenges have only increased in recent years. The MQM's unprecedented grip over the local state, under Pervez Musharraf, has been a major source of conflict with the political parties and organisations claiming to represent the non-Mohajir populations of Karachi, who levelled against Mohajirs the allegation of state 'capture' that the MQM had initially made against Punjabis. The weakening of Pervez Musharraf's regime, following his retirement from the army in 2007, provided a window of opportunity for these groups challenging the MQM's hold over Karachi politics. The events of 12 May 2007 were a watershed in this regard. When the MQM tried to prevent the CJP from visiting Karachi, at a time when he was in open conflict with President Musharraf, gun battles ensued between the MQM and the ANP (whose leaders supported the visit of the CJP) on Sharah-e-Faisal, the road leading to the airport, costing the lives of forty-eight people. Although the majority of the victims turned out to be Pashtuns,[96] these clashes signalled the emergence of a new political and military force determined to challenge the domination of the MQM over Karachi. They marked the beginning of a bloody conflict between the two parties, which endured even after they joined the same coalition government in Sindh and in Islamabad after the 2008 elections. During these elections, the ANP managed to win two Provincial Assembly seats in Karachi, one of which was won against a candidate of the MQM (in PS-128, a Provincial Assembly constituency covering parts of Landhi and Quaidabad). This success owed less to an increase in the ANP's vote share than to its focus on winnable constituencies.[97] For the leadership of the MQM, though, these results were a source of alarm. MQM leaders are aware that the demographic profile of Karachi is changing (cf. Fig. 2), with Urdu-speakers no longer a majority in the city (though still far more numerous that any other linguistic group). In this context, the virtual monopoly of the MQM over Urdu speakers' votes is no longer a guarantee of dominance over Karachi at large. As a result, the MQM has followed a two-pronged strategy: on the one hand, it joined the ANP in provincial and national coalition governments, but on the other it retracted towards its former ethnic and militant posturing. Though it restrained from targeting the Pashtuns explicitly, it used the alleged threat of 'talibanisation' to mobilise its supporters and armed cadres against the ANP and the Pashtuns at large, leading to a resumption of 'target killings' of party activists but also to coordinated attacks against Pashtun street vendors and restaurant owners, in an attempt to roll back the influx of Pashtun migrants and IDPs to Karachi.

The perception that the MQM has captured the state in Karachi has also been a source of conflict with its other coalition partner from 2008 to early 2013, the PPP. The issue of public jobs was at the heart of the political battle between the MQM and the PPP during the summer of 2011, which led to the worst episode of violence witnessed in Karachi since 1995 (see Chapter 6). Besides its own coalition partners, the MQM has been facing armed resistance from the Baloch criminal elements regrouped in the PAC. As we will see in greater detail in the next chapter, this conflict is also focusing on the access to local state institutions, a confirmation that 'the state' (*riyasat*, an Urdu term referring to a permanent power apparatus distinct from more ephemeral governments), far from having withered away in Karachi, remains coveted as a source of physical protection, economic alleviation and political legitimacy by the very same protagonists who trample underfoot conventional notions of sovereignty.

Conclusion

Karachi's dominant political and military force since the late 1980s, the MQM, is the outcome of a student movement, the APMSO, which initially failed to find its public despite an apparently favourable socio-economic context. If most studies of the MQM so far have been locating the origins of Mohajir nationalism in the gradual political and economic marginalisation of Mohajirs from the 1970s onwards,[98] these socio-economic explanations fail to explain the initial erring of Mohajir student activists. The examination of this early phase of Mohajir nationalism complicates the narrative of this movement-turned-party by de-naturalising the electoral successes of the MQM at the end of the 1980s. This examination of the MQM's origins as a student movement is all the more necessary that these 'street fighting years' have left a deep imprint over the MQM leadership's approach towards politics, conceived by the party's ideologues as a state of permanent warfare. The peculiar grammar of consent and authority that has been the trademark of the MQM—and that was projected by its ideologues as the most rational response to the aforementioned 'state of war'—is in fact a legacy of the APMSO. It was only reinforced by the transformation of the Mohajir movement into a mainstream party, a process of institutionalisation that also led to a greater personalisation of authority within the party.

While the militarisation of Karachi's student milieu in the late 1970s/early 1980s left a deep imprint over the founders of the APMSO and precipitated the transformation of this student movement into a political party, the 'ethnic riots' of 1985–1986 brought forth the MQM's military build-up, which only escalated in the course of its battle for local supremacy with the JI and the IJT, examined in the preceding chapter. At the end of the 1980s, the party's weapons procurement spree and its setting up of an elite corps of well-trained fighters made it a force to be reckoned with. Instead of establishing the supremacy of the party, though, these strong-arm tactics were emulated by its rivals, leading to further violent escalation. What truly set the MQM apart from other contenders to political power in Karachi was its ability to fuse militancy and governance, disruption and political convention. Despite what its detractors suggest, the enduring resistance of the party to the incumbency factor was not so much (or not solely) the outcome of its terror tactics, its widespread electoral malpractices or its patronage by successive civilian and military regimes. More importantly, the MQM owes its political longevity—a truly remarkable feat, considering the successive crises faced by the party since its creation—to its ability to reconcile official and unofficial resources, in a permanent dialectic of the legal and the lethal that, as Jean and John Comaroff underline, is essential to the transmutation of power, through its transcendence, into sovereignty.[99] Here lies the 'magic of the state': in the inescapability of the fact that 'might made right no less than right made might'.[100] In postcolonial Karachi, this magic formula was premised on the straddling of the fence separating state and society. This transgression (at least from the point of view of legal-rational models of the modern state which, as we will see further, continue to structure the debate on 'the state' in Pakistan)[101] was facilitated by state agents themselves, who contributed to the fragmentation of state sovereignty with their patronage politics and natural inclination to outsource illegitimate violence through Machiavellian trade-offs with private enforcers. The formula of the MQM's success—reconciling the urns and the arms while operating within and without the confines of the state, in the twilight zone of dis/order—could not be kept secret for long, though. With the passage of time, other contenders to sovereign power tried to replicate it, with varied success. The violence and ever-increasing disorder that resulted from these attempts at replicating the MQM's magic formula were not the symptoms of a worsening state of lawlessness but, on the contrary, a manifestation of the city's increasingly dense architecture of legalities and the advent of a 'horizontally woven tapestry of sovereignties'.[102] Ironically—but as we will see, the paradox is not as blatant as it seems—the most significant contributors to this proliferation of legal orders were two groups commonly identified, in Karachi, as 'criminals' and 'terrorists'. It is this apparent paradox and its consequences for the MQM's hegemonic project that I explore in the next two chapters.

4

THE BANDITS WHO WOULD BE KINGS

Dil ke phaphole jal uthe sine ke dagh se
Is ghar ko ag lag gai ghar ke chiragh se

His heart was burning so hard that his chest was full of blisters.
He set this house on fire with the lamp of the house.

(A two-verse poem accompanying a poster of Rehman 'Dakait' in a lane of Rangiwara, Lyari. Personal observation, August 2012).

In December 2011, as I was driving in an auto-rickshaw across a bazaar of Saddar, the buoyant and decrepit colonial centre of Karachi, I came across a passer-by wearing a t-shirt that proclaimed, 'I own Karachi!' The polarisation of Karachi's political and social life, courtesy of almost three decades of civil strife, gave a highly provocative resonance to that slogan. It reminded me of a conversation I had with one of the most well known public figures of the MQM in the city, Senator Nasreen Jalil, during my first visit to Karachi in 2001. After watching her take the lead of the great Ashura procession[1] on M.A. Jinnah Road without any bodyguard, I had asked her how she dared appear in such a high-risk public event[2] without any armed protection. With a large smile on her face, Nasreen Jalil had replied by reformulating the Mohajirs' sense of entitlement to 'their' city, which is so integral to their identity politics in Karachi: 'Why should we carry guns? This city belongs to us!' Ten years had passed since this conversation and, within that time, Jalil had plenty of occasions to put her statement to the test. In 2005, she became the Deputy Mayor (Naib

Nazim) of the city of Karachi, a post of considerable influence under the newly formed CDGK. The city government of Mustafa Kamal (2005–2010) saw the MQM tighten its grip over the local state, while trying to sell to its constituents and to foreign investors the 'worldclass city' dream. This government had great plans for Karachi. The reference point of its urban utopia was no longer Hong Kong, as it had been two decades earlier for a more militant MQM toying with secessionist projects. This time, Dubai was the model city to emulate for the development of Karachi. To implement its grand projects, the MQM-led CDGK required the support of Karachi's various populations and invited them to develop a feeling of 'ownership' towards their city. 'I own Karachi!' was the slogan adopted in 2008 by Kamal's team to sum up its approach towards development and create a 'sense of ownership among the citizens of Karachi'. The passer-by who had caught my attention could have been an employee of the CDGK—possibly even one of these MQM party workers gratified with a job position on the *sifarish* of the unit-in-charge of their locality. But he could also have earned his t-shirt—along with a 'city owner' badge—after enrolling himself as a volunteer for the numerous citizen initiatives launched by the CDGK in the field of traffic management and 'environmental protection' (in fact, beautification).

This slogan was drawn from the neo-liberal urban governance models, encouraging the 'participatory' management of the affairs of the city, which Kamal and his entourage dreamt to test on Karachi (Kamal did his undergraduate studies in Malaysia, before enrolling at the MBA programme of the University of Wales, and he brought with him a pool of young technocrats familiar with these models). The same idea of 'ownership', conflating the neo-liberal discourse on participatory citizenship with the Mohajirs' sense of entitlement to Karachi was already present in the name of the cultural festival launched by Nasreen Jalil in 2006, *Hamara Karachi* (Our Karachi), though on a less provocative mode. 'I own Karachi!' was indeed of a different calibre. For its detractors, the MQM never tolerated the existence, let alone the development, of other political forces in Karachi, considering the city its personal fiefdom. Coming from an MQM-dominated city government, this slogan sounded like a provocation to the ears of anti-MQM elements. This was particularly true in Lyari, one of Karachi's oldest and poorest localities, which has seen the rise of a fiercely anti-MQM movement in recent years. For Uzair Baloch, the young 'Don' of Lyari,[3] who emerged in recent years as a major adversary of the MQM, the party has 'made the whole of Karachi hostage at gunpoint' (*MQM ne pure Karachi ko banduq ke zor par yarghamal banaya hua hai*). However, Uzair is committed to prevent the MQM from 'owning' the whole of Karachi. 'Their dream will never materialize,' he told me in August 2012, a statement that brimmed with promises of renewed confrontations between Karachi's predominant party and its newly emerged Baloch challengers of the PAC. For Uzair Baloch and other adversaries of the MQM, Karachi's dominant party has not renounced its hegemonic agenda, which has to be resisted politically as well as militarily. Uzair considers himself the rightful owner of his own piece of Karachi—Lyari and its population approaching 2 million—and he is determined not to let anyone snatch it from him. This anti-hegemonic project overlaps with a discourse of autochthony tainted with hostility towards Mohajirs at large, the leadership of the PAC making little distinction between Mohajirs and the MQM, often referring to the former as 'the people of the MQM' (*MQM wale*). As Zafar Baloch, the right-hand man of Uzair Baloch and the 'brain' of the PAC until his murder in September 2013, explained to me in December 2011:

> Basically, they [Mohajirs] are not from here. Basically, we [the Baloch] are from here, because our fathers and grandfathers, they belong to Karachi by birth. The people of the MQM, they are first generation Karachiites. They migrated after 1947. We have been here for more than two centuries.

To reinforce his point, Zafar Baloch resorted to a metaphor comparing Mohajirs to tenants (*kiraedar*s) and the Baloch to owners (*malik*s), an analogy that found its resonance in the battle for space and land rights that is so intimately linked with 'political' and 'ethnic' conflicts in Karachi:

> The owner can evict the tenant at will but nobody can evict the owner. These people of the MQM, they're just like tenants. They have grabbed the property of someone else. When the owner is weak, he gets his land grabbed. But when he gets strong again, he will say, 'Let's recover our property!' [*Hamara* property *waguzar karao*!]

While accusing the Mohajirs at large of having 'captured' Karachi, the leaders of the PAC point to the ethnic bias that allegedly informed the development works of the MQM-led CDGK between 2005 and 2010. According to Zafar Baloch, 'During these four years, they upgraded their area in a big way [*unhon ne apne elaqon ko bahut* up *kiya*]. [...] The MQM claims to speak for everyone but they won't give up their bias against others [*i.e.* non-Mohajirs].' As this statement suggests, the conflict between the PAC and the MQM is not primarily of an ethnic nature. Although the PAC's politics can be seen as the coming of age of an armed politics of autochthony in Karachi's oldest locality, it is also fuelled by a political rivalry over the 'control' (Zafar Baloch often used the English term, while speaking in Urdu) of the local state that emerged in 2001. This access to public resources is all the more pressing, for the leaders of the PAC, that the Baloch of Lyari have been bearing the brunt of the downsizing of public companies and institutions, a complaint that I often heard in Lyari, from sportsmen (who saw their perspectives of titularisation fade away with the closure of the 'departments', that is, the teams funded by Pakistan's leading public banks, companies and institutions) to semi-educated candidates to government jobs. Zafar Baloch summed up this process: 'The downsizing of [public] institutions is going on. Until recently, when your father had been working for 20, 25 years in a public office, it was customary that, when he got retired, you would replace him. This used to happen in all [public] institutions: the KPT [Karachi Port Trust], the KESC [Karachi Electrical Supply Corporation], the banks, the Steel Mill... But when downsizing started, you would no longer inherit your father's position.' Elaborating further on the impact of this estrangement of the Baloch of Lyari from public institutions, Zafar Baloch points at a persisting desire of the state—not of an ethnically blind apparatus distinct from society, but more realistically of a locus of power whose penetration by society is seen as the only way to redress social and ethnic inequalities. Ironically, Baloch—who used to head an organisation accused of harbouring some of the most hardened criminals of Karachi—used the example of the police to make his point:

Take the case of Mr Gulabi Samo, who was recruited as a DSP [Deputy Superintendent of Police]. Well, today he is a DIG [Deputy Inspector General; a one-star rank of the Police Service of Pakistan]. He has made the pride of his family and community. Now he can provide support to his children and offer them a good education. If, instead of only one, 20 young men had been made DSPs, today there would be 20 DIGs or AIGs [Assistant Inspector General; a two-star rank of the Police Service of Pakistan]. Then maybe the gang war, the infighting, the drug-trafficking and all other criminal activities would be under control. 20 DSPs can control crime and they can spread awareness, proving to the people that anyone with education can become an officer. Then, out of 20 DSPs, maybe 4, 6, 10 will be appointed assistant commissioner. Then, gradually, they will provide us with [state] support. Nowadays, why do these MQM-people, the Mohajirs, succeed? Because they are in the administration and can influence the policy-making.[4]

It is the story of this emerging challenge to the MQM's predominance that the present chapter retraces. The politics of the PAC is irreducible to this anti-hegemonic indigenist project, though. It is, first and foremost, the illegitimate child of a complex and unstable politico-criminal configuration involving a group of Baloch 'bandits' (*dacoits*) who, after decades of loyal service to the PPP, attempted to join the political fray on their own terms and form the state for themselves.

The profile of the 'bandits' studied here as well as the context of their interactions with PPP leaders are highly specific to Lyari, which despite its central location stands apart from the rest of the city, whether ethnically (in the late 1990s, 40 to 50 per cent of its population was estimated to be Baloch)[5] or politically (Lyari remains a stronghold of the PPP in a city otherwise dominated by the MQM). Nonetheless, these interactions raise larger questions about the dynamics and inner tensions of other politico-criminal configurations at work in the rest of the city. Moreover, however specific to Lyari the collusions between Baloch *dacoits* and PPP politicians may be, their impact over politics in the city at large has been increasing since the 2000s, which saw Lyari's 'gang war' politicise, escalate and spill over into other neighbourhoods.

Lyari and its Dacoits

The Making of a Degraded Inner-City Neighbourhood

Lyari derives its name from the word *lyar*, a tree said to bloom in graveyards. It is one of Karachi's oldest settlements, often referred to by its residents as 'the mother of Karachi' (*Karachi ki maan*). According to the legend, it is here that Mai Kolachi, the fisherwoman who gave her name to Karachi, lived with her seven sons, six of whom lost their lives to a gigantic crocodile (or shark, according to some versions), until the last one—the physically challenged Mororo—defeated the mighty beast (today, the tombs of the seven brothers take the dust on a non-descript roundabout, at the feet of a flyover, in the locality of Gulbai, on the other side of the Lyari river). Lyari's first residents were Sindhi fishermen and

Baloch nomads (*pawans*) from Makran, Lasbela and Kalat districts, fleeing drought and tribal feuds. A first influx occurred around 1725, a few years before Sindhi *banyas* settled in Karachi and committed to expand it. A second wave of Baloch settlers arrived around 1770, when Karachi came under the control of the Khan of Kalat, following an accord between the Khan and the Kalhora rulers of Sindh. A third wave of Baloch migration took place after 1795, following the annexation of the city by the Talpur rulers of Sindh, which attracted Baloch tribesmen from interior Sindh and the Seraiki belt, many of whom found employment as guards, particularly at the Manora fort. Finally, in the second half of the nineteenth century, the British occupation of Sindh and the modernisation of Karachi's port, as well as the construction of railway connections between Sindh and the Punjab, brought to Karachi a number of Baloch settlers from the Iranian part of Balochistan, most of whom settled on the banks of the Lyari river, currently the largest sewage drain in Karachi but a clean source of water, with abundant fish, until the 1950s. This migration increased after the subjugation of the Persian part of Balochistan by Iranian forces in 1928. Iranian Baloch were generally better-off than Lassis (from Lasbela, 200 km north-west of Karachi) and Katchis (from Katch, in Balochistan, to be distinguished from Gujarati Kutchis). Today, these Baloch of Iranian descent would constitute the largest share of Lyari's Baloch population.[6]

The bulk of these men found employment at the nearby port (as stevedores, boatmen, donkey-cart pushers, date palm packers, etc.), while others worked in the city's first tanneries, oil-pressing mills and wool-washing factories.[7] Women, for their part, sold embroidery from door to door or worked at home, fashioning packages from date palm leaves (dates and date palm leaves were imported from Masqat; Lea Market, currently one of the most vibrant commercial areas of Lyari, was one of the great date markets of Karachi in the nineteenth century). The Baloch/Makrani workforce employed at the port was among the first to organise in Karachi (shortly after railway workers), and the Karachi Port Workers Union emerged among the stevedores during a series of strikes in 1930.[8] Religiously, most of these Baloch settlers were Sunni Hannafis, although at the end of the 1990s it was estimated that Lyari was home to 50,000 Zikris.[9]

The presence of the nearby port and the development of important *mandis* (markets) in Lea Market, as well as in Baghdadi and Shah Baig

Lane (two neighbourhoods of present-day Lyari Town), also attracted workers, traders and entrepreneurs from Gujarat (Kutchi Memons, in particular, a community which became known for its mercantile abilities as much as for its piety and charitable works),[10] while a number of Black Africans added to this cosmopolitan mix (currently known as Sheedis or Makranis, the descendants of these African slaves and soldiers are estimated at 5,000 in Karachi [probably a gross underestimation], most of whom are found in Lyari, particularly in Baghdadi and Shah Baig Lane; they are now part of the larger Baloch society, though well below the tribal Baloch). By 1886, with a population of 24,600, Lyari had become the largest of the twenty-four districts of Karachi, and the only one with a population over 8,000.[11] One of the most populated areas of Karachi (with the largest concentration of Muslims in a city demographically and economically dominated by non-Muslims), Lyari was also one of the most neglected in terms of development. The Hindu mercantile communities that founded the modern city of Karachi and oversaw its early developments were not particularly keen on investing in the infrastructures of this predominantly Muslim working-class area, which developed in a haphazard way around unplanned settlements of *jhuggis* or single-storey stone houses without access to sewerage and water. The British did not show much concern either for the appalling state of the neighbourhood, which degraded further in the late nineteenth century after Karachi's most polluting factories were relocated there. This structural neglect continued after Partition: the primary concern of Pakistan's ruling class was not with the living conditions of the indigenous labour force but with the resettlement of migrants from India. Thus, the two new planned colonies that were developed on the western corner of Lyari, Agra Taj Colony and Bihar Colony, were reserved for the Urdu-speaking *muhajirin*.

In the years following Partition, Lyari experienced a spectacular demographic growth, with its population increasing from 81,768 in 1941 to 360,000 in 1956.[12] Despite the dismal state of large parts of the neighbourhood, which had no basic civic amenities until the 1960s, the residents of Lyari remained attached to their locality. The attempt by General Ayub Khan's regime, in the late 1950s, to relocate Lyariites in New Karachi, in the northern part of the city, faced such resistance that Pakistan's first military ruler had to renounce his project of sanitising the city centre by expulsing its working-class population to the periphery. The success of this resistance movement was all the more remarkable in that it kept at bay powerful investors, eager to get hold of prime propriety land near the city centre. In the following years, left-oriented student organisations (NSF, DSF,...) and political parties (such as the NAP) became extremely active in the neighbourhood, where they distributed literature and sometimes found shelter from the police and intelligence agencies. These young radicals walked in the footsteps of the nationalists of the late colonial period, who had already made Lyari the base of their political activities. The Khadda Market area, in particular, was a hotbed of nationalist politics. It housed the Mazhar-ul-Uloom, a madrasa run by Hafiz Muhammad Sadiq, which became the centre of anti-colonial movements such as the Reshmi Roomal Tehrik[13] and the Khilafat movement. It is also here that Abdullah Haroon grew up. The Haroons are Memon businessmen who migrated from Kathiawar to Karachi in the second half of the nineteenth century. Born in Karachi in 1872, Abdullah Haroon lost his father at an early age and was raised by his mother. In his early teens, he started working as a hawker, before opening a shop in the Jodia Bazaar of Kharadar. Specialising in second-hand clothing and sugar trading, he made a fortune in the following years, earning the title of 'Sugar King' (*chini ke badshah*). In Pakistan, however, it is primarily for its role in the media that the family made a name for itself, with the ownership of prestigious newspapers such as the English daily *Dawn*. The family's political record is equally impressive. Abdullah Haroon's political career started in 1913, when he was elected to the Karachi Municipality. In 1917 he joined the Congress, and two years later became the president for Sindh of the Khilafat Movement. From 1924 to 1926 he was a member of the Bombay Legislative Council. As the movement for Pakistan was picking up pace, he joined the Muslim League and became its Sindh president in 1938. In the following years, the residence of the Haroons was the nerve centre of the Pakistan movement in Sindh. Abdullah Haroon breathed his last in 1942 and was buried in the same Khadda locality, in a college that he founded and to which he gave his name (two decades later, the same college would be briefly headed by one of the most famous postcolonial Urdu poets, Faiz Ahmed Faiz, under whose tenure leftist teachers such as R.R. Hasan made their imprint on local youths).[14] Abdullah Haroon's sons carried his mantle and the family retained its political clout after 1947. In 1949–1950, Yusuf Haroon was the Chief Minister of Sindh, while his brother Mahmud Haroon was the mayor of Karachi in 1954–1955.

As contemporary Baloch nationalist leaders emphasise, Lyari was also 'the birthplace of Baloch nationalism'.[15] It is here that one of the first Baloch nationalist organisations, the Baloch League, came into being in the 1920s around personalities such as Allah Bakhsh Gabol (1895–1972), the grandfather of the former MNA from Lyari, Nabeel Gabol. Postcolonial Baloch nationalist organisations, such as the BSO, were also founded in Lyari, where they concentrated their efforts on education and political awareness.[16] Lyari's *dacoits* themselves have maintained good relations with Baloch nationalist leaders and Dadal (see infra) was a close friend of Ataullah Mengal, according to one of his nephews.[17]

When Bhutto started searching for a base in the largely Urdu-speaking city of Karachi, in the early 1970s, he naturally found it in Lyari, by then one of the most deprived neighbourhoods of Karachi, but also its most politicised and combative. In turn, the socialist rhetoric of Bhutto found an echo among Lyari's working class, which voted massively for the PPP in the 1970 election. Ever since, the PPP has remained unbeatable in Lyari, whether in provincial or national elections. The romance between Lyari and the PPP culminated in 1987 with the wedding reception (*walima*) of Benazir Bhutto and Asif Ali Zardari in the locality. The following year, Benazir Bhutto was elected from Lyari at the National Assembly, followed by her husband two years later (who at the time was behind bars). In recent years, the PPP has been losing ground in the neighbourhood, but Lyari remains its first if not its only stronghold in Karachi.

The Emergence of Lyari's *Dacoits*

In India and Pakistan, the term *dacoit* (with its variants, *daku* and *dakait*) usually refers to rural bandits, often acting as henchmen for landlords. In Sindh, for instance, *dacoits* are outlaws operating under the protection of tribal leaders and 'feudal' lords (*jagirdars*, *waderas*).[18] In the context of Karachi, the term primarily refers, since the 1960s, to the Baloch 'bandits' of Lyari, pointing at their rural origins and attachment to tribal conceptions of honour and authority. It is, however, at the heart of a battle of (self-)denomination between the bandits aspiring to join the notability, the state and society at large, as the reinvention of Rehman *Dakait* (Rehman 'the bandit') as *Sardar* (Lord) Abdul Rehman Baloch demonstrates (see infra).

Lyari's criminal scene started developing in the early 1960s around Nabi Bakhsh, better known by his alias (*urf*) of Kala Nag (Black Serpent). Bakhsh was a smuggler and bootlegger who made a fortune by providing shopkeepers of the Old City with smuggled goods.[19] He died in 1967 while jumping from a building during a police raid and was replaced at the head of Lyari's burgeoning underworld by two of his former protégés, Dad Muhammad (alias Dadal) and Sher Muhammad (alias Sheru). The two brothers belonged to a family from Afshan, in the Iranian part of Balochistan. This family of Iranian Baloch settled in Karachi in the early twentieth century and still owns large tracts of land in Balochistan (in Sakuran, Hub tehsil of Lasbela district). According to a blood relative of Rehman 'Dakait', Dadal's flamboyant son, whose failed attempt to shift from crime to politics I examine below, it is this prestigious ancestry and the social standing of the family in Lyari, as much as the muscle power at its disposal, that made Dadal and later on Rehman so attractive to successive generations of political leaders aiming to establish themselves in the neighbourhood.[20] Despite this relatively privileged background, Dadal and Sheru had humble beginnings. They started their criminal career by selling 'black' tickets in front of cinemas and peddling drugs for Kala Nag.[21] Like many other Baloch toughs before them, they also rented their muscle power to the rich and mighty. In the early 1960s, they took charge of the dirty work of the ruling party (Ayub Khan's CML), sending their men to intimidate political opponents, disrupt political gatherings and, come election day, spread fear in polling stations.[22] The young men's rising clout brought them into conflict with their former mentor. The 'black serpent' did not go without a fight but, in those days, street battles were fought with knives or clubs and the number of casualties remained low, particularly among bystanders. Following the death of Kala Nag, the two brothers consolidated their hold over Lyari's burgeoning underworld, until they were sidelined by Kala Nag's son, Allah Bakhsh (alias Kala Nag II), who united his forces with those of another local gangster, Muhammad Iqbal (alias Babu Dakait). A former footballer (he played as a defender for the local J Brothers Football Club), Iqbal had seen his career compromised after the police registered a case against him following a minor dispute.[23] The former sportsman went into hiding and joined local criminals, to become one of the main architects of Lyari's drug trade.[24] Kala Nag II and Babu Dakait expanded their sphere of influence by battling it out with another local kingpin, Haji

Lal Muhammad (alias Haji Lalu, a former protégé of Babu Dakait), in what increasingly resembled gang warfare. The inflow of modern weaponry and drugs in the wake of the Afghan Jihad, of which we have already seen the impact upon campus politics and ethnic relations in Karachi in the first half of the 1980s, also made a critical impact over Lyari's underworld. Fists and knives gave way to firearms, while heroin replaced *charas* (hashish) in the local criminal economy.

In the course of the 1970s, this criminal economy became increasingly diversified, while inserting in transnational criminal networks extending from Afghanistan to the Gulf countries and, further, to Europe, Africa and the United States. This diversification was encouraged by Bhutto's policies. In 1977, Bhutto banned the production and consumption of alcohol, as well as gambling. Until then, Lyari had several active distilleries and the production and commercialisation of local brews provided employment to many residents. With the ban on alcohol and gambling, distilleries and gambling dens (*jue ka adda*s) started requiring protection—either from criminals or the police, and sometimes both—to survive. By simplifying the issuing of passports, Bhutto also facilitated the emigration of large number of Lyariites to the Gulf. The Gulf bonanza contributed to the emergence of a new affluent class in Lyari but also to a reorganisation of the local underworld. Powerful smuggling networks emerged around personalities such as Yaqoob Gung, who specialised in the smuggling of Baloch labourers into the Gulf countries.[25] Smuggling was nothing new to the Baloch and the same old routes from the Hub and Makran coastal areas of Balochistan (the notorious *whisky trail*) were used to transport illegal migrants and later on drugs to the Gulf countries. At the end of the 1970s, with the development of the international heroin trade, these ancient smuggling routes were connected by local and international drug traffickers to the 'Alexandrian route' running from the coastal areas of Balochistan to European and African markets.[26] The proximity of Lyari with Karachi's port also contributed to the maturation of its criminal economy and to its insertion in the world economy. The oil tankers stationed at Maripore and Hawke's Bay became favourite targets for local racketeers, while the trucks arriving from the rest of the country and carrying cargo to the port through Lyari also fell prey to protection rackets. The development of the heroin trade had an even more profound impact on Lyari's criminal economy and society. Drug shipments arriving from Afghanistan would often transit through Lyari on their way to the Gulf, Europe or America, and Lyari's *dacoits* (Babu Dakait, Haji Lalu and later on Rehman Dakait) became important intermediaries between the traffickers of the Frontier and international buyers. On the sides of this wholesale market of heroin, a retail market also developed in Lyari, with its centre in Kalakot. Large quantities of cheaper varieties of heroin started being consumed locally, replacing alcohol (which was banned more or less at the time as heroin became easily available). Addiction rapidly spread in Lyari, whose population of heroin users was estimated to be over 20,000 in the mid-1990s.[27] Heroin is both smoked from tin foil (a practice known as *panni*) and, increasingly, injected (with alarmingly high rates of HIV and hepatitis infection among users). It is generally sold in small bundles, known as *puri* or *podri*, which cost around $1 each. Although this commerce has become less visible in recent years, drug dealers still operate openly in some localities, such as Baghdadi.

As long as General Zia ruled over Pakistan, the political affiliation of Lyari's bandits was not an issue: both Haji Lalu and his rivals, Kala Nag II and Babu Dakait, supported the PPP and provided shelter to anti-Zia activists.[28] This consensus around the PPP continued after the return of Pakistan to democracy in the late 1980s, despite the rise of the MQM at the helm of Karachi's city politics. However, this situation started to change at the beginning of the 2000s, with the rise of a new generation of *dacoits* in Lyari. Whereas Dadal's son (and Haji Lalu's former protégé), Rehman Dakait, maintained close links with the PPP, his major rival, Arshad Pappu (the son of Haji Lalu, as well as Rehman's brother-in-law), was rumoured to have sided with the MQM, which started making its presence felt in some pockets of Lyari (Agra Taj Colony, Bihar Colony, Gul Muhammad Lane) around 2003.

The Volatility of Politico-Criminal Configurations

The Baloch of Lyari have always been a popular choice with anyone in search of 'muscle' in Karachi. The bouncers of local cinemas, for instance, have traditionally been recruited among this community. Thus, when Lyari's most prominent business and politicial family, the Haroons, entrusted Dadal and his men with the security of Ayub Khan's political rallies, in the early 1960s, it is implausible that they wittingly engaged in an arrangement with 'criminals'. The Haroons were merely extending to

Fig. 4: Two generations of *dacoits* in Lyari (1960s–2000s)

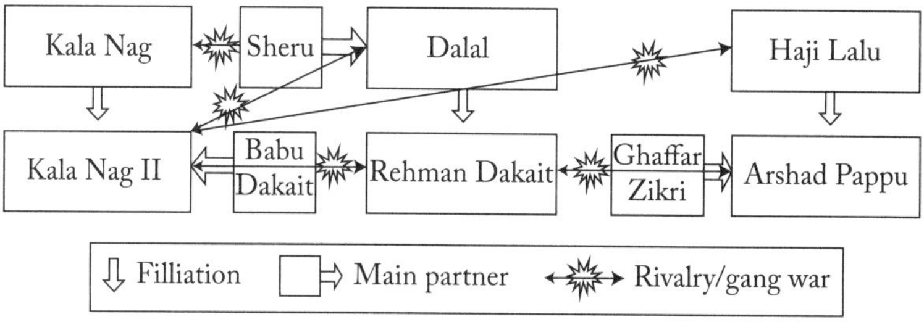

Kala Nag
Sheru
Dalal
Haji Lalu
Kala Nag II
Babu Dakait
Rehman Dakait
Ghaffar Zikri
Arshad Pappu

Filliation — Main partner — Rivalry/gang war

the political realm the security duties that Lyari's Baloch toughs were already entrusted with in other sectors of activity. If these early, pre-democratic arrangements are worth considering, before shifting the focus on Rehman Dakait's career, it is not merely for their archeological value, though. As the incident related below underlines, the prehistory of Karachi's 'gray zone of state power'[29] (that is, the space where the unlawful violence of the state meets with the 'illegitimate' violence of society) attests that fluidity, uncertainty and even conflict are consubstantial to these politico-criminal configurations. If these relations only grew more complex along the years, there never was a time when Lyari's *dacoit*s remained docile executants of their powerful 'bosses'.

On 12 September 1962, Ayub Khan's CML held a public rally at Karachi's Polo Ground. Pakistan's first military ruler was then confronted with students' and workers' unrest and this meeting was intended to be a show of strength, demonstrating that Ayub was still in charge despite the growing agitation in the country. A large stage had been erected by the organisers and all the League's stalwarts had come to show their solidarity with the beleaguered president. But suddenly, all hell broke loose. A group of left-wing activists from the NSF managed to climb on the stage and clashed with Ayub's ministers and party in charge. Among them, Zulfikar Ali Bhutto—who at the time was still the General Secretary of Ayub's party—was infuriated by this impromptu intervention of the students and he engaged in a fistfight with them on the stage. At seventy-three years old, the veteran of the Pakistan movement and former Governor of East Pakistan, Chaudhry Khaliquzzaman, was less pugnacious and he was thrown off the stage by the assailants. After a few minutes of mayhem, the students were brought under control and several of them were arrested and sent to jail. But this mobilisation was not in vain:

Ayub's regime agreed to several of the students' demands, such as the reduction in the Bachelor's degree from three to two years, as well as the diminution of enrolment fees in all educational institutions.

If Pakistani Marxist authors have been projecting this event as a landmark in the country's 'student revolution' of the 1960s,[30] few are aware of the exact circumstances of this incident, and in particular of the role of Lyari's *dacoit*s in it. A few days before the rally, Dadal and Sheru were commissioned by the Haroon family to provide security for the event. Unlike other powerful Memon families such as the Dawoods and the Adamjees, the Haroons had not thrown their lot in with Ayub Khan. But they were seasoned politicians and, although they never compromised the independence of their prestigious newspaper (*Dawn*), they generally avoided antagonising the Field Marshal. Occasionally, they could even cooperate with him on some levels, which occasionally brought some benefits in the long run (Mahmud Haroon became Federal minister for labour in 1965 and Pakistan's High Commissioner in Britain in 1968). It is in this context that the family provided security to the Polo Ground rally, building upon its support network in Lyari, where the family resided until the late 1970s. Since the 1920s, the family has made Lyari (and in particular the area around Khadda Market) the centre of its philanthropic activities, starting with the opening of an orphanage (1923), a madrasa (1927), as well as several colleges, student hostels and mosques.[31] Thirty years later, when Mahmud Haroon became the mayor of Karachi, he allocated a large chunk of the municipality's budget to the development of the neighbourhood.

While pointing at the relations that developed, from the early 1960s onwards, between Lyari's political elites and Baloch strongmen, the events of 12 September 1962 are also revealing of how unreliable the latter could be for their political bosses. The disruption of Ayub Khan's rally was the outcome of a deal that Sheru and Dadal had struck with student leaders behind the back of the Haroons. A few days before the event, Sheru and Dadal were approached by a group of activists from the NSF. The group was led by Mairaj Muhammad Khan (see Chapter 2) and included some female students, who appealed to Baloch notions of honour by placing themselves under the protection of the two kingpins—a movement which was epitomised by their touching the knees of the two bandits in a sign of 'filial' respect. According to Mairaj Muhammad Khan, this gesture greatly embarrassed Sheru and Dadal, who started 'panicking' and, at once, agreed to give the students a ten minutes' window to climb on stage and read a statement. Ayub Khan's project to displace the residents of Lyari at the periphery of the city may also have played in favour of the students, as it had alienated Lyari's residents, including the *dacoit*s. The latter, however, did not anticipate that the students would in turn break their part of the deal. When a group of NSF activists posing as benign students climbed onto the stage, carrying flower pots in their hands (the rose was the electoral symbol of the CML), everything seemed to be going according to plan. But neither the *dacoit*s nor the organisers of the rally had noticed that these flower pots in fact contained stones—which had been gathered at the nearby site of Jinnah Courts, where the Quaid-e-Azam's mausoleum was then under construction. And as soon as the students arrived on the stage, they uncovered their projectiles and started bombarding those present on the dais.[32]

The result of a series of broken, clandestine deals between criminals, economic entrepreneurs and political activists, this incident is revealing of the volatile nexus between Karachi's *dacoit*s and their political bosses. The chronic instability of these collusive arrangements goes against their 'systematisation' in the sense given to the term by Paul Brass in his study of communal riots in North India (essentially that of an unproblematic partnership between violent specialists and political leaders, which can be activated at will, for electoral purposes in particular).[33] If these controversial liaisons are part and parcel of routine politics, particularly of the clientelist variant, they do not follow the same rules as more conventional—i.e. more open—forms of patron/broker relationships. As Enrique Arias underlines in his study of the relations between state agents and drug traffickers in Rio de Janeiro's *favelas*, the ambivalent status of criminals—respected here, despised there, feared everywhere—as well as their position 'outside the pale of government, even while they engage with it', introduces a good dose of uncertainty into the status hierarchies between political 'bosses' and criminal brokers, while making their relations highly unpredictable.[34] When it prolongs itself, this encounter generates informal institutions, that is, 'socially shared rules, usually unwritten, that are created, communicated, and enforced outside of officially sanctioned channels'.[35] However, these rules and the unofficial interactions that make them possible in the first place cannot be considered to be simply 'created' and punctually 'activated' by political entrepreneurs for personal gain, unlike what is suggested by canonical works such as those of Paul Brass.[36] As the political careers of Lyari's *dacoits* exemplify, neither the strategist notion of 'instrumentalisation' nor institutionalist typologies in terms of 'complementariness' or 'accommodation' fully describe what is at stake here.[37] These relations are too unstable to become fully institutionalised and they allow a large part of autonomy, which tends to increase in the course of time, to criminal brokers. The opposite scenarios of a 'substitution' of criminal brokers to their political patrons or of a 'competition' between them are not entirely convincing either. As Jean-Louis Briquet and Gilles Favarel-Garrigues underline, 'violent entrepreneurs are very often satisfied with the existing rules of the political and economic game in which they move'.[38] Rather than uproot the state, most criminals aim to contain it while keeping it in place.[39] Just like 'smugglers need borders', according to a (probably apocryphal) Baloch proverb,[40] criminals need the state to prosper in its folds and ensure the sustainability of their trade. Without the law, crime would not pay. On the other hand, every criminal aims to neutralise the long arm of the law and, whenever possible, to make it subservient to his interests. Both Rehman Dakait and his successors made such an attempt to form the state for themselves by containing it from within, before seizing and rebooting public institutions to establish their writ over Lyari.

Rehman Dakait's Failed Transition from Crime to Politics

The Criminal Career of Rehman Dakait

Rehman 'Dakait' was born Abdul Rehman in the Rexer Lane area of Lyari on 3 July 1974. He only received a basic education (he would later complete his matriculation in prison), but he enrolled at the prestigious, English-medium, Trinity Private School, in Saddar. After dropping out of school at an early age, Rehman started peddling drugs. He is said to have stabbed a man for the first time at age thirteen and, by 1991, he and his men had murdered several members of Babu Dakait's group, including four of his sons. In 1995, Rehman killed his own mother, Fahmida Shireen. According to the FIR filed by the local police, this was a case of murder. It was rumoured that Rehman had planned a hit on Babu Dakait at Haji Lalu's instigation. However, when Rehman came face to face with Babu, the latter would have laughed at him, revealing that he had a long-standing affair with Rehman's mother and that the young man was in fact his own son. Instead of gunning down Babu, Rehman would have headed home and directed his anger against his mother. This version of the events is contested by Rehman's relatives, though, who defend the thesis of an accident: according to them, Rehman's mother would have been killed by a stray bullet, while her son was cleaning his Kalashnikov at home.[41] Whatever its exact circumstances, Rehman's matricide made him a celebrity in Lyari and contributed to the legend of Rehman 'the bandit'.

Rehman's extensive contacts in the police also contributed to make him a folk-figure, endowed with an aura of invincibility. His successive escapes from police custody (in 1997 and 2006) and his claims that he had 'defeated' lie detectors fuelled this reputation ('lie detectors conceived by Punjabis can't trick a Baloch', he allegedly bragged).[42] So did his proximity with top leaders of the PPP, to whom Rehman leased out some of his henchmen for physical protection. Following Rehman's death, his successor at the head of the PAC, Uzair Baloch, claimed that the three men killed alongside Rehman, Aurangzeb Baba, Aqeel Ahmed and Nazeer Balah, had worked as *janissars* (bodyguards) for senior PPP leaders in the past, including Asif Ali Zardari (by then the president of Pakistan), Zulfikar Mirza (by then the home minister of Sindh, and the soon-to-be new political patron of the PAC) and Agha Siraj Durrani (by then the Sindh minister for local governance). Uzair Baloch added that Rehman had helped the PPP get its candidates elected in Lyari by organising and providing security to political rallies, and that the security of the Bhutto's residence at Bilawal House itself was entrusted to Rehman's men. In return, Baloch claimed, senior PPP figures had issued arms licences to some of Rehman's lieutenants, such as Aqeel Ahmed.[43] The leading role played by Rehman during the blast that targeted Benazir's return convoy in October 2007 (see infra) had indeed confirmed the proximity of the top leadership of the PPP with Karachi's most notorious criminal. Rehman was not always in favour with Benazir, though, particularly as far as his political ambitions were concerned. Following the introduction of a three-tier local government system in Karachi under the regime of Pervez Musharraf, in 2001, Rehman started putting up his own candidates as councillors and Union Nazims. Growing more ambitious, he then put up one of his candidates for the post of Town Nazim, a move that was resisted by Benazir herself, who nominated her own men (Khalique Jumma and Malik Muhammad Khan, respectively) for the post of Town Nazim and Naib Nazim. In the next local election (2005), though, the candidate supported by Rehman, Malik Fayaz, managed to defeat the candidate of the PPP. Some foul play was suspected, as the majority of the councillors were with the PPP. According to press reports, some of these councillors changed their stand after they were intimidated by Rehman's men and the police.[44] Asif Ali Zardari seemingly shared his wife's suspicions with Rehman. Members of Rehman's entourage confirmed to me that he had retained close relations with Zardari while the latter was in jail (1990–1993; 1996–2004). This relationship endured after Zardari became the new president of Pakistan in 2008. Not only did Zardari recruit the security staff at his Islamabad residence among Rehman's men,[45] he also allocated two billion rupees for the development of Lyari and entrusted Rehman with the monitoring of these development programmes.[46] But if Zardari acknowledged—and contributed to—Rehman's clout in Lyari, he also suspected that Rehman had his own agenda and could become a threat to the PPP in Lyari.

The relations between Rehman and his former mentor, Haji Lalu, started deteriorating in the late 1990s, after Rehman's men kidnapped a Memon businessman from Kharadar. Haji Lalu asked Rehman to release him, arguing that he was acquainted with him. Rehman obliged, only to discover that Lalu was in fact eager to keep the ransom for himself. The relations between the two men deteriorated further in the following years. Eventually, Rehman split with his former mentor, a move that deeply hurt Lalu's business as the former had been developing extensive contacts with drug suppliers in the preceding years. The conflict between the two groups escalated after Arshad Pappu's men desecrated the graves of Dadal and Sheru with grenades and bulldozers,[47] before kidnapping and killing a transporter, Faiz Muhammad (alias Mama Faizoo, the father of Uzair Baloch), who was related to Rehman. This killing, in 2003, was the opening act of a gang war between Rehman's and Pappu's groups, which raged until 2008, claiming at least 500 lives.[48] Although this claim was never solidly substantiated, this gang war was also suspected to be a proxy war between the PPP and the MQM. As local residents told me, the MQM started making its presence felt in Lyari, particularly in Gul Muhammad Lane, around 2003–2004. Rehman, at that time, remained a devoted *jiyala* (PPP worker). He was determined (and might have been encouraged by his patrons within the PPP) to counter this intrusion and his conflict with Pappu took on strong political undertones.

The arrest of Arshad Pappu in 2006 weakened the position of the MQM in Lyari. Ghaffar Zikri, who took over from Pappu, seemingly pursued the rapprochement initiated by his predecessor with the MQM but the presence of his group was now limited to Ali Muhammad Mohalla, in Baghdadi. With the alleged support of the MQM, though, Zikri managed to gain a foothold in Agra Taj Colony and other neighbouring localities with a substantial Urdu-speaking population—the only vote bank of the MQM in Lyari. Agra Taj Colony thus became the lifeline of Zikri's group, with most of its weapon consignments arriving there (cf. Map 6).[49]

Map 6: Gang turfs and ethnic groups in Lyari (2008)

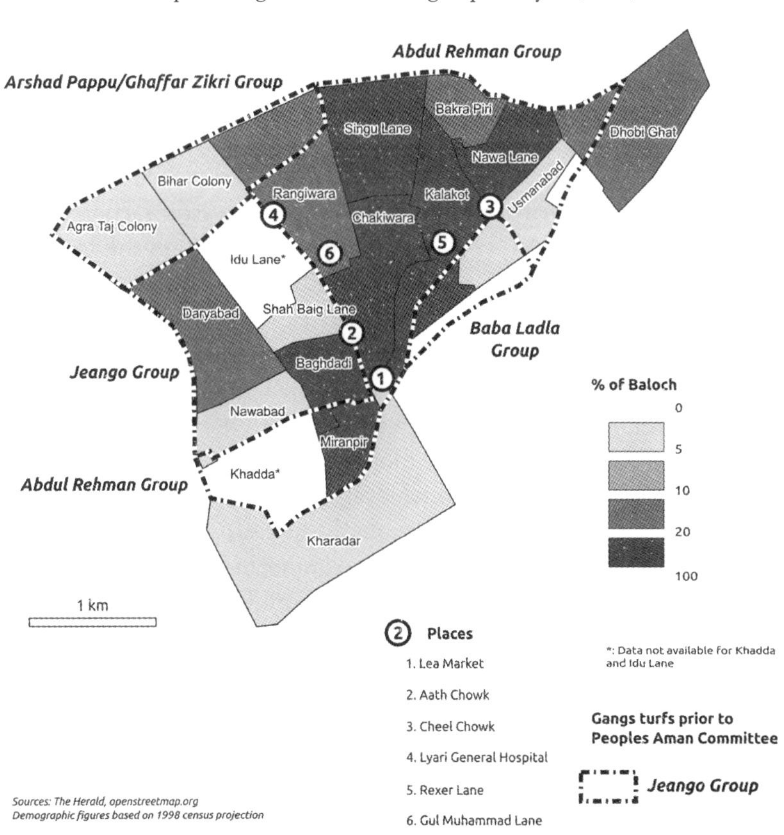

The February 2008 elections—during which the PPP won one of the two National Assembly seats (NA-248) and three Provincial Assembly seats from Lyari—turned out in favour of Rehman. Unlike in 2001, when he had tried to get his own candidates elected as local councillors and Nazims against PPP candidates, Rehman threw his lot in with the PPP this time (he is rumoured to have funded candidates and the party at large, while mobilising voters in favour of the PPP),[50] and he emerged stronger than ever from the elections. Now in a position of strength, Rehman convinced Zikri to accept a truce, which led to the formation of the PAC in 2008.

From Rehman *Dakait* to *Sardar* Abdul Rehman Baloch

Rehman was not merely a ruthless criminal. Following in the footsteps of his father—who, according to members of Rehman's entourage, had opened gymnasiums and boxing clubs, as well as a primary school and a vocational training institute for women in Lyari[51]—Rehman also made a name for himself through his social work, especially after the creation of the PAC in 2008. According to the same members of his entourage, Rehman regularly made donations to Abdul Sattar Edhi's Foundation, Karachi's most active NGO—a rumour that tends to find confirmation in the attendance at Rehman's funeral by Edhi himself. In Lyari, Rehman compensated for the limited presence of the state and competed with other humanitarians by opening tuition centres and medical dispensaries, distributing grain and rations on Eid, reopening government schools, providing children with school uniforms and even starting a small ambulance service. Himself a seasoned footballer, Rehman made donations to some local clubs and ordered the removal of encroachments around Gabol Park, whose status as a football ground was restored. According to a member of his entourage, he also offered grants to boy and girl students from Lyari to enroll at the prestigious Lahore University of Management Sciences (LUMS). To this day, these charitable works remain as the source of Rehman's enduring popularity among large sections of Lyari's population, who continue to refer to him as '*Khan bhai*' (big brother). This popularity transcends ethnic cleavages and I heard Pashtuns, Sindhis as well as Kutchis sing Rehman's praises—praises that were irreducible to fear as several of these respondents no longer resided in Lyari. Naveeda,* a Kutchi social worker whose NGO was looted and set on fire by young men probably affiliated with Rehman's group, following Benazir Bhutto's assassination in December 2007, was not predisposed to support him. Yet, she acknowledged his popularity among Lyariites, partially subscribed to it and unhesitatingly singled it out as the reason for his violent death:

When Rehman founded the Aman Committee [in 2008], he wanted to do something for Lyari. He started some work for the poor. This earned him a position of leader, so this is why he was killed [laughs, as a reminder that there is something puzzling in the normality of the abnormal]. [...] Our leaders at the time [the PPP-led coalition government] didn't like to see other leaders take the spotlight away from them. So they finished him off [*uska patta saf kar diya*, lit. 'they cut his leaves']. What really killed him was politics. [...] After his death, the people got very emotional [public *bahut josh mein thi*]. They were so angry with the government, because the circumstances of Rehman's death were really unclear. At the time of his death, Rehman had become very popular. He was murdered, so he became a hero. The people really worshipped him as a hero. They used to spit on the graves of those who were killed [in the gang war]. But the way he was murdered, this made him a martyr. [...] After his death the people went on the rampage, there was a great fuss [*bahut hangama machaya*]. Until now, people call him *khan bhai*, just like the Mohajirs do with Altaf Hussain.

The successors of Rehman at the head of the PAC, as well as the gang leaders who rallied under them tried to claim a bit of their martyr's charisma for themselves, organising a personality cult around Rehman and his political heir, Uzair Baloch. However prosaic the motives of its promoters (posters of Rehman and Uzair also serve to delineate respective turfs, as they are signed by local *dacoit*s),[52] this cult is irreducible to them. It is the meeting point between the strategies of influence of local criminals, a genuine feeling of sympathy of Lyariites for their martyred bandit, as well as a deep sense of alienation on their part from the mainstream politics of Karachi.

Rehman's welfare activities made him the most powerful patron of the neighbourhood. He surpassed, in his liberalities, Lyari's oldest patrons, the Haroons. So much so that, as of December 2011, Rehman's portrait adorned the gate of Haji Abdullah Haroon Govt. Boys High School, in Khadda, where most of the educational institutions opened with the Haroons' support are concentrated.[53] Besides the Haroons, Rehman also seemed to be winning over the patronage war with the PPP, which had taken over the Haroons as Lyari's prime patron in the 1970s. As early as

1963, Z.A. Bhutto had promised lease documents to Lyariites. He kept his promise and ninety-nine-year leases were issued free of cost after his victory in the 1973 elections. This policy had unanticipated perverse effects, though. It led residents to sell their land titles to developers (many of whom were Memon businessmen), who converted these plots of land into mid-rise apartment blocks. In addition to the price of the sale, the original occupants would be given one or two apartments in the new building, free of cost. The other apartments would be sold on *pagri* (a security deposit equivalent to several years of rent) to lower-middle-class residents, most of them non-Baloch. This construction boom and the new flat culture that accompanied it did not only transform Lyari's cityscape. They added to the congestion of the neighbourhood and, over the years, contributed to the gradual marginalisation of the Baloch in their former stronghold. The increasingly multi-ethnic character of Lyari, and more prosaically the huge sums of money at stake in the construction sector, partly explain the recent flare-up of 'ethnic' violence in the neighbourhood.[54] On a more positive note, Bhutto's government also oversaw the construction of roads and drains in the neighbourhood, which brought a semblance of development to the area. Under Benazir Bhutto's successive governments, Lyari was also promised special development packages, such as an 800 million rupees grant under Benazir Bhutto's first tenure as prime minister (1988–1990). A massive housing scheme for Lyari's residents at Hawke's Bay and an additional grant of 700 million rupees for the development of the neighbourhood were also budgeted for by Benazir's first government but none of these promises materialised: the housing scheme at Hawke's Bay was delayed by administrative bottlenecks while large tracts of land were captured by PPP office-bearers. The additional amount of 700 million rupees, for its part, went to the KMC's Zonal Municipal Committees (which were under the control of the MQM) after the dismissal of Benazir's government in 1990. From the 1990s onwards, Lyariites started growing cynical about their political patron, as it was becoming increasingly obvious that the PPP was unable, and possibly even unwilling, to keep its electoral promises. A report published in the magazine *Newsline* in 1997 quoted local residents for whom all the PPP had done for Lyari was to set-up the infamous Riaz Centre of the Crime Investigation Agency (CIA), whose plainclothes policemen would often 'barge into houses at night, picking up youths only to torture them and release them after extorting thousands of rupees from their families'.[55]

The competing clientelistic practices of Kutchi Memon businessmen, PPP representatives and Baloch *dacoit*s in Lyari unfolded in the context of an inner-city neighbourhood deprived in terms of civic amenities, economic resources, access to justice and integration to the rest of the city, all characteristics that Lyari shares with some Brazilian *favelas*, where the development of the drug trade also contributed to a sudden escalation in levels of violence at the end of the 1970s. More than by sheer absence, the state's footprint in Lyari as well as in these Brazilian *favelas* is best characterised as a form of 'selective presence',[56] as it is essentially limited to punctual repressive actions which tend to be seen as illegitimate by the local population—a trend exemplified, in the case of Lyari, by the protest demonstrations accompanying every police raid, with women often taking a leading role in these public expressions of anger against law and order forces. The following extract of a collective discussion with a group of students and social workers affiliated with one of Lyari's prominent NGOs are revealing of this deep distrust of the police, and of its contribution to a normative disorder metamorphosing the police into the true criminals and the *dacoit*s into protectors:

- [Ahmad,* mid-20s, student in philosophy at KU]: Our greatest fear is the police. The people say that there is no reason to fear the gangs, and anyway so many of them have given up criminal activities. Today, we are afraid that the police will shoot us. As soon as children see policemen, they run away. We are so scared of the police. But we are not afraid of our protectors [*mefhuz karne wale*, i.e. the *dacoit*s]. The world is upside down [*nizam bilkul baraks ho gaya tha*].
- [Aziz*, early 30s, Chief Executive Officer for a private TV channel]: In the 1980s and 1990s, in police stations... When a drug-dealer was struck by the fear of God and decided to give up his trade, he was caught by the police. They would ask him, 'Brother, why are you closing shop? Either you keep on working or we send you to jail.' This is how it worked in those days. [...] The peace promised by the police is worthless [*Pulis aman to bekar hai*]. Our system of local governance works just fine. We are trying to solve our problems on our own. We need neither the police nor the government. We can take care of ourselves [*Jo hamari* boundaries *mein maujud hain, un tak ham ja sakte hain*, lit. 'we can go as far as the boundary wall separating us (from the outside world)'].

While the selective and contested presence of the state opens opportunities for local aspirants to political domination, the high population density of these neighbourhoods of exile guarantees a large impact on even small-scale operations, a point put forward by Camille Goirand in her study of Rio de Janeiro's *favelas*.[57] Among the local aspirants to political domination, criminals have their own reasons for displaying their munificence, the first of them being an imperative of support from the local community, guaranteeing that it will restrain from co-operating with the police.[58] But the good deeds of criminals are irreducible to such calculations and may also partake, in a more ambivalent way, in strategies of re-fashioning for former kingpins aspiring to respectability, within their own community or beyond. After all, as Jean-François Bayart once commented, there are only two options for aging criminals: joining the notability or the graveyard.[59]

According to one of his close relatives, Rehman 'completely changed' after his arrest in Quetta in June 2006, following a year of hiding in Balochistan, during which he strengthened his bonds with some leading Baloch nationalist figures such as Akhtar Mengal. The brutal treatment he was subjected to by the intelligence agencies while in detention in Islamabad and later on by the police after his transfer to Karachi could also have contributed to his political and ethnic awakening. According to the same relative, Rehman became 'a rebel against the Pakistani establishment' after his second escape from police custody the same year. He would have refused 'lucrative posts', deciding that 'his mission was to work for the residents of Karachi's oldest area'.[60] At the same time, he would have drifted towards Baloch nationalism. Some sources even suggest that Rehman financed Baloch guerillas,[61] these suspicions explaining why he was whisked away by intelligence agencies after his arrest from Quetta.

The claim often heard in Karachi's Baloch nationalist circles that Rehman was killed and replaced at the head of the PAC to prevent the spread of Baloch nationalism in Lyari[62] finds some confirmation in the hostile attitude of the post-Rehman PAC leadership towards Baloch nationalists as well as in their apparent patronage by the army. As Uzair Baloch told me in August 2012, 'I am not a Baloch nationalist,' (*Main Baloch parast nahin hun*). His right-hand man, Zafar Baloch, confirmed that, 'We are the kind of people who work within the confines of the [Pakistani] state,' (*ham riyasat ke andar jed-o-jehed ke admi hain*). In fact, the PAC seems to have struck a deal with the army, which guarantees impunity to its leaders as long as they will contain the spread of Baloch nationalism in Lyari—a deal which goes a long way to explain why the Rangers (who are commanded by military officers) did not take part in the ill-fated police operation of April 2012.[63] My visits to Lyari around Independence Day 2012 confirmed this collusion, as the walls of the town were covered with posters representing Uzair saluting the army and the Rangers (see photographs in Appendix).

Nonetheless, the thesis linking Rehman's alleged conversion to Baloch nationalism with his elimination in a police encounter tends to over-estimate his rupture with the PPP and more generally with mainstream politics. More than to the status of rebellious warlord, Rehman was aspiring to a political mandate, ideally at the national level (he had his eyes on the NA-248 seat from Lyari, although the leadership of the PPP let him understand that the party could not afford to nominate candidates with pending criminal cases).

Rehman's process of self-refashioning encompassed two distinct moves. On the one hand, he projected himself as a traditional Baloch leader—a *sardar*. In Balochistan, this title is primarily associated with tribal leaders, and more specifically with petty chiefs heading a particular segment of a given tribe.[64] In Lyari, this term primarily resonates among the populations identifying themselves with a particular tribe (such as the Baloch from Iran and interior Sindh). The figure of the *sardar* has much less relevance for the Baloch tracing their roots to the coastal region of Makran, where a different social system of stratification (closer to a 'caste system') came into being in the eighteenth century, and where patron-client relationships were gradually eroded by transnational migration and trade (including smuggling).[65] Besides the uneven echo of the *sardari* system among the different sections of Lyari's Baloch, this population has seen the emergence of urban-specific, class-based or pan-ethnic identifications that gradually superseded traditional binds based on kin and tribe, although without erasing them.[66] The generalisation of the ethnonym 'Baloch' in Lyari is revealing of this emergence of urban-specific, inclusive identifications, amounting to a process of detribalisation.[67] In this context, it is tempting to see Rehman's endorsing of the title of *sardar*, as well as his use of *jirga*s (tribal assemblies), as a neo-tribal strategy of legitimation, reinventing a long lost tradition. But neither Rehman nor his successor, Uzair Baloch, really went that far by endorsing the title of *sardar* (besides retaining the title of *sardar*, Uzair Baloch has pursued the strategy of the co-opting of local elders put in place by Rehman: in early 2012 he formed the Lyari's Elders Committee, comprising thirty representatives of Lyari's prominent families and clans).[68] As the second in command of the PAC, Zafar Baloch, explained to me in August 2012, 'Rehman was not a *professional* sardar [he used the English term]. It was the expression of the love of the people.' Further, he suggested that Rehman was no more than a primus inter pares: 'in the places where the *jirga* system prevails, ten men will seat and will decide that one of them is a "big man" (*bara admi*)'. In its equation of the Baloch system of social stratification with 'a *jirga* where ten men seat', this statement is indicative of the distant relation of Lyari's bandits turned 'peace janissaries' (*aman ke janissar*, a title that the PAC claims for its leaders and workers) with the tribal political corpus. If this definition would fit Pashtun society, with its political organisation founded on the assembly of equals,[69] it is completely at odds with the traditional patron-client structure of Baloch society.[70] Instead of amounting to a proper neo-traditionalist programme, or even to a technique of domination, Rehman's and Uzair's recourse to this tribal corpus and its 'rhetoric of appeal'[71] were simply an indication that they were claiming grandeur greater than their street credibility. As in every claim to grandeur, Rehman's was an affair of style. In this regard, the sartorial versatility of Rehman and of the promoters of his post-mortem cult deserves attention. On certain occasions (Baloch Cultural Day, in particular), Rehman—and Uzair after him—appeared in traditional Baloch attire, and this is how they are generally represented on the innumerable posters that saturate the visual environment of Lyari today (cf. photographs in Appendix). But Rehman also had a weakness for sporty gangster chic—black jacket, wide collar shirt, jeans and sports watch. This is how I found him represented on a poster of the PAC in August 2012. Behind him, Uzair was wearing a suit, making him a more entrepreneurial figure. The legend accompanying these pictures—'The Great Sardars'—pointed to the various influences informing these two men's charismatic authority, mixing the 'street' with the 'decent' rather than the tribal per se (cf. photographs in Appendix).[72]

'Rehman the noble' also tried to erase his past as 'Rehman the bandit' by launching a campaign against street crime in Lyari, which made him a popular figure well beyond the Baloch population (see Chapter 7). He banned the open selling of narcotics, threatening drug peddlers with death, while forbidding aerial firing during marriage ceremonies (those breaching this rule would expose themselves to a 200,000 rupees fine). Rehman also started enforcing some Islamic-style punishments against criminals who operated without his approval, some residents of Lyari recalling how he cut the hand of a thief who had snatched a mobile phone from its rightful owner.[73]

Rehman's rising clout in Lyari set him on a collision course with local representatives of the PPP, and in particular Nabeel Gabol, the local MNA. Gabol is the heir of a Baloch family from interior Sindh (Thano Bula Khan), which has been dominating Lyari's politics since the 1920s along with the Haroons (Nabeel's grandfather was elected at the legislature of the Bombay presidency in 1927 and was twice the mayor of Karachi [1951–1953; 1961–1962], while his uncle became an MNA from Lyari in the 1970s; more recently [2008], a niece of Nabeel, Nadia Gabol, was elected on a woman's reserved seat from Lyari and became the only woman minister of the MQM in the provincial government). The Gabols were among the richest landlords of Karachi during the colonial period and in the 1930s the British had to impose a ban on further acquisitions of land by the family, 'because at that time almost 70 per cent of Karachi land was bought by the Gabol family', recalls proudly the former representative of Lyari at the National Assembly. Currently, the Gabols own hotels in the Gulf and a car business in Karachi (Gabol Motors). Nabeel Gabol's political career begun in the mid-1980s and he was elected at the Provincial Assembly (where he became the Deputy Speaker) before joining the National Assembly. According to members of Rehman's entourage, the conflict between Gabol and Rehman stemmed from a difference of opinion about the allocation of posts in the police force. After the formation of a PPP-led government in Sindh, it was decided to recruit 3,000 new policemen in Karachi, 700 of them from Lyari. Allegedly, Nabeel Gabol and the president of the PPP in District South wished to allocate some of these jobs 'reserved' to Lyariites to PPP workers from other localities. This would have infuriated Rehman, who was eager to control this important source of patronage and to extend his influence within Karachi's law and order forces. Nabeel Gabol flatly denied this 'allegation' in front of me, only to argue that 'the police quota was directly given to Rehman's supporters from the Home Minister's side [Zulfikar Mirza's]'. Whatever the truth behind these allegations, all parties to the conflict agree that Rehman succeeded in infiltrating the police. A few years earlier, he had already demonstrated the extent of his hold over the security apparatus in Karachi by overseeing the return of Benazir Bhutto to Pakistan. Members of Rehman's entourage confirmed to me that he supervised the security arrangements for Benazir's convoy when she landed in Karachi on 17 October 2007. And when a series of explosions targeted the convoy, Rehman was among those who helped Benazir shift from her armoured bus to a private vehicle, of which he might even have taken the wheel. In a picture published by *The Telegraph* the following day, Rehman can be seen holding Benazir's arm, helping in her transfer.[74] It is therefore in the company and under the protection of Karachi's most wanted criminal that Benazir dealt with this life-threatening crisis, and that she reached the Bhuttos' residence.

After Benazir's death in another bomb blast a few months later, Rehman consolidated his power through the PAC, which was launched in June 2008. The PAC was originally the outcome of a peace accord between two factions of Lyari's underworld: Rehman's and Arshad Pappu's group (then led by Ghaffar Zikri, following Arshad Pappu's arrest). Rehman also conceived the PAC as a rampart against the MQM and a vehicle for his own political ambitions. As we saw earlier, Rehman patronised numerous welfare and development initiatives between the creation of the PAC in 2008 and his death in 2009, while enforcing a form of '*pax traficana*' in Lyari.[75] Paradoxically, the police was infuriated with these developments, as this meant the drying up of an important source of income, since police officers used to collect protection money from local criminals.[76] Besides attracting the animosity of the police, the activities of the PAC were perceived as a threat by the MQM, as the committee rapidly expanded across Karachi and opened contacts with the Haqiqis, the MQM's arch rivals.[77] Finally, Rehman's attempt to join the political fray on his own was resented by the leadership of the PPP. These concerns were summed up by the PPP spokesperson Fauzia Wahab shortly after Rehman's death: 'He was flying high to become a self-proclaimed leader of the area. His ambitions were threatening everyone and he spoiled institutions, culture, peace and everything in the area.'[78] Facing opposition on several fronts, Rehman was allegedly killed in a police encounter in Steel Town (Bin Qasim Town) in August 2009, the exact circumstances of his death remaining a matter of controversy.

Bis Repetita? *The PAC 2.0 and Rehman's Legacy*

After Rehman's death and following internal tussles between aspirants to the throne,[79] a relative of Rehman, Uzair Baloch, took over the command of the PAC. Initially, Uzair accused the PPP of betrayal and, as we saw, started making revelations in the local media concerning collusions between Rehman and the top leadership of the party. However, Uzair rapidly gave up this defiant posture, after he found his own 'boss' in Zulfikar Mirza, the new provincial home minister, who did not shy away from claiming responsibility for Rehman's death, though later repented for 'getting him killed'.[80] Mirza was a newcomer in Lyari's politics, who lacked the assets of more established PPP representatives (such as Members of National Assembly [MNAs] Nabeel Gabol and Abdul Qadir Patel or Members of Provincial Assembly [MPAs] Rafiq Engineer and Saleem Hingoro): he was neither a Lyariite nor a Baloch.[81] He then tried to compensate for these weaknesses by taking the hard men of the PAC under his protection, while reinforcing their clout by issuing them arms licences (Mirza would later claim in a TV interview that he had issued 300,000 arms licences to 'the people' during his tenure, so that they could 'protect their honour, money, and properties' [*apni izzaton, mal aur jaedad ki hifazat kar saken*]).[82]

Following in the footsteps of Rehman, Uzair Baloch and other leaders of the PAC started expanding their activities to social work and dispute settlement in Lyari, settling conflicts over property, divorce... If many Lyariites see them as a wolf in sheep's clothing, others credit them with reviving the local sports scene and containing street crime and shooting incidents. Thus, according to the chief coach of one of Lyari's most respected boxing clubs, which benefited from the patronage of the PAC:

> Today, by the Grace of God, when the news of a firing incident spreads around, people come out of their houses and ask [the shooter]: 'why are you firing?' Some time ago, we banned firing. Shooters will be admonished [*achha khasa* remand *lete hain*]. [...] The people of the Aman Committee are closely monitoring the situation. In one of his speeches, Sardar Uzair Jan [Uzair Baloch] said that these things could no longer be tolerated... that the gang war should cede the way to a sports war... When the time of tournaments approaches, they all come and ask us, 'What's going on? What are you lacking?' And when we organise summer and winter boxing camps, they search for the chief guests [political personalities], and they provide arrangements for refreshments.[83]

Not everyone in Lyari would agree with this statement, particularly as far as the reduction in the level of violence is concerned. In Gul Muhammad Lane, for instance, violence escalated after 2009, following a tussle between Akram Baloch's and Uzair Baloch's groups for the leadership of the PAC. The residents of Khadda Market, for their part, have seen their neighbourhood turn into a battleground between the PAC, the Kutchi Rabita Committee (KRC, see infra) and a Deobandi religious group in July 2011, these clashes apparently focusing on the control of a plot claimed by the three groups. As it extended its control over Lyari, following the death of Rehman, the new leadership of the PAC started competing with other players in the extortion game—and in particular with the MQM, who is credited for systematising the practice of *bhatta khori* (protection rackets) in Karachi. The PAC initially concentrated on the protection of businessmen and traders active in Lyari's markets (Lea Market, Timber Market,...), with non-resident shopkeepers and entrepreneurs being targeted as a priority. Gradually, the PAC started expanding its rackets to the wholesale and retail markets of Karachi's Old City area (Sarafa Bazaar, Jodia Bazaar,...), which the MQM considered part of its turf and where it already collected *bhatta* from traders. This expansion of the PAC's protection rackets also threatened the hold of the MQM over neighbouring Saddar, sometimes referred to as 'Brunei Town' in local parlance for the huge amounts collected by extortionists from local traders and businessmen.[84] Thus, by October 2012, the PAC was extorting hefty sums from traders, businessmen and doctors in Burns Road, one of the strongholds of the MQM in the Old City, at the border with Saddar.[85] According to relatives of Rehman, the PAC also started competing with the MQM for the protection of the transporters carrying goods for NATO troops to Afghanistan. The methods of the PAC also stand out from the more benign forms of protection practised by the MQM, as the massacre of a dozen Urdu-speaking traders at Shershah scrap market, in 2008, suggested. This massacre—which, according to the police, was the brainchild of Noor Muhammad (alias Baba Ladla), the military commander of the PAC—could have been perpetrated in retaliation for the killing of PAC militants and Baloch bystanders by MQM militants. But it could also have been meant to deliver a message to those traders and entrepreneurs who resisted the PAC's offer of protection.

Besides these criminal activities, the fighters of the PAC soon became enmeshed in a new gang war as well as in the turf wars opposing the MQM to the PPP and Sindhi nationalist groups. The gang war between Arshad Pappu/Ghaffar Zikri's group and the PAC soon resumed after Rehman's death. If Ghaffar Zikri and Haji Lalu (who was freed in 2011, and breathed his last the following year) took shelter in Balochistan (in Turbat and Hub, respectively), the connections between their group and the MQM (or at least its local command: the units- and sectors-in-charge) seem to have been revived in recent years. The PAC also targeted the leadership and the workers of the KRC, a platform of organisations representing the Kutchi minority of Lyari, which was formed in 2009 and which in August 2012 claimed to have lost eighty leaders and activists to the bullets of the PAC.[86] The Kutchis have remained steadfast PPP supporters until the 2013 elections. However, even before they announced that they would contest this election on their own (despite the fact that they were offered the ticket for PS-108[87] by the PPP), KRC leaders were suspected of having joined an alliance of anti-PAC elements including the MQM and the gang of Arshad Pappu (who was freed in February 2012). The KRC has also been patronised by Hussain Haroon, the heir of the Haroon family and Pakistan's former representative at the United Nations, who has been trying to carve a niche for himself in Lyari in recent years. Besides the activists and leaders of the KRC, the fighters of the PAC have also turned on ordinary Kutchis, creating an unprecedented drift between this community and the Baloch, to such an extent that in several markets of Lyari, Kutchi traders have started expelling their Baloch employees. The first massive attack on the Kutchi community as such occurred in early July 2011, when around 800 Kutchi families from Khadda Market were chased away from their homes by the gunmen of the PAC, who according to the leaders of the KRC also snatched away community centres, ambulances and buses—all vivid illustrations that the Kutchis live up to their reputation as Karachi's most active community in the field of philanthropy. When the displaced families returned to Khadda a week later, after President Zardari himself intervened to avoid further damage to the PPP's vote-bank in Lyari, they found their houses ransacked and looted.[88] Another round of ethnic violence erupted shortly after the May 2013 elections. For the first time in decades, not a single Kutchi candidate was elected from Lyari under the PPP's banner, leaving the community in the wilderness as the Baloch leadership of the PAC started flexing its muscles and establishing its writ over the last areas escaping its control. In the second half of May 2013, sporadic incidents of violence between the PAC and the KRC (which were thought to be fuelled by a fierce competition over real estate and protection rackets) cost the lives of eighteen people, most of them bystanders. The violence carried on throughout the month of June, before escalating brutally in early July, after Baloch 'gang war criminals', as the local press described them, launched a major offensive on the Kutchi neighbourhoods of Hingorabad, Agra Taj Colony, Phool Pati Lane, Chakiwara, Bihar Colony, Dubai Chowk and Maripur Road. The leaders of the PAC denied any involvement in these attacks on Kutchi homes and blamed the violence on a 'third force' (the MQM, which was suspected of supporting the KRC). However, it is difficult to believe that Baloch 'gangsters' assaulted the Kutchis on their own initiative, especially at a time when the PAC's grip over Lyari had never been so firm, following the electoral victory of its candidates for the NA-248 seat and a couple of provincial seats from Lyari (PS-108 and PS-109). According to Kutchi residents of the affected localities, the military commander of the PAC, Bada Ladla (whose cousin and right-hand man was allegedly killed by Kutchi militants in 2012), used the loudspeakers of nearby mosques to ask Kutchis, Kathiawaris and 'MQM-supporters' to evacuate Lyari within forty-eight hours or face the consequences.[89] Following this announcement, Baloch gunmen launched coordinated attacks on Kutchi *mohallas*. The intensity of the assault was such—besides automatic weapons, Kutchi homes were targeted with RPGs and hand grenades—that the terrified residents had to dig tunnels through their neighbours' walls to escape, a desperate exit strategy reminiscent of the escape of Qasba and Banaras colonies' Mohajir residents in July 2011, at a time when they came under fire from Pashtun militias. However, this time, the gangsters used the same tactic to move into Kutchi neighbourhoods, with a tunnel war adding to the street battles between the PAC and the KRC as a result.[90]

Beyond Lyari, fighters of the PAC have been deployed in areas with a Sindhi or Baloch presence—such as the *goths* (urban villages) of Landhi-Korangi—where they confronted the MQM. Thus, according to MQM sources, the attack by MQM militants on a police bus at Chakra Goth, in Korangi, in August 2011—during which six policemen were killed—was a case of mistaken identity, as the ambushed police commandos were thought to be militants of the PAC in disguise, who were being sent to the area as reinforcements against the MQM.[91]

The arrival of the PAC on the city's multiple frontlines suggested that the PPP, or at least some of its provincial leaders at daggers drawn with the MQM, were inclined to use it as the PPP's own 'military wing'. Despite being Karachi's second political force in terms of vote share (at least until the 2013 elections, when it lost this position to the PTI), the PPP is the only protagonist of the battles for Karachi which does not have its own armed wing. The PSF initially played that role but was rapidly outrun by the MQM's better organised and better equipped militants. In the early years of Operation Clean-up, the PPP also patronised a criminal gang based in Orangi, known as the Salam Group, which abducted, tortured and murdered MQM workers and sympathisers.[92] The deployment of PAC fighters well beyond the district of Lyari served the same purpose—countering the MQM—and probably took place with the knowledge if not the active encouragement of some other PPP leaders.[93] This patronage of the PAC was not a consensual policy within the PPP's ranks, though. Nabeel Gabol, who had recently had to deal with the political ambitions of Rehman, was bitterly opposed to Mirza and his strategy, but his repeated warnings to the PPP leadership went unheard. Frustrated after being sidelined, Gabol moved to the MQM in March 2013 and was elected to the National Assembly from the party's stronghold of Azizabad two months later. Ironically, Gabol claims to be the one who introduced Uzair Baloch to Mirza after the former allegedly came to him 'to surrender', following Rehman's death.[94]

In 2011, the PPP came under increasing pressure from the MQM to clean up its act and disband the PAC, or face the consequences of a withdrawal of the MQM from coalition governments in Sindh and Islamabad. Despite the protests of Zulfikar Mirza (who was replaced as Sindh's home minister), the PAC was banned by the Sindh government in March 2011 and several 'police operations' were launched by the police or the Rangers in Lyari, allegedly to bring the 'extortion mafia' under control. These repressive operations culminated between 27 April and 4 May 2012 in a week-long police operation against the PAC. The operation was supervised by Chaudhry Aslam Khan, a police officer with a sulphurous reputation, who dedicated most of his career to fighting Lyari's criminals and who was in charge of the operation that allegedly cost Rehman his life in 2009. This impressive deployment of police personnel mobilised nearly 3,000 men—as well as a few well-armed women—who were guided into the maze of Lyari's lanes by masked men suspected of being members of Arshad Pappu's gang. Though this police raid was projected as an 'anti-extortion' operation, it singled out the militants of the PAC and the chain of events that precipitated it leaves no doubt about the political motives behind it. In the days which preceded the operation, a local leader of the PPP, Malik Muhammad Khan, was gunned down by assailants suspected of being affiliated with the PAC. A few days later, the leaders of the PAC met with Ghaus Ali Shah, the provincial leader of the largest opposition party, the PML-(N). This meeting followed overtures by the PAC towards other parties than the PPP,[95] which suggested that Uzair Baloch and his companions were considering dispensing themselves from the patronage of the PPP. The MQM was also suspected of having put pressure on the leadership of the PPP to act against the PAC, which despite its official disbanding in 2011 had continued to operate openly, and had even expanded its activities across Karachi (from Trans-Lyari localities such as Old Golimar and Shershah to Landhi and Korangi in the eastern part of the city and to Surjaani Town in its northern outskirts). Finally, the stepbrother of Zardari, Owais Muzaffar 'Tapi', was also suspected of having put pressure on the president for an intervention, as he would have an eye on the NA seat of Lyari.

This operation turned out to be a disaster for the police, whose fire was returned with submachine guns, G3 rifles and RPGs. Armoured Personnel Carriers (APCs) could not find a way through Lyari's lanes and the jamming of cellular networks was largely inefficient as the militants of the PAC used walkie-talkies. After seven days of intense fighting, the police withdrew its forces without any significant achievement to its credit—save for the deaths of five of its own (including an SHO) and, officially, twenty civilians (the police also claimed to have killed eight 'miscreants' but none of the leaders and military commanders of the PAC were either killed or arrested). The number of casualties among the civilian population was probably much higher, though, and the deployment of 'tanks' (as local residents call APCs) had a dramatic impact upon the population, who felt that Lyari had become 'another Afghanistan' or 'another Waziristan', as I often heard during my fieldwork there in August 2012. The incident that came to epitomise the 'tyranny' (*zulm*) unleashed upon Lyariites during this police operation involved one of these tanks, which ran over a ten-year old boy during a demonstration of local residents against the police. Three months later, the death of Amar was systematically mentioned by my respondents to show the injustice done to them. The memory of the whole operation was still looming large—graffiti abusing the police and Nabeel Gabol was ubiquitous (cf. photographs in Appendix), posters of police 'atrocities' adorned the outside walls of local NGOs financed and protected by the PAC, and street corner sit-ins protesting against the operation went on. While the entry of the police into Lyari was seen as an 'invasion' by many residents, its blatant failure galvanised the supporters of the PAC and silenced its critics. As of August 2012, the general mood remained indignant if not belligerent, and the PAC appeared in control of the largest part of Lyari. An arrest warrant was issued against Uzair Baloch by an anti-terrorist court but the police responded that he had 'gone underground'. In fact, as I would discover for myself a few days later, Uzair remained a very public—and accessible—figure. In his Singhu Lane four-storey mansion with swimming pool and dernier cri interior design, guarded by heavily armed men, he held his *darbar* (court), receiving local residents of all social backgrounds, from tribal elders invited to discuss neighbourhood matters to an eunuch (*hijra*) accusing her relatives of trying to evict her and grab her property. Far from being afraid to move across Lyari, Uzair and his lieutenants continued to attend public events (*iftar* parties, football tournaments, cultural programmes,...). Despite the threats against his life, Uzair himself drove his four-wheeler—although with a pistol around his waist and heavy security arrangements, including an escort of armed teenagers on motorbikes. I accompanied him to an Iftar party in Nawa Lane on Independence Day and saw that bystanders, shopkeepers and children all saluted him as he drove through. Though it is difficult to determine whether these rather formal salutes were inspired by fear, respect or even affection for the new 'Don', Uzair has undoubtedly become the most powerful public authority in Lyari, and as soon as he steps out of his car, impoverished residents come to him to plead for help (see photographs in Appendix). Unlike more conventional politicians, Uzair listens patiently, without interrupting his or her interlocutor. Surrounded by his heavily armed guards, the young 'Don' fully endorses his vocation of problem-solver, remaining silent until the last minute, when he promises to look into it.

Following this 'mini-insurgency' (which some Baloch nationalist leaders compared to the Warsaw Ghetto Uprising),[96] Uzair Baloch announced that he was breaking up with the PPP and would run on his own for the NA-248 seat in the 2013 elections. However, Uzair and his lieutenants are pragmatic entrepreneurs of the violent *and* political kind. In August 2012, when I spent some time with them, both Uzair and Zafar Baloch confirmed to me that they were discussing with the top leadership of the PPP, through the mediation of a sister of the president, Faryal Talpur. Following these discussions, the PPP leadership revived its alliance with the leaders of the defunct PAC. This time, however, it seemed that the balance of power between the PPP leadership and Uzair's group had been reversed. In exchange for their return to the PPP's fold, the former leaders of the PAC were allowed to select the candidates of the party to the May 2013 provincial and national elections (in NA-248, PS-108, PS-109, PS-110 and PS-111). The profile of these candidates would only confirm the ground lost to the *dacoit*s: for the first time, the PPP had to grant a ticket to a notorious criminal—or so claim the police and his political adversaries. Shah Jahan Baloch, the PPP candidate for NA-248, was a former Union Council (UC) Nazim. Facing two murder charges, he contested the election from jail, winning with a large margin against the candidate of the PTI (the MQM withdrew from the race after complaining of mass rigging, although it won Lyari's other seat at the National Assembly yet again).[97] The choice of this controversial figure for a safe seat that Asif Ali Zardari destined for his son Bilawal, so as to launch his parliamentary career, was a deliberate provocation on the part of Uzair Baloch and his entourage.[98] It exposed the loss of influence of the PPP over the neighbourhood, while confirming that Uzair had succeeded where Rehman had failed: he had become Lyari's de facto sovereign.

Conclusion

Known as 'Mini-Brazil' for the passion of its residents for football, Lyari presents other similarities with Brazilian *favelas*. Also nicknamed *Masailistan* (the land of problems), Lyari remains one of the poorest and most criminalised localities of Karachi, whose Baloch populations (who claim the title of the first inhabitants of Karachi) are feeling increasingly alienated from the political mainstream and more generally from a city politically and economically dominated by Mohajirs since Partition. The evolutions of criminality in the neighbourhood followed a trajectory similar to that observed in some Brazilian *favelas*. With the arrival of hard drugs and modern weaponry in the late 1970s, criminal rivalries escalated into deadly gang wars. Far from containing this violent escalation, political actors competing for the control of the neighbourhood (the PPP and the MQM) colluded with criminal groups to extend their influence, giving birth to politico-criminal configurations that are once again reminiscent of Brazilian *favelas*. In Lyari, though, these collusions seem to have taken on a more systematic dimension, as they extended from the local office-bearers of political parties to their top leadership (at least in the case of the PPP, since the MQM seems to have entrusted its covert operations to its local office-bearers—the sectors- and units-in-charge—while its provincial and national leadership remained insulated from these controversial practices). This semi-overt political patronage gave a sense of impunity to local kingpins who, with the passage of time, were tempted to do away with their political protections and join the political fray on their own. As the elimination of Rehman Dakait in a police encounter in 2009, as well as the police operation launched against the PAC in April 2012 demonstrated, these attempts at autonomisation were systematically resisted by the *dacoits*' political bosses. Although the 2012 police operation turned out to be a public relations disaster for the police and the PPP leadership, this failure was primarily the result of ill-planning and political pressure over the police force. The deployment of the Rangers would probably have shown better results but it would have compromised the tacit understanding between the PAC and the army, which granted impunity to the PAC leadership in exchange for its support in the containment of Baloch nationalism in Lyari. A year later, when the Rangers did conduct a raid on the PAC's office and Uzair Baloch's palatial mansion, they did not face any resistance (Uzair was not at home at the time, which suited all the parties concerned). It is therefore too early to conclude that the state has withered away in Lyari, the apparent loss of sovereignty over this neighbourhood of exile amounting to an optical illusion, as in other warzones of Pakistan. Karen Barkey's warning in her study of the incorporation of bandits by the Ottoman state is worth keeping in mind while considering the issue of 'state breakdown' in contemporary Pakistan: 'The existence of contending forces in society does not necessarily mean total loss of control on the part of the government. We need to analyse the type of contention and the solutions to this contention before we can make any generalisation about the breakdown of the state.'[99] In Lyari, one cannot fail to notice that political patronage and police/military protection remains essential to the survival of the *dacoits*,[100] while the control of the local state by these bandits projecting themselves as 'peace janissaries' is integral to their project of domination. More than the tribal traditions that they invoked or the 'Robin Hood' syndrome that they nurtured (several of my respondents used this reference while discussing Rehman's career), it is their rebooting of public services (Lyari General Hospital, government schools,...) as much as their social work and repression of street crime that has enabled these bandits to take the advantage in the patronage war raging in Lyari. The *pax traficana* that emerged in Lyari in the process provides a vivid illustration of the frequent 'counterfeiting of the culture of legality by the criminal underworld'. As Jean and John Comaroff suggest, such criminal architectures of legalities 'feed the dialectic of law of disorder', for 'once government begins seriously to outsource its services and to franchise force, and once extralegal organisations begin to mimic the state and the market by providing protection and dispensing justice, social order itself becomes like a hall of mirrors: at once there and not there, at once all too real and a palimpsest of images, at once visible, opaque and translucent'. The logical outcome of this 'copresence of law and disorder' is the coming into being of a new geography: 'a geography of discontinuous, overlapping sovereignties'.[101]

This presence of the legal in criminal, counterfeited forms of sovereignty, never erases the possibility—the necessity, even—of the recourse to violence. As Thomas Blom Hansen underlines in his study of competing repertoires of authority in contemporary India, sovereign power is a fundamentally 'unstable and precarious form of power', which finds its origins and sustains itself through 'acts of violence characterised by excess—not merely in their brutality but also in their apparent lack of intention and moderation'.[102] This duality of sovereign power, which materialises in the dialectic of the legal and the lethal (in the Comaroff's terms) or in that of terror and generosity (in Hansen's terms), is exemplified by the ambivalent rule of the PAC over Lyari. In March 2013, as it seemed to be winning the battle for hearts and minds in the neighbourhood through its social work and its control of street crime, the group organised a public execution which, even by Karachi standards, was unprecedented in its brutality. The exact circumstances of this event remain shrouded in mystery, but Lyariites claim that, following the abduction of Arshad Pappu (the arch rival of the PAC leadership and the murderer of Uzair Baloch's father) and two of his companions (including his brother Yasir Arafat), the residents of Afshan Gali were invited through the loudspeakers of local mosques to attend, and even, according to some accounts, to take part in his 'punishment'. Pappu would then have been tortured/beaten to death, tied to a car, dragged naked, before being beheaded with a knife. As graphic photographs published by the local Urdu press attested, his headless corpse, along with that of his brother, was later paraded on a donkey cart around the area of Gabol and Aman

Park, until it was chopped into pieces and burnt, with the ashes being dispersed in a *nallah* (open sewage canal). This gruesome performance would have culminated in armed cadres of the PAC—including the military commander of the group, Baba Ladla—playing football with his severed head. At least some parts of the event were filmed—such as Pappu's beheading at anonymous hands—and the video went viral in the next few hours, thus enlarging the audience of this foundational moment of violence. From a political point of view, this macabre performance seemed counter-productive, as many residents of Lyari formerly sympathetic to the PAC started questioning their affiliation with such a brutal group.[103] However, this apparently senseless act of excessive violence—further magnified by rumours—was also a political statement of the strongest kind, aiming to publicise the absolute, unbound power of Lyari's de facto sovereigns. This statement did not go unnoticed by the official state. Confirming the commitment of the judiciary to restore the 'writ of the state' (see Chapter 6), the Sindh High Court ordered the arrest of Uzair Baloch and his lieutenants. To date, these court orders and the subsequent raids conducted by the police on Uzair's house have failed to produce any result. The attempt of the judiciary to re-monopolise the right to kill and reclaim sovereignty for the state should be accounted for nonetheless, as it indicates that the fragmentation of authority at work in Karachi remains contested in principle, if not yet in practice.

(*As this book goes to print [March 2014], Lyari's political landscape presents a significantly different picture from the one depicted here. The main source of Uzair Baloch's public authority used to lay in his political connexions, which were managed by his right hand man, Zafar Baloch. Following the assassination of the latter, in September 2013, Uzair's hold on the myriad 'commanders' of the PAC became increasingly tenuous. Thus, when the most powerful of these gang leaders, Baba Ladla, broke with the young 'Don' the next month, the PAC imploded and a new gang war erupted in Lyari. Once again, former foes turned into circumstantial allies and, possibly with some encouragement from the security apparatus, Baba Ladla turned to his former arch rival, Ghaffar Zikri. While the truce between the two former foes remains fragile, it has significantly weakened Uzair's forces' hold on large parts of Lyari. So much so that, by the end of November, Lyari's* 'sardar' *was but the shadow of his former self. These recent developments serve as a reminder that the political survival of 'deviant' aspirants to sovereignty is as much premised on their ability to secure the protection of some sections of the state (if only against other state agencies) as on their ability to stabilise their sovereign power by overcoming their own founding violence and bringing their most mercurial elements into the ambit of some legal order, official or otherwise—a rare feat that, in Karachi, has evaded every political force but the MQM).*

Image 1: MacLeod Road (I.I. Chundrigar Road) in the early 1950s (Courtesy *Dawn*)

Image 2: MacLeod Road (I.I. Chundrigar Road) today

Image 3: Paramilitary Rangers in front of the gates and wall constructed by the MQM in its stronghold of Azizabad, June 1992 (Courtesy *Dawn*)

Image 4: Army soldiers in Karachi after the launch of Operation Clean-up (June 1992) (Courtesy *Dawn*)

Image 5: An alleged torture cell of the MQM unearthed by the army in the course of Operation Clean-up (Courtesy *Dawn*)

Image 6: Afaq Ahmad and Amir Khan, the leaders of the MQM (Haqiqi), return to Karachi in June 1992 (Courtesy *Dawn*)

Image 7: Cover of a calendar issued by the MQM in 2001, with Altaf Hussain guiding the 'Mohajir Nation'. The slogan in Urdu reads, 'Rise! Gather your forces and be the arm of the leader.'

Image 8: Poster celebrating the 30th anniversary of the APMSO. The slogan in Urdu is a verse: 'In every circumstance, we have protected the garden [the nation]'

Image 9: A cover of the magazine edited by the APMSO, *Naqīb* (The Scout)

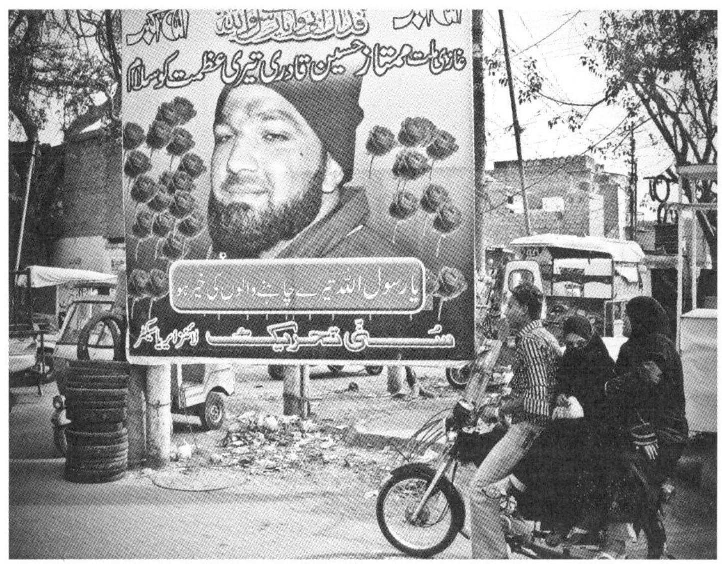

Image 10: Poster of the Sunni Tehrik celebrating the 'holy warrior of the nation' Mumtaz Hussein Qadri, the murderer of former Governor of Punjab Salman Taseer. Lines Area, 2011

Image 11: Jihadist mural. Lyari, 2012

Image 12: Demonstration organised by the Ahl-e-Sunnat wal Jama'at (formerly Sipah-e-Sahaba Pakistan). Saddar, 2011

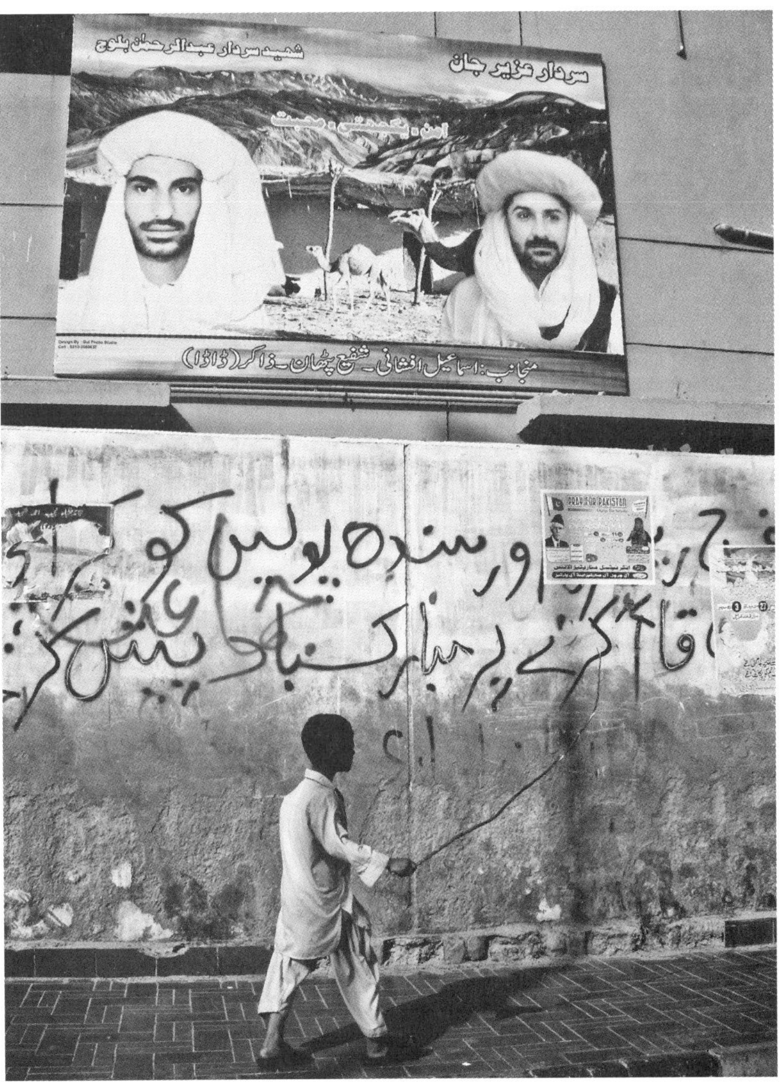

Image 13: Poster of the Peoples Aman Committee (PAC), with the late Rehman 'Dakait' (left) and his successor at the head of the PAC, Uzair Baloch (right). The graffiti on the wall abuses the Sindh police, following an operation that targeted the leadership of the PAC. Lyari, 2012

Image 14: Poster of the PAC, with the late Rehman 'Dakait' (right) and his successor at the head of the PAC, Uzair Baloch (left). Lyari, 2012

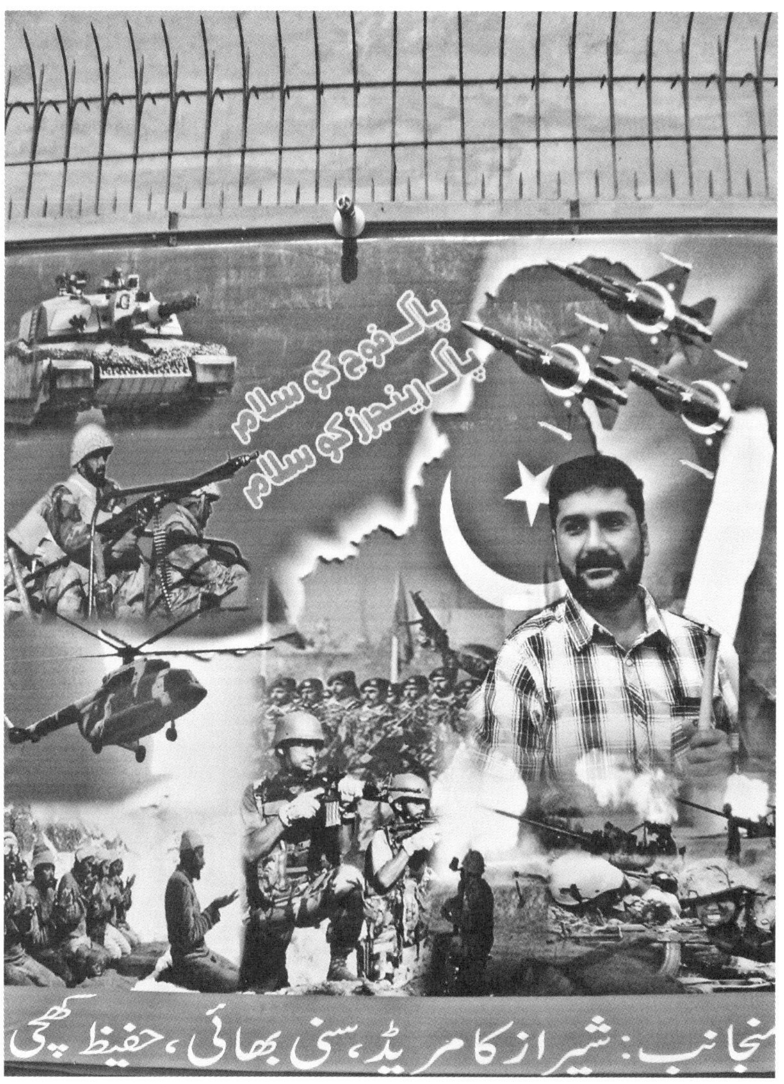

Image 15: Poster issued by the PAC on the occasion of Independence Day 2012. Uzair Baloch (right) presents his respects to the army and the Rangers. At the bottom, the poster is 'signed' by notorious gangsters active in the locality of Khadda Market: Shiraz 'Comrade', Suni Bhai and Hafiz Kutchi. Lyari, 2012

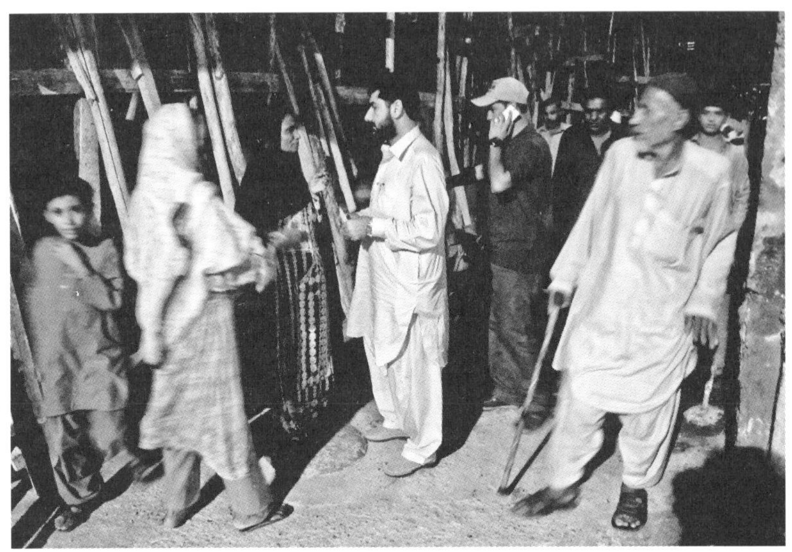

Image 16: Uzair Baloch hearing the plight of an elderly resident of his neighbourhood. Lyari, 2012

Image 17: Uzair Baloch receiving Baloch elders in his palatial mansion. Lyari, 2012

Image 18: Graffiti abusing the former MNA from Lyari: 'We cannot accept Nabeel [Gabol] the dog. Nabeel is a dog.' Lyari, 2012

Image 19: 'Wall-chalking' by the Sunni Tehrik: 'We are all soldiers of the Sunni Tehrik.' Clifton, 2011

Image 20: Entrance to a colony contested by the Sindhi nationalists of Jiye Sindh Qaumi Mahaz (JSQM) and the MQM. The banner above the gate proclaims that the neighbourhood is 'Altaf [Hussain]'s Fort'. Gulistan-e-Jauhar, 2011

Image 21: Qasba Colony and Orangi seen from the hills of Kati Pahari, 2011

Image 22: The 'border' between Urdu-speaking and Pashto-speaking localities in Kati Pahari/Qasba Colony. Notice the bullet holes riddling the walls, which are revealing of the intensity of the clashes that took place here during the summer of 2011, a few months before this picture was taken

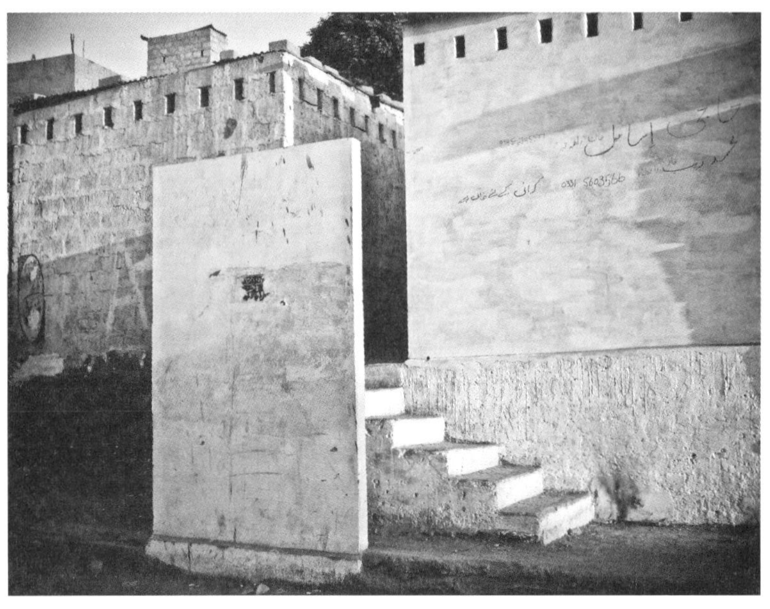

Image 23: Protective wall or *morcha* (shooting post)? Kati Pahari, 2011

Image 24: Kati Pahari seen from the Qasba Colony side, 2010

5

JIHAD COMES TO TOWN

This is a warning for Altaf Hussain to cease his statements against the Taliban and end his kingdom in Karachi, otherwise we will launch attacks against the MQM and its leaders.

Maulvi Umar, TTP spokesman, Karachi, 2008.[1]

As the MQM was struggling to contain the growing influence of the PAC—which in recent years expanded its activities from Lyari to Landhi by taking a foothold in the Baloch-populated urban villages (*goths*) that dot the city—another front opened early 2013. Five years after its first verbal attacks against Karachi's predominant party, the Pakistani Taliban started carrying out their threats. On 1 January 2013, a political rally of the MQM was for the first time the target of a bomb blast. Four people were killed and at least forty-two others were injured in the attack, which took place in the MQM's stronghold of Federal B Area. It is not that jihadi groups—which had already struck on several occasions in the city since 11 September—had no grudge against Karachi's aspiring hegemon. On the contrary, the MQM's secularist stance and its growing aggressiveness towards religious militants of all hues, post-11 September, were a matter of concern for jihadi and sectarian groups, who have been operating in the city since the days of the Afghan Jihad. But until then, none of these groups had dared to declare an all-out war on the MQM. The party leadership was therefore taken by surprise and a party worker present on the site of the blast told me that his leaders were in a state of complete shock after the explosion, as they were totally unprepared for such an event. They could have seen it coming, though. For the past few months, the Tehrik-e-Taliban Pakistan (TTP) had been renewing its threats against the MQM. But as the Pakistani Taliban were already busy targeting their Pashtun rivals of the ANP in the city, the MQM leadership probably thought that these would remain just that—threats. The Taliban had other plans, though, and as their offensive against the ANP was nearing its end—within a year (January 2012–January 2013), the ANP was virtually wiped out of Karachi—they turned their guns against the MQM and started carving their own dominion across the city. Ten days after the 1 January blast, the TTP claimed responsibility for the killing of an MQM MPA from Orangi Town, Manzar Imam. In the coming months, the MQM repeatedly came under attack from the TTP—particularly during the campaign for the general elections—while entire neighbourhoods of the city fell under the grip of the Taliban, who now felt confident enough to operate openly and deliver their own brand of justice in plain sight. Clearly, there was a new sovereign in town.

If the offensive of the Taliban against the ANP and later on against the MQM, as well as their shift to a logic of territorialisation, took party activists, social workers and political analysts alike by surprise, these developments were not as sudden and unpredictable as they seemed. While the remnants of Pakistan's progressive intellectual class continue to project Karachi as 'Pakistan's secular centre',[2] these secular credentials are open to question and jihadist organisations have been taking root here since the Afghan Jihad of the 1980s. Thus, the first Pakistani jihadist organisation, the Jamiat-ul-Ansar (Society of the Partisans), was formed in Kabul in 1980 by a group of madrasa students from Karachi.[3] Among the thousands of mosques and seminaries that dot the city, a handful have undoubtedly been flag bearers of radical Islam and vocal supporters of global jihad, the most notorious of which has been the Jamia-ul-Ulum Islamia, better known as 'Binori Town'. There is however some danger in singling out such hotbeds of militancy, when retracing the trajectory of sectarianism and jihadism in Karachi, a tropism inevitably leading to discriminate between 'good' and 'bad' Muslims according to their alleged level of 'moderation'.[4] As we will see, the madrasa of Binori Town, often perceived outside Pakistan as a citadel of Muslim radicals somewhat cut-off from mainstream religion and society, is in fact one of Pakistan's most respected centres of Islamic learning. On the other hand, the increasing tendency of Western media and academics to portray 'Sufis' (that is, Barelwis, in the context of Pakistan) as 'good', 'moderate' Muslims, finds a strong denial in Karachi in the shape of the Sunni Tehrik (The Sunni Movement—ST). A sectarian group formed in the early 1990s, the ST has used its strong-arm tactics to protect the interests of the Ahl-e-Sunnat wal Jama'at (lit. 'the group of the followers of the Tradition', an expression referring to Sunnis in general but used by the Barelwis to designate themselves) against rival Sunni sects (the Deobandis and the Salafis of the Ahl-e-Hadith school of thought).

With the exception of some militants of the global jihad connected to al-Qaeda, most sectarian and jihadi organisations maintaining a presence in Karachi have seen their religious struggle melt into urban turf battles in recent years. Instead of redefining the terrains and patterns of conflict that have become the trademark of the city since the mid-1980s and signalling a shift from 'ethnic' to 'religious' conflicts, these new turf wars bear testimony to the acclimatisation of religious militants to Karachi's conflictive politics while pointing at their growing insertion into the city's unofficial economy. Even the Pakistani Taliban, for all their professed commitment to fight against crime and restore order in their strongholds, have become enmeshed in criminal networks while contributing to the deregulation of the city's market of protection.

A Secular City?

The description of Karachi as the most secular and cosmopolitan city in Pakistan, and thus as a haven of moderation and liberalism in a country threatened by Talibanisation, remains a common trope among liberal Pakistani scholars, journalists and political activists. Granted, Karachi developed as a colonial rather than as an Islamic city, where mosques and shrines never played a central role in the structuring of space and everyday life. As Michel Boivin underlines, 'One sometimes has to wait for Fridays to notice the presence of a mosque.'[5] The assignation of secular credentials to 'Karachi' rarely proceeds from such social or topographic considerations, though. It is a modernist myth—a historicist construction which equates Karachiites with Mohajirs and reifies the latter by assigning them, with no concern for their internal differentiations or for their idiosyncratic arrangements with modernity, a liberal ethos heavily indebted to the European Enlightenment, both as philosophical corpus and as historical trajectory.[6] 'The Muhajirs believed in secularism, liberal politics, laissez-faire economics and could not agree to a federal and tribal set-up,' thus writes Amtul Hasan, a Karachi-based international relations scholar, in a recent book on the Mohajirs' predicament.[7] The refugees who settled down en masse in the city after Partition were indeed more educated, more urbane and, on some issues, more 'liberal' than the Pashtun migrants who arrived in the following decades. Assigning to the *muhajirin* a belief in secularism seems somewhat far-fetched, though. Not only because the term 'secularism' remains a loose, under-theoreticised concept in Pakistan (to date, the English term remains in use among its proponents, whereas its critics prefer to use the Urdu term *ladiniyat*, which translates literally as 'irreligion'), but also because a variety of attitudes towards religion and politics prevailed among early *muhajirin*. In the years following Partition, the influence of religious clerics (*ulama*, *maulvi*s, mullahs,...) was far greater over the *muhajirin* than over indigenous populations, be it the Pashtuns, the Baloch or the Sindhis (who in the latter case were more attached to Sufi *pir*s). This trend, informed by the structures of religious authority that prevailed in colonial North India, translated into specific patterns of political representation. As Sarah Ansari points out, clerics were over-represented in the social and political organisations set up by the *muhajirin* in the years following Partition.[8] The most influential patron of the *muhajirin*, among these religious elites, was Maulana Shabbir Ahmad Usmani (1886–1949), a *muhajir* from Bijnaur (UP) and the only leading Deobandi figure who had lent his support to the creation of Pakistan. In the two years following Partition, Usmani repeatedly pleaded the case of the *muhajirin* in front of Sindhi elites, to whom he reproached their insensibility and lack of Islamic solidarity.

If most accounts of Pakistan's first episode of sectarian violence, which targeted the Ahmadis[9] in the early 1950s, generally focus on the Punjab, Karachi was not immune to this movement. In May 1952, riots broke out after the Karachi Ahmadiya Association tried to hold its yearly convention in Jahangir Park, in the heart of Saddar—which at that time remained the centre of political, intellectual and leisurely activities in the city. If the incidents reported on the first day of rioting remained relatively benign, the following day saw thousands of assailants loot and set on fire Ahmadi property and businesses in central Karachi.[10] As would often be the case in future incidents of rioting in the city, the police were slow to react, suggesting some connivance with the rioters. The anti-Ahmadi movement gained momentum in the city in the following months. On 21 May, prominent Karachi *ulama* called for the government to declare the Ahmadis a non-Muslim religious minority (a demand which would finally be met by Z.A. Bhutto in 1974). Then, in July of the same year, 50,000 people gathered at Arambagh Garden under the leadership of the same *ulama* and called for drastic action against the Ahmadis. Among these *ulama* were Maulana Ehteshamul Haq Thanvi, a prominent Deobandi cleric who would become the chief imam of one of Karachi's largest mosques in the 1960s (the Jama Masjid Thanvi, in Jacob Lines), Maulana Hamid Badayuni, the president of Pakistan's largest Barelwi organisation, the Jamiat-e-Ulama Pakistan (Society of the Islamic Scholars of Pakistan—JUP), 'who had made a name for himself as leader of some of the more 'noisy' elements of Karachi's refugee population'[11] as well as various members of the Majlis-e-Ahrar, a sectarian organisation which predated the Sunni extremist groups that bloomed in the late 1980s in the Punjab.[12]

In March 1953, several leaders of the anti-Ahmadi movement, including the *amir* of the JI, Maulana Abul Ala Maududi, were arrested. The following month, a protest was organised by the JI in Karachi, demanding Maududi's liberation. It was well attended, an indication that the social base of the organisation was gradually expanding from its Punjabi bastion[13] to Pakistan's southern capital.[14] Over the years, Pakistan's prime Islamist organisation had accumulated a strong capital of sympathy among the *muhajirin*, for various reasons. First of all, the bonds between the JI and the refugees were strengthened by its social work. Shortly before Partition, the JI set up a relief camp for Muslim victims of communal violence in Patna (Bihar), which was placed under the supervision of Maulana Amin Ahsan Islahi and Abdul Jabbar Ghazi. According to a later leader of the Pakistani JI, this humanitarian work primarily aimed to 'help Muslims stand on their own feet' by 'raising their spirits' (*unke pust hosle buland karna*). In the JI's perspective, however, this goal was inseparable from a project of socio-religious reform and could only be achieved by bringing Muslims back onto the 'true Islamic path' (*sahih islami roh*).[15] In Pakistan itself, while government services proved unable to cope with even the most basic needs of the refugees, the JI proved more responsive to their quandary. Maududi himself had to camp in

Lahore's Islamiyah Park for several months, after his arrival from Delhi by truck in July 1947. This sensitised him to the plight of the refugees and his call to the public in their favour was well received.[16] Between 1947 and 1954, 1.5 million *muhajirin* benefited from welfare activities ranging from the burial of unclaimed dead bodies to the management of refugee camps and the distribution of food, medicine and clothing. The success of this campaign was instrumental in the incorporation of social work into the structure of the party,[17] leading to the creation of a branch devoted to the 'service to the people', the Shu'bah-e-Khidmat-e-Khalq, which would later on be replicated by the MQM with similar success. In Karachi, the JI ran a fleet of mobile dispensaries and, by 1958, also provided medical care in fifty permanent dispensaries and 100 medical centres.[18] In early 1958, when the refugee-dominated Anjam Colony burned down, activists and social workers of the JI were the first present on the scene, well before state authorities. However limited, the role played by the JI in local trade union politics was also a source of its popularity among the *muhajir* workforce.[19]

The growing popularity of the JI among Karachi's refugee population was attested by the results of the party in the 1958 KMC election, where it won eighteen out of the twenty-three seats that it contested. Beyond the capital of sympathy it had accumulated with its social work, the JI could also rely on a more efficient electoral machine than its rivals, an advantage which was brought to light by 'the way that the JI selected its candidates [who were not professional politicians and whose number was never greater than the number of seats in a given ward], its more thorough-going approach towards voters, its sympathetic and targeted campaigning, and its ability to turn out supporters on the day of the polls'.[20]

Besides the JI, the JUP, which represents the interests of the Barelwi sect (*maslak*), also benefited from the reorientation of the *muhajir* vote from the Muslim League to politico-religious parties in the aftermath of Ayub Khan's coup (1958). In the 1960s and 1970s, these two parties competed for the votes of the *muhajirin* and found support among Urdu- and Gujarati-speaking traders, entrepreneurs and lower middle classes. Thus, in the 1970 National Assembly election, the JUP secured three National Assembly seats from Karachi and the JI two, with the five other seats in the city going to the PPP. The entrenchment of the JI and JUP in Karachi was confirmed ten days later during provincial elections, when they won respectively one and four of the fifteen constituencies of Karachi (eight went to the PPP).[21] Nevertheless, the landslide victory of the PPP in Sindh showed the limit of this electoral support to politico-religious parties: the *muhajirin* were now left in the wilderness, their political representatives sitting in the opposition with little prospect of ever getting closer to power. At the same time, the assertion of ethno-linguistic identities by the four indigenous 'nationalities' of Pakistan, starting with the Sindhis, demonstrated the limits of the official nationalism, rooted in the 'two nation theory', that had remained the framework of *muhajir* identity politics until then. As we saw in Chapter 3, it is in this context that Mohajir nationalism emerged in the course of the 1970s.

If some of the founders of the APMSO and the MQM came from the left (Azim Tariq, in particular), others were originally sympathisers of the JI (Altaf Hussain himself took an active part in the anti-Bhutto Pakistan National Alliance movement of 1977, which was led by the JI). However, they broke with the Islamists after acquiring the conviction that Urdu-speaking party workers were being discriminated against, to the benefit of Punjabis (a claim that did not verify itself in later years, as the Karachi *amir* of the JI is systematically a Mohajir, while the local leaders of the IJT have often been, even more specifically, Mohajirs with roots in Hyderabad, Deccan). During the municipal election of 1987 and the general elections of the following year, the MQM made a major dent in the JI's and other religious parties' vote-bank (the JUP's in particular). On three occasions, the Islamists managed to regain some power in later years, but without seriously challenging the political dominance of the MQM. In 1995, the JI won the municipal election but this was a pyrrhic victory, as the MQM had boycotted the polls. The JI's victory in the 2001 municipal election also followed their boycott by the MQM. On this occasion, the JI's Karachi *amir*, Naimatullah Khan, became the first City Nazim and head of the CDGK. At seventy-three years old, this former lawyer born in Ajmer (Rajasthan) committed to 'gradually turn Karachi into an Islamic, welfare society'.[22] The liberal media anxiously watched the new CDGK take measures to 'islamicise' education (by making the hejab compulsory for girl students in public schools, for instance). In practice, though, the local Mohajir leadership of the JI is far less conservative than its Pashtun leaders and never had the project of enforcing a strict programme of Islamicisation in Karachi. According to Professor Ghaffoor Ahmad, who started his political career by getting elected at the KMC in 1958, before becoming an MNA in 1970 and a senator in 2002, some of the initiatives taken by JI/IJT activists in the Frontier, such as the blackening of female models' faces on billboards, were opposed by Karachi-based leaders of the JI.[23] During the 2002 elections, the JI and its coalition partners within the Muttahida Majlis-e-Amal (United Action Committee—MMA) fared surprisingly well in Karachi. This success was short-lived, though, and was primarily the expression of public outrage against American intervention in Afghanistan in the aftermath of 11 September (the Islamists' show of unity also benefited them in the context of a first-past-the-post electoral system, while their campaign against *bhatta* and corruption struck a chord with the public).[24] In the following election (2008), the Islamists were nowhere to be seen, though, and the MQM registered one of its highest scores ever in Karachi, particularly in the constituencies of District Central, where Urdu-speakers are concentrated. The 2013 elections confirmed the marginality of Islamist forces. Although the JI registered 3 per cent of the votes polled in the provincial election and 5 per cent of those polled in the National Assembly election, while the Sunni sectarian groups gathered in the Muttahida Deeni Mahaz (United Religious Front—MDM) came a close second in one Provincial Assembly constituency (PS-128, which covers the Pashtun-dominated localities of Quaidabad and Future Colony, where the Sipah-e-Sahaba Pakistan [SSP][25] has a sizable presence), the Islamists could not win a single seat in the city.

Even if we consider them genuine (which is not evident, considering the malpractices registered down the years and the large number of unregistered voters), electoral results are only one part of the picture. Throughout Pakistan, the influence of politico-religious groups is irreducible to their vote share and it primarily exerts itself through social networks operating from below. In this domain, the MQM has had to contend with a serious competition since the late 1990s, both on the city streets and on the campuses, where the IJT retains an influence completely disproportionate to the electoral weight of its parent body. To date, Noman Baig's study on the transformations of the MQM at the end of the 1990s is the only work to have captured these local challenges to the MQM's supremacy in its bastions. The greatest challenge for the MQM came from Barelwi organisations (Barelwi Islam remains predominant among Mohajirs) such as the Dawat-e-Islami and ST (see below). The 'green turbans' (*hari pagri wale*), as they are commonly known in Karachi, were at the forefront of this Islamic revival, which led to the revitalisation of religious rituals and celebrations that replaced the MQM's political gatherings as 'major attractive cultural events'.[26] Green flags started competing with the MQM's tricolour, while the celebration of the birthday of Prophet Muhammad (Eid Milad-un-Nabi) started being celebrated with the same fervour as Altaf Hussain's in the past. Finally, the street corner meetings of the MQM paved the way for Quranic lessons (*dars-e-quran*), with people assembling in public squares (*chowks*) to listen to preachers who often happened to be former MQM activists or leaders.[27] The MQM leadership acknowledged this new public culture and, around the early 2000s, started patronising it to steal the show from the green turbans. Since then, every year, the welfare branch of the MQM (the KKF) oversees the celebrations across Karachi, which include processions and public religious gatherings (*mehfil-e-milad-un-nabi*). However, the MQM's response to the increasing visibility of religious activists was not limited to this counter-offensive in the field of public culture. The MQM also defended its turf militarily.

Sectarian Turf Wars

As we have seen, the anti-Ahmadi movement of the 1950s found some echo among Karachi's Urdu-speaking populations. So did anti-Shia currents, which emerged right after Partition. Thus, shortly before his death in 1949, Maulana Shabbir Ahmad Usmani signed a fatwa declaring the Shia infidels. Some incidents of anti-Shia violence were recorded in the late 1970s, such as the attack on a Shia procession in Ali Basti, Old Golimar, in 1978 (fourteen dead).[28]

For long, however, these currents remained marginal until their patronage by the army, in the context of the Afghan jihad, reinforced them. In 1980, a Deobandi cleric, Maulana Saleemullah Khan, founded the Sawad-e-Azam Ahle Sunnat (the Great Sunni Majority). The core of this group, which was believed to enjoy the support of the military regime of Zia-ul-Haq, was composed of Pashtun Deobandi *ulama*. It also counted Haq Nawaz Jhangvi, the future founder of the SSP, among its members, and it was the first group in Pakistan to pressurise the state to declare the Shia infidels.[29] Soon after the creation of the group, incidents of sectarian violence broke out in Karachi and some of its members were suspected to be involved in attacks against Shia homes and religious gatherings.[30] Far from being imported from the Punjab, as is often suggested in the Pakistani media,[31] Karachi's sectarian movement developed in parallel with it and contributed significantly to it, as exemplified by the trajectory of leading figures of sectarian/jihadi movements based in the Punjab, such as Azam Tariq and Masood Azhar (who were both educated at the Binori Town madrasa and who both started their career as teachers in Karachi seminaries).

Until the mid-1990s, incidents of sectarian violence remained relatively scarce. In 1994, fifty-seven people were killed in sectarian attacks and sectarian violence gained in frequency and lethality in the following years (seventy-four of the 1,742 murders registered in 1995 were attributed to sectarian militants).[32] If sectarian violence in Karachi as in the rest of the country took the shape of bomb (and later on suicide) attacks against Shia places of worship, it also singled out Shia professionals (doctors, engineers, lawyers,...). Doctors, who make soft targets because they can be easily located in clinics and hospitals, bore the brunt of these attacks and seventy-two of them were murdered between the early 1990s and 2002, with this campaign intensifying after 1999.[33] Doctors could also have been targeted following the diffusion in Pakistan of anti-Shia literature (probably of Saudi origins) claiming that Iran was conspiring to spread Shiism in Pakistan through medical practitioners.[34] Ironically, although there was no evidence of such a link between Iran and Shia doctors in Karachi, two prominent Sunni physicians were accused of links with al-Qaeda, namely Akmal Waheed and his brother Arshad Waheed, both from Karachi (the latter was killed in a drone strike in South Waziristan while the former was subsequently cleared of all charges in Pakistan).[35] Unlike ethnic and political violence, this sectarian violence did not subside after General Musharraf's coup and 450 people lost their lives in sectarian attacks in Karachi between 1999 and 2002.[36] But instead of redefining Karachi's pre-existing conflicts, sectarian militants got enmeshed in a complex set of ethnic, political and criminal conflicts, with their sectarian war blending into the city's turf wars.

Madrasas and the Spread of Sectarianism in Karachi

Sectarianism gradually took the shape of a social movement in Karachi, with its base and ideologues in some of the city's madrasas, whose numbers have continually expanded since the 1980s. In 1950, there were only four major madrasas in Karachi. In 1971, there were twenty, a majority of them affiliated with the 'traditionalist' Barelwi *maslak* (only four were Deobandi and one Shia).[37] Thirty-five years later, according to an estimate by the International Crisis Group, this number had shot up to 1,800. Although this figure is already twice higher than official ones, the actual figure is probably even higher, with the federation of Deobandi madrasas alone claiming 1,500 seminaries of its own *maslak* in the city in 2007.[38] However contested this madrasa arithmetic may be, scholars tend to agree on two points: in Karachi as in Pakistan at large, the number of madrasas (especially those affiliated with the Deobandi *maslak*) has considerably increased since the 1980s; on the other hand, though, the number of students enrolled in madrasas across the country remains insignificant compared to those attending 'secular' schools.[39] The madrasas of Karachi have large contingents of students hailing from other parts of the country, whose parents were attracted by the reputation of these schools but also by the fact that sending their children to a distant city will make it more difficult for them to run away.[40] Contrary to a common perception, though, madrasas are not only catering to the educational needs of poor Pashtun children but also to large numbers of poor Bengali children, as well as significant numbers of lower-middle-class Punjabis, with smaller contingents of Mohajirs. Out of the four largest (all Deobandi) madrasas in the city (Binori Town, in Guru Mandir; Jamia Dar-ul-Ulum Karachi, in Korangi; Jamia Binoria, in SITE Town; Jamia Farooqia, in Shah Faisal Colony), only one would have a large majority of Pashto-speaking students (Jamia Dar-ul-Ulum Karachi).[41]

The relocation of large numbers of Deobandi *ulama* from North India to Karachi after Partition, as well as the migration of Pashtuns to Karachi in search of work both contributed to make Karachi a stronghold of Deobandi clerics, some of whom promoted jihad and sectarianism.[42] This has been the case, in particular, of the *ulama* who, in India, had been affiliated with the anti-Pakistan faction of Husain Ahmad Madani at Deoband, who have made Binori Town their stronghold (the followers of the pro-Pakistan Ashraf Ali Thanvi group, for their part, gathered around the Jamia Dar-ul-Ulum, in Korangi).[43] The most prominent of these madrasas, as far as the promotion of sectarianism is concerned, is the Jamia-ul-Ulum Islamia of Binori Town (thereafter Binori Town), one of the largest and most influential seminaries of Karachi (spread over six acres, it presides over a network of twelve smaller seminaries spread across the city, and 12,000 students would currently be enrolled in the different departments of the Jamia and its branches).[44] The Binori Town mosque and madrasa complex was founded in the mid-1950s by Muhammad Yusuf Binori (1908–1977), a Pashtun from the north-west (he was born in Basti Mahabatabad, near Peshawar), who studied at Deoband before Partition, under the guidance of Maulana Shabbir Ahmad Usmani.[45] In 1953, two years after migrating to Pakistan, Maulana Yusuf Binori founded his first madrasa in Karachi, the Jamia Arabia Islamia. Taking the lead in the campaign against the reformist Islamic scholar Fazlur Rehman, he also took part in the anti-Ahmadi movement Khatm-e-Nabuwat, which was one of the crucibles of the Sunni sectarian movement that would emerge in Pakistan in the 1980s.[46] His influence and that of his seminary grew under the regime of General Zia-ul-Haq, who appointed him to the Council of Islamic Ideology (CII).

From the 1980s onwards, Binori Town has been at the forefront of Pakistan's sectarian wars. In 1986, one of its founders, Mufti Wali Hasan Tonki (the former Chief Mufti of Pakistan and head of Binori Town's Dar-ul-Ifta, or Fatwa Department), issued a fatwa of apostasisation against Shias, arguing that they were 'outside the pale of Islam' as they believed that the Quran was created and altered in the course of time, while only accepting literally Muhammad as the last prophet and rejecting the consensus (*ijma*) prevailing among Sunnis on the caliphates of Abu Bakr and Umar.[47] Other *ulama* of Binori Town were propagators of sectarianism, the most influential in this regard being Maulana Yusuf Ludhianvi, who earned the nickname of 'media mufti' for his frequent contributions to the press, starting with a special column on Islam in the Urdu daily *Jang* in 1978.[48] An influential 'sectarian polemicist',[49] Ludhianvi directed his hostility against Ahmadis as well as Shias, and along with another influential cleric from Binori Town, Nizamuddin Shamzai, he endorsed Maulana Wali Hasan Tonki's anti-Shia fatwa of 1986. Anti-Shia fatwas from Indian and Pakistani Deobandi *ulama* would later be collected in a book edited and distributed at Binori Town, which included religious decrees such as this one, which came from Maulana Rasheed Ahmed, the head of the Darul Irshad (a Deobandi madrasa in Nazimabad):

> Undoubtedly, Shias are infidels [*kafir*s], there is no doubt about this. All of them, including literate, illiterate man, woman or child are of the same belief so they are all infidels. Shias are more dangerous than other non-Muslims because they are entrenched in Muslim communities and are trying to destroy this world and the world to come. May God protect us from their mischief [*shar*].[50]

These leading *ulama* did not explicitly call their partisans to murder Shias, but by projecting the latter as infidels or even worse, apostates, they provided justifications to more peripheral *ulama* and their henchmen to unleash violence against the renegades. As Muhammad Qasim Zaman points out, the fact that Ludhianvi himself was murdered—probably by Shia militants, in 2000—suggests that, 'in view of their opponents, there are no firm boundaries between the militants on the ground and those seen as urging them from a distance'.[51] This perception was reinforced after the creation of the Jaish-e-Muhammad (Army of Muhammad—JeM) in 2000. A jihadist organisation whose main theatre of operation was initially the Indian province of Jammu & Kashmir, the JeM had organic links to sectarian Deobandi *ulama*, those of Binori Town in particular. The JeM's founder, Masood Azhar, is a Binori Town alumnus and he taught there for two years (1988–1989), before joining the jihad in Kashmir and getting captured by Indian security forces (he was released after the hijacking of an Indian Airlines flight from Kathmandu to Kandahar in December 1999). A Pashtun from Swat, who graduated from Jamia Farooqia (another Deobandi, Saudi-funded seminary of Karachi), Nizamuddin Shamzai openly patronised the group and Masood Azhar even held a press conference at his apartment after his release in early 2000.[52] Shamzai, who would become notorious for his October 2001 fatwa calling for jihad against the United States and its allies in Afghanistan, was the fourth scholar from Binori Town to be murdered by unknown assailants in 2004 (after Maulana Yusuf Ludhianvi, Dr. Habibullah Mukhtar and Mufti Samiullah). Despite his involvement in the anti-Shia sectarian movement, his patronage of the JeM, his support for the Taliban and his proximity with Bin Laden (he attended the wedding of his eldest son in 2000),[53] Shamzai was perceived as a moderate scholar in Pakistan, at least until his 2001 fatwa against the United States.[54]

Until 11 September, sectarian militants were protected from police interference by their proximity with jihadist organisations. The latter were patronised by intelligence agencies and the police did not dare question, let alone detain, anyone connected to these organisations. When police officers dared to arrest some of these militants, they faced pressure from their superiors or directly from the intelligence agencies to release the suspects. In December 2000, for instance, a police officer of District East, Captain Mir Zubair, arrested some activists of the SSP after they went on the rampage when they were prevented from staging a demonstration in the middle-class colony of Gulshan-e-Iqbal. Shortly thereafter, Captain Zubair was ordered to release the detainees. He refused to comply but a police officer who was known for his links with intelligence agencies intervened to get the men released. Captain Zubair, in turn, was transferred from his post.[55] As with Lyari's *dacoits*, the thesis of a 'failure' of the state to contain sectarian elements is deceptive. Thus, when the army and its intelligence agencies finally decided to disassociate themselves from sectarian groups aligned with jihadi organisations, in 2002, the police easily overpowered and (briefly) detained the entire leadership of the SSP during a raid on its headquarters, the Jama Masjid Siddiq-e-Akbar, a mosque located in the lower-middle class, Mohajir-dominated neighbourhood of Nagan Chowrangi, in North Karachi.[56]

It is here that Azam Tariq officiated before being spotted by Haq Nawaz Jhangvi and Zia-ul-Rehman Farooqi—the main ideologue of the SSP—who invited him to Jhang to head the SSP's alma mater, the Jamia Mahmudia madrasa.[57] A graduate (*fazil*) from Binori Town, Azam Tariq was instrumental in developing the party in the city. As the Khateeb of the Jama Masjid Siddiq-e-Akbar, he often led the Friday prayers. A firebrand orator—he was said to be able to 'ignite water'[58]—he brought many young men from the surrounding localities into the SSP's fold. Following his departure from Karachi, in 1990, Qari Saeed took charge of the organisation in Karachi but he was murdered in 1994 and the SSP lost some ground in the city in the following years, until it was revived by Abdul Ghafoor Nadeem and Ilyas Zubair (respectively president and general secretary of the party in Karachi).

Despite its claim to the contrary, the SSP has been actively involved in the killings of Shias in Karachi since 1994. It recruited local militants to launch attacks against the Shias in the city but hit men were also sent from the Punjab and were apparently paid hefty sums for each operation in Karachi.[59] These sectarian militants often financed their operations through criminal activities (car theft and robberies), a practice which had been systematised by the militants of political parties in the preceding decade. Sectarian militants replicated other methods of the henchmen affiliated with political parties, such as the use of torture cells where they would detain, question, maim or kill their rivals. This transfer of experience between the armed wings of political parties and sectarian groups (both Sunni and Shia) was accelerated by the shift of a number of militants formerly affiliated with political parties to these organisations in the course of the 1990s.[60] Azam Tariq met Amir Khan, one of the MQM (Haqiqi) leaders, in 1993. Shortly thereafter, Haqiqi militants united their forces with the SSP. While the former took part in attacks against Shia places of worship, sectarian militants showed their solidarity by targeting activists of the MQM (Altaf).[61] Activists of the MQM (Altaf) faction, for their part, are suspected of having lent a hand to the (Shia) Sipah-e-Muhammad, although the latter was never particularly active in the city.[62] Usually, these hit men are unaware of the identity of their target and only learn about it later on in the news. In some cases (and the same holds true for non-sectarian target killings), these killers are hired to settle personal enmities, business rivalries or financial scams. Thus, one the most high-profile 'sectarian' murders ever perpetrated in Karachi (the killing of Shaukat Raza Mirza, managing director of Pakistan State Oil, in July 2001) could have been related to financial scams in the PSO, though it was made to look like a sectarian murder.[63] Among the victims of Sunni militants were also Sunnis mistaken for Shias by virtue of their name, such as Dr. Ishrat Hussain, a Sunni medical practitioner murdered in 2001, or Syed Ali Imran Jaffrey, a deputy general manager of the KESC, who was killed in North Nazimabad in June 2012.

Although the leadership of the SSP in Karachi is traditionally dominated by Punjabis and Pashtuns, its stronghold of Nagan Chowrangi is located in an Urdu-speaking area, which suggests that the party has found some support among Deobandi Mohajirs. In Karachi, the party replicated the organisational grid of the MQM, dividing the city into units and sectors. Besides North Karachi, the group is reputed to have a strong presence in other parts of the city dominated by Mohajirs, such as Malir, Landhi and Korangi (in Landhi at least, this presence seems rather limited in Urdu-speaking areas, though, which remain firmly controlled by the MQM). Over the years, the SSP and the Lashkar-e-Jhangvi (LeJ—the unofficial armed wing of the SSP)[64] have expanded their influence to some Pashtun localities of the west (Ittehad Town and Tori Bangash Colony in Orangi, Muhammad Khan Colony, Gulshan-e-Ghazi, New Saeedabad, Abidabad, Swat Colony and Sarhad Colony in Baldia Town) and the east (Quaidabad and Future Colony in Landhi), as well as Lyari (according to some sources, Abdul Malik Rigi, the founder of the anti-Shia group Jundullah active in the Iranian part of Balochistan, who was executed in Iran in 2010, was a former member of the Baloch Liberation Organisation who changed his ideological stand, from Baloch nationalism to Sunni sectarianism, after interacting with SSP activists in Lyari).[65]

Street Sectarianism: The Rise of the Sunni Tehrik

In parallel with the emergence of a Deobandi sectarian movement, Karachi has seen the development of a Barelwi sectarian organisation, the ST, which arrived as a direct challenge to the MQM and other (Deobandi, Ahl-e-Hadith) sectarian organisations, but also to more quietist Barelwi religious parties such as the JUP. The ST was founded in Karachi in 1990 by Saleem Qadri, an auto-rickshaw driver whose family migrated from Gujarat to Karachi after Partition. Born in 1960 in Karachi, Qadri started his political career in the ranks of the APMSO. He soon drifted away from the MQM, though, and became a disciple of Maulana Ilyas Qadri, the leader of the Barelwi missionary organisation Dawat-e-Islami, which was founded in Karachi in 1984 along the same lines as its major rival, the (Deobandi) Tablighi Jama'at.[66] The creation of the Dawat-e-Islami was meant to be a wake-up call for the 'silent majority' of the Barelwis in the face of the growing visibility and militancy of rival sects, be they Sunni (Deobandi or Ahl-e-Hadith) or Shia. Indeed, if the Barelwis are thought to be numerically dominant among Pakistan's Muslims, their lack of state support (either from the Pakistani state or from foreign countries funding Sunni groups in Pakistan, such as Saudi Arabia and to a lesser extent Iraq) and their long-time opposition to militancy contributed to their rapid marginalisation by smaller but better endowed sects. Incidentally, the militant stand of the ST against Saudi-backed groups seems to have earned it the financial support of Iran, with the ST's turf wars against the SSP and the Jama'at-ud-Dawa (JuD, the public face of the jihadist organisation Lashkar-e-Taiba) presenting elements of a proxy war between Iran and Saudi Arabia as a result.[67]

One of the major strengths of Dawat-e-Islami lied in its capacity to bridge the gap between the two sources of religious authority among Barelwis—the *pir*s and the *ulama*—by stressing *zikr* (devotional practices) without ignoring *shariat* altogether (as many contemporary *pir*s tend to do).[68] This middle path between devotional and legalistic approaches towards religion, as well as the group's allegiance to the major Sufi orders (*tariqa*s) active in Pakistan (such as the *zikr*-oriented Qadiriya and Chishtiya, as well as the more *shariat*-concerned Naqshbandiya and Suharwardiya), contributed to the success of the organisation. It enabled the Dawat-e-Islami to find financial support and recruit manpower in all the sections of the Barelwi population, from the Memon business community to madrasa students (Dawat-e-Islami alone claimed around 200 madrasas in Karachi in 2004,[69] while the leadership of the ST argued that it controlled seventeen madrasas in the city in 2006).[70]

Saleem Qadri's fiery rhetoric earned him a solid reputation within his organisation, and he was made responsible for the branch of the Dawat-e-Islami in his locality (Saeedabad, in Baldia Town). His charisma also gained him recognition from the JUP, which provided him with a ticket in the 1988 provincial election, where he lost. Following this electoral defeat, Qadri gave up his job as an auto-rickshaw driver and launched a cloth and poultry business.[71] In the meantime, he diverged from the leadership of the Dawat-e-Islami and found himself at odds with the primarily religious and resolutely quietist agenda of the green turbans, and after breaking away with his former mentor, launched his own organisation. In the same way as the SSP, though (which never completely broke away from mainstream Deobandi political parties such as the Jamiat-e-Ulama-e-Islam–JUI), the ST retained strong links with the Dawat-e-Islami and the membership of the two groups often overlap. Moreover, some members of the Dawat-e-Islami have been involved in acts of violence despite the quietist orientation of their organisation. A case in point is that of Mumtaz Hussein Qadri, the former bodyguard of the governor of Punjab Salman Taseer, who murdered his employer in 2010 after the latter took a stand against Pakistan's controversial blasphemy law. This murder was eulogised by the ST, whose graffiti and billboards celebrating the '[holy] warrior of the nation' (*ghazi-e-millat*) appeared in all the localities where the ST has established a presence (cf. photographs in Appendix).

From its inception, the ST adopted a militant posturing against its rivals and specialised in muscular operations meant to reclaim mosques 'occupied' by rival sects—one of its most popular slogans was, 'We will sacrifice our youth to save mosques!' (*Jawania larenge, masjiden bachenge!*).[72] When I met with the central leader of the ST, Shahid Ghauri, in June 2006, he told me that his group had already regained control of 20 to 25 per cent of the mosques it had set its eyes on across Pakistan. This came at a cost: according to Ghauri—thirty workers of the ST were killed during these operations between 1990 and 2006.[73] The founder of the group himself, Saleem Qadri, was killed in 2001, allegedly by SSP militants, while his successors were killed in a bomb blast in April 2006. The blast occurred as the group was holding a congregation on the occasion of Eid Milad-un-Nabi in Nishtar Park, a popular location for political and religious gatherings in Karachi. Fifty people died in the attack, including the whole leadership of the ST. Three militants of the LeJ were charged with plotting the attack but they have not been convicted until now. In any case, even their conviction would probably not put an end to a persistent rumour attributing this attack to a prominent political party aiming to cut the ST down to size.

Intra-Sunni sectarian violence brutally escalated in 2011, which saw several deadly clashes between the ST on one side and the SSP or the JuD on the other. Whereas the ST confronted the SSP in its strongholds of North and New Karachi, its militants fought with those of the JuD in Landhi, where a clash between the ST and the JuD over the control of a mosque (the Jamia Masjid Ummul Qura) produced one victim in early July 2011. What initially started as a competition over the control of places of worship—and their financial resources—gradually evolved into turf wars similar to those involving political parties. In the New Karachi locality of Godhra Camp, for instance, the gun battles that erupted between the ST and the SSP in early July 2011, costing the lives of eight persons, revolved around the control of a mosque and a hospital (the Godhra Muslim Community Hospital). During the 1990s, public hospitals became a favourite place for stashing arms and ammunition for Karachi's warring groups, a practice which was systematised by the MQM at the Abbasi Shaheed Hospital, in Nazimabad. Today, the MQM is still reputed to control this hospital—its armed militants are no longer visible but there remains a unit office on the premises of the hospital—as well as the Civil Hospital, in Saddar. The ANP, for its part, exerts its influence over the Valika Hospital, in SITE, while the PAC has taken control of Lyari General Hospital, in Rangiwara, after evicting drug peddlers and users from its premises and putting the medical staff back to work.[74] Patients are now expected to visit the 'good' hospital, in accordance with their ethnicity.[75] The conflict between the SSP and the ST in Godhra Camp should be replaced in the larger context of the turf wars between Karachi's major stakeholders, for whom the capture of hospitals has become an important element in their strategies of patronage, allowing them to redistribute as a 'favour' to their constituents—and to their constituents only—what was originally a public good.

These new aspirants to local domination face severe hindrance while trying to enforce their sovereignty over their turf. Whereas the police and—to a lesser extent—the Rangers have generally refrained from interfering in the turf wars involving political parties, especially the MQM, the more marginal status of the ST and the SSP have exposed them to state repression. Thus, on the night of 14 October 2011, 500 paramilitaries of the Frontier Constabulary (FC, a paramilitary force which, like the Rangers, was initially focused on the protection of Pakistan's borders but which is increasingly involved in domestic 'law and order' operations)[76] cordoned off the locality of Godhra Camp and conducted door-to-door searches. More importantly, they brought down street barriers erected by the SSP and the ST, as well as their banners and hoardings, all visual markers of urban space serving to demarcate one's turf in Karachi. Finally, the buildings used by the two groups as their local offices were razed to the ground by bulldozers provided by the local administration, which suggested that the entire operation had been approved by the ruling coalition of the PPP, MQM and ANP.[77] The last time such drastic measures were taken against a protagonist of Karachi's turf wars was in Landhi in 2003, when the MQM bypassed the local government and sent bulldozers to tear down Bait-ul-Hamza, the headquarters of the rival Haqiqi faction. Despite their rarity, these operations confirm that more than the capacities to enforce 'law and order', what is often missing is the political will to make an impartial use of these resources. With their status as newcomers on the verge of legality (the SSP was banned in 2002 while the ST was put 'under observation'), lacking the political capital of more established parties and thus more dependent on volatile political protections, sectarian groups cannot pretend to establish their sovereignty over a turf in the same way as more resourceful criminal groups, such as the gangs of Lyari, and a fortiori as mainstream political parties. The sectarian divide that has been growing in these neighbourhoods over the years makes it relatively easy for these groups to reassert themselves after every police operation. Thus, the ST and the SSP lost no time in reopening their offices in Godhra after the 2011 operation. Today, the lanes in Godhra are divided along sectarian lines and activists of the two rival groups guard their entrance, with residents avoiding venturing into the 'wrong' streets.[78] However, this growing sectarian divide is yet to translate into electoral support, which would enable these groups to institutionalise their domination and better resist the pressure of their more mainstream political adversaries. Thus, during the May 2013 elections, the ST and the MDM (a platform of Sunni sectarian groups including the SSP) were nowhere to be seen in NA-244 (the National Assembly seat covering Godhra Camp, among other localities of New Karachi, Buffer Zone and Federal B Area), where the two groups registered only 1,162 and 7,045 votes, respectively, against 133,885 for the MQM.

Despite their growing clout in some parts of the city, the leaders of the SSP and the ST complain that the persisting domination of the MQM over local politics has been a major hindrance to their expansion. In June 2009, a few months before his assassination in Karachi, the provincial information secretary of the SSP/ASWJ, Qari Shafiq Rehman Alvi, told me that, had it not been for the MQM, the SSP would have succeeded in expelling Shia *kafir*s from Pakistan and establishing its writ over Karachi. Three years earlier, Shahid Ghauri had argued in front of me that the MQM was a much more fearsome rival than the SSP and the JuD: according to him, seventy-five workers of the ST were killed after the group adopted a more political stance and entered local politics, in 2004. 'Most of our activists were martyred by the MQM with the help of the police,' Ghauri told me, a few minutes before gunshots were fired at the building by policemen from the local *thana* (police station), who according to the ST leader were loyal to the MQM (see Chapter 7 for more details on this incident).

As of today (October 2013), the relations between the MQM and the ST remain fraught with tensions. The social base of the two groups is roughly the same and they compete, in particular, for the financial support of the Memon business community (which is believed to be backing financially the ST since its creation) as well as for the votes and manpower of the Urdu-speaking lower-middle-class. ST offices are frequently located on MQM's turf. Although the MQM tolerates their presence, it has been less indulgent with the attempts made by ST workers to replicate its own tactics of disruption. In the Babar Market area of Landhi, for instance—the former stronghold of the Haqiqis, under the control of the Altaf faction since 2003—the ST opened a small but highly visible office, in front of Landhi Hospital, in 2011. The MQM did not protest, and ST activists started making their presence felt in the area, through 'wall-chalking' or through the organisation of religious gatherings outside their office. However, when ST activists tried to enforce a shutdown of the area in August 2012, the local unit of the MQM sent armed workers to reclaim the streets. Following an attack on Salim Naqshbandi, the imam of a nearby mosque affiliated with their group (the Hanafiya Alamgir Jama Masjid), ST activists tried to force shopkeepers in and around Babar Market to pull down their shutters. In response, armed workers of the MQM deployed themselves in the area, determined to reassert their sovereignty and their monopoly over disruption. A few gunshots were fired, but no one was killed and the ST backtracked. When I visited a friend living in the area a few days later, there was still tension in the air. Salim Naqshbandi—who had probably been targeted by the SSP rather than by the MQM—was between life and death and everyone feared that clashes would erupt once his death was announced. Eventually, the cleric breathed his last a few days later and no untoward incident was reported. For once, the Rangers had deployed themselves in the area before trouble erupted. Nevertheless, the whole episode was revealing of the precarious balance of power that prevails in these disputed turfs.

Towards the 'Talibanisation' of Karachi?

While sectarian groups have taken root in Karachi since the mid-1980s, the city has also been a haven for jihadi groups active in Kashmir and Afghanistan. Some madrasas such as Binori Town provided encouragement and legal justifications to anti-Shia sectarian groups and to anti-Indian or anti-Western jihadists, while some prominent cadres of al-Qaeda are known to have operated from Karachi prior to 11 September and thereafter. It is here that the two masterminds of the 11 September attacks, Khaled Sheikh Muhammad[79] and Ramzi Binalshibh, were staying when they gave their first—and sole—interview in the aftermath of the attacks (to Yosri Fouda, a journalist for al-Jazeera).[80] It is also here that Ramzi Binalshibh was captured on 11 September 2002. Besides providing a refuge to Pakistani and foreign jihadis, Karachi repeatedly came under attack from these militants. Although the first suicide-bombing was registered in 2000 (to date this remains the only suicide-attack perpetrated by a woman in the city),[81] the frequency of these incidents increased after 11 September. As of April 2012, fifteen suicide-bombings had been registered in Karachi, targeting foreign workers (such as the French engineers of the Direction des Constructions Navales, in May 2002), diplomatic missions (the American Consulate, in June 2002), Shia places of worship (Imambargah Hyderi and Imambargah Ali Raza, in May 2004), Sufi shrines (the *dargah* of Abdullah Shah Ghazi, in October 2010), political gatherings (of the ST, in April 2006; of the PPP, following Benazir Bhutto's return to Pakistan, in October 2007), and so on. These attacks have been well documented by local and foreign journalists and I do not have much to add to their often courageous work.[82] Moreover, most of the groups behind these attacks (Jaish-e-Muhammad, Harkat-ul-Jihad Islami,...) do not have any political stake in Karachi and remain focused on a regional or even global jihad. The presence of the Pakistani Taliban in the city, which started being felt around 2009, is a different issue altogether. After keeping a rather low profile until the summer of 2012, the militants affiliated with the TTP shifted to logics of territorialisation from then on and committed to reclaim the bastions of the ANP. After wiping out secular Pashtun nationalists, they consolidated their position in these localities and started enforcing a parallel justice system blending elements of Islamic and tribal 'traditions', as understood by these militants. It is at this point, in the early months of 2013, that the Taliban revealed themselves as an emerging public authority in some neighbourhoods of Karachi, a 'coming out' that was bound to put them in conflict with the MQM. But Karachi's predominant party was already engaged in myriad conflicts and its military capacities were getting overstretched, a strategic weakness that the Taliban exploited by striking repeatedly against the party. Surprisingly, for a party that had built a large part of its reputation on its military capacities and street power, there were no reprisals, no strike, no demonstration, not even the 'referendum' that the party had briefly considered organising against the Taliban in November 2012. For the first time in its history, the MQM was traumatised by the violence unleashed against its workers and leaders and did not know how to respond, a disorientation that became even more flagrant during the bloody election campaign of April–May 2013. This lack of response on the part of the MQM only emboldened the Taliban, who constrained the MQM to give up its usual mass-meetings and retain an unusually low profile throughout the campaign. This did not prevent the party from registering another victory in the 11 May elections (amidst allegations of mass rigging). However, the MQM's public authority—including in its own bastions—emerged severely diminished from this offensive of the TTP, which would prove to be the opening act of a long war of attrition. The killing of a newly elected MPA of the MQM, along with his son, a month after the election, pointed in this direction. As the TTP claimed responsibility for the attack against Sajid Qureshi, it threatened to carry out more attacks against the party in the near future.

Talibanisation in Trompe-l'Oeil Style

MQM-affiliated publications started raising the alarm about the presence of the 'Pakistani Taliban' in Karachi around 2000, well before the term gained common usage in Pakistan, following the foundation of the TTP in 2007. Initially, this 'Taliban' threat took the shape of pro-jihad clerics and madrasa students, which the MQM leadership anxiously watched replicate its own disruptive tactics to get its voice heard. The emerging street power of the pro-jihad madrasas, and of Binori Town in particular, was for the first time demonstrated in November 1998, when they enforced a complete shutdown of the city following the murder of Maulana Habibullah Mukhtar and Mufti Abdus Sami. A similar mobilisation took place after the murder of Maulana Yusuf Ludhianvi two years later. An article published in June 2000 in *Naqīb*, the journal of the APMSO, denounced the acts of 'rioting' (*hangama arai*) and 'terrorism' (*dahshatgardi*) committed by madrasa students affiliated to Binori Town and other seminaries on this occasion. The author of the article was particularly outraged to watch the city at the mercy of these 'armed militants of religious parties', though he was confident that this attempt to bring back the city to the dark ages would be defeated by the educated and enlightened people of Karachi.[83] This definition of the Pakistani Taliban by the MQM was in phase with a context which saw Islamist groups regain some power on the streets and shortly thereafter at the town hall, following the election of Naimatullah Khan as city mayor in 2001. This 'Islamic revival' in Karachi politics was short-lived, though, and if the coalition of Islamist parties gathered in the MMA made a dent in the MQM's vote-bank the following year, the MQM reasserted its dominance over local politics at the next elections. From 2007 onwards, while the Islamist threat was declining, the ANP started emerging as a new military and electoral challenge. In this new configuration, the features of the Taliban started changing for the MQM. Under the garb of its 'anti-talibanisation' movement, the party started targeting ANP activists and ordinary Pashtun migrants and IDPs, who were perceived as a far greater demographic and political threat to the MQM's supremacy than the actual Taliban. This political instrumentalisation of the 'talibanisation' threat by the MQM only facilitated the implantation of the jihadis in Karachi, by weakening the secular forces that could have contained them in Pashtun settlements while allowing them to build up their forces and prepare themselves for a showdown. This (mis)calculaltion of the MQM relied upon the conviction that Pashtun jihadis were not a direct threat to its rule over Karachi as they had no political stake in the city. And when the party leadership understood that the Pakistani Taliban were getting ready to turn their guns against their party after having cut the ANP down to size, it was too late. The Taliban were now too entrenched in Pashtun settlements to be uprooted from a city they also laid some claims upon.

The Implanting of the Pakistan Taliban in Karachi

If some of Karachi's violent entrepreneurs, such as the *dacoits* of Lyari or the city's most powerful land suppliers (see Chapter 7), have tried to contain the state from within, through their proxies, others (or the same ones at other times, as the resistance of the PAC to the April 2012 police operation demonstrated) strived to contain it from without, by resisting militarily against the encroachment of their de facto sovereign enclaves by state agencies. The growing disequilibrium between the military capacities of these violent entrepreneurs and those of public enforcers (especially the police), to the benefit of the former, makes this option increasingly attractive for non-state aspirants to sovereignty. After Lyari's *dacoits*, the Pakistani Taliban recently started using strong-arm tactics to carve their own sovereign spaces in Karachi. Since 2012, the Pakistani Taliban operating in Karachi have increased their attacks on the police, so much so that eleven of the eighty policemen killed in the city between January and October 2012 have fallen to the bullets of 'Taliban-style elements', according to police sources.[84] As in the north-west, these groups are divided along tribal and factious lines. The Mehsud faction of the TTP seems to maintain the strongest presence in Karachi. It is organisationally divided between a faction loyal to TTP chief Hakimullah

Mehsud and another paying allegiance to the second-in-command of the TTP, Wali ur Rehman—at least until the latter was killed in a drone attack in May 2013. Besides these groups operating under the command of the TTP's central leadership, the group of Maulana Fazlullah (alias 'Maulana Radio') has taken root in the suburban neighbourhoods where Pashtun IDPs from Swat settled down from 2009 onwards. Thus, while the TTP Mehsud faction exerts its influence over Mehsud-dominated settlements of Baldia Town, Orangi Town and Gadap Town, the Fazlullah faction took root in Pathan Colony (Orangi Town) and Future Colony (Landhi Town). The consolidation of this influence was often brutal: dozens of anti-Taliban tribal elders living in or travelling to Karachi were killed from 2011 onwards.[85]

Beginning in January 2012, TTP militants also started targeting ANP leaders,[86] capturing offices of the party and hoisting the flag of their group on the 'liberated' buildings. Despite Rehman Malik's—Pakistan's home minister—claim to the contrary, it was becoming obvious that the Pakistani Taliban were no longer coming to Karachi to 'spend vacations'.[87] Instead, they were now fighting for their own turf, while getting involved in local sectarian wars in collaboration with anti-Shia armed groups active in the city, such as the Ataur Rehman group of the LeJ. These two groups are suspected to be behind the recent upsurge of sectarian killings witnessed in the city, which has been targeting Twelver Shias as well as Bohras, although on a smaller scale in the case of the latter.[88] Thus, according to the Human Rights Commission of Pakistan, the number of Shias murdered in Karachi shot up from fifty to 200 between 2011 and 2012.[89]

The recent transformation of Manghopir, at the edge of Orangi Town, into a 'no-go area' for the police, bears testimony to the Taliban's shift to the logics of territorialisation. With military operations in the 'tribal areas' of the north-west gaining momentum, from 2009 onwards, large contingents of IDPs started settling down in Manghopir, Sultanabad, Pakhtunabad, Kunwari Colony, Awan Colony and New Mianwali Colony, which at the time remained sparsely populated (cf. Map 7). Among these IDPs were a handful of Taliban fighters, who were initially planning to stay briefly in Karachi before heading back to the war-zones of the north-west. However, with the passage of time, these militants realised that Karachi provided a safe haven, where they could escape drone attacks and easily generate funds to finance their activities in the north. The militants then turned to local land suppliers, who unofficially allotted them large numbers of plots at minimal rate—Rs 30,000 to Rs 40,000 for 100-square-yard plots. Building upon ethnic solidarity networks, the Taliban encouraged their ethnic brethren—Mehsuds, in particular—to settle down in these localities. These newcomers often bought several plots, which they would reallocate to their relatives or re-sell to new settlers. The ethnic composition of these localities was drastically altered in the process, as more ancient residents of other ethnicities resented this influx and relocated to other areas. As a result, these colonies became ethnically homogeneous clusters virtually overnight. Once the ethnic composition of the neighbourhood was drastically altered in their favour, the Taliban started recruiting local criminals that provided them with a skilled workforce, who knew how to handle Karachi's law and order forces. In turn, these local criminals used their alliance with the Taliban to uproot their rivals. Thus, a notorious extortionist known as 'Bhaloo', who lives close to the summit of the Manghopir Hills, started working in tandem with the TTP, while his main rival, known as 'Kami', joined a sectarian group.[90] Following this recruitment drive, the militants started flexing their muscles. They resisted every incursion of the police on their turf and a raid of the SHO of the Pirabad police station on a local mosque used as a gathering place for religious militants, in the spring of 2012, ended up with the policemen getting roughed up and forced to negotiate their release against that of the heavily armed militants they had captured.[91] Moreover, the Taliban repeatedly targeted the local police station, killing eight officers.[92] Feeling emboldened, they started enforcing a ban on 'immoral activities' by cutting down internet and cable TV services, shutting down shops selling CDs and DVDs, while setting up 'peace committees' settling property and business disputes, as well as family feuds. These mobile courts (the date and venue—which changes from time to time—are only announced shortly before the hearings, for safety reasons) blend elements of Islamic and tribal 'traditions' as understood by the Taliban. They are presided by a *qazi* but operate in the manner of a *jirga*, bringing together local figures of authority such as tribal elders and clerics. In some cases, tribal elders or local clerics can also be appointed by the Taliban to solve the issue.[93] Although these parallel courts have been hearing complaints from the public for a while, they only started delivering punishments—including physical ones—from January 2013. For the first time, a convicted thief was publicly administered lashes after stolen goods were recovered from his possession, before being returned to their rightful owner.[94] For now, however, the most common punishment inflicted on the guilty is a fine.[95] It remains to be seen whether this rough justice will have a dissuasive effect on local criminals (a highly improbable outcome, considering that the Taliban themselves often patronise extortionists and other petty criminals). For now, though, it seems to have become a popular instrument of dispute settlement and contract enforcement, as business partners and/or parties in conflict are convinced that no party to the settlement will dare disobey the decision of a Taliban-controlled *jirga*.[96]

This recourse to the familiar repertoires of justice and authority—which are perceived as less intrusive, more legitimate and more efficient than the so-called 'rule of law' enforced by corrupt policemen and judges—has certainly facilitated the consolidation of the Taliban's hold over these Pashtun localities (at least in the case of the Mehsud faction, as the Fazlullah group does not meddle in family feuds and business disputes).[97] As they garnered substantial popular support through these dispute settlement mechanisms, the militants also went on a massive funds procurement spree, through extortion and kidnappings for ransom (some sources suggest that the escalation of the Pakistani Taliban's fundraising efforts in Karachi, in recent years, aimed to compensate for their financial losses, following the toughening of anti-terrorism financing measures in Pakistan).[98] Manghopir has a thriving marble industry: each year, the 350 medium- to large-size factories of the area process around 400,000 tonnes of marble, which is extracted from the hills of Balochistan and transported by truck to Karachi.[99] This industry was a prime target for extortion and factory owners as well as traders generally complied, fearing retaliation while hesitating to move out, out of fear of falling into the clutches of other extortionists—the Taliban and the criminals they sheltered had become the evil they knew. At the end of this almost two-year journey, the Taliban of Manghopir were confident enough to operate openly within the neighbourhood but also elsewhere in the city, where they started taking a more proactive stand against law and order forces, including the Rangers.[100] The electoral campaign of April–May 2013, for its part, provided them with the opportunity to demonstrate their capacities of disruption of the political process in Karachi, as they targeted repeatedly the three largest secular forces in the city, the MQM, the ANP and the PPP, killing dozens of party workers and bystanders in a series of bomb blasts. This campaign of terror had the result of bringing the

MQM and the ANP together, although MQM officials privately confided that Pashtun nationalists had become 'irrelevant' in Karachi following the upsurge of the Taliban.[101] Indeed, between January 2012 and May 2013, seventy cadres of the ANP were killed by the Pakistan Taliban,[102] and as of July 2013 the party had closed down 70 per cent of its offices across the city, abandoning the terrain to religious militants.[103] The public standing of the party was so damaged that some of its workers started shifting to the MQM.[104]

The modus operandi of the Taliban in Manghopir suggests that, while advertising virtuous credentials (one of the TTP's offices in the Manghopir area thus bears the name of Anti-Crime Control Committee), these jihadis have become enmeshed in the city's criminal economy, both directly (through extortion, land grabbing, kidnappings for ransom, bank robberies, unofficial water supply, etc.) and indirectly (by recruiting known criminals and patronising others). The hefty sums generated by these traffics have sometimes brought dissensions within the ranks of the movement, and in early 2013 the leader of the Hakimullah Mehsud faction of the TTP in Karachi was reportedly murdered after his superiors learned that he was embezzling money collected through extortion and bank heists (jihadist and sectarian militants are suspected to be behind eleven bank robberies that took place in the first four months of 2013, generating a revenue of $800,000).[105]

The Taliban's double standards, as far as 'crime control' is concerned, could rapidly erode their capital of sympathy among the Pashtun residents of their strongholds. Not that this really matters for them: more than on popular support, their political grip over these localities rests upon their capacity to carry out their threats, in Karachi as well as in the place of origins of local residents. Thus, one should not misread the Taliban's attempt to enforce their own legal order as an attempt to legitimate their rule. It primarily amounts to a power statement, giving visibility to their growing public authority. By resorting to lawfare, that is, 'to the violence inherent in the law, to commit acts of political coercion, even erasure',[106] the Taliban nonetheless profess their firm belief in the power of legal instruments—a fetishism of the law that has no parallel among other aspirants to sovereignty in Karachi.

Map 7: Taliban influence in Karachi

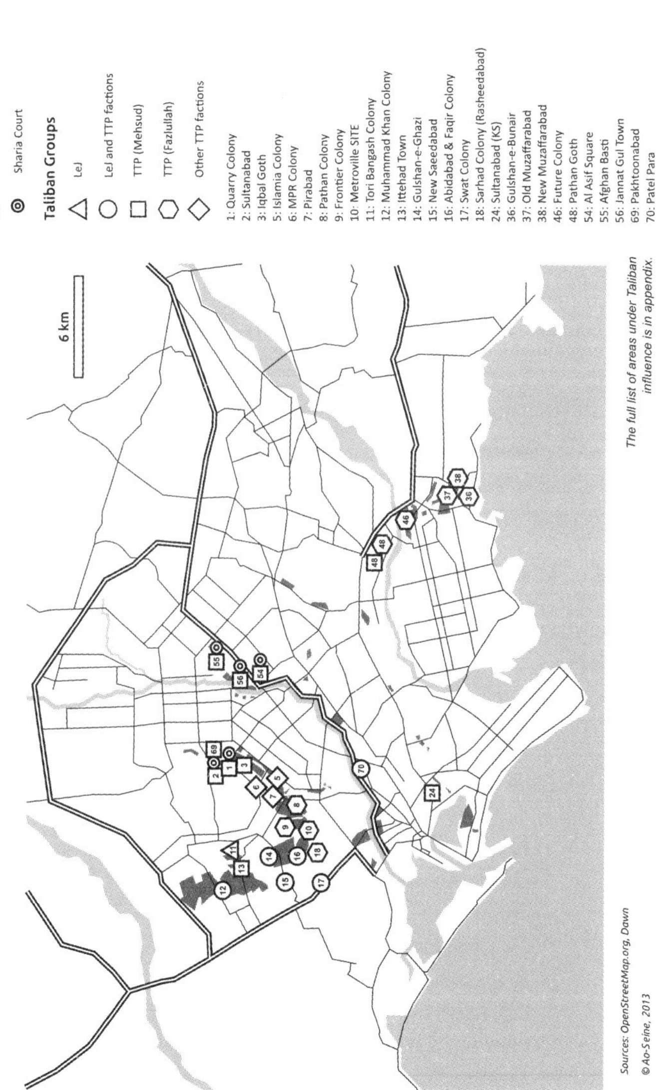
Taliban Influence
Area under Taliban influence
Sharia Court
Taliban Groups
LeJ
LeJ and TTP factions
TTP (Mehsud)
TTP (Fazlullah)
Other TTP factions
1: Quarry Colony
2: Sultanabad
3: Iqbal Goth
5: Islamia Colony
6: MPR Colony
7: Pirabad
8: Pathan Colony
9: Frontier Colony
10: Metroville SITE
11: Tori Bangash Colony
12: Muhammad Khan Colony
13: Ittehad Town
14: Gulshan-e-Ghazi
15: New Saeedabad
16: Abidabad & Faqir Colony
17: Swat Colony
18: Sarhad Colony (Rasheedabad)
24: Sultanabad (KS)
36: Gulshan-e-Bunair
37: Old Muzaffarabad
38: New Muzaffarabad
46: Future Colony
48: Pathan Goth
54: Al Asif Square
55: Afghan Basti
56: Jannat Gul Town
69: Pakhtoonabad
70: Patel Para
6 km
The full list of areas under Taliban influence is in appendix.
Sources: OpenStreetMap.org, Dawn
©Ao-Seine, 2013

Appendix: Colonies with a sizable Taliban presence

SL	*Name of the Colony*	*Population*	*Group*
1	Quarry Colony	4,986	TTP (Mehsud)
2	Sultanabad	4,450	TTP (Mehsud)
3	Iqbal Goth	7,391	TTP (Mehsud)
4	Mianwali and New Mianwali Colony	10,310	TTP (Mehsud)
5	Islamia Colony	13,377	TTP
6	MPR Colony	14,697	TTP
7	Pirabad	12,591	TTP
8	Pathan Colony	47,873	TTP (Fazlullah)
9	Frontier Colony	49,784	TTP (Fazlullah)
10	Metroville SITE	51,336	TTP (Fazlullah)
11	Tori Bangash Colony	15,320	LJ
12	Muhammad Khan Colony	66,417	TTP/LJ
13	Ittehad Town	33,774	TTP (Mehsud)
14	Gulshan-e-Ghazi	80,920	TTP/LJ
15	New Saeedabad	21,756	TTP/LJ
16	Abidabad and Faqir Colony	32,605	TTP/LJ
17	Swat Colony	11,096	TTP/LJ
18	Sarhad Colony (Rasheedabad)	13,085	TTP (Fazlullah)
19	Bawani Chali	38,321	N.A.
20	Gulbai	N.A.	N.A.
21	Gulistan Colony (South)	27,656	N.A.
22	Niazi Colony	22,901	N.A.
23	Lea Market	8,039	N.A.
24	Sultanabad (KS)	13,978	TTP (Mehsud)
25	Tekri Colony	17,103	N.A.
26	Gulshan-e-Sikandarabad	86,499	N.A.
27	Shireen Jinnah Colony	7,635	N.A.
28	Generalabad	9,655	N.A.
29	Reti Lane	7,049	N.A.
30	Pak Jamhuria Colony	N.A.	N.A.
31	Hazara Colony (South)	N.A.	N.A.
32	Massom Shah Colony no. 2	13,655	N.A.
33	Muhammad Nagar	16,916	N.A.
34	Sherpao Colony	15,441	N.A.
35	Bilal Colony	10,839	N.A.
36; 37	Gulshan-e-Bunair/Old Muzaffarabad	57,527	TTP (Fazlullah)

38	New Muzaffarabad	50,089	TTP (Fazlullah)
39; 40; 41	Firdous Chali/Dand Chali/Moinabad	59,144	N.A.
42	Moinabad no. 2	21,637	N.A.
43	Quaidabad	N.A.	TTP (Mehsud)
44	Laiquabad	N.A.	N.A.
45	Gulistan Colony (Malir)	N.A.	N.A.
46	Future Colony	44,246	TTP (Fazlullah)
47	Hazara Colony	N.A.	N.A.
48	Pathan Goth	17,202	TTP (Fazlullah)/ (Mehsud)
49	Natha Khan Goth	52,366	N.A.
50	Pehalwan Goth	28,256	N.A.
51	Bhitaiabad	N.A.	N.A.
52	Hussain Hazara Goth	5,796	N.A.
53	Bajaur Para	18,380	N.A.
54; 55	Al Asif Square, Afghan Basti	N.A.	TTP (Mehsud)
56	Jannat Gul Town	N.A.	TTP (Mehsud)
57	Shafiq Mill Colony	13,386	N.A.
58	Jehangirabad	4,301	N.A.
59	Chawla Market	4,932	N.A.
60	Feroz Colony	6,515	N.A.
61	Jalalabad and Musarrat Colony	12,867	N.A.
62	Natal Colony and Dera Saifullah	29,381	N.A.
63	Khyber Ajab Bangash Colony	16,810	N.A.
64	Umer Farooq Colony	41,910	N.A.
65	Usman Hgani Colony	23,745	N.A.
66	Bilalabad	891	N.A.
67	Khalilabad	13,228	N.A.
68	Yaqoob Shah Basti	N.A.	N.A.
69	Pakhtoonabad	25,321	TTP (Mehsud)
70	Patel Para	17,275	TTP/LJ
71	Darwesh Colony	10,371	N.A.

Source: Zaman, Fahim and Naziha Syed Ali, 'Taliban in Karachi: the real story', art. quoted.

Karachi's Homegrown Taliban

While the TTP was taking roots in Karachi through migratory flows originating from the north-west, it also induced circulations—though on a much smaller scale—in the opposite direction by recruiting local youths and dispatching them to the northern warfronts of Waziristan and Afghanistan. The following section focuses on this lesser known aspect of the Taliban presence in Karachi, all too often reduced to the disruption of an allegedly modern and secular city by its tribal margins. The two life-stories examined below challenge this dominant narrative—at least among the educated Urdu-speaking elites—of an urban paragon of reason and civility under siege from uncouth and fanatic tribals freshly descended from their mountains. These two life-stories do not claim any form of generality (they are not conceived to be ideal-types in the Weberian fashion) but are sufficiently distinct to point at the variety of radicalisation processes leading to the enrolment of Karachi-based youths in the ranks of the Pakistani Taliban. These differences are not merely idiosyncratic (they are not merely related to personal developments or 'career contigencies', in Erving Goffman's terms)[107] but proceed from a generational gap between these two men: whereas the radicalisation process of Wali Khan* was a byproduct of 11 September and its immediate aftermath, the enrolment of Abu Hamza* was characteristic of the previous generation of jihadi fighters, ideologically trained in madrasas and militarily trained on the battlefields of Kashmir and Afghanistan with the support of Pakistan's army and intelligence agencies. As we shall see, this generational hiatus has strongly impacted the worldviews of these jihadi fighters, particularly as far as their representations of the Pakistani army and (inter)nationalism are concerned.

A child of 11 September: Wali Khan's journey from Karachi to Waziristan

Wali Khan remembers vividly the day the towers fell down. Like twenty-five thousand other students in Karachi, he was preparing for his Matriculation examination when the news of al-Qaeda's attacks on New York and Washington started doing the rounds. The images of the Twin Towers' collapse broadcast over all Pakistani TV channels made a strong impression on the young man, who until then had not shown any particular concern for politics or religion. He measured the enormity of the event and the changes yet to come in the region and beyond. A new global war had started, and he wanted to be part of it. 'These events inspired me to join the jihad,' he told me in July 2009. However, this motivation did not immediately translate into political mobilisation. His parents wanted him to complete his studies and become an engineer. These aspirations found a particular resonance in this family of first-generation Pashtun migrants, who had left South Waziristan shortly after Wali Khan's birth, in the hope that Karachi would provide better opportunities for their children than their rugged homeland. The prospect of seeing their son make the return trip to Waziristan, even more so as a jihadi, must have been a serious source of concern for the young man's parents. But Wali Khan was inflexible, and his mediocre results in the Matriculation examination closed the doors of engineering colleges to him. He then enrolled in the BSc programme at KU, which he completed in 2004. During these years, he became acquainted with radicalised students at KU and the adjacent NED University, who invited him to attend lectures and 'workshops' on jihad, before offering him to join summer camp organised by radical Islamists. This new circle of friends and the prospects of engagement and adventure that they opened for Wali Khan could have compensated for his sense of personal failure and shrinking opportunities. Even more importantly, these friends helped Wali Khan translate his motivation into actual mobilisation. Some of them were connected with jihadist groups active in Pakistan's tribal belt and Wali Khan felt emboldened by these like-minded companions. In 2004, while the results of his final exams were still due, he set off for the north-west in the company of four Urdu-speaking friends, whom he had met during the aforementioned 'summer camp' (three of them were students at NED University whereas the last one studied at KU). In the following months, Wali Khan underwent training in a camp located in South Waziristan, following which he joined the ranks of the Pakistani Taliban, a movement that had begun to take shape in 2002 and that would only grow in the following years, leading to the formation of the TTP in 2007.

For this young Pashtun educated in Karachi, the return to his 'homeland' was an exhilarating experience. In his eyes, Waziristan looked like 'paradise' (*jannat*), a perception which probably had less to do with the anticipation of a fantasised hereafter than with a nostalgic longing for a lost world of pristine natural beauty, in complete contrast with the urban environment of Karachi. The city-dwellers who enrolled themselves in the Taliban insurgency were probably not so different from the young American men they were so eager to fight. At least initially, war resembled a summer camp; it was a liminal experience beyond parental reach, with promises of great adventures in the outdoors. The representations of 'nature' that young American soldiers and young Pakistani Taliban carried with them could have been structured by distinctive cultural frames. The Arabic term in use in Urdu to refer to nature, *qudrat*, is infused with religious connotations: this is nature as the manifestation of God's will in its primordial form, prior to human interference (thus, *qudrat* also carries the idea of 'power'). But even if it found a particular echo among the religiously-inclined, city-dwelling recruits of the Pakistani Taliban, this encounter with nature had little to do with a mystical experience. More prosaically, it offered an escape from the city and the material world at large, with its temptations and deceptions. One should not lose sight of the most essential dimension of this experience for its participants, though: first and foremost, this great escape into the wild was as 'fun' (*maza khez*) as 'appeasing' (*pur sakun*). This peculiar form was epitomised by the food they were served (in Urdu, the term *maza* both refers to 'fun' and 'taste'). Thus, when Wali Khan tried to explain to me why he 'didn't like living in cities', he started talking of the food he was served in the jihadi camps where he stayed: 'even the best meal served in the city cannot compare to a simple *roti* served there [in Waziristan]. This is the food of the victorious [*fatehin ki khorak*].'

On the contrary, the fighters born and bred in the north-west who episodically take shelter in Karachi have often found it difficult to acclimatise themselves to this new urban environment. The crowds, the traffic and, worst of all, the sight of women driving cars come as a shock for these residents of Pakistan's highlands. The brutality of this uprooting, however temporary it may be, was brought to light by my brief and unfruitful encounter with another young fighter of the Pakistani Taliban in June 2009. The young man hailed from Bajaur Agency, a tribal area on the border with Afghanistan. This was his first trip to the big city, and it showed. With the help of a Pakistani journalist friend, I arranged a meeting with him in the office of a news agency located in one of the high-rise buildings of I.I. Chundrigar Road, where the head branches of most Pakistani banks and press organisations are located. In order to reach the office, which was located in the upper floors of the building, one had to take the lift. This proved to be a daunting task for the young fighter, who had never used such a mode of transportation. When he came out, he was pale and dizzy. We tried to comfort him but to no avail: this hellish experience only added to his apprehensions about our meeting—he apparently suspected us to be intelligence sleuths—and despite all our assurances, he promptly put an end to the conversation and left (through the stairs, I would guess).

For Wali Khan and his companions, the ravishing experience of their discovery of nature was short-lived. Soon enough, they were enrolled into more martial activities than those expected in a traditional summer camp. In the first few weeks of their stay in South Waziristan, they received a general instruction in the handling of weapons and IEDs, before undergoing more specialised courses on the basis of their respective abilities. Wali Khan stayed a full year in South Waziristan. In 2005, the pressure of the army on the insurgents started to increase and he went back to Karachi. By then, he already had a solid experience of combat, as he had fought for 'more than forty days' against the Pakistani army. His recollection of his first experience of combat points at the initial reluctance of these young radical Islamists to fight their own army, but also at the mechanisms through which they contained their fears and disquiet:

> The first time that I took part in an ambush [against a Pakistani military convoy], I was scared. But my companions told me to practice *zikr* [recitation of the names of Allah] and when I did, by the grace of God, my fear vanished. That day, we killed at least 20 soldiers. [...] When we see our flag on the vehicles [of the Pakistani army], we feel reluctant to attack them. But we have no other option and when we think of all the women and children killed by the army, we want revenge.

After returning to Karachi, Wali Khan thought for a while of putting his jihadi activities on hold. He considered applying for an MBA but finally gave up the idea, as his political engagement was too compelling. After a few months, he returned to Waziristan—alone, this time. In 2006, he crossed over to Afghanistan and stayed in Khost for four months, taking part in combat operations against American forces, which he described as even less fearsome adversaries than Pakistani soldiers: 'they never engage into combat and immediately call for aerial support'. At the end of 2006, Wali Khan returned to Karachi to rest and receive some medical treatment for a pain in the knee (according to him, Taliban fighters only have access to first aid on the frontline, so much so that 'many of our companions were martyred because of the lack of medical facilities').

In 2007, he went back to Waziristan and stayed there for a few months before returning to Karachi to complete 'some work' he did not elaborate upon. He then spent the whole of 2008 in Waziristan and when I met him, he had just returned from there. When I asked him if he was not exhausted by all this travelling, he denied any weariness: 'Insha'allah, we will rest in paradise!' A few months later, his wish was granted: he died while preparing a bomb that was meant for Pakistan's home minister, Rehman Malik.

A veteran jihadist: Abu Hamza, from one jihad to the next

I met Abu Hamza during the same month of July 2009. Our meeting took place in a roadside restaurant in the lower-middle-class locality of Gulistan-e-Jauhar, in full view of other customers. Abu Hamza did not seem to care much about potential eavesdroppers, though, which is not to say that he did not have any concern about confiding himself to a foreign academic—he did make the distinction, indeed, between a 'researcher' and a 'journalist', something that my respondents rarely do, if only because the Arabic term in use in Urdu for 'researcher' (*muhaqeq*) is rarely understood by common people. The fact that Abu Hamza fully understood the term and its implications was an indication of his upbringing in Karachi's most famous madrasa in Binori Town, where he had learned Arabic. But as I said, this understanding of the nature of my work was no guarantee of an interaction based on mutual trust. I do acknowledge the limits of my encounters with Pakistani Taliban, which, each time, were limited to a single interview session that I was not allowed to tape. In the case of Abu Hamza,* these suspicions extended to my first batch of questions on his family background and childhood: he flatly refused to answer any question related to his family, probably out of fear that my writings could expose them to the scrutiny, or worse, of Pakistan's intelligence agencies. I therefore had to restrict my questionnaire to his formative and later years, following his admission at Binori Town. His experience there already offers much to ponder over, though, while significantly departing from Wali Khan's own radicalisation process.

Abu Hamza joined Binori Town in the early 1990s. He went for the full Dars-e-Nizami course,[108] which is normally completed in sixteen years. During his stay at Binori Town, he became convinced that 'jihad is one of the pillars of Islam' and the spectacular rise of the Afghan Taliban, in the second half of the 1990s, inspired him. For him, these victories boded well for the jihadi movement, which was bound to expand from Afghanistan, eventually to 'conquer the whole world'. In 1998, Abu Hamza left for Afghanistan with a dozen friends from Binori Town. By then, the hold of the Taliban over Afghanistan was at its peak and Abu Hamza was enthralled with what he discovered: 'It had been such a long time that a purely Islamic system of government had not been in place in Afghanistan.' Once in Afghanistan, he was dispatched to Jalalabad, where on his own admission he remained cantoned to clerical work, though he took part in some fighting around the city for around three weeks. Apparently, this experience of combat left a mitigated impression over the young man (he was eighteen years old by then) and he decided to return to Karachi to complete his education at the end of his summer holiday. He was not alone in contenting himself with this brief exposure to combat: among his group of fifteen young *tulaba* from Binori Town, ten made the choice to return to Karachi, which probably made it easier for Abu Hamza to make the trip back home and prioritise his education over a glorious death on the battlefield. This decision, similar to that taken by Wali Khan after his first trip to Waziristan, deserves attention as it points at the discontinuous, incremental and contingent nature of the radicalisation process of these young jihadis. This radicalisation process did not follow a linear trajectory and, at times, even seemed to have been put on hold. This is not to say that these militant careers were erratic or purely contingent, but that the radicalisation of these two students is best understood as a process of trial and error rather than as the outcome of a definitive conversion.

Temporarily renouncing jihad for the sake of his studies, Abu Hamza returned to Karachi, passed his exams and then decided to pursue further studies at KU, where he completed an MA in Islamic Studies—another indication that the boundaries between Karachi's supposedly secular/moderate and religious/radical centres of learning are much more porous than commonly acknowledged. While studying at KU, Abu Hamza retained strong links with the Deobandi jihadi movement inspired by the *ulama* of Binori Town. Though he remained elusive on the extent of his connections with the group, he made no mystery of his sympathy for the JeM and its leader, Masood Azhar. This sympathy was made explicit at the end of our meeting, when Abu Hamza said that he had a 'gift' (*tohfa*) for me, which turned out to be a copy of Masood Azhar's

Fazail-e-Jihad (The Virtues of Jihad), a voluminous book offering historical and theological justifications for the JeM's conceptions of holy war. The proximity of Abu Hamza with the JeM also became clear in the course of the interview, when he lamented that the events of 11 September had 'broken the chain of command' that Pakistani jihadis used to be familiar with. What Abu Hamza meant by that was that until Pakistan sided with the United States—even half-heartedly—Pakistani jihadi groups took their orders from the Pakistani army (he used the generic term *fauj*, which refers to the military at large rather than its intelligence agencies). The division of work was clear and the foot soldiers of jihad saw themselves—and were recognised as such by their powerful patron—as agents of global change as much as Pakistani patriots, promoting the country's interests in the region. Even if he was roughly the same age as Wali Khan, Abu Hamza was radicalised in a different context—almost a different political generation—at a time when jihadi groups fought side by side with the Pakistani army in Kashmir and Afghanistan. It was therefore even harder for Abu Hamza to cope with the rupture of these relations after 11 September. Even though he does not seem to have been personally involved in military operations against Pakistani soldiers, he expressed the same malaise as Wali Khan at seeing jihadis target coreligionists and alleged defenders of the country. His justification for such attacks was slightly different, though. On the one hand, he recalled his sense of moral outrage at seeing these soldiers slaughter 'innocent girls' during the operation against Islamabad's Lal Masjid in July 2007—a landmark in the history of Pakistan's jihadi movement, which precipitated the formation of the TTP. In a more ideological vein, Abu Hamza also suggested that the Pakistani army had lost the moral high ground to the jihadis as far as the defence of Pakistan was concerned, thus adhering to a form of jihado-nationalism insufficiently acknowledged by analysts of the Pakistani Taliban. For Abu Hamza, Musharraf had 'sold Pakistan on one phone call [from US authorities]', and if the army itself had abdicated its sacred mission of protecting the land of the pure, the jihadis had to take over, for the sake of Islam as much as for the sake of the country.

Unlike Wali Khan, Abu Hamza did not seem to have joined the ranks of the TTP. When I met him in 2009, he had recently 'visited' Waziristan, but according to him, 'the situation was peaceful by then' and he did not take part in combat. He also pointed at a feeling of cultural estrangement from the local Taliban. Though himself a Pashtun, Abu Hamza admitted that he had some difficulties understanding the Pashto dialect spoken in Waziristan, and he did not stay long enough to blend in. Once again, he returned to Karachi, slightly disillusioned at what he had seen in Waziristan, particularly as far as ethno-linguistic divisions among the Pakistani Taliban were concerned (he resented the physical separation of militants on the basis of language, with the 'Punjabi Taliban' staying and training on their own). When I met him, Abu Hamza was teaching in a madrasa, and though he had not broken his ties with the jihadi movement, his fighting days—which were not as challenging as those of Wali Khan, anyway—seemed to be over. While Wali Khan aspired for martyrdom on the battlefield or even better in a suicide-bombing ('the ideal way to go to Allah is in smithereens', he told me, a few months before his wish was granted), Abu Hamza, at twenty-nine, was already a disillusioned veteran. He had renounced martyrdom to content himself with a mundane life, only interjected with brief escapades in what remained, in his urbanite's eyes, the wild north-west. More than a terrorist, Abu Hamza had become a tourist of jihad, like so many madrasa students and alumni before him.

Conclusion

The sectarian undercurrents which appeared in the city as early as the 1950s and matured into a proper social movement in the 1980s challenge the representations of Karachi as Pakistan's 'secular centre', a representation that was reinforced from the mid-1980s onwards by the predominance of the 'liberal' MQM. This predominance did not prevent some Karachi-based Deobandi *ulama* from playing a leading role in the ignition of Pakistan's sectarian wars and later on in the emergence of jihadi organisations such as the JeM. The militant careers of two Karachi-based Pakistani Taliban surveyed here also points at the porosity of the boundaries between supposedly secular/moderate institutions of higher learning (such as KU or NED University) and religious seminaries suspected of 'radical' leanings (such as Binori Town), as far as the circulation of jihadist worldviews and role models are concerned. In practice, ideas and individuals circulate between these institutions. Significantly, among these two young jihadi militants, the one who seemed the most dedicated to the cause of jihad—by putting forward an ardent desire to die as a martyr—was the one entirely educated in the 'secular' system of education, which speaks volumes of the artificiality, if not the fallaciousness, of the madrasa/university divide (and thus of the lower-/middle-class one) as far as the spread of jihadism among Pakistan's youths is concerned. However limited the career options offered to madrasa alumni, the seminaries provide some sort of safety net to their graduates, if only by guaranteeing them some sustenance through a teaching position. The access to the job market is often more complex, and a source of greater anxiety, for graduates of secular universities and colleges, as the sense of personal failure related by Wali Khan suggests. This role of secular centres of learning in the Islamist networks linking Karachi to Afghanistan is not new. In the 1980s, the IJT was already sending KU students to take part in the Afghan Jihad.[109] After 2001, however, IJT cadres have been divided on this issue, as the JI was firmly against sending volunteers to fight the Americans in Afghanistan and, a fortiori, the Pakistani army in South Waziristan. According to a professor in the science department of KU, these debates gained intensity around 2006–2007, after the local chapter of the IJT was infiltrated by *takfiri* elements. In 2007, these aspiring jihadists were expelled from the IJT and founded their own group, known as the Punjabi Taliban. Some of these young radicals from KU then left for South Waziristan, where several of them would be killed in drone attacks in the following years. The leader of the group, Qari Shahid, who had a Masters' degree in political science from KU, was killed during a police raid in Karachi in December 2011. His wife, Sabiha Karim, was also an active member of the group and revealed that it had been involved in several high-profile attacks against military installations and Shia worshippers or activists in Karachi since 2010.[110] Thirty years after the hijacking of a PIA flight from Karachi to Damascus, which marked the entry of KU's student activists into the annals of international terrorism (see Chapter 2), this university was more than ever a site of radicalisation.

Until recently, the spread of sectarianism and jihadism in Karachi remained contained by the political dominance of the self-professed 'secular' MQM—and even more importantly by its military capacities. More than on ideological grounds, the conflict between the MQM and religious militants is premised on political calculations, and on battles for local supremacy. This conflict escalated into armed confrontations after some religious groups started displaying political ambitions and draining some of the militants from the MQM, while competing with it for the collection of donations in cash and kind (animal hides remain a major source of funding for the MQM). This was the case, in particular, of the Dawat-e-Islami (which started beating the MQM in *zakat* collection around 2006)[111] and the ST (although most former MQM workers within the ST, such as Shahid Ghauri, came from the Haqiqi faction). Besides the ST, the SSP has also joined the political fray and fielded ninety candidates in Karachi in the 2005 local elections, as well as five National Assembly candidates and sixteen Provincial Assembly candidates during the 2013 general elections. These sectarian groups remain electorally insignificant, though, and until recently the MQM was more concerned with the concurrence of the ANP, fearing that its vote-bank could expand with the arrival of hundreds of thousands of new Pashtun migrants into the city. Thus, if MQM-affiliated writers started raising the alarm on Karachi's 'talibanisation' as early as 2000, the party's leadership was for long more concerned about the growing presence of Pashtun migrants and IDPs than about the spread of jihadism, as a movement and an ideology, in Karachi. This fear proved to be misplaced, though, and by focusing its attacks on the ANP while sparing the actual Taliban, the MQM ended up facilitating the rise of the latter.

Taking every political force in the city by surprise, the Taliban recently traded their low-key strategy of sanctuarisation for the logics of territorial control. This shift was premised on the most explicit dialectic of the legal and the lethal to have emerged from Karachi's ordered disorder as yet. The MQM, at the peak of its power, became a law unto itself by superseding the state. The *dacoit*s of Lyari, for their part, have enforced a *pax traficana* by regulating their own criminal activities while containing the state from within and, to a certain extent, from without. Until now, though, only the Taliban went as far as setting up parallel courts, which owe their efficacy to the relative 'legitimacy' of their Islamic and tribal referents, at least in comparison with a formal justice system widely perceived as corrupt and inefficient. The credibility of the Taliban's parallel courts also proceeds from the unrivalled coercive capacities of their judges-cum-executioners. Besides their firepower and battle-hardened fighters, which guarantees them against interference from the police, the Taliban can pressurise the Pashtuns of Karachi by using the threat of reprisals against their families in the north-west.

The Taliban are not merely adding another thread to Karachi's tapestry of sovereignties: they are taking the practice of lawfare—an expression that should here be understood literally as the militarisation of 'the law', or it simulacra—to an unprecedented level. And before pathologising or exoticising such 'aberrations', one should remember that it is precisely on this violence of the law that the project of the European modern state was premised, although Walter Benjamin's caveat remains in order: to sublimate itself as sovereignty, power must transcend the violence inherent to the process of law-making-as-power-making. As an architecture of legalities, sovereignty demands an order of rules beyond the state of exception.[112] It is not the least of Karachi's recent history's paradoxes that the most elaborate attempt to establish such a legal order came from Pakistan's most infamous band of 'terrorists'. But this paradox disappears when one considers this 'legal' order, however counterfeit, in the backdrop of the permanent state of exception enforced by the official state (especially the police, with their systematic recourse to extrajudicial methods of 'law enforcement'). When state agents operate systematically beyond the ambit of the law, including in their official assignments, while informality rules in the economy and the market of protection becomes increasingly deregulated, the terrain becomes ripe for alternative, community-based forms of law enforcement. Which is precisely what the rough justice dispensed by the Taliban is all about—rough, but familiar and predictable. Unlike the police, the Taliban judge, punish and kill by the book—and a highly revered one at that. The enforcement of this parallel legal order is premised upon a contradiction, though: as the Taliban relied upon local criminal groups to take root in Karachi, they rapidly took exception to their own rules and regulations while providing a roof to the very forces of the shadow economy they initially aimed to discipline and bring within the ambit of the law.

6

A CITY ON THE EDGE

In Charles Tilly's terms,[1] collective violence has acquired a strong 'salience' in Karachi politics: the infliction of damage, whether actual or potential, has come to dominate political interactions. This is not to say that Karachi is frozen in conflict. As Ann Frotscher points out, what we are dealing with, here, is 'a densely-woven fabric of group conflicts fought out on a number of different levels, the causes of which interrelate and interact'.[2] Over the years, this translated into an ordered disorder—less a fixed, closed and harmonious *system* of social regulation and political competition than a patterned but fluid *figuration*, in Norbert Elias' sense of a 'web of interdependence'[3] formed by individuals or social groups, which transforms itself and its participants in the course of their interactions. The rules governing such configurations can be changed, bypassed or openly transgressed—in this case, the absence of sanction is often the preliminary to a banalisation of the transgression, as demonstrated by the systematisation of gunfights and targeted killings at KU following the murder of Hafiz Aslam (see Chapter 2). However, in such configurations, no player ever has a complete control over the game and its rules, even when he has invented them. This is what the IJT discovered after the rise of the MQM in the mid-1980s, and what the MQM itself realised after the Pashtun militants of the ANP, the Baloch *dacoits* of the PAC and finally the Pakistani Taliban decided to beat it at its own game, by resisting militarily its hegemonic project and replicating, with more or less creativity, its muscular style of governance. Today, even if the MQM proceeded to a complete *aggiornamento* of its repertoire of action by giving up violence, it is doubtful that armed conflicts would recede in the city. Karachi's predominant—but increasingly contested—party currently resembles the apprentice sorcerer of Goethe's poem, who stands 'before the spirits he has conjured up and which, once at large, are no longer in his power'.[4]

The unprecedented escalation of violence witnessed in Karachi since 2007 confirms that major changes are currently underway in the social and political regulation of the city, and that the checks and balances that used to contain armed conflict within certain bounds are no longer in order. Not only did the number of murders reach an all-time high in 2012, never, in the history of the city, did homicidal violence continue to rise unabated over such a long period of time. To make matters worse, a new record could be set in 2013, with already 2,058 killings between 1 January and 30 September, according to CPLC data. If the city experienced several sequences of violent escalation in the past (1985–1986; 1989–1990; 1994–1995; 1996–1998), violence systematically receded after a couple of years at the most, following a political settlement between the various forces competing for the city and/or the intervention of 'law and order forces'. Despite the apparent loss of control of the Pakistani state over its most turbulent city, there remained some scope for the containment of violence, including by state agencies. After recalling the major premises of this tensile equilibrium, the present chapter factors in the recent developments examined in the last two chapters and their contribution to a re-configuration of Karachi's ordered disorder, an ongoing process with a high potential for further violent escalation.

The Institutional Fabric of Karachi's Armed Conflicts

As already suggested in the general introduction, the political trajectory of Karachi over the past three decades raises two complementary questions: how did armed conflicts become endemic in the city since the mid-1980s? And what spared Karachi a general conflagration, despite repeated sequences of violent escalation accompanied by ethnic, political and, more recently, religious polarisation? As the following section argues, these two questions might have the same answers: the institutional mechanisms sustaining violent conflicts in the city have also contained them within certain bounds, at least until recently. Particularly decisive in this regard has been the peculiar mode of government of the city's predominant political party, which is premised upon a capacity to *order* disorder in both senses of the term—that is, a capacity to unleash but also to tame civil strife at will. Second, Karachi has been characterised, since the mid-1980s, by the inability of any actor to exert a complete domination over local politics and monopolise the means of coercion *and* the ability of one actor—the MQM—to dominate the game nonetheless. Third, the city's armed conflicts have been fuelled but also moderated by a genuine yet unconsolidated democratic context, which saw the development, in the shadow of military interventions, of an armed consociationalism regulating the tense relations between ethnic-based and partly militarised political parties. Last but not least, one has to acknowledge the ambivalent role of state agencies—and in particular of the army—whose repeated attempts to restore order through performances of legitimate violence, through the outsourcing of illegitimate violence and through a politics of patronage has had mitigated effects, both nurturing and moderating violent conflicts in the city.

Ruling on the Edge: The MQM's Power over Disorder

The peculiar positioning of the MQM in Karachi politics—that of a dominant political party cultivating its marginality and disruptive capacities—goes a long way to explain the formation and the reproduction over time of a configuration of ordered disorder in the city. While systematically denying any involvement of their party in violent or illegal activities, the leaders of the MQM have built their party's reputation over its capacity to disrupt life in the city. As the MQM made a name for itself through its frequent and well-attended strike calls, its charismatic leader earned the surname of '*Hartal Hussain*' (Hussain the Strike). The street power that this surname alluded to was not merely disruptive, though. It did rely upon a capacity to bring the city and its economy to a halt (the cost of a single day of strike, around 1995, was estimated at $37 million and there were twenty-two days of strikes in the first ten months of this year;[5] in recent years, daily trade and industry losses caused by outbreaks of collective violence were estimated at $31.5 million and $73.6 million, respectively).[6] However, this capacity of disruption always went along with the ability to restore normalcy at short notice. More than its violence or its sheer power of disruption, it is this capacity to command (over) disorder that has made the party an indispensable ally for successive civilian and military governments. More often than not, these disruptive capacities remain at the discursive level of mere threats. However, to be credible, these threats have to be actualised occasionally in violent flare-ups. This constantly reactualised street credibility explains that more mainstream political forces (the PPP, the PML-[N]) prefer to bring the party on board whenever they form a government at the centre or in the province, however difficult it might prove to accommodate in the long run (see Chapter 2).

Such 'power over disorder', to use the term of Andrew Abbott, is common in many professions (strangely enough, Abbott omitted politics from his list of professions where the taming of disorder is of particular importance, such as medicine, psychiatry, law and the clergy). Following Abbott, I would suggest that the aura of Altaf Hussain and his party outside the MQM amounts to a 'charisma of disorder': a particular form of power drawing its efficacy from a prolonged exposition to the realm of the disorderly, which is only heightened by the risk of failure—of being irremediably defiled by these social impurities.[7] In the realm of politics, the risk inherent to these close encounters with the disorderly is also a loss of control with disastrous consequences for public order. This risk looms large over all attempts to rule on the edge of disorder and gives them their efficacy, allowing strategies of negotiation or legitimisation that oscillate between the demiurgic and the most mundane forms of racketeering. Thus, when Karachi faced one of its worst episodes ever of political violence, following the resignation of the MQM from the PPP-led government, during the summer of 2011 (cf. infra), its leaders in Karachi claimed that the party, far from instigating violence, was in fact restraining the Urdu-speaking population of Karachi. In the process, they claimed to have spared the city 'such mayhem and bloodshed that the people would not be able to count the bodies'.[8] This valorisation of the regulating capacities of the MQM could obviously be read backward as a veiled threat, by suggesting that the party had the power to unleash an urban apocalypse at will.

The MQM's Predominance as a Factor and Regulator of Conflict

The political and military predominance of the MQM introduced an element of stability and predictability in a political configuration otherwise characterised by chronic uncertainty and informality. This is exemplified by the institutionalisation of a market of protection in the late 1980s. If critics of the MQM complain that the collection of *bhatta* causes great distress to the shopkeepers, entrepreneurs and citizens of Karachi,[9] this system was not without merits for its participants, however coerced into it they might have been. First of all, it was institutionalised. Most 'donations' were collected through the KKF on a monthly basis as well as on some specific occasions—religious festivals, in particular—and these donations were duly acknowledged through 'receipts' (*rasiden*). Moreover, the sums collected remained minimal (and inferior to those previously collected by the police).[10] At the time of Eid, for instance, shopkeepers would be asked to contribute around 1,000 rupees as *zakat* or *fitra*. In a country where only 0.6 per cent of the population paid income tax in 2012, and where VAT efficiency, at 25 per cent, is the lowest in the world,[11] the MQM proved that it was possible to enforce a rational system of taxation—a process which, let us recall, always implies a certain amount of coercion, although it also sets the basis for a relationship of reciprocal obligations.[12] However coercive the *bhatta* system enforced by the MQM might be, it is not arbitrary, which distinguishes it from a rudimentary form of booty. Moreover, along with its contributors' votes, it buys them certain 'rights' (physical protection against rival groups and the MQM itself, non-interference from the police or the bureaucracy, etc.). As we will see further, it is less this unofficial form of taxation per se that causes distress to Karachi's mercantile and industrial classes than the recent deregulation of the market of protection, following the gradual loss of control of the MQM over revenue collection (but also, it seems, following the increasingly disorganised collection of *bhatta* by MQM activists)—a process which paved the way for increasingly violent and arbitrary forms of extortion.

The MQM's predominance is the result of a disequilibrium in interdependencies between the various forces competing for the control of Karachi's populations and economic rents. The MQM is more powerful than other forces because it is less dependent on them than they are on its policies, tactical coups and political alliances. On certain occasions, this disequilibrium was such that the party's adversaries withdrew from the competition, with violence reaching an all-time low as a result. This was the case, for instance, between 2002 and 2007, when the MQM was patronised by the President-cum-COAS Pervez Musharraf. This patronage by the army chief himself, combined with the party's full control over the local administration, following its electoral victory in the 2005 municipal election (which gave it control of 14 towns of Karachi, the remaining four going to the PPP), operated as a strong deterrent against potential rivals. If we except some brief and relatively low-key incidents of pre-electoral violence between the MQM and the JI in 2005, as well as some clashes between the MQM and the ST throughout the period, the years 1999–2007 (excluded) were the most peaceful in Karachi since the mid-1980s. However, it should be kept in mind that the number of murders decreased significantly *before* the return of the MQM to power following the 2002 general elections and that it escalated significantly from 2007 onwards, while the party was still in full control of local bodies and to a large extent of the provincial administration. These two significant variations in homicidal violence had less to do with the political fortunes of the MQM per se than with incidents of regime change in Islamabad. Thus, the sudden decrease in the level of violence witnessed in the city in 1999 was a direct outcome of the return of the army to the helm, following Pervez Musharraf's coup. By the same logic, violence escalated once again during the past few years of Musharraf's rule, which saw the army chief gradually lose control of the political process in the country, retire from the army (November 2007) and finally resign from the presidency (August 2008). The predominance of the MQM and its contribution to the moderation of the level of violence in the city should thus be qualified: more than on the electoral strength or the military capacities of the party, it is premised on its alliances of convenience with the rulers of the day, which are always shaky in the volatile context of Pakistani politics. The political configuration of the 2000s, from which the MQM derived unprecedented power, was a rare occurrence and did not survive the return to 'unguided' democracy, following which the MQM was relegated to the status of an aspiring but contested hegemon. As we saw in the two previous chapters, this cutting down to size of the MQM emboldened its new rivals. It was also a source of tension with its political 'allies' of the time, with which it maintained uneasy relationships oscillating between conflict and co-operation.

The Democratic Fabric of Karachi's Ordered Disorder

Since the mid-1980s, Karachi's ordered disorder thrives in a democratic environment that remains more formal than substantial but which appears eligible for the title of a (weak) polyarchy nonetheless. Although Pakistan's democracy remains unconsolidated, this state of affairs has less to do with the lack of 'institutionalisation' of democracy in the country—a notion which, in comparative democratic politics, often leads to reserving the title of 'proper' democracies to Western political regimes[13]—than with the persisting threat from the military over its existence. Clearly, democracy is not yet seen as 'the only game in town', to use Juan Linz's formula.[14] Far from invalidating the link between Karachi's conflicts and their democratic environment, though, this unconsolidated nature of Pakistani democracy is crucial to understanding the regulation of Karachi's armed conflicts through a form of armed consociationalism.

This volatile coalition politics culminated between 2008 and 2013, when the PPP, the ANP and the MQM—three parties with distinct ethnic constituencies (Sindhis and Baloch, Pashtuns and Mohajirs, respectively)—ruled together in Sindh and in Islamabad. During this period, conflicts between coalition partners punctually came to a head during episodes of 'broken negotiations',[15] which saw the MQM withdraw its support to the government, a development sometimes followed by outbreaks of violence (in the form of 'riots' or coordinated attacks against political activists and civilians affiliated with the ruling parties). Once the demands of the defector were accommodated, though, violence swiftly receded and coalition politics resumed. During its previous period in power (1993–1996), the PPP could afford to govern alone in Sindh and in Islamabad. As a result, it was less inclined to accommodate the MQM, so much so that it did not hesitate in unleashing 'legitimate' violence against the latter—including through extrajudicial means. This was no longer the case between 2008 and 2013, at least at the centre, where the PPP was around fifty seats short of forming a majority. With twenty-five seats at the National Assembly, the support of the MQM was critical to the survival of the PPP-led central government, which provided the MQM with greater leverage than in the past. The participation of the ANP in this coalition was an additional source of tension, as the PPP-ANP alliance operated as a check on the MQM's hegemonic designs in Karachi and boosted the sense of confidence of each party.[16] The MQM was uncomfortable with the intrusion of its two uneasy partners on its turf and on numerous occasions threatened to quit the government, starting in May 2009 when it announced that it would part ways with the PPP-led coalition if it did not sever ties with the 'criminals' of the ANP, alleging that its leaders were protecting the Taliban and providing a cover to various 'mafias' in Karachi.

These tensions reached their climax during the summer of 2011, following the decision of the PPP-led Sindh government to repeal the SLGO 2001, and to revive instead the commissionerate system put in place by the Zia-ul-Haq regime.[17] The SLGO had given birth to a three-tier local government in Karachi, with the CDGK at the top, eighteen town municipal administrations in the middle and 178 Union Councils (UCs) at the bottom. Following this institutional reform, the powers of the local state were considerably expanded, as various departments were transferred from the provincial to the city government. As a result, local officials were given unprecedented authority in matters of land use, housing, urban planning and transport, as well as recruitment, education and health (the police, though, remained under the control of the provincial government, to the great dismay of the MQM, which had been demanding that they were placed under the city government). Moreover, Union councillors (neighbourhood representatives) were allowed to recruit armed guards directly, raising fears that political parties could use this opportunity to legalise their armed wings by recruiting their militants as bodyguards. By 2005, the MQM had gained the upper hand over these local government structures, through its City Nazim, Town Nazims and UC Nazims. This provided the party with unrestrained access to the city's resources, while enabling it to strengthen its hold over law and order forces, which became increasingly subservient to the party's leadership. For the MQM, the decision of the Sindh government to return to the commissionerate system jeopardised thousands of jobs, many of which had been attributed to MQM party workers, sympathisers or potential voters. At the time of their dissolution in 2001, the two major municipal institutions, the KMC and the KDA, had respectively 10,000 and 4,000 employees. Ten years later, the CDGK had 80,000, including 50,000 from the departments merged into the city government.[18] With the dissolution of the CDGK, the fate of this staff hung in the balance, and the MQM feared that a major instrument in its politics of patronage could slip from its hands. More fundamentally, the restoration of the commissionerate system threatened the MQM with losing its grip over the local state, as it would have transferred back the management of city affairs across the province to the bureaucracy, where Sindhis were better represented than Mohajirs. The MQM responded to this bleak prospect by quitting the coalition government in Sindh and at the centre in late June 2011.[19] Following this resignation, violence brutally escalated (mostly in the western part of the city), before receding briefly, only to escalate once more in mid-August (this time, the worst affected neighbourhoods were those of District South, such as Kharadar and Lyari).[20] Instead of involving a continuous sequence of escalation, though, each of these rounds of violence consisted in a succession of outbursts that, in their briefness as much as in their calculated brutality (against civilian populations, in particular), provided evidence of their strategic nature and of their sponsors' capacity to control the rate of terror. As the Human Rights Commission of Pakistan noted in a report published shortly after the events:

> Although the city has a history of political, ethnic and sectarian violence, the year 2011 saw horrific bloodshed that was unprecedented even by Karachi's standards. This latest violence would erupt without a warning, claim dozens of lives and would subside as abruptly and inexplicably as it had emerged. This sequence of killings was often repeated several times a week. In July alone, at least 358 people were killed in flare-ups of violence that paralysed the city. Many of the victims were tortured, shot and stuffed in burlap sacks that were dumped in the streets or in sewerage drains.[21]

In the following month 229 more people were killed,[22] before violence subsided markedly. This sudden decrease followed the return of the MQM to the negotiating table, where it was given some assurances about the restoration of the post-2001 local government system in Karachi and Hyderabad, following which it announced its return to the coalition in October 2011. Although the MQM was certainly not the only group to have benefited from these successive violent outbreaks, the fact that violence suddenly receded after the resumption of negotiations between the PPP and the MQM suggests that a large part of it partook in an episode of 'broken negotiations'.

While electoral contests, the competition over state resources and the management of coalition politics fuel political violence, the structural weakness of the democratic framework within which this volatile coalition politics unfolds tends to moderate it, as the threat of a suspension of the game by the military looms large over the protagonists. No political party in Karachi can allow violence to escalate towards a general conflagration, which could provide the army with an excuse to suspend democracy, as it already did on several occasions in the past (1958, 1977, 1999).

If democratic institutions sustain these clashes, their weakness contains them. Even the MQM, which was formerly patronised by a general-president, had to take this constraint into consideration, as Musharraf's elective affinities with the MQM had less to do with his position as the army chief than with his ethnicity. His successor, General Ashfaq Parvez Kayani, was a Punjabi from whom the MQM could not expect the same leniency, in case the army was brought back to power. Thus, if the level of control of these parties over their armed cadres is open to question, one cannot fail to notice that violent flare-ups never last more than a few days, following which the Rangers reclaim the streets from armed militants. In order to factor in this resilience of 'the state' in the regulation of Karachi's armed politics, it is however necessary to disaggregate it and consider on their own terms, without systematically denigrating them, the 'non-Weberian practices of power'[23] of Pakistan's ruling elites.

State Ambivalence

Down the years, the multiple violent entrepreneurs and political forces competing for the control of Karachi have co-evolved in a complex ecology of violence that has produced ever escalating levels of insecurity for the city's population. Karachi's tryst with ordered disorder cannot be reduced to a spiral of state decline, though, and has also seen repeated instances of state intervention to establish new if inherently unstable compromises between public and private aspirants to sovereignty. This reiteration of state power, at a time when it seemed to be fast eroding, primarily took the shape of public performances of 'legitimate' violence—targeted police, paramilitary or military operations, aimed at killing or capturing certain challengers to state sovereignty and more fundamentally to 'restore the writ of the state', to use one of the favourite expressions of Pakistan's ruling elites. These attempts to make state power more visible by countering the '"weakness" of everyday stateness'[24] are not always successful and may end up reinforcing narratives of state decline, as the calamitous police operation conducted in Lyari in April 2012 exemplified. However, the apparent 'failure' of such operations can be misleading, as it is often the outcome of political (mis)calculations rather than of state weakness per se.

Performances of 'legitimate' violence

Far from being a passive spectator of Karachi's conflicts, state agencies regularly orchestrate performances of 'legitimate' violence through which they aim to reassert their sovereignty, if only symbolically. These performances generally take the shape of police or paramilitary operations during which the security forces conduct raids on public offices of political parties or hideouts of criminals, at the behest of civilian authorities. Between June 1992 and November 1994, the army itself conducted a massive operation in Karachi, which aimed at breaking the backbone of the MQM's secondary state and reclaiming the territories under its control. From a military point of view, operation Clean-up was a partial success: the MQM's 'secondary state' was dismantled, state sovereignty was re-established over Mohajir-dominated neighbourhoods and the newly exiled leadership of the MQM had to acknowledge its inability to sustain a campaign of urban warfare in the face of its more powerful opponent. However, the operation backfired on several levels. The violence unleashed upon MQM workers and Urdu-speaking civilians further alienated the freshly invented Mohajir community, while exposing the army to severe critiques from the local media and international NGOs as far as its human rights violations were concerned. Last but not least, the army's support to the dreaded Haqiqis, who established their own 'no-go areas' in a short span of time, further eroded the myth of the Pakistani state's neutrality. All in all, the army failed to reassert what Thomas Blom Hansen, in the context of Mumbai, refers to as the 'sublime' dimensions of the state—impartiality, restraint and justice.[25] On the contrary, Operation Clean-up and subsequent operations targeting the MQM—such as the ruthless campaign overseen by Major-General (retired) Naseerullah Babar in 1995–1996 (at a time when he headed the federal Home ministry, during Benazir Bhutto's second term in office)—were tainted with ethnic and political bias, while being premised on the systematisation of extrajudicial violence. Thus, according to a report on the situation in Karachi published by Human Rights Watch in 1997:

> As part of a tightly coordinated effort with a streamlined chain of command headed by Home minister Naseerullah Babar, the police, backed by paramilitary Rangers with sweeping powers of search and arrest, conducted systematic pre-dawn cordon-and-search operations in pro-MQM localities, indiscriminately rounding up all able-bodied males and parading them before informants for pur-

poses of identification. Between July 1995 and March 1996 an estimated 75,000 Urdu speakers were reportedly rounded up in this way; toward the end of the year, hundreds remained in jail awaiting trial.

Several key MQM militants were the victims of extrajudicial executions, either during targeted police raids; or in custody, allegedly after being tortured or severely beaten; or in staged 'encounters,' often during transit between prisons. Police rationalised the illegal killings on the grounds that witnesses' reluctance to testify against militants in open courts made it nearly impossible to secure convictions.[26]

By condoning extrajudicial violence against alleged enemies of the state, the military, and later on the civilian authorities, unleashing sovereign violence upon the MQM institutionalised a permanent state of emergency that normalised state terror. This is precisely how Michael Taussig, in his readings of Walter Benjamin in the face of Colombia's history of violence, understands the notion of 'ordered disorder'. Although my own understanding of this notion is slightly different—rather than as a zone of anomie resulting from a permanent state of exception *à la Agamben*, I see Karachi's ordered disorder as a violent configuration nurtured by a clash of sovereignties within and without the state apparatus—it is undeniable that these performances of state violence and the culture of terror that they institutionalised played a crucial role in de-legitimating 'the state' in the eyes of large sections of Karachi's population, thus preparing the ground for alternative loyalties and claims to sovereignty.

Two years and a half after deploying itself in Karachi, the army withdrew its troops and the task of maintaining law and order was transferred back to the police and, increasingly, to the Rangers. This paramilitary force, whose original mandate was focused on the protection of Pakistan's border with India, established a permanent presence in Karachi in 1989 to assist the civilian government in the face of a fast deteriorating 'law and order situation'. The Rangers then seconded the army during Operation Clean-up, before being called in for reinforcement by Benazir Bhutto's government in 1995. Since then, the Rangers have become an essential component in the maintenance of 'law and order' in Karachi, with 11,500 of their personnel deployed across the city (against 30,000 policemen). Although this presence has been mired in controversy,[27] the Rangers are generally perceived by Karachi's population and political class as more neutral and efficient than the police. At the same time, though, their peculiar line of command (the Pakistan Rangers

[Sindh] are led by a Major-General and operate under the control of the Interior Ministry and the V Corps of the Pakistan Army in Sindh) raises questions about their neutrality, as they are often suspected of being in the hands of the army and its intelligence agencies. Despite these suspicions of partiality and the controversies surrounding their extra-professional activities in Karachi and Sindh at large, the Rangers have seen their mandate continuously expand over the years, another indication of the normalisation of exception in Karachi. Thus, in August 2011, powers of police were conferred upon the Rangers, allowing them to arrest individuals suspected of serious crimes, terrorism in particular.

Conducted by the army over a two-year period, Operation Clean-up proved to be an extraordinary attempt at 'restoring the writ of the state' in Karachi. Since then, such attempts have been less spectacular. More often than not, a few party workers or criminals will be rounded up and arrested, before being set free a few days later. Much less frequently, some senior personalities will also be detained, in order to send a message to the targeted group. This is what happened across Karachi in the months preceding the May 2013 elections. In Landhi, for instance, the Rangers raided MQM offices and detained a dozen workers and cadres of the party, including its sector-in-charge, in March 2013. The detention of such a high-ranking MQM cadre, at a time when the MQM was protesting about the redrawing of constituencies in Karachi in preparation for the general elections, sent shivers through the spines of MQM activists in the neighbourhood. One of them, who informed me of this raid by e-mail, suggested that 'arresting a sector-in-charge means that law-enforcement agencies have their own agenda before the elections', and more specifically that the 'agencies' were once again backing the rival Haqiqi faction in view of a weakening of the MQM on the eve of the elections. The same worker added that 'everyone in Landhi who belongs to MQM is now frightened', as the rumours of a return of the Haqiqis in Landhi were doing the rounds. For this party worker and his comrades, the detention of a sector-in-charge by the Rangers signalled a major policy shift within the security establishment, which put their lives in danger. Such suspicions of state partiality have been fuelled by decades of unofficial partnerships between sections of the security apparatus and private enforcers operating in Karachi and elsewhere in the country. At this point, it is necessary to recall the peculiar trajectory of the Pakistani state as far as the relations between public and private enforcers are concerned.

The occult realm of state power

At the time of Partition, the rulers of Pakistan inherited from the British a repertoire of indirect rule that, in parallel with the formation of a regular, bureaucratic army,[28] had prolonged pre-colonial practices of warfare. This comes as a reminder that, in south Asia as elsewhere, the fallacious idea of a 'colonial legacy' often blinds us to the nonlinear provenance of modern repertoires of state power and in particular to the fructuous interactions between colonial rulers and the imperial powers that preceded them.[29] In order to quell insurgencies in the Punjab and later on in the North-West Frontier, the British subsidised tribal leaders (*khasadars*) and encouraged them to raise private armies to maintain 'law and order' in their zone of influence.[30] These militias bore strong similarities to auxiliary forces of the past, such as the 'half-troopers' of the Mughal period: matchlockmen and archers paid by the emperor but serving under the military aristocracy (*mansabdars*).[31] This recourse to private militias in the field of counter-insurgency was later extended to the diplomatic realm. From the 1920s onwards, the colonial state started enlisting tribal militias (*lashkars*) to influence the political game in neighbouring Afghanistan, a policy which enabled British colonial rulers to serve their interests while maintaining plausible deniability in the face of Afghan and Russian allegations of interference.[32] In 1924, the British provided covert support to some Pashtun tribes living on the Afghan side of the Durrand line to overthrow King Amanullah, whose social reforms and diplomacy were a matter of concern in London. Five years later, tribal *lashkars*, recruited among the Wazir, Mohmand, Mangal and Jadran tribes, were encouraged to overthrow the Tadjik 'bandit', Bacha-i-Saqao, who had succeeded Amanullah and proved unable to restore order in Afghanistan.[33]

As Ian Talbot has shown, the imprint of the 'British security state', which relied upon practices of indirect rule through local intermediaries (landlords, tribal chiefs and princes …), has been greater over Pakistani political and military elites than over their Indian counterparts.[34] I do not have the ambition to produce a history of this legacy here. Suffice it to say, for the purpose of my argument, that the devolution of violence that was consubstantial with the Afghan policy of the Raj from the 1920s onwards was rejuvenated—and perfected—by the civilian and military elites of Pakistan right after Partition. The colonial repertoire of 'frontier warfare', both in its open and covert dimensions, was 'passed on' to the indigenous leadership of the Pakistani army and put to good use right after Partition.[35] The first India-Pakistan war of 1947–1948—during which Pashtun *lashkars* invaded Jammu & Kashmir under the supervision of Pakistani military officers—was a case in point, and British officers serving in the nascent Pakistani army were suspected by Indian officers of having organised the 'base facilities' used by the invading tribesmen.[36] The secret war waged by Pakistan in Kashmir in the following decades and, later on, the proxy war waged in Afghanistan by Pakistan's military and civilian governments would only confirm the pervasiveness of this legacy.

Whereas this devolution of violence had initially been tested in the domestic field of counter-insurgency by the colonial state before expanding to covert diplomacy, it followed the opposite trajectory in Pakistan. In Karachi, the MQM was rumoured to have received the support of the Zia-ul-Haq regime at the time of its creation, whereas the rival Haqiqi faction was widely believed to be supported by the army and its intelligence agencies in the early 1990s. The return of the Haqiqis in army trucks, at the beginning of Operation Clean-up, confirmed these collusions between the most powerful public enforcer of the country and this newly emerged politico-military faction claiming its own share of Karachi. These unofficial partnerships between military agencies and certain factions operating in Karachi have been well documented in the local media and have given credibility to a conspiratorial representation of politics projecting the Pakistani state as 'both separated from society as well as capable of manipulating society totally'.[37] This occult cosmology is particularly significant among the workers and sympathisers of the MQM, who have been the prime targets of the army's 'operational conspiracies' in Karachi, that is, of its attempts to shape the political game through covert and often illegal means. As Daniel Hellinger suggests in his review of popular conspiracy theories in the United States, such operational conspiracies are integral to the functioning of intelligence agencies.[38] The repeated use of this repertoire of action and its occasional uncovering by investigative journalists or public commissions of enquiry give credence to conspiratorial representations of politics that extrapolate these open secrets to craft broader occult cosmologies, thus bringing the hidden realm of state power into the ambit of popular comprehension. Premised upon the conviction that 'there is more to power than meets the eye',[39] such conspiracy theories are also raw material for alternative forms of power and representation. When politics becomes a game of shadows, whose true nature is imperceptible in laymen's eyes, the need for seers arises. This is one explanation for Altaf Hussain's singular appeal over his followers. Within the MQM, the personality cult surrounding Altaf Hussain can be related, among other things,[40] to the extraordinary foresight that his followers attribute to him in anticipating the agencies' dirty tricks. This is what most of my respondents within the MQM's leadership as well as in its rank and file suggested when I questioned them on the rationales of the title of *Pir*, traditionally reserved to Sufi figures of authority, conferred by MQM followers to their leader. According to MQM leader Hyder Abbas Rizvi, this title was for the first time attributed to Altaf Hussain by a political worker, Sardar Ahmed (who would later join the rival Haqiqi faction), after the death of General Zia-ul-Haq in a plane crash in 1988. According to this worker, the conditions of Zia's death confirmed the prediction made by Altaf Hussain a few years earlier: 'One day, the Almighty will lay his vengeance upon this tyrant and he shall evaporate without leaving a trace' (*Allah ta'ala is jabir wa zalim par apna azab nazil karega aur voh ek din khak mein mil jaega aur logon ke pas uska nam wa nishan tak nahin rahega*, lit. 'One day, the Almighty will lay his vengeance upon this tyrant and oppressor and he will be found into the dust and people will not even remember his name and mark').[41] The belief in Altaf Hussain's foresight is indeed widespread among MQM party workers. In 2006, Abdullah,* a party worker based in Landhi, explained to me that Altaf was gifted with a 'knowledge of the unknown' (*ilm-e-ghaib*). This esoteric knowledge did not provide Altaf with an access to otherworldly realities, but with a supernatural political foresight that endowed the MQM with a unique strategic asset:

> It is not that Altaf *bhai* is an astrologist [*Altaf bhai ko ilm-e-najum nahin*]. Praise be to God, we are Muslims. We call 'insight' [*basarat*] the faculty to see through the eyes, and 'foresight' [*basirat*] the faculty to see through the soul. God Almighty has gifted Altaf *bhai* with such spiritual power [*ruhani itni taqat*] that he can guess the intentions of his friends and enemies. [...] He used to reveal to us the intentions of the agencies, of political leaders... Because of this spiritual foresight, the nation started calling him *Pir Sahib*. [...] In fact, in Urdu and Arabic, one calls 'knowledge of the unknown' [*ilm-e-ghaib*] this faculty to see what will happen in one moment, one hour, one day, one year. I do not know what stands behind this wall, this is the 'knowledge of the unknown'. But he who has 'foresight' can. God Almighty has given so much spiritual *power* to Altaf *bhai* that he can *define* the things which are yet to be. This is a God-gifted quality.

The Limits of Control

The spectacular and unabated rise in Karachi's body count since 2007 is the syndrome of far-reaching transformations in the city's increasingly complex ecology of violence. As we saw in detail in previous chapters, the predominance of the MQM, which endowed Karachi politics with some stability and predictability, is increasingly contested. These challenges to the MQM's hegemonic ambitions have come from various quarters and have taken different forms, from armed resistance to electoral disavowal. As the MQM was gradually losing its grip over the city's electoral and armed politics, it also saw its regulatory power over the unofficial economy being cut down to size (see the next chapter). Unlike what detractors of the MQM hope, though, this gradual—and still relative—'decline' of Karachi's predominant party will probably not lead to a pacification of the city. On the contrary, it carries the potential for further violence and disorder, threatening the tense equilibrium upon which the survival strategies of the city's population, as well as the sustainability of its otherwise highly resilient economy, were premised. It is however too early to predict a general disordering of Karachi's politics and economy. If, on the one hand, the cutting down to size of the MQM could nurture increasingly atomistic—but also increasingly lethal—forms of violence, the response of the state to the current reconfiguration of Karachi's ordered disorder remains uncertain. The recent evolutions of Karachi politics are an invitation to consider the current transformation of indirect rule in Pakistan at large, and the possibility of a shift from a politics of patronage to more distant and intermittent forms of arbitrage. On the other hand, the recent attempt of the Supreme Court to 'restore the writ of the state' in Karachi's 'no-go areas' suggests that there remains some scope for a reaffirmation of more direct forms of state power in the country's most troubled spots.

Post-Hegemonic Disorder: The Case of the Market of Protection

While the number of protagonists involved in the battles for Karachi never ceased to increase, the scope of their activities kept on widening, extending from mainstream politics to practices of wealth accumulation (through extortion and land grabbing, in particular). Even the PPP has recently joined the fray, by using the PAC as its own military wing, while getting involved in land grabbing.[42] The spreading of illicit activities across the political spectrum does not simply amount to a process of criminalisation of Karachi politics, which would translate into, in Charles Tilly's words, atomistic forms of 'opportunistic violence'. The rise in extortion is primarily the result of an economy of scale, as the presence of armed men within political or religious groups makes it possible to apply violence to one context (political strife) and then to another (economic accumulation) for a limited additional cost, a phenomenon witnessed in other situations of armed conflict such as that of Northern Ireland.[43] The motives behind land grabbing are more complex and cannot be reduced to the logics of economic gain, as *qabza* (capture) also applies to political projects. As a recent report in the *Herald* magazine suggested, 'Land also has a political role to play in a city as polarised as Karachi. Here land means housing, housing means inhabitants, and inhabitants mean potential votes.'[44] As we will see in detail in the next chapter, housing can also partake in the grand strategic designs of political parties, and in particular in their attempts to control the major entry and exit points to/from the city.

As a result of these developments, Karachi's protection rackets have become increasingly disordered in recent years, with an ever increasing number of racketeers—including bogus ones, posing as collectors for political, religious or criminal groups—competing with each other, unhindered by mechanisms of cartelisation.[45] Although it is difficult to estimate the sums collected by extortionists in the city, if only because most demands for *bhatta* remain unreported, police sources suggest that these payments could run into tens of millions of dollars annually, with 2013 all set to be a record year.[46]

Far from interfering in these protection rackets, the police themselves have systematised *bhatta*, especially at the lower level of the constables, preying on rickshaw, bus and taxi drivers, as well as on passers-by. The Pashtun owner of a beach resort in Hawke's Bay, who used to organise 'first class parties' for VIPs until a few years ago, explained to me how this voracity of the police had put him out of business, scaring his customers away. He tried to reason with local constables, by warning them against the non-sustainability of their racket, but to no avail:

> I told them, 'Eat the eggs, not the chick. If you eat the chick, where will you get your eggs from? If you took less money [from unmarried couples visiting the beaches of Hawke's Bay], people would continue to visit and I would still be able to pay my rent.'[47]

The deregulation of the market of protection has important consequences for Karachi-based traders and entrepreneurs, as it makes protection more expensive and yet less reliable, effectively turning it into a form of extortion. The competition over *bhatta* is also making extortion more violent, as demonstrated by the attack on Shershah scrap market in October 2010, in which fifteen traders were killed. Besides the growing involvement of Lyari's criminal groups in the game, the recent arrival of the Pakistani Taliban on the extortion scene has significantly contributed to the rise in violent incidents. Not only do the Taliban practice a more aggressive style of extortion (their demands for *bhatta* are carried through letters where the sum demanded is often accompanied by a bullet attached with Scotch tape); they are also notorious for carrying out their threats and killing recalcitrant businessmen, with a predilection for grenade attacks.

This problem is becoming increasingly acute, as competing offers of protection do not only emanate from rival political parties and religious groups but also from different officials within the same party: in matters of protection, 'unfair' competition often begins at home.[48] As a Karachi-based builder, who planned to shift his activities to Saudi Arabia, explained to me in December 2011:

- It has become impossible to do business in this city. I work in the construction sector and it's been two years that I cannot conduct any project. The single reason for this is extortion, which has reached unprecedented levels [*inteha par hai*]. I have to spend so much money just to ensure the feasibility of a given project. And *bhatta* has become so sophisticated: instead of being direct, it is now largely indirect. Let me give you an example. The last project I conducted involved the construction of a building to which I decided to add one more floor, which was not included in the original plan. In this case, the normal procedure consists in requesting permission from the relevant government office.... There, they told us, 'You won't get the permission but it's ok, you can go on with your project. We will just ask you to give us two million rupees.'
- Were they affiliated with any political party?
- Yes. [Lowering his voice.] They belonged to the MQM. This department is full of them and we had to pay them. Then we went to the local sector office [of the MQM], where the sector-in-charge told us, 'Yes, we will make your project feasible.' For such a 20 million rupees project, they would generally ask for 1 to 3 million rupees. Then, when the project was almost completed, the elder brother of [names a prominent political personality] submitted a petition against the project at the High Court, which argued that this was an

> illegal construction and that it should be demolished.... He told us that we had to give him three million rupees and that he would withdraw the petition. After much bargaining, he agreed to bring down this sum to 1.5 million rupees.... In order to save ourselves some trouble [*jan churane ke liye*], we gave the money, and within an hour, the petition was withdrawn [laughs]. I invested 20 million rupees in this building and all I earned from this operation was a big headache. After this, I put all my activities in Karachi on hold. Because in addition to this [the aforementioned practices of extortion], there are also people [party activists] who come to you asking for donations for x, y, z function, and the minimum contribution is 100,000 rupees... and such functions take place every week.

The same entrepreneur also made it clear that episodic outbursts of violence were less of a hurdle than the increasing cost of protection, as 'riots only last two to three days [and then recede]'. In other words, more than Karachi's endemic violence, it is the deregulation of its protection rackets which is currently threatening its economy, forcing leading local entrepreneurs to shift their activities to other parts of Pakistan (such as Lahore or Islamabad) or abroad (Dubai, Saudi Arabia, Bangladesh, and so on). It should however be emphasised that such delocalisations, particularly in the textile sector, are not new and are not always related to insecurity and extortion. Thus, the appeal of Bangladesh for textile industrialists is primarily related to the low cost of the workforce and the preferential access of Bangladeshi exports to European markets.[49]

The Transformation of the Patterns and Terrains of Violence

While the number of protagonists in Karachi's battles and the scope of their activities expanded, their violence mutated and spread to new areas. Following the armed clashes of 12 May 2007 between MQM and ANP gunmen, dead bodies stacked in gunny bags reappeared across the city. As in the past, these corpses would often be tied up and bear torture marks. More often than not—and this is a more recent trend—they would also be beheaded or castrated. In the most extreme cases, only torsos are found. These increasingly 'cruel methodologies', to use the terms of the CJP Iftikhar Muhammad Chaudhry,[50] seem to be the answer of Karachi's 'violent specialists' to the routinisation of violence in the city. As murder alone no longer catches the attention of the public, assassins and their political patrons have shifted to terror tactics to 'tip the scales', a trend also witnessed in Colombia in the late 1980s.[51] Target killers are thus paid more to mutilate their victims in a certain way to frighten the public.[52] These mutilations also make it more difficult for the police to identify the victims and trace down their killers.

The upgrading of the weaponry of the belligerents has also been contributing to the recent escalation of the city's turf wars. The episodes of collective violence witnessed during the summer of 2011 are a case in point: even by Karachi standards, these gun battles were of unprecedented intensity. In the worst affected localities, such as Qasba Colony and Banaras, those residents who were not chased away by armed fighters, looters and arsonists had to stay indoors for four consecutive days, deprived of electricity, food and water, only to escape through the holes they dug in the walls of their homes so as to find a safe passage to their neighbours. Two years later, Lyari's Kutchi residents resorted to the same exit strategy after they came under heavy fire from Baloch gunmen (see Chapter 4). The increasing ruthlessness of the city's armed fighters can also be gauged by the fact that even ambulances are now being targeted, while hospitals are being pressured to select patients on the basis of their ethnicity.[53] Hospitals have even become battlefields, where gunmen related to political parties or criminal gangs no longer hesitate to 'finish off' their wounded rivals after street battles.[54]

These transformations of the patterns of violence point to its increasingly indiscriminate nature, or more precisely at the deliberate targeting of civilian populations. Attacks against civilians were common during the early phases of Karachi's conflicts, as exemplified by the December 1986 massacres of Qasba and Aligarh colonies or by the aftermath of Hyderabad's Black Friday (30 September 1988), which saw MQM militants retaliate against the killing of dozens of Mohajirs by Sindhi nationalists, in turn opening fire randomly on Sindhi bystanders. The testimonies of MQM's target killers gathered by Nichola Khan, for their part, offer ample evidence of these militants' involvement in acts of blind terror against Pashtun civilians during the same period.[55] During the following decade, young Mohajir men were also exposed to the threat of extra-judicial killings on the part of security agencies, which at the time were battling it out with the MQM. From 1999 to 2007, though, the level of violence decreased considerably in the city and the residual violence was far more 'targeted' than it used to be, as it generally spared ordinary citizens and primarily affected party activists. The gun battles that erupted on 12 May 2007 between MQM and ANP militants brought an end to this lull and marked the beginning of a new sequence in Karachi's conflicts. In the following months, civilians bore the brunt of riotous episodes and armed clashes between rival parties.

Following the murder of Benazir Bhutto in Islamabad, on 27 December 2007, riots erupted across Sindh. In Karachi, the worst affected city in the province, forty-four people were killed, twenty banks were burned or looted and fifteen factories, ten petrol pumps and more than 1,000 vehicles were torched during three-day long disturbances.[56] The Karachi Chamber of Commerce and Industry estimated losses in Karachi and the rest of Sindh at $1.3 billion.[57] As the PPP's bastion in Karachi, Lyari was one of the worst affected localities in the city (besides Landhi). Local youths went on the rampage, attacking police stations and banks, torching cars, trucks and buses, looting shops, godowns and NGO offices. 'They destroyed everything and did not even leave one electric cable behind them,' recalls one of the persons in charge of Lyari's oldest NGO.[58] Five years later, when I visited the offices of this NGO, the damage caused by the riots could still be gauged by the blackened walls of the rooms set on fire by the rioters, which had not been renovated due to a lack of funds (many outside donors stopped funding this particular NGO after the riots, considering that it was no longer sustainable in Lyari's degraded security environment) and to the absence of any compensation whatsoever from public authorities. But Lyari and Landhi were not the only towns affected by this outbreak of violence, and numerous incidents of arson and looting were also reported in residential neighbourhoods such as Clifton.

If the gun battles of May 2007 and the riots of December 2007 terrified ordinary citizens and forced most of them to stay indoors for several consecutive days, deliberate attacks on civilians started increasing from 2008 onwards. In late November 2008, clashes between the MQM, the ANP and the respective populations they claim to represent caused around fifty deaths and led to the destruction of dozens of houses, shops and factories. From Banaras Chowk, these clashes spread across the city, from Orangi in the west to Landhi in the south-east. And if this violence initially targeted rival party activists, it rapidly extended to bystanders and daily labourers without any political affiliation. According to a reporter for the *Herald* magazine, who visited several hospitals across the city, hundreds of patients were admitted after being assaulted by armed men. Many of the victims, who included women and children, were badly mutilated, with numerous cases of ears and noses cut off.[59] The massive recourse to mutilations against civilians was unknown of in Karachi's history of violence and revealed a generalisation of violent rituals initially cantoned to inter-party rivalries. In recent years, the level of violence unleashed upon bystanders, local vendors and commuters—all these transient, vulnerable populations, unable to melt into the crowd despite being perpetually on the move—has only increased. This terror unleashed on the common man (*aam admi*) is both low-tech in nature and high-tech in its circuits of diffusion—the most gruesome acts of torture, killing and post-mortem mutilation, which are perpetrated with knives or blades, are sometimes filmed on cell phones[60] and these low-grade but highly suggestive snuff movies are later on used to intimidate the captives abducted by armed gangs. Some of these videos also end up circulating on the Internet, in view of spreading terror or outrage (depending on who posts them) among the general public. This war on civilians culminated in August 2011, when passers-by were abducted, tortured and killed, bus passengers were burned alive or offloaded to be executed on the spot on the basis of their ethnicity, while houses were shot at, bombed or torched. This time, however, the violence no longer concerned exclusively the MQM, the ANP and the respective ethnic groups they claim to represent. The PAC also played a major role in this round of violence, signalling the arrival of a new protagonist on Karachi's multiple battlegrounds, from the battle for space to the battle for votes and *bhatta*.

Another emerging trend in the city's conflicts is the multiplication of arson attacks against shops and homes—a possible indication of the escalation of the battle for real estate in Karachi. Following the attacks on Shia mourners of 28 December 2009, fires destroyed one of the city's largest wholesale markets on M.A. Jinnah Road, with some evidence pointing to the involvement of builders or real estate agents with political protections. In the meantime, violence expanded to areas that, until then, had remained relatively safe, such as the old vegetable market of Sabzi Mandi and several localities in the middle-class colony of Gulshan-e-Iqbal. Last but not least, new turf wars have begun, in which the MQM does not seem to be even remotely involved. In New Karachi, as we saw in the preceding chapter, it is two Sunni sectarian groups, the SSP and the ST, which confront each other. The Pashtun working-class settlements of District West and District East, for their part, have been the theatre of a bitter turf war between the ANP and the Pakistani Taliban between January 2012 and January 2013, which concluded with the eviction of the ANP from its former strongholds.

Few places illustrate this increasingly complex political landscape better than the *goth*s and *katchi abadi*s around Future Colony, in Landhi. Within a 1 sq. km. area, almost every armed faction active in Karachi maintains some visible presence. Future Colony itself has a majority of Pashtun and Hazarawal residents—most of them daily wagers or factory workers employed in the neighbouring Korangi industrial area. Until recently, the neighbourhood was dominated by the ANP but like elsewhere in Karachi, the party started losing ground in 2012, to the benefit of sectarian and jihadi groups. In February 2013, the office of the ANP was the target of a grenade attack, which local residents attributed to religious militants affiliated with the TTP (Future Colony is one of the strongholds of the Fazlullah faction in Karachi). According to these residents, the motive of the attack was not political but financial and followed the refusal of the local office-bearer of the party to pay *bhatta* to the Taliban. When I visited the locality in February 2013, there were no signs of the Taliban's presence (such as their notorious black flags) but the same could not be said of Sunni sectarian groups such as the SSP, which competed with the ANP for control of the colony's visual environment. Pro-SSP graffiti were ubiquitous and I came across a small roundabout where SSP activists had painted the inscription 'Jhangvi Chowk' (Jhangvi's roundabout, a reference to the controversial cleric who founded the SSP and would later inspire the anti-Shia terrorist group LeJ). The rising clout of the SSP in the neighbourhood found confirmation during the 2013 provincial election, when the MDM, of which the SSP was a component, registered its best score in Karachi in PS-128, which covers Future Colony and the neighbouring localities of Landhi II as well as the Pashtun-dominated settlements of Quaidabad. On the whole, electoral success eluded the sectarian parties which, for the first time, tried to make inroads into national and provincial elections in the city (this failure was even more blatant in the case of the Shia groups gathered in the Majlis Wahdatul Muslimeen). However, in PS-128, the candidate of the MDM, Aurangzeb Farooqi (who happens to be the leader of the Karachi chapter of the SSP and runs a madrasa located in the Old Muzaffarabad area of Landhi, the Amir Moavia/Masjid Ibrahim),[61] registered 23,625 votes and came a close second to the MQM's candidate, Waqar Hussain Shah, who won with 23,827 votes. This was another warning call for the MQM and, even more so, for the ANP, which in Landhi at least was literally wiped out by this emerging sectarian vote.

On the same side of Korangi Road, the next neighbourhood, known as Baloch Para, has a majority of Baloch residents. According to one of my respondents, who resides in a Christian *katchi abadi* of Landhi II, on the opposite side of Korangi Road, this neighbourhood fell under the control of the PAC around January 2013. Posters of Uzair Baloch and pro-PAC wall-chalking confirmed this. According to the same respondent, the PAC has also extended its influence to the Sindhi-dominated *goth* facing Future Colony, Ismail Goth, where the Sindhi nationalist group JSQM (Jiye Sindh Qaumi Mahaz, an offshoot of the Sindhi nationalist group JSM, which was launched in 1995) is also active. At the time of my visit, the situation was extremely tense around Ismail Goth and the street separating this urban village from the aforementioned Christian *katchi abadi* (which comes under the control of the MQM) had become the frontline of a new turf war between militants of the PAC and the JSQM on one side and of the MQM on the other. Bullet holes riddled the walls and local residents complained that they could not find sleep at night due to continuous firing from both sides. Clearly, the PAC no longer confined its activities to Lyari and was now firmly entrenched in Baloch and Sindhi-populated *goth*s across the city, from where its militants engaged in fierce turf wars against the MQM, with the support of Sindhi nationalists but also of Haqiqi militants, who were trying to reassert their authority over Landhi and Korangi. The situation of the ANP looked even more precarious as it did not seem to have the capacity to survive a siege from the Taliban and their sectarian allies. And once the party would be rooted out from the area as well as from the strategic neighbourhood of Quaidabad, on the other side of the National Highway, it would only be a matter of time before they would turn their guns against the MQM. A new battle for Landhi had just begun, reflecting the power struggles brewing in the city at large.

Contrasting Trends of State Intervention

As Karachi grows ever more fragmented, socially, politically and spatially, 'political' and 'criminal' violence—two categories that constantly overlap—take increasingly atomistic forms. More than ever, Karachi seems to be on the verge of a general implosion, as the struggle for the city disseminates into myriad battles for turf and rents. More than a descent into chaos, though, the current transformations of the city's increasingly complex ecology of violence should be seen as a re-configuration of its ordered disorder. The response of state agencies will be decisive in this regard. And for now, this response is far from consensual. As 'the' Pakistani state remains a multi-vocal conglomerate of institutions, different possible paths of state intervention are taking shape.

Towards a referee state?

In many areas of Karachi, from Lyari to the Pashtun-dominated localities that recently fell under the control of the Taliban, the presence of public enforcers seems to have been reduced to a nominal one, with private enforcers now providing security, settling disputes and allocating resources (land, water, jobs,...). The understaffed[62] and poorly equipped police force, in particular, seems to have been outrun by unofficial 'protectors'. The most powerful land suppliers, for instance, provide their clients with a protection against police interference. Thus, the residents of Muhammad Khan Colony, which is spread over 2,500 acres in Baldia and Gadap Town, were instructed by the land supplier who gave his name to the colony (see the next chapter) that, 'if the police come to ask for bribes or trouble you then just tie them and call me, I will take care of them'.[63] This apparent containment of the state by an increasingly militarised society does not reveal the full picture, though. As weak as it may seem, Karachi's police force continues to play a key role in the regulation of the economy, legal and otherwise. In fact, the more violent and disorderly the economy gets, the more crucial police protection becomes. As Arif Hasan and Mansoor Raza emphasise, real estate transactions have become increasingly risky in Karachi with the rising scale of litigation in courts, the increasing competition between powerful interest groups with an easy access to firearms and the absence of coordination between myriad land-owning agencies—a problem which became even more acute as new regulatory powers over land use and acquisition were transferred to local authorities by the 2001 devolution plan. In this context, the only way for developers to reduce uncertainty and gain the upper hand over their rivals is to have the police on their side. The frequent disputes between builders, real estate agents and buyers during land transactions are also settled by 'power': cash, connections to persons of influence and 'the possibility of using the police for pressurising each other or simply killing the opponent and as such making an example of him.'[64] In other words, what the various protagonists of the real estate market buy from the police, through payments in cash or kind (plots, apartments,...), is their arbitrage in the conflicts that are bound to emerge between the various corporate interests involved in these transactions. The real estate market is not an isolated case in this regard, and this power of arbitration between militarised interest groups has become the defining attribute of state agencies in Karachi. What seems to be at stake, here, is the self-confining of state agencies to the role of a non-neutral referee. No more, but certainly no less.

A similar evolution towards the referee state can be observed in the response of other state institutions to the consolidation of non-state public authorities in Karachi. The army, in particular, seems to have shifted from a politics of close-contact patronage, exemplified by its promotion of the Haqiqis in the early 1990s and by its alliance with the MQM (Altaf) under Pervez Musharraf's rule (2002–2008), to more distant forms of arbitration. The army's refereeing is still far from neutral, though, and it continues to take sides in these conflicts, as its covert support for Uzair Baloch's group suggests. The same could be said for civilian elites, and for the PPP leadership in particular. The open patronage of the PAC by Zulfikar Mirza was only momentary. The conflict that this policy ignited with the MQM led to Mirza's sacking, to the ban on the PAC and to the police intervention of April 2012, following which the relations between the PAC and the PPP leadership were revived but in a more discrete mode. This shift found confirmation in the response of the newly elected PPP government to the violence unleashed upon Lyari's Kutchi community in the summer of 2013. As the PAC leadership was accused by a section of the media and the leaders of the KRC of orchestrating coordinated attacks on the Kutchi minority, the provincial government set up a commission that concluded on the involvement of 'outside militant groups with political backing' (read MQM) in the recent flare-up of violence.[65] Instead of ordering 'law and order forces' to set up permanent check-posts in the affected areas of Lyari, as the KRC leaders demanded, the PPP leadership chose to limit its role to that of a distant, though blatantly biased, mediator.

This increasingly distant mode of government leaves a significant degree of autonomy to private enforcers in their everyday operations.

However, as the erratic relations between the PPP leadership and Lyari's *dacoits* demonstrate, this does not preclude the possibility of state-impulsed renegotiations of the contract, through targeted police or (para-)military operations for instance. Rather than as a retreat of the state, this form of governmentality should be thought of in terms of influx and reflux of state power in the face of private enforcers encroaching on state sovereignty without necessarily challenging it—and in fact, more often than not, claiming it for themselves. In this increasingly complex configuration, state agencies are no longer the organisers of the world—supposing they ever claimed that role, which, in Pakistan at least, is highly debatable. They cannot even claim to be a patron ensuring the loyalty of his protégés through more or less formal ties of allegiance, frequently reactualised through face-to-face interactions. The distant government that is emerging here amounts, instead, to a form of arbitrage, by certain arms of the state (the army and its intelligence agencies, the ruling parties,...), of the competitive relations between the holders of 'illegitimate' violence.

The short arm of the law?

The emerging forms of indirect or distant rule roughly sketched above are not the only horizons of state intervention in Pakistan. In the opposite direction, the recent attempts by the judiciary to pull Karachi back from the brink provide the ground for an interrogation on the possibilities of a reassertion of direct rule in the city and in Pakistan at large. Since his nomination as the head of the Supreme Court, the CJP Iftikhar Muhammad Chaudhry has been struggling against the military and, after the elections of 2008, against civilian elites, to reaffirm the autonomy of the judiciary. His judicial activism set him on a collision course with Pervez Musharraf—who suspended him in 2007, before reinstating him a year later, after an unprecedented mobilisation of Pakistan's lawyers—and, between 2008 and 2013, with the PPP-led coalition government. The CJP's weapon of predilection, in this war of position, has been the *suo motu*, whereby the Court opened investigations on a particular issue on its own initiative. It is through this procedure that the CJP tried to reassert the rule of law in Karachi, at a time when political, criminal and sectarian violence was fast escalating. In August 2011, the CJP took notice of the fast deteriorating 'law and order situation' in the city and commissioned a full enquiry about those responsible for the spiralling violence. In order to fully understand the motives of the CJP, it is necessary to rewind and go back to the events of 12 May 2007. By then, the lawyers' movement demanding the restoration of the CJP was in full swing—at least in the Punjab, since Karachi was under the tight control of the MQM, which at the time was a key ally of the military-backed regime of Pervez Musharraf and which was commissioned to contain the spread of the lawyers' movement in its stronghold. Although he was well aware that his move would be resisted by the MQM, the CJP landed in Karachi in the early hours of 12 May 2007. As expected, the MQM used all its power to prevent the magistrate from reaching the city, by blocking all its major access points and deploying its armed fighters at strategic locations. What was unexpected, though, was the resistance of the ANP, whose armed activists confronted the MQM's, transforming several parts of the city into a virtual warzone. As we already saw, these gun battles were the opening act of a bitter conflict between the two parties. This episode also reinforced the CJP's hostility towards the MQM, which would inform all his later moves while addressing Karachi's situation. The CJP's own commitment to 'restore the writ of the state' in Karachi would thus overlap with a more personal dispute, fuelled by a desire to downsize Karachi's predominant party.

Between 2011 and 2013, the Supreme Court made repeated attempts to restore 'law and order' in the city by substituting itself to what its judges identified as a defaulting if not complicit government. The first round of this protracted conflict started with the publication of a vitriolic judgment on the situation in Karachi (October 2011), which unambiguously singled out political parties—and the MQM in particular—as the main culprits of Karachi's deteriorating law and order situation. On this occasion, the Apex Court ordered the police and Rangers to 'restore the writ of the state' in the city within a year. In October 2012, the Supreme Court took up the case once again to assess the progress made in this direction. The implementation of its order was transferred to a five-member bench acting under the Karachi registry of the Supreme Court and headed by the CJP himself. This bench resumed its proceedings in November 2012, with the Apex Court once again ordering the police to move in against well-known criminals and militants. The CJP and his entourage were increasingly concerned with Karachi's spiralling violence, and more specifically with the growing presence of the Pakistani Taliban in the city.

However, the Court's orders remained unanswered and the police operation that the CJP was calling for never happened. With the dissolution of Parliament and the installation of a non-partisan caretaker government, in March 2013, a new window of opportunity opened for these activist judges, though. On this occasion, the Court ordered all security forces deployed in Karachi—including the Rangers—to move into the city's 'no-go areas' and reassert the authority of the state against the gangsters, religious militants and armed political activists who had allegedly taken the law into their own hands. For the first time, Karachi's police authorities reluctantly admitted the existence of 'partially no-go zones' for law and order forces. This admission and the reports submitted by police authorities on the actions taken to 'clear' these so-called 'no-go areas' failed to satisfy the Supreme Court, though, and the judges raised doubts about the reports submitted by the police and the Rangers, unequivocally accusing them of blatant failure in restoring law and order in the city, even threatening them to 'call honest officers from other provinces' to complete the task. The critiques of the Supreme Court did not stop with the police and extended to the Rangers. In the aftermath of the Abbas Town bombings of March 2013—which targeted the apartment complexes of a Shia-dominated locality in Gulshan-e-Iqbal, killing forty-five of their residents—the Supreme Court accused the paramilitary force of incompetency and threatened the director general of the Rangers in Sindh, Major-General Rizwan Akhtar, to 'take action against him for failure in discharging of duties and exercising powers under the law', if he did not comply with a court order assigning his force the task to 'clean the city' at the earliest.

For the Supreme Court judges, the reason for this failure is the 'politicisation' of the security forces, which has made the law and order forces subservient to political parties, thus eroding the confidence of the public. These accusations are compatible with the particular brand of judicial activism promoted by the Court since 2006, which aimed at rescuing the state from politicians, or to reassert the more sublime dimensions of the state by immunising it against the impure realm of politics. In contemporary Pakistan, this commitment to restore the myth of the state is not specific to the Supreme Court[66] and the recent movement of former televangelist Tahir-ul-Qadri similarly made a claim to rescue the state from politics (the major slogan of the movement, '*siyasat nahin, riyasat bachao*', literally translated as 'Save the state, not politics!'). Ironically, this movement—which promoted a brand of populist justice similar to that pursued by the activist judges of the Supreme Court[67]—was quashed by a court order from the very same judges eulogised by Qadri. Questioning Qadri's loyalty to Pakistan by virtue of his Canadian citizenship and allegiance to 'the Queen of England', the CJP and his entourage sent him packing after two weeks of intense mobilisation in Islamabad.

To date, the results of this judicial offensive remain mitigated. Following an order of the Supreme Court, the police and Rangers conducted several raids across Karachi in April 2013, during which they arrested hundreds of party activists and alleged criminals, including some target killers. However, most of these men were booked under minor charges and subsequently released on bail. Two alleged target killers, who confessed respectively to 115 and 47 murders, were thus let loose after their FIRs only charged them for taking part in an armed encounter with the police and possession of illegal weapons. This infuriated the Supreme Court, whose judges ordered the police to re-arrest the two men and charge them with more serious offences. On this occasion, the CJP and his colleagues directed once again the security forces to clear all no-go areas in the city, to which the Inspector General of Police (IGP) Sindh, Shahid Nadeem Baloch, replied that it would be impossible to ensure the sustainability of these actions, as criminals could return in the future. Other police officers also admitted that all it took to set arrested criminals free was a phone call from their powerful patrons. While the commanding officers of the Rangers resisted better the pressure (probably because of their affiliation with the army), police officers started showing obvious signs of nervousness from March 2013 onwards. At this point, some of them decided to let it all hang out. On 21 March, the acting IGP Sindh, Ghulam Shabbir Shaikh, handed over a list of 224 suspects involved in 'target killings' and other serious crimes—with their political affiliations. The message to the judges was crystal clear: stop using the police as a scapegoat and move against the real culprits if you dare. The next hearings of the 'Karachi violence case' suggested that the judges were not yet willing to move against the political patrons of the city's criminals. Instead of treating the problem as a political issue—in conformity with its own diagnosis of October 2011—the Court retracted to a reading of the situation in terms of 'law and order'. As of July 2013, the most significant outcome of this *suo motu* procedure was the adoption of a working definition of a no-go area as a locality 'where the Rangers need to send a battalion of at least 200 personnel to step into the area'.[68] Ghulam Shabbir Shaikh, for his part, was retired at the end of April. Although this retirement was imminent, this police officer (who had orchestrated the arrest of the two main leaders of the LeJ in Sindh) had become an embarrassment to his corrupt colleagues because of his moral probity after he prepared a list of 400 police officers who had benefited from out-of-turn promotions or were involved in serious crimes.

Conclusion

The unprecedented escalation of homicidal violence witnessed in Karachi since 2007 is the outcome of far-reaching transformations in the city's ordered disorder. The checks and balances moderating the violence of this peculiar configuration have been uprooted over the past few years: the predominance of the MQM has been increasingly challenged through the urns and through the arms, while state interventions are more ambivalent, if not contradictory, than ever. The dissemination of public authority, the militarisation of society and the deregulation of the market of protection have only increased in the process, three overlapping dynamics that, in each in its own right, carries a potential for high levels of violence. Although it seems to be moving in this direction, Karachi—and Pakistan at large—has not yet reached the stage of what Achille Mbembe, in African contexts, refers to as 'private indirect government'.[69] If the informalisation of state power and the proliferation of public authorities point in this direction, there remains some scope for a reassertion of direct rule and the more 'sublime' dimensions of state power, through the dispensation of justice in particular. However limited its results for now, in the context of Karachi at least, the recent reassertion of the judiciary in Pakistani politics confirms that for all its violence and instability, Pakistan is anything but a lawless society. On the contrary, the realm of the law has become one of its major battlefields over the past few years and the culture of legality has come to saturate even its most unlawful enterprises, which counterfeit sovereignty by enforcing their own brand of 'popular' justice. The more disorderly Pakistan gets, that is, the more atomised its patterns of domination become, the more scope there seems to be for unofficial public authorities and idiosyncratic legalities. Here, as in many other seemingly disordered societies, 'politics is migrating to the courts',[70] be they formal tribunals promising to deliver a new brand of populist justice or kangaroo courts restoring the local order of things in the name of custom or religion. Sadly, this judiciarisation of social struggles and economic conflicts does not preclude ever increasing levels of violence and insecurity. The proliferation of the legal is no guarantee against the propagation of the lethal.

7

GEOGRAPHIES OF FEAR

Aisi shiddat hai ab ke mausam mein
Bach ke jaen to kis taraf jaen
Ag se maut dhalta suraj
Akhri saeban mein utra hai
Khauf is shehr be nahayat ki
Har gali, har makan mein utra hai

These are really hard times.
Where shall we flee?
There is no longer any refuge
from the deadly fire of the sun.
In this endless city, fear
has descended upon every alley, every home.

Harris Khalique, 'Karāchī Merā Shehr',
My City Karachi, 2006.[1]

The escalation and proliferation of violence witnessed in Karachi since the mid-1980s has instilled a climate of pervasive fear that permeates everyday life, lurking under the surface of an apparent normality. While projecting even the most banal experiences of the city into the realm of the uncanny, this chronic state of fear disrupts the relations between and within ethnic groups (*qaums*), which owe most of their political relevance to violent conflict. It also silences internal opposition and reinforces the walling-in of ethnic groups within citadels protected and governed by political parties or their versatile proxies. This ethnic partitioning of urban space is supplemented by a new division of the city between its high-security zones and its 'tension-prone areas', a division that only reinforces pre-existing dynamics of socio-spatial segregation. In Karachi, the fast increasing gap between the haves and the have-nots can also be measured by the uneven distribution of resources for the management of fear in everyday life.

Fear as a chronic condition is experienced differently across the social divide and the social and spatial contours of perceived threats are at great variance from one group to another. It is to these geographies of fear that I turn now, drawing most of my material from interviews and conversations with present or former residents of Lyari, most of which were recorded in August 2012, a few months after a massive police operation targeted the leaders of the PAC, failing to achieve its goal but costing the lives of dozens of civilians in the process. This focus on Lyari—one of the localities of Karachi currently inspiring the greatest fear among those who do not reside there—will help us to understand that Karachi's geographies of fear are irreducible to a media-induced stigmatisation of certain localities as 'no-go areas', or to a moral panic among the barricaded city elites. Which is not to say that everyone has the same urban nightmares.

By 'geographies of fear', I do not merely refer to socio-spatial representations of danger, but also to 'spatial formations of violence':[2] territorial formations and circulatory systems informed by these representations. It is primarily through this angle—the provision of security to frightened citizens, within and across a fragmented city—that I consider here the larger questions of urban governance, segregation and land grabbing (*qabza*). Throughout this chapter, I try to expand Linda Green's argument on the 'socialization to terror' in the context of Guatemala. As Green points out on the basis of her ethnography of Mayan widows, 'terror's effects are not only psychological and individual but social and collective as well'.[3] 'Fear as a way of life' also has important socio-spatial repercussions. In a context possibly more relevant to our case study, Loïc Wacquant shows how, in Afro-American 'hyperghettos' such as Chicago's Southside, 'acute physical danger floods everyday life and creates an oppressive climate of terror that has caused the near complete disappearance of public space'.[4] In Karachi, though, less than on public space per se (which resisted better, especially in lower-income neighbourhoods), this state of fear wrought havoc on pluralistic urban living, that is, on the coexistence of populations of various ethnic or sectarian backgrounds. Karachi's ordered disorder has its own territoriality and the following pages are an exploration of the multifarious ways residents, urban planners, land developers and political parties are rethinking and reshaping their city in the face of endemic violence.

City of Fear

Malformations of Violence

Karachiites often claim to have learned to cope with violence, to such an extent that they would have become immune to it. As a fifty-five-year-old Urdu-speaking bookseller at Burns Road's Urdu Bazaar told me in December 2011, a few months after Karachi witnessed its worst episode of political warfare since the mid-1990s, 'Today, so many people are dying that [whenever someone is killed], we are less affected than if a flea was creeping over our ear' (*Ab itne log mar jate hain, to logon ke kan par jun tak nahin ringti*). However common such assertions may be, it is doubtful that the populations of Karachi have become a fearless and heartless lot. Nor are they more 'resilient' than other populations affected by armed conflict. They have simply adjusted their everyday life, as best as they could, to the virtual or actual threat of political, ethnic and criminal violence. Rather than coping *with* crisis, they have learned to cope *in* crisis.[5] Their 'bystander tactics'[6] are only 'tactics' in the sense of Michel de Certeau[7] because they operate *within* a system of domination characterised by a high salience of violence. This 'art of survival', as a local journalist recently described it,[8] encompasses routines of representation and routines of action that were gradually internalised by Karachiites, the fastest learners being, as always, children. In his gripping account of the December 1986 massacres of Qasba and Aligarh colonies and their echo across the rest of the city, which I have already quoted extensively (see Chapter 1), the writer and critic Asif Farrukhi recalls how his young daughter reacted, in his absence, to her first experience of a gun fight at close range:

> On my way back from the office, I peeped into the room of my children. I noticed that the shelves where Anusha was keeping her dolls and stuffed toys had been emptied. I was surprised and the first thought that came to my mind was that there had been a burglary. The toys which my children kept with so much care

had vanished! Panicking, I made some noise. Anusha came to me laughing. 'I hid the dolls, so that they wouldn't be hit by a bullet.'[9]

To amount to a form of social navigation, such coping in crisis demands some predictability in the patterns, timing and locales of recurring episodes of violence. This is undoubtedly the case in Karachi, where the major tension spots of the city (Banaras Chowk, Qasba Colony, Orangi, Sohrab Goth, the Teen Hatti bridge to Liaquatabad, etc.) have shown a remarkable continuity since the mid-1980s, while certain public events (religious festivals, strikes, days of mourning for 'martyred' political or religious leaders, etc.) are collectively identified as life-threatening, inciting people to stay indoors. The routinisation of violence, in Karachi as in other societies confronted by situations of chronic civil strife, should not be mistaken for a 'habituation' of conflict by its populations. As Henrik Vigh emphasises in his study of soldiering in Guinea-Bissau, situations of prolonged political turmoil see the disappearance of habits and their replacement by more flexible routines that 'rather than being imponderable sets of actions and interpretation, are constantly evaluated and related to new movements of the socio-political environment'.[10] In the most violence-prone localities of Karachi, the management of 'ordinary' violence by local residents is challenged by the continuous transformation of this violence in the course of the conflict. Here lies the source of the Karachiites' enduring sense of fear: violence will always transform faster than their attempts to cope with it.

More than the frequency of violent occurrences, what has been upsetting the residents of Karachi over the past few years is the blurring of the categories of violent events, that is, their increasingly indiscriminate morphology—'malformations of violence', so to speak. Schematically, three different types of collective violence could be distinguished until recently. Ethnic and sectarian 'riots' (*hangamas*) were the most encompassing form of collective violence: anyone singled out as a member of a rival group on the basis of his phenotypical features, sartorial style and even haircut[11] could become a target. However, these incidents remained limited in time and space: they would generally flare up on specific occasions at well-identified places (particularly at the interface between ethnically differentiated neighbourhoods), before expanding around this epicentre, only to recede after a few days of disturbances and the deployment of security forces in disturbed areas. The most exposed to these episodes of collective violence were daily labourers, itinerant merchants and the homeless, who could not take shelter from the violence unleashed by rioters and militants acting under the cover of the 'riotous crowds'. Political violence, for its part, was more targeted, singling out party activists while sparing 'apolitical people' (*ghair tanzim log*, lit. 'people without [any affiliation to] an organisation'). Although bystanders could always fall prey to a stray bullet during a 'clash' (*tasadum*) between rival groups, the gradual professionalisation of target killers limited collateral damages. The most unpredictable form of violence—and thus the most dangerous for civilians—was criminal violence, which took the shape of 'gang wars' between rival groups (with a high potential for collateral damages among bystanders) and, more rarely but with even more dramatic consequences for the general public, of coordinated attacks against civilian populations (such as in Qasba and Aligarh colonies in December 1986).

Until recently, the quasi-institutionalisation of these forms of violence made them amenable to safety routines containing the level of the threat for those in the know and with the resources to take shelter, at the right time, from public disturbances. This is no longer the case. First of all, the upgrading of the belligerents' weaponry has increased the risks of collateral damage even during targeted attacks. As a young Pashtun who grew up in Gul Muhammad Lane told me in August 2012, '[The gang war of the 2000s] was not such a big deal. Living in Lyari, I'm used to these things. When incidents of firing happened, it was ok [firing *agar ho gai, to bas thik hai*]... it was just everyday matter.' This situation changed in recent years, though. The same respondent thus recalls how RPGs started replacing Kalashnikovs, with devastating consequences for bystanders:

> I remember that near my house... last year [2011]... a clash happened between them [rival gangs]. There was this man, Akram Baloch [a gangster affiliated with Rehman Dakait's group, who disputed to Uzair Baloch the leadership of the PAC after the death of the former], who lived near my house... He was in charge of the security at Bilawal House... He used to live in the same *gali* where my house was located. When clashes took place [with the PAC], they [the assailants] would climb on the 5th or 6th floor of a nearby apartment building and shoot rockets [rocket-propelled grenades] from there. Sometimes, some of these rockets went astray [*kahin bhi gir jata tha*]. Once, a rocket hit a PMT [electric transformer] and the whole area was plunged into darkness for almost 10 days. People of the KESC would not come because the situation was so bad. They [the assailants] did not know how to use these rocket-launchers with precision [Precise *unka koi nahin tha ki kaise marun*]. Once, they hit someone's house and three people were killed.[12]

This young Pashtun and his family were relatively 'lucky', in that they owned the apartment they lived in and managed to sell it in 2011—though for well below its market value—before moving to a much safer and upscale locality. Other, less fortunate residents of Lyari do not have the luxury to exercise such exit options, though, and are constrained to survive in an increasingly dangerous environment.

Besides these technological transformations of Karachi's conflicts—which affect all forms of collective violence, particularly criminal and political rivalries—one should factor in the increasingly indiscriminate nature of this violence, and the deliberate targeting of civilians in order to spread terror and outrage among rival groups (see Chapter 6). According to Mujahid,* a middle-aged, lower-income Mohajir who used to live in Liaquatabad and was a witness to some of the worst episodes of fighting between the MQM, the Haqiqis and security agencies in the course of the 1990s:

> If you were neutral… I mean, if you didn't have any relation with a political party… It was not as difficult [as it is now]. Today, linguistic prejudice [*zuban ka t'asub*] prevails… So much so that we cannot venture into non-Urdu speaking areas, such as in Pashto-speaking or Baloch-speaking areas. In those days [the 1990s], it was not difficult but today it is. […] It has become very difficult to venture into some localities of Karachi. For instance, in Liaquatabad, there is a road starting at the old vegetable market, heading towards Hasan Square. On the way, there is a Pashtun locality where the situation often gets bad. Firing can erupt at any time, passers-by [*rahgir*] get abducted and beaten up… It's been like that for the last three years or so… So it is very dangerous… Before that, they would not grab passers-by and beat them… Back in the days, the violence was more targeted. They would say 'This guy is with the MQM, take him out.' Then they would take him away and maybe send him to some [torture] cell. […] But today it is very dangerous for the common man, and if people have to come back from work at night, they will ensure that they don't have to cross through a Baloch or Pashtun neighbourhood.[13]

This sentiment of vulnerability to ethnic violence is not limited to Urdu-speaking Mohajirs bearing the brunt of an ethnic backlash spearheaded by Pashtun and Baloch political groups (the ANP and the PAC, respectively). The same feeling of insecurity can be detected, for instance, among the younger Baloch of Lyari. As one of them, a social worker affiliated with one of Lyari's oldest NGOs, told me in August 2012, 'I'm really reluctant to go out [of Lyari]' (*Mera dil jane ka karta hi nahin*, lit.

'My heart does not desire to go out'). He referred to a particular incident, which took place shortly before Eid-ul-Fitr 2011, to explain this fear of the 'outside'. Six Baloch youngsters from Lyari were kidnapped, most probably by MQM activists, while shopping at Zainab Market, a popular commercial area of Saddar, located a few kilometres away from Lyari. The following day, their mutilated bodies were found in gunny bags in the middle-class and primarily Urdu-speaking locality of PECHS,[14] a fate which used to be reserved for political activists but to which the 'neutral people' referred to by Mujahid above are no longer immune. These changes in the rules of armed conflict are a major source of anxiety for those residing or working in the most volatile areas of the city, as they disturb individual and collective attempts at managing violence in everyday life through idiosyncratic evasive tactics or collective, community-based procedures of containment (see infra).

In such a context, it does not take much more than a wrong turn to expose oneself to life-threatening risks, or so it seems. This is exemplified by the following online chat I had in November 2012 with a party worker of the MQM based in District East:

- Just today i was lucky to be alive when I entered in a Baloch PAC area in Malir accidently.
- What happened?
- I have seen posters and banners of Uzair Baloch and ppl where staring at us strange my God those moments.
- What were you doing there?
- My friend's dad died today and we were going to the cold storage or morgue today in Malir. I just lost my way due to an ISO [Imamia Students Organisation; a Shia student group] rally at Malir and accidently we entered into that area all of them were baloch ppl [...] i was lucky that today was friday and most of the ppl were out to offer prayers.
- Did people look hostile?
- Yes but we were 4 ppl on 2 motor bikes and wearing pent shirts looking like muhajirs we were lucky no one tried to stop us there.

To make matters worse, it is not merely 'by mistake'—that is, by tampering unintentionally with everyday safety routines—that the residents of Karachi's most volatile localities expose themselves to life-threatening situations. Such safety routines can also become a liability when episodes of collective violence no longer conform to the patterns one thought to be well-established. This is what Nadim,* a middle-aged Pashtun minibus driver working in the city's largest vegetable market and living in the strife-torn locality of Kati Pahari, explained to me in December 2011. On 5 July 2011, Nadim was coming back home after a long day at work. On his own admission, the situation had been 'pretty bad' for the past four days but it seemed that the violence between ANP and MQM militants in Kati Pahari was receding, making it safe to venture out. However, while he was approaching his home, Nadim came across a group of masked young men who started beating him up and might have killed him if a police mobile had not miraculously turned up, chasing the assailants away. Nadim had misread the situation and its potential danger, a mistake that could have proved fatal and that he explains by the discrepancy between this round of violence and the usual patterns of political warfare in his locality:

> I was coming from work. The situation was still a little bit bad [*thora thora halat kharab chal raha tha*] but we never thought that it would get that bad. [...] We live in a place where... if anything happens, we stay indoors and see how things turn out [*agar koi masla hua to yahan baithe baithe dekhi jaegi*].

The Hermeneutic of Danger and its Blind Alleys

The looming threat of political, ethnic, criminal and increasingly sectarian violence, as well as its actualisation through quasi-ritualised violent performances, has imbued Karachiites with an acute sensitivity to their surroundings. This sensitivity amounts to a hermeneutic of urban life, interpreting the city's social text through the decryption of signs, clues, rumours and moods, always fluid and uncertain, and thus prone to misinterpretations. This perspective on urban life is first and foremost a hermeneutic of *danger*, which consists of reading the 'environment' (*faza*) and anticipating potentially life-threatening 'situations' (*halat*). As such, it is a tool of social navigation on a volatile terrain: it does not only interpret the city but informs actual practices, and in particular certain ways of moving safely *across* the city. Far from being specific to the residents of Karachi, this ability to divine a frightening city seems to be shared by all city-dwellers exposed to situations of protracted armed conflict. In the strife-torn Indonesian town of Ambon, which was the theatre of large-scale communal violence between Muslims and Christians between 1999 and 2002, Patricia Spyer observed a similar development. There as well, the climate of fear permeating everyday life led to the emergence of what Spyer refers to as a 'hyperhermeneutic': 'a compulsive need to interpret and mine just about everything for hidden meaning, to see any trivial occurrence as a sign or omen of what might come'.[15]

As Linda Green points out, one can never be permanently on alert and 'fear as a way of life' involves a succession of emotional climaxes and anti-climaxes, followed by longer periods of apparent tranquility.[16] In its most banal, everyday forms, this hermeneutic of danger is illustrated by the taxi driver precipitously closing the doors and windows of his car after entering a zone of lesser population density, or by the friend driving you back home after a dinner party and suddenly stopping the car, taking the time to clarify whether the traffic jam further down the road is indeed a traffic jam or the beginning of a 'power riot'. During episodes of collective violence or right after, the level of alertness is at its highest, and imagination is running wild. This is, for instance, how a friend teaching at KU recalled his experience of the violent events of July and August 2011:

> Since 1995, it was the first time where I went out, with my family, and even if a motorcycle was coming from behind, I was just, you know... scared. Literally, I was scared. You know, I'm married now and have to provide for my family so it matters now... And there were random incidents, you know. People sitting and people coming, shooting them... Mohajirs killing Pashtuns, Pashtuns killing Mohajirs. You just didn't know and the city went completely dark. Then Ramzan came and people started saying 'It's Ramzan, nothing will happen'. [...] But damn, they slaughtered each other during the month of Ramzan. 250 people died, for nothing. This has contributed to make people more... Well, they were always scared anyway, but this has made them more weary about this violent activity.

The eruption of actual situations of violence is not, per se, a cause of alarm for these 'weary' Karachiites, and risk assessments continue long after firing has started, focusing on the potential of violent escalation. My sole first-hand experience of such a violent situation—during a visit to the Markaz Ahl-e-Sunnat (the headquarters of the ST, which is located in Saddar Town, near the Civil Hospital)—was particularly revealing in this regard. When the sound of gunshots resonated from the street below, the first reaction of the journalist friend accompanying me was to make a guess on the type of gun that had fired them. He opted for a TT pistol, the favourite weapon of MQM militants. Meanwhile, Shahid Ghauri, the ST leader whom we had come to interview, seemed much more preoccupied. He picked up the phone and started making calls to identify the origins of the shooting and thus assess the level of the threat. A few months earlier, the entire leadership of the ST had been decimated in a bomb blast in Nishtar Park and Ghauri had reason to be worried, as his organisation had made numerous enemies, from the MQM to the SSP to the jihadis. The more he spoke on the phone, the more preoccupied he looked, and the tension in the room escalated. When he finally hung up, it was to announce that the gunshots had been fired by policemen from the local *thana*, whose SHO (officer-in-charge) was known to be aligned with the MQM. There was no retaliation from the ST's strongmen, who had suddenly gathered around their leader, and the tension gradually died down. Ghauri agreed to continue the interview, concluding that this was, after all, nothing more than a banal act of intimidation with little potential for escalation.

While Karachiites cling to their experience of past violent events to navigate safely across their volatile city, the increasingly indiscriminate nature of ethnic, political, criminal and sectarian violence, as well as its growing unpredictability, compromise these routines of action and interpretation. As one of my respondents complained, the common (wo)man can no longer 'breathe freely' in her own city. In this context, the 'evasive tactics'[17] used by parents to keep their children at bay from the dangerous world of party politics or by the residents of localities dominated by another community than their own to avoid raising the attention of the dominant party tend to become obsolete. This sense of increasing vulnerability to collective violence nurtures a deeper urban malaise. For its fearful residents, the city has become undecipherable. As Naveeda, the Kutchi social worker whom we encountered earlier, told me in August 2012, 'Such a strange environment has developed in our city that it seems to have become a foreign land' (*Ajib tarah ki faza hamare shehr mein ho rahi hai ki hamko apna shehr ajnabi lagne laga hai*).

The growing uncertainty surrounding extraordinary disturbances (bombings, large-scale arson or firing attacks,...), as well as more 'banal' violent incidents (targeted killings, abductions, extortion,...), only adds up to this malaise. As every group in the city denies involvement in violent or illegal activities, the identity of the perpetrators and their rationales are anybody's guess. This opacity sustains a form of 'epistemological uncertainty'—a doubt about what one knows about one's social relations and environment—that obfuscates norms and relationships.[18] Fear as a way of life, in the context of Karachi, thrives on this opacity of violent occurrences. While upsetting even the most intimate relationships (what can really be known of one's friends, neighbours and even relatives in such a game of shadows?), it reinforces, a fortiori, the boundaries between ethnic groups (if one cannot be sure about one's own, how could one see through ethnic 'others'?). Thus, the urban malaise conveyed above by Naveeda is irreducible to a sense of personal vulnerability. It is also the expression of a lament for the pluralistic city and its promiscuities, a city where, in the words of Naveeda, people of all ethnic stock 'interacted closely, sat together in restaurants, ate and drank together'. The transformations of violence recalled above—its increasingly indiscriminate, unpredictable and opaque nature—compromise the prospect of pluralistic urban living by equating the significant presence of ethnic 'others' in one's vicinity with life-threatening risks, while reducing the opportunities of cross-ethnic or cross-sectarian leisurely and ritual exchanges. Mujahdid, who professes a passion (*shok*) for football, has given up attending matches in Lyari, out of fear of being targeted by the gunmen of the PAC. According to him, this fear factor has seriously affected the football scene in Karachi: 'Tournaments still take place in Malir, Orangi Town and other areas, but on a reduced level, because of the situation in tension-prone areas [*kashidgi wale elaqon mein*]. Many Karachi clubs who used to play in Lyari don't go there anymore, because the situation there is so unpredictable [*ghair yaqini halat hai*]. Nobody can predict whether something will happen or not.' Besides the somewhat anecdotal example of football, the decline in sectarian intermingling during religious performances is revealing of this shrinking of the pluralistic public space. Several of my Sunni respondents, in Lyari but also in Urdu-speaking localities, told me that they grew up offering *namaz* indifferently in Sunni mosques and Shia *imambargah*s, privileging the closest to home. However, they stopped doing so after Shia places of worship started being targeted by Sunni religious extremists in the mid-1990s. Sunnis also used to offer support to their Shia neighbours at the time of Muharram by setting up *sabeel*s (kiosks, where refreshments would be served) on the path of mourning processions, a practice which was discontinued in recent years in an atmosphere of growing mistrust (in 2008, arrested Sunni sectarian militants revealed that they had planned to poison the *sabeel*s with cyanide).[19] Today, if the celebration of Imam Hussein's martyrdom continues to bring together Sunnis and Shias, as well as Hindus, in some *basti*s of Karachi, the great Ashura procession along M.A. Jinnah Road is now restricted to Shias and cordoned off by an impressive deployment of police personnel ensuring that no 'intruder' (that is, no non-Shia) breaks into the *julus*. These security measures were put in place after the terrorist attack of 2009 against the same Ashura processions—both attacks and state responses that effectively put an end to an old tradition of cross-ethnic and cross-sectarian intermingling in the context of a religious celebration joyfully mixing the sacred and the profane within its more carnivalesque elements.[20]

This chronic state of fear and its social ubiquity set Karachi apart from Bombay/Mumbai, a city which has had its own share of political, religious and criminal violence since the 1980s but which, according to Thomas Blom Hansen, 'is not regarded as a dangerous place in terms of everyday occurrences'.[21] On the contrary, fear has become a chronic condition in Karachi—a 'way of life' indeed. However ubiquitous this sentiment of vulnerability to life-threatening situations may be, it is experienced differently from one social group or one residential community to another, while presenting important context-related variations of intensity. The following section explores these everyday geographies of fear, both relative (mental maps are deeply idiosyncratic) and contingent (these maps are context-dependent, with the presence of others, as well as the hour and the political temperature of the day affecting risk evaluations).

Everyday Geographies of Fear

In June 2008, after taking me on a tour of his constituency, the Nazim of Union Council 6 of Landhi Town, Imran Ahmed Khan, drove me back to the guest house where I used to stay, which was located in Clifton. It was night time and as we entered the neighbourhood, Khan opened the glove compartment, pulled out a pistol and placed it on the dashboard. I would have thought that Clifton—an upper-class locality inhabited by the city elites and top politicians, including the Bhutto family—was much safer than Landhi, which for a decade had remained a no-go area for the supporters of the MQM and outsiders, and where gun fights continued to erupt occasionally between the supporters of the MQM and the Haqiqis. When I mentioned this to Imran Ahmed Khan, he flatly denied my assessment: 'No, these posh colonies are much more dangerous than Landhi. There is so much money here, so it attracts plenty of thieves.' Khan was particularly wary of young armed thugs on motorbikes and he explained to me that if some of them were to approach his car, he would not resist, hand out his valuables to them, and then later, as they sped off, shoot at them, 'because no bike can drive faster than a bullet'. Khan's risk assessment was proven wrong by the circumstances of his own death three years later: he was murdered in broad daylight by Haqiqi militants while visiting a shop in his locality. However flawed his judgement proved to be, it pointed at the relativity of urban geographies of fear among Karachi's residents, which primarily take the shape of mental maps used to make daily decisions informed by personal experience as well as the media.[22] If the city's elites are increasingly uncomfortable with venturing out of their gated communities, this fear of the outside is equally prevalent among the city's poorer inhabitants.

This sentiment of insecurity often begins once one leaves the *mohalla*—a couple of blocks, comprising a few hundred houses at the most and characterised by at least a relative ethno-linguistic homogeneity. Thus, Aziz,* a Sindhi resident of Lea Market, in Lyari, who works for an NGO based in Clifton, told me in August 2012 that:

> Before [the creation of the PAC, in 2008], the situation was not that bad. When there was a clash between them [rival gangs], one could still move freely [across Lyari]. But today, if you live in Lyari and have to go to another place [within Lyari], you will consider whether it is indispensable to do so. [...] Nobody wants to face trouble without a good reason [*Bas yeh hai ki banda yeh chahta hai ki voh bela wajah kisi pareshani mein na pare*]. If we still want to go, we will be questioned [by the gunmen of the PAC], they will give us some trouble, and if they'll end up letting us through, they will waste our time [*bande ka time zaya hota hai*]. This will not happen in one's *mohalla*, but in other areas of Lyari. Generally, people don't venture out [of their *mohalla*] alone, they will be accompanied by a child, for instance, and then only they will feel safe [*phir voh apne apko* safe *mehsus karte hain*]. If you are a Baloch, then you won't be facing any problem, but if you're not, you will do some thinking before going.[23]

As this testimony suggests, everyday geographies of fear are deeply contingent. The presence of a child on one's side—supposed to soften gunmen—can thus be experienced as a form of protection, in a complete reversal of the familiar order of things. Aziz also emphasises how the *mohalla* can be turned into a sanctuary, in a 'spatial retrenchment' predicated upon a dissection of space partitioning the urban topography 'not only into ethnic categories but also into categories of life and death', as Allen Feldman observed in the case of Belfast.[24] The militarisation of such sanctuaries by irregular armed groups tends to compromise their sanctity, though. The entrenchment of militias in community space transforms the latter into a battlefield, exposing it to raids and incursions by state enforcers and rival paramilitaries, leading to the 'proliferation of chronic violence'.[25] Going back to Aziz, this was exemplified by his personal losses during the police operation of April 2012, in which a hand grenade thrown at the police by gunmen of the PAC exploded near his garage and caused damage to his car. The repairs cost him around 12,000 rupees ($125); yet he considers to have been lucky: 'If the [CNG] cylinder and the tank had caught fire, the whole building would have collapsed.'

The overlapping of political conflict and crime also contributes to the imperfect partitioning of the 'domains of violence' from the 'domains of kinship and residence', in Feldman's terms.[26] While raids and hit-and-run attacks by external adversaries challenge the sanctity of the *mohalla* from without, the occupation of the streets by local specialists of violence threatens its integrity from within. This dual threat compromises the whole 'spatial metaphysic' pitting the safety of sanctuary space—supposedly guaranteed by face-to-face prolonged interactions, kinship and mutual obligations—against the dangers of the outside. Thus, the political and economic rise of violent specialists, in Karachi's major conflict zones, destabilises local hierarchies and, most notably, intergenerational relations. In the lower-middle-class Mohajir neighbourhoods that became hotbeds of militancy in the 1990s, such as Liaquatabad or Landhi, the rise of the MQM's 'street nationalism'[27] was part of a larger movement of youth assertion, challenging the authority of previous local leaders (*dallal*s, *izzatdar*s, *muezazin*s, etc.).[28] In Lyari, the occupation of the streets by drug-dealers and aspiring bandits has had the same effect, while inducing even greater anxiety among elder residents. A middle-aged resident of Baghdadi, working for a local Baloch nationalist organisation, thus related his fear of the young drug-dealers of his locality, without even trying to hide his sense of shame and powerlessness in the presence of other men (this interview was recorded in the midst of a *soyem* ceremony [prayers for the soul of the departed, on the third day of his demise]):

> Lyari used to be very safe. The people did not even use locks for their house. If they had to visit someone at the hospital or attend a wedding, they would leave their house under the care of neighbours. It was so safe, so peaceful [*Itna tahaffuz, itna aman tha*]. There was no fear of any sort [*Kisi kism ka koi khauf nahin tha*]. Today, in the same Lyari, and although I have reached the age of 57, I am scared when I come home. I will be hoping that in the very street where I live,

I won't encounter a kid who will misbehave with me and will pull out his gun for one reason or another and… *thaen*!, *thaen*! [shoot me]. If somebody asks him why he shot me, he will say that I was passing through or that I was staring at him. These days, this is enough to justify murder and massacres.

This perception of an internal threat over community space and the resulting sentiment of disempowerment—both at the individual and at the collective level—are also manifest in the crisis of local procedures for the management of violence. Thus, another of my respondents, a Sindhi fisherman from the Dhurai community, who has spent all his life in Khadda Market, points out how local populations gradually lost their grip over 'trouble-makers', and how the containment of violence within certain boundaries became increasingly difficult in the process:

[When there is an incident of firing], people of this locality tend to go home and lock themselves in, for their own sake. This is the present situation. In the past, whenever some people started creating trouble, everyone used to get out, and tried to solve the matter [*voh jakar suljha dete the*]. They tried to identify the culprits and the nature of the issue, before chasing the troublemakers away [*usko markar bhaga dete the*]. If a grave injustice [*zulm*] or a theft was committed by someone, he would be exposed to a scolding, maybe a beating, or he would be tied up to a pole normally used for horses, and people would pour tar [*kala thel*] over him and throw eggs at him. That was the custom. But today the situation is such that if someone comes across a group of troublemakers, he avoids getting involved and heads home [*agar koi panchayat ho rahi hai, to chalo bhai, ghali mein, ghar mein, aur derwaza bandh*]. If one of your blood relatives is involved, you might interfere, but otherwise you'll prefer to stay out of it, without putting your life at risk. It was different in the past. When there was some noise in the middle of the night, the whole neighbourhood would wake up, get out and congregate to see what was going on. If a husband was beating his wife, they would knock on the door. 'Why are you beating your wife, what is the reason for that?' They would force the husband to get out and provide shelter to his wife. Then, in the morning, relatives would settle down the issue. Today, things are different. I try not to get involved [*Aisa hota hai ki main bhi koshish karta hun ki a dekhun*].[29]

These sentiments of being disempowered and humiliated from within by local criminals and to be exposed to the wrath of the state as punishment for their transgressions do not exhaust the complex relations between Lyariites and their bandits, though. First of all, the presence of drug peddlers and users in public space has always been greater in certain localities (Kalakot in the past, Baghdadi today) than in others. Second, the perceptions of this threat seem to be strongly gendered. The narrative of disempowerment by the Baloch nationalist activist quoted above deserves to be put in context with its antithesis, which comes in the shape of a narrative of female empowerment hinting at the 'emasculation' of Lyari's men by local bandits. For the past two decades, Naveeda has been working with Lyari's oldest NGO. As we recalled above, the head office of this NGO was looted and partially torched during the riots that followed Benazir Bhutto's death. Shortly thereafter, the directors of the NGO were alerted that local gangsters had their eyes on the 200-yards terrain occupied by the organisation's head office. Naveeda then took it upon herself, in the face of male fear and apathy, to defend the organisation's property:

> At a point, I was the only one sitting in office. I did everything. There was the danger of seeing the terrain captured in case we closed down. There were so many groups involved in the gang war and all of them had set their eyes on our office, ready to capture it. [...] So I decided to fully dedicate myself [*Ham apne sar ki kimat laga li thi*; lit. 'I fixed a price on my own head,' *i.e.* I got ready to sacrifice my life] and just sat there. Maybe because of the presence of *ladies*, they did not lay their hand on it. The presence of *ladies* deters the grabber [*churane wala*]. There were three or four of them then. The men were terrified [Male *jo the, voh bahut dare hue the*]. The problem in those days was that when you travelled from one area to another you could be abducted. So I gathered all my courage [*jawanmardi*] and faced the challenge. Then the situation improved gradually.[30]

If I am inclined to nuance the attitudes of Lyariites towards the PAC it is also because almost all my respondents, Naveeda included, insisted that the expansion and consolidation of the PAC's hold over Lyari resulted in a significant decline in street crime. Even Aziz, otherwise critical of bandits he considered unsympathetic towards his own ethnic group, conceded that incidents of petty criminality had almost disappeared and that Lyari was much safer than other, more privileged areas of Karachi: 'Those of us who live in Lyari, when we go outside [*bahar*], we are afraid that we could get our cell phones or anything snatched at gunpoint. When we re-enter into Lyari, this fear vanishes.' Even their critics do not exclusively look at street-level, plebeian specialists of violence as parasites of community space. As with the MQM, the domination of the PAC over Lyari, however coercive and contested it may be, does not preclude contractual relations with the local population. These relations are crucial for the perpetuation of the PAC's hold over Lyari.

The security of the streets, the rebooting of public services and the redistribution of the manna of drugs and extortion through welfare programmes sustain this informal pact, with its guarantees of mutual protection: while these political bandits protect their constituents—essentially from their own violence, or from that of their retainers—these constituents are a human rampart against the police, which grows only thicker after each new raid. However, these contractual relations do not amount to a universal social contract mimicking citizenship. Despite the PAC leadership's claims to the contrary, these relations of mutual protection primarily concern the Baloch population of Lyari, to the exclusion of other ethnic groups. Thus, when the Sindhi fisherman quoted above turned to Uzair Baloch for some support in the refurbishing of a school in Khadda, his request was turned down by the PAC's leader, who suggested that his interlocutor was knocking on the wrong door: 'I am not your [Sindhis'] patron' (*Main ne ap logon ka theka to nahin liya hai*), replied the young 'Don'. For Lyari's self-proclaimed 'social' bandits, not all the poor are created equal. (N.B. this section was written before the implosion of the PAC and Uzair Baloch's dramatic loss of authority during the last months of 2013)

The Architecture of Safety

Karachi's geographies of fear are irreducible to the mental maps of the city's residents. These representations inform and are actualised by territorial formations and transit systems reshaping the cityscape. Before turning to these spatial formations of violence, two caveats are in order, though. First of all, one should remember that Karachi has a 'long' history of ethnic clustering, which predates the escalation of violence in the second half of the 1980s. In Karachi as elsewhere in south Asia, the separation of ethnic and religious groups in urban space combined logics of social exclusion (as exemplified by the Hindu ghettos that remain in existence to this day in Ranchore Lines and Lyari)[31] and cultural autonomisation. This *mohalla* system developed along a mosaic pattern, with different groups coexisting while remaining separate. It emerged incrementally in pre-colonial Karachi, without the formality it had assumed in the great, planned cities of medieval India. Moreover, in this modern city of migrants whose demographic growth, in the nineteenth century, was the outcome of rapid economic development, the dynamics of ethnic clustering were over-determined by economic factors. The largest ethnic clusters developed around the port during the colonial period and around trading and industrial estates after Partition, as successive generations of migrants relied upon their kin already settled in the city to find work and accommodation. This process of in-grouping, which facilitated the acclimatisation of newcomers to the city, is exemplified by the transformation of Baloch semi-rural settlements along the banks of the Lyari river into Karachi's largest working-class neighbourhood during the nineteenth century, and by the consolidation of the Pashtun presence around industrial areas such as SITE, in the west, or Landhi/Korangi, in the south-east, during the 1960s. In both cases, the 'ethnic' component in the formation of these working-class neighbourhoods was more social than ideological: ethnicity, in the restrictive sense of kinship, place of origin and language, played a major role in the demographic growth of these neighbourhoods but it only recently became a marker and a device for public claims (some local struggles for regularisation in postcolonial squatter settlements used ethnic bonds as a tool of mobilisation but rarely explicitly). Even in this restrictive sense, the ascribing of a central role to ethnicity or kinship in the formation of Karachi's 'ethnic enclaves' can be deceptive. It tends to negate the multiplicity of dynamics at work in the formation of these largely unofficial neighbourhoods, particularly in the postcolonial period. The inflow of Urdu-speaking refugees, in the aftermath of Partition, also led to the formation of ethnolinguistic clusters. However, many of these *muhajir* squatter-settlements (such as those that developed in and around Saddar) displayed a multiclass character that set them apart from other, lower-income migrant colonies.[32] Moreover, the magnitude of these migrations and the subsequent 'invasion' of entire neighbourhoods by the *muhajirin* limited their dependence on middlemen already established in the city. Last but not least, these refugees received some assistance from the state—however insufficient it may have been—for their installation and rehabilitation. The conditions of arrival and settlement of later rural migrants, whether Punjabi or Pashtun, were radically different. These migrants arrived more gradually in the city, which made them more dependent on their 'fellow villagers' (*ghar wale*) already settled and set the basis for unequal patron-client relationships. And unlike the *muhajirin*, these migrants from the countryside or the highlands did not receive any support from the state, which further increased their dependence on 'community patrons' in terms of access to housing, employment or credit.[33]

Besides acknowledging the historicity of these dynamics of ethno-linguistic clustering shaped by migration, labour relations and state intervention, one has to stress that Karachi's ethnic divide remains incomplete. Spaces of ethnic or sectarian mixing have not completely faded away in the city. Even within localities displaying a strong degree of ethnic cohesion and under the control of a single political party—two identity markers that often coexist and reinforce each other—a handful of families from different ethnic stock can be found coexisting peacefully with the dominant group. As Laura Ring points out, such coexistence is not devoid of tensions,[34] but these are not necessarily (and in fact rarely) related to ethnic or political differences.

Having said that, it is undeniable that the proliferation of violence has reinforced the Karachiites' pre-existing inclinations towards ethnic enclosure. A study conducted by a team of local economists in 1993, on the basis of a socio-economic survey of 6,275 households, concluded that 'Patterns of mobility in the city indicate that around 24 per cent of all moves are from neighbourhoods which are reputed to be violent to peaceful ones. The concentration of households with similar ethnic backgrounds and observed patterns of mobility make ethnicity and the level of violence possible determinants of choice of location in the city.' Further, the authors of this study predicted 'increased segregation of people by their ethnic backgrounds'. More originally, they raised the alarm concerning the risk of a new partitioning of the city between 'high-risk' areas and 'safe-rings'.[35] These ominous predictions were validated in later years, to such an extent that 75 per cent of Karachi's population currently live in ethnically or religiously tainted, if not homogeneous neighbourhoods.[36] In present-day Karachi, the traditional mosaic pattern survives in some lower-income neighbourhoods and *katchi abadi*s, from Lyari to Orangi, whose residents sometimes take pride in the ethnic or religious diversity of the area (this is particularly true in Lyari, where the presence of Hindus was often invoked by my interlocutors to demonstrate the liberal spirit of their neighbourhood). The escalation of ethnic violence has been compromising the survival of these mixed neighbourhoods, though, the brutal eviction of thousands of Kutchis from Lyari during the summer of 2013 being a case in point (see Chapter 4). Apartment buildings, for their part, continue to show a significant degree of ethnic mixing.[37] However, some changes are starting to take place there as well, following the attempts made by political parties to take control of some of these buildings and evict the residents affiliated with rival ethnic groups. This was exemplified by the combat between the MQM, the ANP and the JSQM in the Rabia City apartment complex of Gulistan-e-Jauhar in 2011. Finally, residential 'colonies' show contrasting trends. While the upscale areas concentrated in the south of Karachi (Defence and Clifton) continue to show high levels of ethnic mixing and are more organised on a class than an ethnic basis, middle- and lower-middle-class 'colonies' and 'societies' have been diversely affected by the phenomena of enclosure related to the degradation of the city's security environment.

Violence and Ethnic Segregation in Karachi

The first neighbourhoods to be affected by the spiral of violence that engulfed Karachi in the 1980s were the *basti*s (which came to be known, more pejoratively, as *katchi abadi*s from the 1970s onwards).[38] The formation of these *basti*s was predicated upon various logics of (self-)segregation, the most significant of which were language and place of origin. But these *basti*s were also integrative in the sense that they emerged as a 'quasi-domestic space of Muslim solidarity and national integration'. While partially a continuation of the north Indian *mohalla* system, this organisation of urban space also relied upon a notion of the locality as an extension of the home,[39] which made the *basti* 'neither totally public nor entirely private', a place where *parda* rules could be relaxed and where ethnic or sectarian parochialism could be transcended in the realisation of a Pan-Islamic nation—more a political project to be fulfilled than an everyday reality, but a galvanising moral and political programme nonetheless.[40] And if cultural homogeneity was searched for and preserved within the *basti*, these lower-income neighbourhoods were tightly knit with each other, which 'enabled recent settlers to feel fully integrated as new citizens'.[41] All this changed during the 1980s, when the modes of access to these *basti*s, the power dynamics behind their formation and control, as well as the resistance they encountered, were drastically altered in the wake of the Afghan Jihad. *Dallal*s, who guaranteed a minimal sense of security to *basti*-dwellers, were then sidelined by a new breed of slumlords. The 'riots' of 1985–1986 provided a cover for the Pashtun 'land mafia' to extend its sphere of influence, and the resistance of Urdu-speaking communities to this attempt had less to do with ethnicity than with an attempt to resist eviction or alienation at the hands of these new, ruthless slumlords (see Chapter 1). As they became sites of violent contests between land suppliers and later on political parties with distinct ethnic bases, the *basti*s ceased to be widely romanticised 'quasi-domestic' urban settlements. In the eyes of outsiders, they became increasingly associated with poverty, crime and parochial hatreds—not merely slums but urban jungles threatening the more 'civilised' parts of the city. In the eyes of *basti*-dwellers themselves, the experience of quasi-domesticity was 'hollowed out' from its original meaning.[42] Streets, parks, playgrounds, schools and even sewerage lines became battlefields or sites of performative violence, where dead bodies were dumped or exhibited.

Between its first electoral victories (1987–1988) and the dismantling of its 'secondary state' during the course of army, police and paramilitary repression (1992–1996), the MQM seemed to have succeeded in reviving the old *basti* ethos and enthusiasm of yore. Whereas outsiders saw the formation in MQM strongholds of ethnically homogenous, barricaded enclaves, as a manifestation of the party's propensity towards separatism or as an illustration of its 'fascist' tendencies, the residents of these neighbourhoods—especially the disenfranchised Mohajir youth—initially celebrated what could pass for a revival of quasi-domesticity, with its afferent notions of security, authenticity and spontaneity.[43] At the same time, though, these ethnic enclaves were fortified and turned into citadels, which became sites of brutal, sometimes grotesque excesses—a darker side to Mohajir neighbourly life that was epitomised by the MQM's torture cells, whose existence was an open secret (cf. photographs in Appendix). The intervention of the army in 1992 broke the backbone of these de facto quasi-sovereign spaces. The gates and walls erected by the MQM at the entrance of its strongholds (cf. photographs in Appendix) were brought down by the army, which implemented a strategy of counter-insurgency that had several affinities with that of Ariel Sharon in Beirut, as it relied upon a matrix of strategically located observation points and checkpoints (army posts were built on major roundabouts and checkpoints at the entrance of Mohajir neighbourhoods), which was supplemented by a wide network of informers and undercover agents in public spaces, offices and educational institutions.[44] In the meantime, the army helped recreate other no-go areas in the city, which were left to the control of the Haqiqis. To date, this remains the most extreme case of ethnic segregation ever witnessed in Karachi, in the shape of a coercive occupation and control, through terror tactics, of large urban settlements. The *reconquista* of these 'no-go areas' by the MQM in 2003 put an end to this exception. In these former strongholds of the party, there was no return to the euphoric local politics of the late 1980s/early 1990s. A large part of that enthusiasm had now shifted—at least temporarily—to revivalist religious groups such as the Dawat-e-Islami (see Chapter 5). But segregation along ethnic lines continued to be viewed as the best protection against everyday and extraordinary violence, a perception which was even reinvigorated in recent years, following an escalation of ethnic violence.

At present, every ethnic group in the city has its citadels, guarded by self-proclaimed (though occasionally elected) representatives of the community, with access to military resources. In these turf wars, the frontline takes the shape of the 'interface': points of contact between ethnically and politically distinct localities with a history of confrontation, where rioting or targeted attacks serve to expand the limes of the sanctuary, not only by capturing land but also by forcing the most uncertain populations to take sides more unambiguously than they were ready to. Today, the most volatile of these interfaces are signalled by barriers painted in the colours of locally dominant political parties and by the number—and size—of bullet holes riddling the walls of the homes and shops awkwardly sitting on these border areas (sometimes explicitly referred to as such by local residents, as in the case of the 'India-Pakistan border' separating warring Urdu-speaking and Pashtun localities in Kati Pahari)[45] (cf. photographs in Appendix).

Qabza: The Politics of 'Capture', Between Land Contests and Urban Cleansing

The competition over land and the involvement of political parties in this tussle is another important factor of ethnic consolidation—spatially at least, if not necessarily mentally. The argument that Karachi's conflicts would merely be the outcome of greed and rivalries between local 'mafias' does not resist evidence. As Haris Gazdar and others have been emphasising consistently, Karachi's conflicts—and in particular the episodes of collective violence somewhat hastily qualified as 'ethnic riots'—are primarily political in nature.[46] But this is precisely why contests over land rights and uses are an integral part of the battles for Karachi. For land suppliers, the battle for real estate may well be primarily economic in nature (around 2010, 3,000 acres of land were converted annually into

100,000 plots in areas formerly occupied by urban villages [*goths*], the commercial value of these plots being estimated at 25 billion rupees [$250 million]).[47] But the motives of their political patrons are more complex, as they are not only concerned with the economic exchange value of land but also with its political usage value. As I already suggested in the previous chapter, in a city such as Karachi, which has been subjected to tremendous pressure to accommodate newcomers since Partition, the provision of accommodation to one's constituents has been a key element in the formation and sustaining of political clienteles.

The complex status of land in Karachi must be recalled to understand the nature of the conflict. Currently, thirteen public agencies are involved in the control and development of land in the city. Besides the provincial and local governments, the federal government and the army (which inherited its cantonment areas from the British), the Railway, Port Qasim, the Karachi Port Trust (KPT), the Defence Housing Society (DHS), the Katchi Abadi Authority (KAA), Recent Allocations (Educational City), the Lyari Development Authority (LDA), SITE, as well as the Malir Development Authority (MDA) all own and control land in Karachi.[48] To the exclusion of residential 'societies', such as DHS, only 3.9 per cent of the land in the city is in private hands. This share is insignificant, especially if one compares it with that of the provincial government (17.7 per cent) and even more so with that of the CDGK (30.9 per cent after the merger of the KDA and the KMC under the devolution plan implemented in 2001; cf. Fig. 5).[49] Rampant corruption within these public agencies and, over the past two decades, their search for additional funding, has led them to 'auction off the family silver', as Ardeshir Cowasjee puts it.[50] This unofficial privatisation of state-owned land has been at the heart of real estate speculation in Karachi since Partition. But it is also the only form of access to housing for more than half of the city's population, which continues to reside in unofficial settlements developed through exchanges between land suppliers, middlemen, policemen, politicians and bureaucrats.

While political leaders have been facilitating the occupation and subdivision of public land since the early days of Pakistan, political parties as institutions started coveting state-owned land for clientelistic purposes from the 1970s onwards. The PPP was the first political party to use land redistribution as a political tool, by instructing the KDA to sell large parts of Korangi, Gulshan-e-Iqbal and North Karachi to party loyalists at give-

Fig. 5: Distribution of land ownership rights in Karachi (in %)

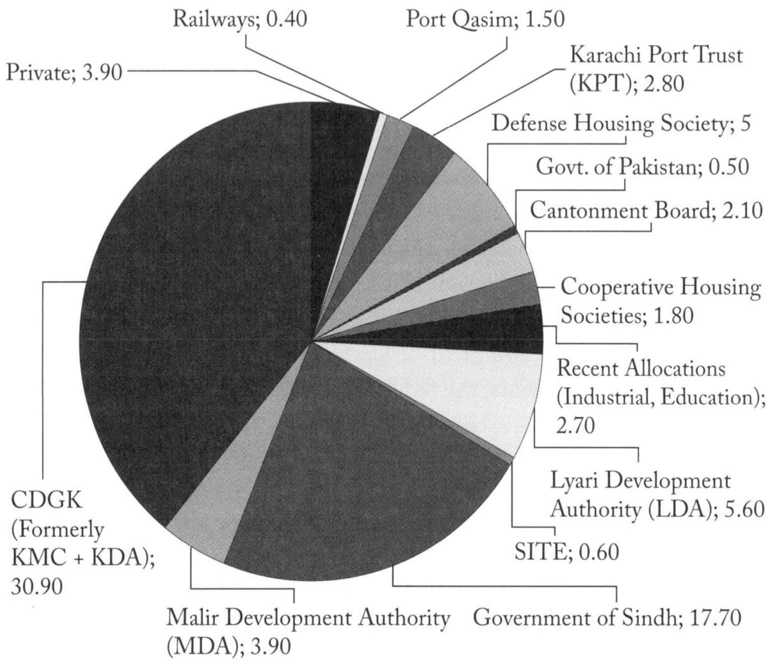

Source: Hasan, Arif and Mansoor Raza, *Karachi. The Land Issues*, op. cit., p. 15.

away prices, while issuing ownership rights to the Baloch population of Lyari. These practices were continued by the regime of Zia-ul-Haq, during which the Chief Minister of Sindh, Ghous Ali Shah, 'distributed thousands of plots of land in Karachi to government followers, who later made huge profits by selling this land to real estate traders'.[51] Benazir Bhutto emulated her father's policy when she sought to transfer vast tracts of undeveloped land in Hawke's Bay to her constituents. As we saw earlier (see Chapter 4), this project failed in the face of red tape and misappropriation of the projected land by some cadres of the PPP. Nevertheless, the first PPP government outdid its predecessors when it came to selling off land to supporters: within a couple of years, more than 3,000 plots of land were sold below their market value by the KDA, on the instruction of the Ministry of Housing and Town Planning.[52] Many building permits issued by the PPP government were however cancelled by Jam Sadiq Ali, the chief minister of Sindh in the following PML-(N) government, who re-allocated them to his own protégés, a practice which would be continued by all following governments.[53]

This land-grabbing spree was accelerated by the implementation of the SLGO 2001. This devolution plan led to a considerable increase in malpractice, as it transferred from the provincial to the local government the responsibility of overseeing land use, housing and settlement in the city. By then, the most common form of unofficial land development was through the illegal—but unofficially state-sanctioned—conversion of agricultural land surrounding the city's urban villages (*goth*s) into residential/commercial/industrial land. At present, the exact number of these *goth*s remains uncertain. While the OPP puts the figure at 2,173, this figure has been disputed. Officially, Karachi had 808 villages in 2008, 458 of which were regularised while 350 still awaited regularisation.[54] The lands attached to these villages are sanctioned for agricultural purposes by the provincial government's land/revenue department (a sanction known as *sanad*) in the name of *goth* elders. Normally, such land cannot be sold, as the *sanad* merely provides permission to use it for agriculture and the related housing over a certain period of time (thirty years, after which the sanction can be extended). Such sanctioned land can be officially converted into residential or commercial land (it is then known as *sikni*) but its selling being illegal, it always takes place unofficially—which is not to say that government officials are not involved in the process.

Following the creation of the CDGK, the Nazims (the new mayors of the city's 'Towns') supervised the demolition of several *goth*s across Karachi. These evictions partook to a land-grabbing contest that was particularly intense along the ring roads and highways linking Karachi with the rest of the country (the Northern Bypass, the Super Highway and the National Highway). Besides economic incentives (the value of land in outlying districts increased manifold following the construction of heavy-traffic roads), these real estate operations were informed by strategic concerns. Thus, by settling its constituents along these roads, the MQM aimed to deny an important source of leverage to its rivals (the ANP, in particular) by hampering their capacity to cut off the city from the rest of Pakistan during episodes of ethnic violence. The same parties were also planning to keep an eye on the goods—legal and otherwise—entering Karachi, with a particular concern for weapons shipments, which were susceptible to alter significantly the balance of power in the city. The control of these highways through programmes of land acquisition and the development of new colonies was an act of power in the sense of Elias, as they aimed to provide tactical advantage to respective political parties over their rivals by making them less dependent on others. Those controlling strategic roads could expect to introduce a disequilibrium in interdependencies, to their advantage. This proved to be a more complicated task than anticipated. The residents of some *goth*s took up arms to resist the attempt of local authorities to demolish their settlements and make way for new colonies, as in Sikander Goth, in Gulshan-e-Iqbal town, in 2006. And when some town Nazims did manage to demolish some of these *goth*s with the backing of political parties and the support of municipal bodies, they had to cope with the interference of some powerful land suppliers, who sided with *goth* elders in exchange for the latter's permission to develop new colonies on surrounding agricultural lands. This is exemplified by the story of Altaf Nagar, in Gadap Town.

Between October 2006 and July 2007, bulldozers of the KDA demolished more than 300 houses in a section of Gulshan-e-Zia colony, in Orangi Town, as well as in several *goth*s situated at the border between Orangi Town and Gadap Town, in order to make way for a new residential colony called Altaf Nagar (The City of Altaf [Hussain]). This unofficial operation by public officials[55] was overseen by the Nazim of Orangi Town (who was affiliated with the MQM), who claimed that the area came under his jurisdiction, although this was disputed by the Nazim of Gadap Town (who was affiliated with the PPP). After the first demolitions, local *goth* elders (all these settlements have a Baloch/Sindhi population) felt that they were caught between two 'snakes'. The 'black snake' (*kala sap*) consisted of the political parties coveting their land, while the 'yellow snake' (*pila sap*) took the shape of the land suppliers who guaranteed them protection against the former in exchange for their permission to develop surrounding agricultural lands. After considering these two options, *goth* elders decided to go with the yellow snake—a land supplier whose political clout and military resources forced the Nazim of Orangi Town to back down, fearing a major clash. The career of this particular land supplier, Muhammad Khan, an Afridi Pashtun from Khyber Agency, bears testimony to the complex relations between the so-called 'land mafia' and state agencies. Far from forming a 'parallel government' or a 'para-state system',[56] these land suppliers have built their reputation—and fortune—on intimate relations with state agents, which provide them with political protection but also with operational resources.

A former driver in the KESC, Khan began his career in real estate in 1990 by subdividing and selling land reserved for a poultry farm. This unofficial operation also involved an officer of the KMC, a senior police officer of the town's police station and a councillor of the town's administration.[57] The volume of these activities only increased over the years, after Khan was approached by *goth* elders who were eager to sell unofficially their sanctioned lands. From 1995 onwards, industrial areas were also set up in the *abadi* (settlement), which took the name of Muhammad Khan Colony. In the following years, this settlement kept on expanding, reaching 2,500 acres in 2012. A conservative estimate puts the funds generated by the sale of the colony's 75,000 plots at 11.25 billion rupees ($112 million).[58]

In order to extend his influence within public institutions, Khan encouraged his two sons to join the local administration. One of them contested elections for the town's Nazim seat and lost but the other was elected in 2005 as a general councillor of a Union Council. Besides infiltrating the state through his proxies, Khan patronised politicians and supported a local MNA and an MPA, who got elected with his support. The police, for their part, were neutralised, after succumbing to the persuasiveness of Khan's intermediaries, usually on a per plot sold rate. As a result, not only did Khan ensure the protection of his activities on the verge of legality, he also mobilised his contacts within the bureaucracy for the development of his unofficial colonies, which got access to water lines, electricity, sewerage systems, road networks, bus routes, and so on. By 2006, Khan had become one of the most powerful land suppliers in Karachi, and in the following years, even the MQM—which, at that time, was at the peak of its power—had to acknowledge his clout. This realisation came after a series of fierce clashes between the police and MQM militants on one side and militiamen recruited by *goth* elders and Muhammad Khan on the other. During one of these clashes, the Naib Nazim of Orangi Town and a police officer were injured. A couple of months later, the two parties reached a settlement which was formalised by a *hathbandi* (delimitation agreement) in late 2008.[59] At the end of the day, the MQM had to revise its ambitions from a fear of a showdown with this major figure of the unofficial economy, a development with far-reaching consequences. Not only did the party lose control over a strategic area of Karachi, this episode signalled the emergence of a new challenge to the MQM's hegemonic ambitions, as the balance of power between Karachi's predominant political force and its new real estate magnates started shifting to the advantage of the latter. It should however be mentioned that the mobilisation of the media by experienced activists as well as the support of the Nazim of Gadap Town also contributed to the success of this anti-eviction movement.

For Perween Rahman, the late director of the OPP, who took an active role in this case (on the *goth* elders' side), the failure of the MQM to implement its agenda was a blessing for the city as it 'stopped the polarisation of Karachi'. A few weeks before her tragic disappearance in March 2013, Rahman told me that, currently, 'the area has a mixed population'. She was so thrilled with the outcome of this affair that she looked at it as one of the five defining moments in the postcolonial history of Karachi, after Partition ('when the population shot up from 400,000 to 1.5–2 million, which gave birth to the unofficial housing sector'), the Green Revolution ('when the rural population was displaced by mechanisation and came to settle here'), the 1971 war in East Pakistan (which brought another influx of refugees to Karachi) and the pro-poor mobilisation of the PPP (when Z.A. Bhutto's regime passed a bill to regularise unofficial settlements).[60]

As the story of Altaf Nagar exemplifies, the use of coercion in real-estate operations is becoming increasingly risky in a context of general militarisation of Karachi's society.[61] Another way for political parties to gain control over apartment buildings and housing societies is through their residents' committees, which are generally elected for two years and whose composition is often exhibited by the colour of the flags flying on top of apartment buildings or at the gates of a specific colony. Religious organisations have also used these committees to establish their writ over some residential societies. This is the case, for instance, with al-Akhtar Trust, an organisation listed by the United States Treasury Department as a terrorist group in 2003 for its alleged links with the Afghan Taliban and al-Qaeda, which has controlled the residential committee of the Sindh Baloch Cooperative Housing Society, in Gulistan-e-Jauhar, since 2010. Local residents do not seem to be particularly concerned with the ideological leanings of the organisation. One of these residents told me in August 2012 that he had heard that the trust was somewhat controversial for its activities in Afghanistan, but that to his knowledge it was merely involved in the construction of hospitals in that country, an activity which from his point of view could hardly be considered reprehensible. A more pressing concern, for this middle-class resident, was the provision of health facilities and security, two points on which he considered that the trust had delivered on its promises, though he resented the ban enforced on the annual cultural festival previously organised by residents. The provision of security by the trust actually predated its control of the local residents' committee: it manages a local madrasa, the Jamia Ashraf-ul-Madaris, which had its own security system in the shape of AK-47s-toting private security guards, who according to this resident often hailed from Waziristan. This presence of armed men providing security to the madrasa seems to have had a trickle-down effect on the security of the neighbourhood at large, or at least on the feeling of security of its residents. Some years ago, a clash occurred between the guards of the madrasa and militants of the Shahid Bhutto faction of the PPP (led by Ginwa Bhutto, the Lebanese widow of Murtaza Bhutto), who tried to occupy a student hostel located on the outskirts of the colony. Two people were killed but for this resident, 'these madrasa people demonstrated that they had power, that they had a kind of deterrence over others'.[62] Another violent incident took place on 6 November 2012, when the Rangers raided the premises of the trust's seminary while searching for a 'high-valued militant' from Swat, who had come to visit Maulana Hakim Akhtar. An exchange of fire ensued, and although no loss of life was reported, two madrasa students were injured in the crossfire, while the wanted militant managed to slip away.[63] One would have thought that such incidents would compromise the feeling of security of local residents. However, when I asked the resident quoted above how he and others in the locality had reacted to the incident, I was told that, 'it didn't bother residents of the locality much since many people believe that these types of raids are just cosmetic [...] People did talk about it for a couple of days and then it was business as usual.'[64]

Another mode of penetration into residential colonies used by political parties, and most notably by the MQM, is through the leasing of security personnel. According to the same resident of the Sindh Baloch Cooperative Housing Society, who was a witness to such practices in neighbouring colonies, 'The MQM offers local residents to erect barriers and to station guards at the entrance of their locality, who sometimes happen to be students with licensed arms. This happens with the support of the people. They don't have a choice, because the police don't help them'.[65] This form of armed clientelism does not stop with the provision of physical security, though. Once they establish their writ over a locality, MQM cadres promptly deliver basic services as a 'favour' to their new protégés. On the contrary, the localities escaping the control of the party are often deprived of these facilities. Thus, the Sindh Baloch Cooperative Housing Society, where the MQM only has a limited presence, is the only locality in this part of Gulistan-e-Jauhar without a water supply.

To what extent do these practices of land grabbing and territorial expansion or consolidation reinforce ethnic boundaries and affiliations? On the one hand, the example of the Sindh Baloch Cooperative Housing Society suggests that the control of a political or religious organisation over a certain locality is not necessarily detrimental to its ethnic mix (the population of that particular colony remains much more diverse than its denomination suggests). It also shows that support to the said organisation, as far as it programme of local governance is concerned, does not mechanically translate into adhesion to its larger social or political agenda. However, the control of residents' committees by political or religious organisations may indeed be seriously detrimental to ethnic and social pluralism. Besides the rather benign example of the Sindh Baloch Cooperative Housing Society and the ban on its annual festival, another illustration of this is provided by the MQM's attempt to evict Pashtun labourers from the residential colonies and apartment buildings under its control, working towards the advent of 'clean' urban spaces, where all signs of ethnic otherness would have been erased. In Rizvia Co-operative Housing Society, for instance—a Shia-dominated colony in Nazimabad, where the residents' committee is under the control of the MQM—Pashtun restaurant owners and shopkeepers started receiving threatening letters such as this one in 2008:

Salam Aleikum!

Through this letter I would like to bring to your notice that your hotel has become a gathering point for unpleasant individuals [*napasandida afrad ka markaz*]. Local residents [*ahl-e-mohalla*] complain that suspicious individuals [*mushtaba-o-mashkuk afrad*] visit your restaurant and spend hours in a row there. For this reason, local residents are concerned that some untoward situation [*naghani surat-e-hal*] could develop in the near future, which could result in a loss of lives and damages to properties.

Therefore, we request you to close down your restaurant on short notice.

Sincerely,

[Signed by the Honorary Secretary of Rizvia Co-operative Housing Society—name withheld].[66]

This attempt at 'urban cleansing' resembles that of Mumbai's Shiv Sena in the 1990s, which 'translated the problem of scarce space into the imaginary of cleansed space'—in that case, 'a space without Muslim bodies'.[67] In Karachi, elements of this project can be discerned in the violent campaign of the MQM against Pashtun restaurant owners, street vendors and daily labourers under the garb of a movement against 'talibanisation' since 2008. But whereas this project of urban cleansing was primarily informed by a battle for space, however spectral, in the case of Mumbai,[68] it was primarily related to a battle for votes in the case of Karachi. The hostility of the MQM was not directed against the Taliban per se but against the ANP and the growing number of Pashtuns at large, which were seen as a greater challenge for the MQM's hegemony over Karachi—a (mis)perception which would help the actual Taliban strengthen their hold over certain parts of Karachi from 2012 onwards (see Chapter 4). The violence unleashed by MQM target killers against ordinary Pashtuns became integral to a proper project of ethnic cleansing, a vain but bloody attempt at reversing demographic trends in the city. Whereas the violence of the Shiv Sena against Muslims could be read as a 'bizarre utopia of urban renewal',[69] the MQM's war on ordinary Pashtuns and the ANP proceeded from a no less fantastical project of exclusive urban ownership.

In the opposite direction, ethnic cohesion can also become a tactics for land grabbing. Thus, a notorious Sindhi nationalist leader and land supplier is currently trying to attract lower-income members of the Christian minority to capture some vacant land along the National Highway. In August 2012, a middleman involved in this operation explained to me that plots of 80 to 120 yards were allocated to 'poor people' at a 'very low price'. Preference was given to Christians as they were thought to be harder to evict: any attempt to displace them would be met with accusations of 'anti-minority bias'. Although the motives of this particular land supplier were primarily economic, the same could not be said of his political patrons. As the aforementioned middleman explained, such operations help the PPP 'strengthen its vote bank on tips of the National Highway' and 'break the chain of ANP supply routes'.

Mass Transit and the Relegation of Neighbourhoods of Exile

Far from being neutral, urban development projects are an answer to the estrangement between ethnic communities, while reinforcing it. This politicisation of urban development culminated under the mandate of Mustafa Kamal, City Nazim (mayor) between 2005 and 2010. Kamal's dynamism and his commitment to transform Karachi into a global city on par with Dubai gained him acclaim from the Urdu-speaking middle and upper classes as well as from foreign experts, going a long way towards the rehabilitation of the MQM's image, from a violent and disruptive party to a responsible and competent manager of Karachi's urban affairs. Kamal committed much of his time and energy to the alleviation of Karachi's structural transport problem. This issue has a particular resonance in Karachi, where everyone remembers the spiral of violence ignited by Bushra Zaidi's death in a traffic accident, and where the creation of a mass transit system has been a matter of debate since the first attempts at urban planning conducted in postcolonial Karachi in the early 1950s (the MRV Plan, for instance, recommended a mass transit rail system). 'Mass Transit', in Karachi, is not merely a matter of concern for urban planners and commuters in a hurry, but also for poets and novelists concerned with the human fabric of their city, as exemplified by Maniza Naqvi's acclaimed eponymous novel. *Mass Transit* was published in 1998 and tells the story of Safina, a young woman recently returned to Karachi after a long stay abroad. The city which she confronts is both buoyant and chaotic, torn apart by spasmodic outbursts of violence. And for Safina, all of Karachi's problems come up to one key issue—its lack of a mass transit system:

> The problem with the city, she decided, was that it didn't have some sort of a mass transit system like a subway. [...] Buses, rickshaws, taxis, motorcycles, vans, and cars. Everyone was in a compartment. No matter what the size of the confinement may be, everyone remained isolated.[70]

Mustafa Kamal had a different conception of mass transit, though. For the young mayor of Karachi and other promoters of the 'megacity dream',[71] mass transit was essentially a matter of 'smooth and hassle-free traffic flow', as a promotional document issued by the CDGK in 2009 emphasised. The first section of this document advertising the accomplishments of the MQM city government is devoted to 'flyovers', 'underpasses' and other 'interexchanges', with their promises of a fluid and un-promiscuous circulation. The text accompanying the pictures of these various projects reveals, in hesitant English, the quasi-erotic resonance of these fantasies of circulation: 'First time people are enjoying the driving pleasure, which had been a dream in the past.'[72] The flyover was the fetish of the hyperactive mayor and his entourage, the symbol of their commitment to speed and urban modernity. And so Karachi became a city of flyovers: forty-six were commissioned between 2001 and 2012, while four were still under construction in July 2012.[73] Rumours of corruption have been doing the rounds, arguing that the MQM's leadership was falsifying the tenders and collecting huge sums from builders for each project, and that the attraction of the city government for these emblems of modernity was much more profane than it seemed. But the rumours remained unsubstantiated—no one was prosecuted, let alone convicted—and despite occasional collapses of these hastily built structures,[74] their construction continued. Karachi's upper and middle classes were jubilant: they could now drive across the city—to visit friends, relatives or clients, for instance—by bypassing 'tension-prone areas'. The completion of the Lyari Expressway and, more recently, the inauguration of a flyover linking Orangi-5 and North Nazimabad, made it possible for drivers to bypass two of the most volatile parts of the city: Lyari and its impoverished inner city, as well as the Pashtun-dominated areas stretching between Banaras Chowk and Orangi. As such, the Lyari Expressway and the Banaras Chowk flyover were primarily meant to cater to the electoral base of the MQM—middle-class and lower-middle-class Mohajirs—by ensuring that they could circulate freely and safely across the city, without any risk of a confrontation with their ethnic others, whether Baloch or Pashtun. If these projects were justified by the necessity to reroute traffic and alleviate the burden of this traffic over the city centre, it also had an important and self-conscious political dimension. Whereas the Safina of *Mass Transit* dreamt of de-compartmentalising transport across Karachi, the promoters of the 'world class city' fantasise about tension-free corridors linking 'safe rings' by bypassing 'high risk' areas. Nausheen Anwar, an assistant professor of urban studies at the Institute of Business Administration, does not say otherwise: 'Think of "bypassing" Lyari or "bypassing" the lower-income colonies that pepper the margins of the KPT Expressway,' as if the merits of that 'bypassing' were obvious to her middle-class Urdu-speaking interlocutor (incidentally, it was not, and the author of the article felt the need to disassociate herself from Anwar's language).[75] The partition of space that Nizat Ahmad and his colleagues at the University of Karachi had anticipated in the early 1990s was becoming a reality. Fear, ethnic politics and urban modernity collided within the MQM's flyovers and their dead spaces, which effectively partitioned the city between those flying over and those living down under. This strategy of bypassing lower-income, ethnically 'other' and politically volatile areas was not lost on the residents of these localities. As a Baloch nationalist activist from Lyari told me in August 2012, 'Today, Lyari has become so isolated from the rest of the city [*ham garhi mein gire hue hain*; lit. 'we have been thrown into a pit']. They have built new roads such as the Northern Bypass [between 2002 and 2007], and none of these newly built roads ever turns towards Lyari. Even in colonial Africa, people were treated better than in Lyari today!' One does not need to be a Baloch nationalist to acknowledge the social cost of such contributions towards a mass transit system in Karachi. Besides reinforcing feelings of alienation among the residents of what increasingly resemble neighbourhoods of exile, these megaprojects involve the demolition of lower-income housing and the displacement of already disenfranchised populations on a massive scale (the construction of the Lyari Expressway thus required the displacement of 24,000 families), not to mention their controversial impact on the environment. If this was not enough, these megaprojects partake of the symbolic marking of the city by its predominant party and end up reinforcing the idea that Karachi belongs to Mohajirs and their political representatives. Thus, the flyover inaugurated in April 2012 in SITE Town was initially approved by the Sindh government as the 'Habib Bank Flyover', in reference to the famous intersection where the four-lane flyover was erected, the Habib Bank Chowrangi. But during the inaugural ceremony for construction, in April 2011, the (MQM) Governor of Sindh, Ishrat-ul-Ebad, announced that the bridge would be renamed 'Afza Altaf Flyover', after Altaf Hussain's daughter. SITE officials were apparently 'left in a daze' at the move, which also embarrassed the Sindh government, as the (PPP) chief minister had approved the construction under a more neutral name.[76]

Conclusion

The increasing sense of vulnerability of ordinary men, women and children of Karachi to political and criminal violence is upsetting individual and collective routines ensuring the containment of this violence in everyday life, and thus preventing its habituation. Daily routines can even be turned against themselves: instead of providing a sense of confidence in repetition, they can become a source of vulnerability. This is particularly true of Karachi's middle- and upper-class families, who have been exposed to extortionists using their intimate knowledge of the daily schedules of their victims or their children to threaten them. At the other end of the social spectrum, itinerant vendors, who usually follow the same route every day, can also become soft targets for kidnappers and killers settling scores for their political patrons. And while the evasive tactics and measures of containment of the past tend to become obsolete, the hermeneutic of urban danger no longer provides comfort. The urban environment becomes increasingly difficult to decipher, its moods no longer as predictable as they used to be.

Besides compromising the routinisation of violence, fear is literally reshaping Karachi, as the public policies of the CDGK in the field of mass transit or the increasing regrouping of the city's population on self-conscious ethnic patterns illustrate. And in a city where uncertainty on all levels is fast increasing, even the devices against fear are subject to contradictory interpretations, their function unfixed and contested. This rudimentary architecture of slabs, sandbags and iron barriers is never what it seems. A ten-feet high concrete slab at the entrance of a street, as in the Pashtun settlements of Kati Pahari, could well be a protective device for the local residents against gunfire (this, at least, is what local ANP activists told me). But it could also be turned into a *morcha* (shooting post) during the next round of interparty violence (cf. photographs in Appendix). Similarly, the rudimentary barriers of corrugated iron, often painted with the colours of the party, that block the entry to every lane in many MQM-dominated localities, are officially meant to prevent 'dacoities' (thefts) by making it more difficult for motorised thieves to enter and escape from these localities. But these barriers are also a protection against target killers, and as such constitute visual reminders that the war is going on, unabated.

CONCLUSION

Unlike other situations of prolonged urban warfare, such as those witnessed in Beirut in the 1980s or in some Colombian cities during the 1980s and 1990s, Karachi's ordered disorder has stood the test of time. Almost thirty years after the death of Bushra Zaidi and the 'ethnic riots' that followed, Karachi is more contested than ever. The original conditions of possibility of this ordered disorder were updated by a series of demographic, strategic and economic developments, through which they also sustained each other. The re-internationalisation of Afghan conflicts and Pakistan's contribution to the 'war on terror' led to the displacement of tens if not hundreds of thousands of Pashtuns to Karachi, with the conflicts around its 'ownership' and its relations with the rest of the country taking on a new intensity in the process. These large-scale displacements of population also reinforced trends towards the informalisation of the city and its development, be it in the field of housing, water-supply, employment, security, dispute settlement,... Another outcome of Pakistan's contribution to the war on terror was the rise of a new war economy around the transport of NATO cargo from Karachi to Afghanistan—a highly profitable trade (generating approximately $500 million a year in 2010)[1] that nurtured an equally lucrative unofficial economy through the pilfering of NATO supplies, the extortion of transporters and the smuggling of foreign goods under fake ISAF documents forged by officials at the Karachi Port Trust (KPT).[2] Paradoxically, those who profited the most from this trade were the Afghan and Pakistani Taliban, who received millions of dollars as 'protection charges' from NATO and ISAF.[3] But this trade also had significant repercussions over 'political' and 'ethnic' conflicts in Karachi. Thus, the conflict between the MQM and the PAC was fuelled by a competition for the control of Karachi's market of protection, including that of the transporters carrying NATO cargo transiting through the city. This 'NATO factor' in Karachi's conflicted politics is bound to remain topical in the years to come, as large quantities of equipment used by these troops will have to be shipped back from Karachi's port—a matter of serious concern for NATO countries.[4]

The reasons for the perpetuation of Karachi's chronic disorder should also be looked at further, in the response—or the lack thereof—of foreign powers to this protracted crisis. While the regionalisation of Lebanese conflicts contributed to their escalation, their international politics also participated in their resolution and to the gradual normalisation of the situation in Beirut.[5] The threat of their extradition to the United States, for its part, seems to have accelerated the demobilisation of Colombian paramilitaries, a development which significantly impacted the level of violence in a city like Medellin.[6] On the contrary, in the case of Karachi, the imperatives of the war on terror seem to play in favour of the status quo. The position of the British government towards the MQM could significantly evolve in the coming months, as the enquiry into Imran Farooq's murder follows its course.[7] Until now, though, the accusations of remote-controlled political violence waged against the exiled leadership of the party have fallen on deaf ears in Britain. For all the controversies surrounding him and his party, Altaf Hussain has served British and American interests by standing against religious 'extremists' and giving visibility to a moderately enlightened if not pro-Western public at a time when anti-Occidentalism seemed to rule supreme over Pakistan. After all, this is the party that organised mammoth 'anti-terrorism rallies' in the wake of the 11 September attacks, at a time when the jihadis aimed at demonstrating their street power throughout urban Pakistan. The MQM also provided the British government with access to Pakistan's corridors of power and to information on the ground, making Karachi 'one of the few places left on earth in which the Americans let Britain take the lead'.[8] In return, the prolonged complacency of this 'long-time stakeholder in Karachi politics'[9] towards the MQM and its disruptive tactics undoubtedly contributed to the sustainability of Karachi's violent government.

While the original circumstances of Karachi's ordered disorder and the MQM's predominance found a source of sustenance in these national and international developments, new actors and thus new power relations started emerging. The violent escalation witnessed since 2007 is not the sign of a descent into chaos but of a series of reconfigurations of Karachi's ordered disorder, from an oligarchic two-tier game to an increasingly democratic multi-level one.[10] The years 2008–2013, during which time the MQM maintained an uneasy co-operation with the PPP and the ANP in Sindh and in Islamabad already signalled a transition in Karachi politics, which saw the MQM's power being curtailed by an increasingly affluent, numerous and vocal Pashtun community, represented by the ANP. This transition involved a certain amount of violence, as exemplified by the events of 12 May 2007 and the vain attempt made by the MQM to roll back the influx of Pashtuns into Karachi in the following years. The predominance of the MQM—which culminated between 2005 and 2008, when the party controlled tightly the local government while keeping the provincial government at bay—was already challenged by these developments. With the advent of a three-sided coalition in the province and at the centre, the MQM was downgraded to the position of a primus inter pares, within a configuration increasingly resembling an inter-party oligarchy (the military, which in the 1990s did not hesitate to intervene directly in Karachi politics, had now backtracked and contented itself with a more distant observer role). However divided, political parties were still calling the shots—sometimes literally, as the events of July and August 2011 demonstrated. In recent years, however, the power differential between the players on the upper level of the game (political parties) and those on the lower levels (violent entrepreneurs of different kinds, such as land suppliers, sectarian and jihadist organisations, criminal gangs,...) has been decreasing. This shift in Karachi's 'constellations of the balance of power'[11] was the combined outcome of the growth in military capability achieved by these lower-level players, of their rising economic clout (as a result of a fast liberalising market of protection and a thriving unofficial housing sector, in particular) and of the self-confining of the so-called 'law and order forces' to the role of a referee arbitrating the violent conflicts among the players of the upper and lower levels as well as between them. These violent entrepreneurs, who had often been instrumentalised by political parties in the past, now started standing toe-to-toe with their former patrons, when they did not try to revert the terms of domination. As multi-level games democratise, lower-level players tend to consider that they are no longer the retainers of upper-level players and that, on the contrary, the latter are there for their benefit.[12] In Karachi, this general trend finds its best illustration in the recent transformation of the relationship between the PAC and the PPP. This is not an isolated case, though, and other political parties—including the MQM—are increasingly constrained by the actions of criminal groups and unofficial entrepreneurs whom they used to consider their dependents.

Despite what many adversaries of the party would like to believe, it is therefore highly unlikely that the weakening of the MQM—which remains relative, but which is now indisputable, whether in electoral, military or financial terms[13]—will bring durable peace to the city. As this book aims to demonstrate, the crystallisation of an ordered disorder in Karachi during the late 1980s/early 1990s was irreducible to the strategies of the political parties that competed for the control of the city and its resources, even the most powerful ones. Moreover, the predominance of the MQM brought some order to the city. It translated into contested but relatively stable patterns of domination, which introduced some predictability up until the violence and disorder that were consubstantial to the reproduction of this domination. As a result, the marginalisation of the MQM in the urns and in the armed politics that has become the trademark of Karachi over the years will probably bring greater instability and uncertainty, as well as a continuous rise in the level of violence.

This phase of terror could be temporary, as the demographic changes at work in the city and the increasing difficulty faced by individual political parties to contain violent entrepreneurs on their own could constrain these parties to soften their ethnic stance and build cross-ethnic coalitions.[14] The growing threat posed by the Pakistani Taliban's shift to logics of territorialisation, since 2012, could provide such a meeting ground for self-declared secular parties such as the MQM, the PPP and the ANP. However, as the volatile coalition politics of 2008–2013 demonstrated, the advent of such coalitions is no guarantee, in itself, of a pacification of Karachi politics. Moreover, even if political parties committed collectively to a more civil code of conduct, the shift in power balances described above suggests that this will not suffice in allaying Karachi's endemic violence. Recent developments, such as the tussle between the PAC and the PPP in Lyari, the showdown between the MQM and Muhammad Khan in Altaf Nagar or the eviction of the ANP from its former strongholds at the hands of the Taliban unequivocally demonstrated that mainstream political parties have lost some ground to a new breed of de facto sovereigns in several parts of the city. A growing number of stakeholders, all of whom have formidable economic and military resources, are determined to defend their sense of entitlement to the city. In this context, the culture of terror sponsored by political parties and violent entrepreneurs could continue to upset everyday life and compromise pluralistic urban living in the city, radically altering its cosmopolitanism.

At the same time, there is little scope for this increasingly disorderly configuration—or, more precisely, for this democratising multi-level game—to lead to a proper situation of anarchy or to a full-blown civil war. The political landscape of Karachi remains too prone to state intervention (by the various branches of the security apparatus but also, and this is a more recent trend, by the judiciary) to descend into utter chaos. This is what the crackdown against alledged 'target killers', 'extortionists' and 'gangsters' launched by Nawaz Sharif's government in early September 2013 demonstrated. Hundreds of suspects were arrested and this grand operation overseen by the Rangers brought some respite in the violence plaguing the city. Although many residents doubted that this lull would last, considering the astoundingly low rate of conviction of suspected criminals in Pakistani courts and the extent of their political protections in a city like Karachi, the state once again demonstrated its resilience nonetheless. While remaining prone to such state interventions—however flawed these may be—Karachi has also become too atomised to lend itself to a conventional civil war between incumbents and insurgents. Instead, the city faces a proliferation of highly localised turf wars that result from an increasingly even competition—and thus from more balanced power relations—at all levels of the game. As the number of players increase, any 'figuration' runs the risk of becoming increasingly disorganised and of seeing its functioning deteriorate.[15] But the game may pursue its course nonetheless. Save for a few emerging protagonists of Karachi's battles (such as the Pakistani Taliban), most stakeholders do not challenge the order of things—namely, parliamentary democracy and a liberalising economy—but aim to maximise their gains within the prevalent conditions. In this context, the creative reproduction of Karachi's ordered disorder, that is, its continuous reconfiguration in the course of its actualisation, is all set to pursue its course. And if past regulatory mechanisms, which relied upon strong power differentials between the state security apparatus and political parties but also between the latter and violent entrepreneurs, may no longer be in order, others seem to be emerging at the lower levels of the game, from the very violent interactions that have repeatedly brought the city to a halt in recent years.

The ongoing mutations of real estate politics in the city, which played such a critical role at every stage of Karachi's conflicts, are a case in point. The escalation of violence witnessed in recent years was fuelled by a fierce competition between the various land suppliers operating in the city, both within and without political parties. This race focused, in particular, on the subdivision and development of agricultural land attached to the city's urban villages. It begun at the tail-end of Pervez Musharraf's rule and culminated in 2011 before receding, as there was simply less and less available land. Between 2008 and 2013, the PPP government started approving land titles for the *goth*s, first at the collective level of the *abadi* (settlement) and later on at the individual level of residents. According to Perween Rahman, the late director of the OPP, more than half of the city's *goth*s had been approved in this way by February 2013, providing their residents with some security against land grabbers of all kinds. As Rahman emphasised, 'There is still some land [to grab], but not huge chunks.' As a result, practices of land grabbing have become less spectacular, which is not to say that illicit real estate operations have stopped altogether. A new practice emerged recently in the shape of 'doubling', which consists, for a land supplier, in reselling land to several buyers at the same time, letting them fight among themselves for ownership rights. Moreover, various forms of encroachments are still taking place in graveyards, parks and drainage channels, as well as on coastal land.[16]

If the days of the great land rush seem to be over in Karachi, people still kill 'instantly' for land, Perween Rahman added. Her assumption was tragically validated a few weeks later by her own murder, which was probably commissioned by the so-called 'land mafia' she had so consistently engaged, and occasionally antagonised. No one was more familiar with the ground realities of Karachi's roughest neighbourhoods than she was. Rahman's observations thus deserve to be kept in mind at the time of closing this book. This sensitive analyst of Karachi's contested terrain was well aware that the battles for the city involved an ever increasing number of protagonists, but also that the dividing lines between this growing number of belligerents increasingly ran across them, with a large number of killings currently taking place *within* political parties, in relation to personal or financial disputes. This development has important implications. It suggests that Karachi's ordered disorder is not a zero-sum game, where the weakening of some players (state agencies, political parties,...) would mechanically translate into the strengthening of others (criminal groups, religious organisations,...). Not only do the members of these groups circulate between them: they can also occupy several positions at the same time, these dynamics of straddling being exemplified by the involvement of public officials in the unofficial housing sector, by the participation of the police in criminal activities and by the sheltering of petty criminals by political parties and jihadist organisations. Karachi's ordered disorder is not only growing more complex but also more opaque, so much so that its participants have lost the capacity to represent themselves in the game in its entirety as much as in deciphering individual moves, including those by their own 'team'. In such opaque and uncontrollable configurations, the game starts to take on a life of its own and the individual player 'gradually becomes *aware* of his inability to understand and control it'.[17] If the growing opacity of Karachi's ordered disorder and the chronic uncertainty descending upon its protagonists and their audience are a case in point, a similar phenomenon seems to be at work in the reconfiguration of the jihadist/sectarian scene in Pakistan at large: nobody knows any longer who works with whom, for whom and under whose protection.

Despite this opacity and the awareness growing among individual players (even the most powerful ones) that they cannot figure out, let alone control the whole game, Perween Rahman remained convinced that Karachi was *not* an anarchic metropolis, and she doubted that the evolutions of recent years could be the prelude to a general conflagration. According to her:

> Different land suppliers might be supporting certain political parties but at the bottom line they are partners... They often come from the same area... And they have to work... Sultan Bhai can work with Subhan [Rahman is here referring to two notorious land suppliers], it's not a problem... That's why, after a while, there has to be peace. [Episodes of collective violence] cannot extend for too long... The bottom line is more about personalities: who gets along with whom. It's the same for political parties: they can make statements against each other but this won't prevent them from working together in land supply, like the MQM and Sindhi nationalists for instance.[18]

One does need to subscribe to functionalist or peace through commerce paradigms to endorse this statement. More subtly, Rahman pointed out that even those violent entrepreneurs—such as land suppliers—who owe their economic and political clout to decades of violence and disorder tend to recreate incrementally, through their interdependencies, a 'flexible lattice-work of tensions'[19] moderating their endemic conflicts while setting the conditions for their reproduction. Beneath the apparent chaos descending upon the city, an emerging order is profiling itself. The configuration that it will give shape to—and that will reshape it in turn—could well be more violent, more volatile and even more intractable than the one that preceded it, though. Granted, the continuous escalation and increasingly random nature of political and criminal violence in Karachi are no hindrance to its routinisation, that is, to its management through everyday procedures aiming at reducing the level of threats. As Perween Rahman used to say, 'There's always a way of working when there's chaos.' She emphasised, for instance, how Karachi's commuters like herself started stocking food in their cars after the riots that engulfed large parts of the city in the aftermath of Benazir Bhutto's killing, so that they wouldn't be caught unprepared by another prolonged episode of rioting.[20] However, such routines for the management of violence are never more than an attempt to adapt to a fast-changing and irreducibly unpredictable environment. If one can work one's way around 'chaos', there is no business 'as usual' in such fluid situations. And on such a rough sea, even the most experienced and prudent navigators are never guaranteed to return safely to port. Perween Rahman was well aware of this, and this is what made her commitment to improving the living conditions of Karachi's denizens so striking. One can only hope that her callous murder will be vindicated by a new generation of political activists and social reformers who, without losing sight of the realities of Karachi's mean steets, will be as committed as she was in upholding the possibility of a common world for Karachi's battle-weary populations.

This task is more pressing than ever, for Karachi but also for Pakistan at large. Because of Karachi's enduring centrality in the national economy but also because of the city's increasingly complex ethnic mix, the country will not pull itself back from the brink without bringing Karachi on board. Among many others, Karachi bears the nickname 'mini-Pakistan' for its ethnic, linguistic and religious diversity. Since the mid-1980s, Pakistan's only megalopolis has also become a microcosm of the multiple fault lines running across the country. Sadly, the story recalled in this book is not unique to Karachi. Instead, it is revealing of the increasing difficulties faced by Pakistan's ethnic, linguistic and sectarian groups to coexist peacefully, even separately. It also bears testimony to the informalisation of state power and development policies, to the militarisation of society, to the criminalisation of politics and to the politicisation of criminals that have been reshaping state and society, while blurring their boundaries, over the past decades. As a commentator observed in the columns of the Lahore-based weekly *The Friday Times* in the midst of Karachi's worst episode of urban warfare since the mid-1990s, 'All of these things are also happening in other parts of Pakistan, but are scattered over a greater area. In Karachi, they come together, and create a horrifying scenario, which, one only hopes, is not a precursor of how things may develop in Pakistan if the current wave of divisiveness on every count continues.'[21]

To a great extent, this 'horrifying scenario' is the ransom of success, for a city that never ceased to whet the appetite of its aspiring hegemons and captivate the imagination of generation after generation of immigrants, ready to risk losing it all for a second chance in the 'city benevolent towards the poor' (*gharib nawaz shehr*, yet another nickname for this city of dreams, however broken). These famous verses by Mirza Ghalib, who saw his own share of political turmoil and urban decay in late-Mughal Delhi, convey this predicament with more eloquence than any contemporary writer could ever dream of:

Meri t'amir mein muzmir hai ek surat kharabi ki
Hayola barq-e-khirman ka hai khun-e-garm dahqan ka

Inherent in my creation is the seed of my destruction.
The passion of my creative endeavour creates instead the force which strikes me down.[22]

NOTES

INTRODUCTION

1. Sahil, Zeeshan, 'Ek Dīn' (Urdu) (One Day), in *Karāchī aur Dūsrī Nazmen* (Urdu) (*Karachi and Other Poems*), Karachi: Aaj, 1995, p. 124. I am grateful to Hidayat Hussain for bringing Zeeshan Sahil's work to my attention.
2. This figure was taken from the preliminary results of the 2011 Census. It indicates a 115 per cent increase in Karachi's population since the previous census, which was conducted in 1998 (cf. Table 1). Even if the city's growth slowed down substantially, Karachi could become the largest city in the world by 2030; cf. Cox, Wendell, 'Pakistan: where the population bomb is exploding', *NewGeography.com*, 7 February 2012; http://www.newgeography.com/content/002940-pakistan-where-population-bomb-exploding (Accessed 3 October 2013)
3. In June 2013, the painter Naiza H. Khan curated an exhibition in Karachi on art and violence in Pakistan, where she presented a drawing of a corpse stashed in a gunny bag under the title, '*bori band lash*'; cf. Ali, Syed Hassan, 'Violence has influenced art tremendously in recent times', *Dawn.com*, 26 June 2013; http://dawn.com/news/1020670/violence-has-influenced-art-tremendously-in-recent times/?commentPage=1&storyPage=1 (Accessed 3 October 2013)
4. Taussig, Michael, 'Terror as usual: Walter Benjamin's Theory of History as a state of siege', *Social Text*, 23, Autumn-Winter (1989), p. 4.
5. The 1951 Census defined '*muhajirs*' as 'persons who entered Pakistan on account of partition or for fear of disturbances connected therewith'; *Census of Pakistan, 1951*, vol. 1, Table 19-a, note 1, pp. 19–2.
6. The Arabic term *muhajir* (pl. *muhajirin*) refers to the 'migrants' who accompanied Prophet Muhammad from Mecca to Medina in 622 AD. This migration (*hijrat*) marks the beginning of the Muslim calendar.
7. Russell, Ralph, 'The pursuit of the Urdu Ghazal', *The Journal of Asian Studies*, 29, 1, November (1969), p. 124.
8. Zamindar, Vazira Fazila-Yacoobali, *The Long Partition and the Making of Modern South Asia. Refugees, Boundaries, Histories*, Delhi: Penguin, 2008 [2007], p. 156.

9. Source: Citizens Police Liaison Committee (CPLC), http://www.cplc.org.pk/content.php?page=26 (Accessed 3 October 2013)
10. Chaussée, G. A., 'Translator's note', in 'Zeeshan Sahil, *Karachi and Other Poems*: a selection', *Annual of Urdu Studies*, (1996), pp. 90–1.
11. Khan, Nichola, *Mohajir Militancy in Pakistan. Violence and Practices of Transformation in the Karachi Conflict*, London: Routledge, 2010, p. 64.
12. Pécaut, Daniel, 'From the banality of violence to real terror', in Koonings, Kees and Dirk Kruijt (eds), *Societies of Fear. The Legacy of Civil War, Violence and Terror in Latin America*, London/New York: Zed Books, 1999, pp. 141–67; Taussig, Michael, 'Terror as usual', art. quoted, pp. 3–20.
13. Michael Taussig, 'Terror as Usual', art. quoted, p. 4.
14. See for instance the autobiographical account of political scientist Noman Baig, who grew up in Liaquatabad in the 1990s, in Baig, Noman, *From Mohalla to Mainstream. The MQM's Transformation From an Ethnic to a Catch-All Party*, BA Thesis (Political Science), University of Oklahoma, 2005, pp. xiii-xxiii.
15. I am grateful to Mahim Maher for this information.
16. Baig, Noman, *From Mohalla to Mainstream*, op. cit., p. xviii.
17. 'Back from the brink', *The Herald* (Karachi), September 2002, p. 90.
18. On this distinction between the 'routinisation' and 'habituation' of violence, see Vigh, Henrik, *Navigating Terrains of War. Youth and Soldiering in Guinea Bissau*, Oxford/New York: Berghahn, 2007, pp. 154–5.
19. Rozema, Ralph, 'Medellin', in Koonings, Kees and Dirk Kruijt (eds), *Fractured Cities. Social Exclusion, Urban Violence and Contested Spaces in Latin America*, London/New York: Zed Books, 2007, p. 65.
20. As Thomas Blom Hansen and Finn Stepputat argue, 'communal riots' are too often constructed by state agencies—but also by local and foreign analysts—as 'events without actors', characterised by their spontaneity. This line of argument does not only deny rationality to supposedly impressionable masses, but guarantees impunity to the perpetrators of these episodes of collective violence, which are generally much more organised than they seem; cf. Hansen, Thomas Blom and Finn Stepputat, 'Introduction', in Hansen, Thomas Blom and Finn Stepputat (eds), *Sovereign Bodies. Citizens, Migrants, and States in the Postcolonial World*, Princeton/Oxford: Princeton University Press, 2005, pp. 28–9.
21. Names followed by an * have been changed to preserve the anonymity of my respondents.
22. Interview, Karachi, December 2011.
23. The comparison of Karachi with Beirut at war is in fact much more ancient and started being made by Pakistani journalists in the mid-1980s; see for instance Hussain, Zahid, 'The war within', *The Herald*, August 1987, p. 69.
24. See for instance Abbas, Qaswar, 'World's most dangerous city', *India Today* (Delhi), 27 August 2011.
25. See Alvi, Suroosh, 'Vice guide to Karachi', http://www.vice.com/the-vice-guide-to-travel/the-vice-guide-to-karachi-part-1 (Accessed 3 October 2013) and

Kemp, Ross, 'Extreme world: Karachi', http://www.youtube.com/watch?v=-QukrBRg38s (Accessed 5 October 2013)

26. Hashim, Asad, 'Karachi's killing fields', *AlJazeera.com*, 7 September 2012; http://www.aljazeera.com/indepth/interactive/2012/08/201282210292095l929.html (Accessed 3 October 2013)
27. Yusuf, Huma, *Conflict Dynamics in Karachi*, Washington: United States Institute for Peace, 2012, p. 4.
28. Hasan, Arif, *Participatory Development. The Story of the Orangi Pilot Project-Research and Training Institute, and the Urban Resource Centre, Karachi, Pakistan*, Karachi: Oxford University Press, 2010, p. 16; Asian Development Bank, *Karachi Megacities Preparation Project: Final Report*, vol. 1, 2005.
29. Marshall, Andrew, 'To live and die in Karachi', *Time*, 16 January 2012, pp. 24–9.
30. Tambiah, Stanley J., *Leveling Crowds. Ethnonationalist Conflicts and Collective Violence in South Asia*, Delhi: Vistaar, 1997, p. 193.
31. I am indebted, here, to Vigh, Henrik, *Navigating Terrains of War*, op. cit.
32. Ibid., p. 166. Although the author sees a form of 'ordered disorder' in Guinea Bissau, his demonstration suggests otherwise, pointing towards a form of chaos.
33. Hashim, Asad, 'Interactive: killings sweep Karachi', *AlJazeera.com*, 7 September, 2012, http://www.aljazeera.com/indepth/interactive/2012/08/201282210292 0951929.html (Accessed 5 October 2013)
34. Ibid.
35. 'Seven most violent flashpoints in Karachi', *The Herald*, September 2011, pp. 62–3.
36. Richards, Paul (ed.), *No Peace No War. An Anthropology of Contemporary Armed Conflicts*, Oxford: James Currey, 2005.
37. Kalyvas, Stathis N., 'The ontology of "Political Violence": action and identity in civil wars', *Perspectives on Politics*, 1, 3, September 2003, pp. 475–94.
38. For an overview of these practices, see the first chapter of Khan, Nichola, *Mohajir Militancy in Pakistan*, op. cit.
39. Elias, Norbert, *The Civilizing Process*, Oxford: Blackwell, 1994 (1939), p. 444.
40. Quoted in Taussig, Michael, 'Terror as usual', art. quoted, p. 7.
41. Ibid.
42. For a recent re-appraisal of this classical line of thought, see North, Douglass C., John Joseph Wallis and Barry R. Weingast, *Violence and Social Orders. A Conceptual Framework for Interpreting Recorded Human History*, Cambridge: Cambridge University Press, 2009.
43. The German term *figuration* used by Elias has generally been translated into English as 'figuration', and less frequently as 'configuration'. Although my own preference goes to this more commonly used term, each of its occurence refers directly to Elias' figurational sociology.
44. Elias, Norbert, *What is Sociology?*, New York: Columbia University Press, 1978, pp. 130–1.
45. Elias, Norbert, 'Figuration', in Schäfers, Bernard, (ed.), *Grundbegriffe der Soziologie*, Opladen: Leske en Budrich, 1986, p. 162, quoted by van Krieken, Robert, *Norbert Elias*, London: Routledge, 1998, p. 48.

46. Burger, Thomas, 'Talcott Parsons, the problem of order in society, and the program of an analytical sociology', *American Journal of Sociology*, 83, 2, September 1977, pp. 320–39.
47. Elias, Norbert, *The Civilizing Process*, op. cit., p. 444.
48. Hansen, Thomas Blom, 'Sovereigns beyond the state: on legality and authority in urban India', in Hansen, Thomas Blom and Finn Stepputat, (eds), *Sovereign Bodies*, op. cit., p. 170.
49. Debos, Marielle, *Le Métier des Armes au Tchad. Le Gouvernement de l'entre-guerres*, Paris: Karthala, 2013; Lund, Christian, 'Twilight institutions: an introduction', *Development and Change*, 37, 4 (2006), pp. 673–84; Raeymaekers, Timothy, Ken Menkhaus and Koen Vlassenroot, 'State and non-state regulation in African protracted crises: governance without government', *Afrika Focus*, 21, 2 (2008), pp. 7–21.
50. Richards, Paul, 'New war: an ethnographic approach', in Richards, Paul, (ed.), *No Peace No War*, op. cit., p. 4.
51. Kalyvas, Stathis N., *The Logic of Violence in Civil War*, Cambridge: Cambridge University Press, 2006.
52. Coronil, Fernando and Julie Skurski, 'Introduction: states of violence and the violence of states', in Coronil, Fernando and Julie Skurski, (eds), *States of Violence*, Ann Harbor: University of Michigan Press, 2006, p. 2.
53. Taussig, Michael, 'Terror as usual', art. quoted, p. 14.
54. Taussig, Michael, *Law in a Lawless Land. Diary of a Limpieza in Colombia*, Chicago/London: Chicago University Press, 2003, p. 17.
55. Richards, Paul, 'New war: an ethnographic approach', art. quoted, p. 14.
56. Ahmad, Tania, 'Bystander tactics: life on turf in Karachi', *SAMAJ*, 5 (2011); Ali, Kamran Asdar, 'Men and their "Problems": notes on contemporary Karachi', in Ali, Kamran Asdar and Martina Rieker (eds), *Comparing Cities. The Middle East and South Asia*, Delhi: Oxford University Press, 2009; Khan, Nichola, *Mohajir Militancy in Pakistan*, op. cit.; Chaudhry, Lubna Nazir, 'Reconstituting selves in the Karachi conflict: Mohajir women survivors and structural violence', *Cultural Dynamics*, 16, 2/3 (2004), pp. 259–90; Ring, Laura, *Zenana. Everyday Peace in a Karachi Apartment Building*, Bloomington and Indianapolis: University of Indiana Press, 2006.

1. A CONTESTED CITY

1. Riaz, Fahmida, *Karāchī*, reprinted in Kamal, Ajmal (ed.), *Karachī kī Kahānī* (Urdu) (*The Story of Karachi*), Karachi: Aaj, 2007 [1996], vol. 2, p. 476.
2. *Guide to Karachi*, Karachi, *circa* 1943.
3. Hasam, Zinat, 'Guzre dīn, guzarte dīn' (Urdu) (Past days, passing days), in Kamal, Ajmal (ed.), *Karāchī kī Kahānī*, op. cit., vol. 2, pp. 617–53.
4. Siddiqi, Anwar Ehsan, 'Parwarish-e-loh-o-qalam (khud nawisht)' (Urdu) (Literary upbringing: an autobiography), in Farrukhi, Asif (ed.), *Dunyā Zād*, 32 (2011), p. 272.

5. Hasam, Zinat, 'Guzre dīn, guzarte dīn', art. quoted, p. 622.
6. On this character, emblematic of Karachi's nightlife during the 1960s and 1970s, see Yusuf, Huma, 'City of Lights: violence and Karachi's competing imaginaries', in Anjaria, Jonathan Shapiro and Colin McFarlane (eds), *Urban Navigations. Politics, Space and the City in South Asia*, Delhi: Routledge, 2011, pp. 298–318, as well as Inskeep, Steve, *Instant City. Life and Death in Karachi*, Penguin: New York, 2011.
7. A famous militant of the MQM, who was arrested and charged with numerous murders in 1999.
8. See for instance the presentation of Karachi on the website of the City District Government of Karachi, which claims that, 'It is locally termed as the City of Lights for its liveliness'; cf. 'Karachi the gateway of Pakistan'; http://www.karachicity.gov.pk/ (Accessed 3 October 2013)
9. Verkaaik, Oskar, 'At home in Karachi: quasi-domesticity as a way to know the city', *Critique of Anthropology*, 29, 1 (2009), pp. 65–80.
10. Shaheed, Zafar, *The Labour Movement in Pakistan. Organisation and Leadership in Karachi in the 1970s*, Karachi: Oxford University Press, 2007, p. 258.
11. See for instance Harris Khalique's poem 'Rush' (Urdu), in *Ishq kī Taqwīm mein. Harris Khaliq kī Nazmen, 1985–2005* (Urdu) (In the Calendar of Love. Poems by Harris Khalique, 1985–2005), Karachi: Danyal, 2006, p. 137.
12. Ali, Kamran Asdar, 'Strength of the state meets strength of the street: the 1972 labour struggle in Karachi', in Khan, Naveeda, (ed.), *Beyond Crisis. Re-Evaluating Pakistan*, Delhi: Routledge, 2010, p. 210.
13. Karachi's first major 'ethnic riot' took place in the wake of the January 1965 presidential election, when a victory procession led by Gohar Ayub, the son of Field Marshall Ayub Khan, led to clashes between the (mostly Pashtun) armed supporters of Ayub and Urdu-speakers as the procession was passing through Liaquatabad.
14. Shakir, Parveen, 'Karāchī', in *Khud Kalāmī* (Urdu) (Monologue), 1990.
15. Quoted by Prakash, Gyan, *Mumbai Fables*, Princeton: Princeton University Press, 2010, p. 25.
16. Ibid., p. 11.
17. Jalal, Ayesha, *Self and Sovereignty. Individual and Community in South Asian Islam Since 1850*, Delhi: Oxford University Press, 2001, p. 11.
18. Bhopali, Mohsin, *Shehr-e-Ashob* (Urdu) (Lament for the City), Karachi: Aiwan-e-Adab, 1997.
19. See for instance the analysis of Jurat's 'Mukhammas-i-Shahr Ashob', in Pritchett, Frances W., 'The world turned upside down: sahr-asob as a genre', *Annual of Urdu Studies*, vol. 4 (1984), p. 39. On the anti-plebeian bias of the *shehr-e-ashob*, see also Haqe, Ishrat, *Glimpses of Mughal Society and Culture*, Delhi: Concept Publishing Company, 1992, p. 71 sq.
20. Prakash, Gyan, *Mumbai Fables*, op. cit., p. 30.
21. Ibid.

22. Lefebvre, Henri, *Le Droit à la Ville*, Paris: Anthropos, 1968.
23. Verkaaik, Oskar, 'At home in Karachi', art. quoted, p. 69.
24. Ibid.
25. Tan, Tai Yong and Gyanesh Kudaisya, *The Aftermath of Partition in South Asia*, London/New York: Routledge, 2000, p. 185.
26. *Census of Pakistan 1951*, vol. 1, Table 19-A, pp. 19–2.
27. Boivin, Michel, 'Karachi et ses territoires en conflit: pour une relecture de la question communautaire', *Hérodote*, 101 (2001/2002), p. 182.
28. The introduction of this passport system was preceded by the unilateral adoption of a permit system by India in July 1948, with the Pakistani state adopting similar restrictions a few months later; cf. Fazila-Yacoobali Zamindar, Vazira, *The Long Partition and the Making of Modern South Asia*, op. cit., p. 82.
29. Ansari, Sarah, *Life after Partition. Migration, Community and Strife in Sindh, 1947–1962*, Karachi: Oxford University Press, 2005, p. 122.
30. Nichols, Robert, *A History of Pashtun Migration, 1775–2006*, Karachi: Oxford University Press, 2008, p. 151.
31. On the difficulties of quantifying the Afghan presence in Karachi, see *Afghans in Karachi. Migration, Settlement and Social Networks*, Karachi: Collective for Social Science Research, 2005, p. 4.
32. Ibid., pp. 2, 34.
33. Hasan, Arif, *Understanding Karachi. Planning and Reform for the Future*, Karachi: City Press, 1999, p. 27.
34. Haroon, Fariha Razak, 'The police is bankrupt', *The Friday Times* (Lahore), 17–23 August 2001, p. 5.
35. Supreme Court of Pakistan, Suo Motu Case No. 16 of 2011 [suo motu regarding law and order situation in Karachi], 2011 [thereafter SMC 2011], p. 75.
36. Mansoor, Hasan, 'Aliens set up seminaries in Karachi', *The Friday Times*, 18–24 April 2003.
37. *Afghans in Karachi*, op. cit., p. 4.
38. Yusuf, Huma, *Conflict Dynamics in Karachi*, op. cit., p. 8.
39. A projection merely based on the population growth rate of this population as provided in the 1998 Census would already approach 3 million.
40. Rehman, Zia ur, 'Demographic divide', *The Friday Times*, 15–21 July 2011.
41. Ansari, Sarah, *Life after Partition*, op. cit.; Zamindar, Vazira Fazila-Yacoobali, *The Long Partition and the Making of Modern South Asia*, op. cit.; Daechsel, Markus, 'Sovereignty, governmentality and development in Ayub's Pakistan: the case of Korangi township', *Modern Asian Studies*, 45, 1 (2011), pp. 131–57.
42. If most Hindu elites left Karachi in the months following Partition, the departure of affluent Parsi families (the Minwallas, Katraks, Dinshaws, etc.) was a later development. So much so that in the 1970s, these Parsi families still controlled the port sector and the shipping industry; cf. Boivin, Michel, 'Karachi, "mère des immigrés": business, violence et politique identitaire', *Hérodote*, no. 139 (2010), p. 130.

43. I am grateful to Thomas Blom Hansen for bringing this discrepancy to my attention.
44. Tahir, Tanvir Ahmad, *Political Dynamics of Sindh, 1947–1977*, Karachi: Pakistan Study Centre, 2010, p. 171.
45. The One Unit system aimed to counterbalance the demographic weight of the Bengalis by regrouping all the provinces of West Pakistan under a single administrative unit.
46. On cosmopolitanism as 'the ethical idea of living together with strangers', see Mayaram, Shail, 'Introduction: rereading global cities: topographies of an alternative cosmopolitanism in Asia', in Mayaram, Shail, (ed.), *The Other Global City*, Delhi: Yoda Press, 2013 (2009), p. 9.
47. Zamindar, Vazira Fazila-Yacoobali, *The Long Partition and the Making of Modern South Asia*, op. cit.
48. Interview with Shahi Syed, Islamabad, July 2007.
49. Interview with Zafar Baloch, Karachi (Lyari), August 2012.
50. Budhani, Azmat Ali, Haris Gazdar, Sobia Ahmad Kaker and Hussain Bux Mallah, 'The open city. Social networks and violence in Karachi', Crisis States Research Centre working papers series 2, 70, Crisis States Research Centre, London: London School of Economics and Political Science, 2010, p. 1.
51. 'Karachi: SC dismisses pleas in Major Kalim case', *Dawn.com*, 14 August 2007; http://dawn.com/news/261106/karachi-sc-dismisses-pleas-in-major-kalim-case (Accessed 3 October 2013)
52. *The Herald* (Karachi), September 2000.
53. Source: http://www.cplc.org.pk/content.php?page=26 (Accessed 3 October 2013)
54. One of the most elaborate endeavours, in this regard, was the design of Shahjahanabad (Old Delhi) in the seventeenth century; cf. Blake, Stephen P., *Shahjahanabad. The Sovereign City in Mughal India 1639–1739*, Cambridge: Cambridge University Press, 1991.
55. Hotchand, Seth Naomul, *The Memoirs of Seth Naomul Hotchand*, Karachi: Pakistan Herald Publications, 2006, p. 3. The autobiography of Seth Naomul Hotchand was originally published as *A Forgotten Chapter of Indian History, as told by Seth Naomal Hotchand, CSI, of Karachi (1804–1878), Written by Himeself and Translated by His Grandson Rao Bahadur Alumal Trikamdas Bhojwani, BA, Edited with an Introduction by Sir H. Evan M. James, KCIE, CSI, Commissioner of Sindh, 1891–1899, Printed for Private Circulation Only*, Surat, 1915.
56. Ibid., p. 9.
57. Gazdar, Haris, et al, 'The open city', art. quoted.
58. The model of the dual city, which had already been experimented in Madras before being expanded to Karachi, aimed to limit the contacts between the British and the 'natives', prevent the spread of epidemics, defend the colonial quarters against 'communal riots' and demonstrate the cultural superiority of the colonisers. On the history of Karachi's dual city, see Lari, Yasmeen and Mihail S. Lari, *The Dual City. Karachi During the Raj*, Karachi: Oxford University Press, 2001.

59. On the contribution of Seth Harchandrai Vishandas to the modernisation of Karachi, see Boivin, Michel, 'Les hindous de Karachi dans la perspective historique: de la domination socio-économique à la marginalisation minoritaire', *Revue des Mondes Musulmans et de la Méditerranée*, 107–110, September (2005), pp. 61–96.
60. Amrohvi, Rais, 'Pagrī', *Jang*, 9 May 1948, reproduced in *Qat'āt Raīs Amrohvī*, vol. 1, Karachi: Rais Academy, 1987, p. 16.
61. Ansari, Sarah, *Life After Partition*, op. cit., pp. 126, 127.
62. Tahir, Tanvir Ahmad, *Political Dynamics of Sindh*, op. cit., p. 502.
63. Ansari, Sarah, *Life After Partition, op. cit.*, p. 141.
64. Ibid., p. 188.
65. On these discrepancies between Ayub Khan's and C.A. Doxiadis' imaginings of Korangi as a 'space of discipline' and a 'space of governmentality' respectively, see Daechsel, Markus, 'Sovereignty, governmentality and development in Ayub's Pakistan', art. quoted.
66. Ibid., p. 148.
67. Hasan, Arif, *Understanding Karachi*, op. cit., p. 26.
68. Appadurai, Arjun, 'Spectral housing and urban cleansing: notes on millenial Mumbai', *Public Culture*, 12, 3 (2000), pp. 627–51.
69. Interview with Perween Rahman, head of the Orangi Pilot Project (OPP), Karachi (Qasba Colony), February 2013.
70. Frotscher, Ann, *Claiming Pakistan. The MQM and the Fight for Belonging*, Nomos: Baden Baden, 2008, p. 60.
71. Hasan, Arif, 'Development and change in Pakistan', *City* (Karachi), 1 July 2002, p. 9.
72. Ibid.
73. Ibid., p. 10.
74. The OPP started in Orangi (Karachi's largest unofficial settlement, with a population of 1.5 million) in 1980. Encouraging self-help initiatives, it initially focused on the provision of low-cost sanitation to the residents of Orangi. Over the years, the activities of this NGO expanded to housing, health, education, micro-credit and research (mapping, in particular).
75. Interview with Perween Rahman, director of the OPP, Karachi (Qasba Colony), February 2013.
76. Roitman, Janet, 'The politics of informal markets in sub-Saharan Africa', *The Journal of Modern African Studies*, 28, 4 December (1990), pp. 671–96.
77. Mbembe, Achille, 'Du gouvernement privé indirect', *Politique Africaine*, 73, March (1999), pp. 103–21. On these transformations of sovereignty and state-society relations in contemporary African contexts, see also Mbembe, Achille, 'Sovereignty as a form of expenditure', in Hansen, Thomas Blom and Finn Stepputat (eds), *Sovereign Bodies*, op. cit., pp. 148–66.
78. 'Violent entrepreneurship' refers to 'a set of organizational solutions and action strategies enabling organized force (or organized violence) to be converted into

money or other valuable assets on a permanent basis'; Volkvov, Vadim, *Violent Entrepreneurs. The Use of Force in the Making of Russian Capitalism*, Ithaca/London: Cornell University Press, 2002, p. 25.

79. Between 1987 and 2010, 376 *katchi abadi*s have been notified for regularisation out of a surveyed number of 702 settlements. Only *katchi abadi*s that came into existence before 30 June 1997 are eligible for regularisation; cf. Hasan, Arif and Mansoor Raza, *Karachi. The Land Issues* (first draft), Karachi: NED University, Urban Research and Development Cell, 27 June 2012, p. 22. This legalisation policy has sometimes been resisted by the residents of these colonies themselves, as it led to an increase in land prices, rents and even building material costs; cf. Van der Linden, Jan and Frits Selier (eds), *Karachi. Migrants, Housing and Housing Policy*, Lahore/Karachi: Vanguard, 1991.
80. The *dallal* (middleman; the word also means 'pimp' in Urdu) was the original middleman who subdivided illegally government land and allocated plots to lower-income tenants after ensuring the complacency of the police and the bureaucracy through his network of relations; this somewhat benevolent figure was sidelined by more ruthless slumlords with links to the drugs trade in the 1980s (see infra and Chapter 7).
81. *Thalewala*s provide building materials on loan to the residents of squatter settlements.
82. Hasan, Arif, 'The growth of a metropolis', in Khuhro, Hamida and Anwer Mooraj (eds), *Karachi. Megacity of Our Times*, Karachi: Oxford University Press, 1997, p. 185.
83. Frotscher, Ann, *Claiming Pakistan*, op. cit., p. 50. For an ethnography of neighbourly relations in one of these apartment buildings, see Ring, Laura, *Zenana*, op. cit.
84. Hasan, Arif, *Participatory Development*, op. cit., p. 19.
85. Verkaaik, Oskar, 'At home in Karachi', art. quoted.
86. Appadurai, Arjun, 'Spectral housing and urban cleansing', art. quoted.
87. Siddiqi, Ahmad Hussein, *Karāchī. Gohar-e-Buhīrah 'Arb* (Urdu) (Karachi. The Pearl of the Arabian Sea), Karachi: Fazli Sons, 1995, p. 4.
88. Baillie, Alexander F., *Kurrachee. Past, Present and Future*, Karachi: OUP, 1997 [1890], p. 6.
89. Webb, Montagu de P., 'Editor's Foreword', in *The Karachi Residents Directory for 1932*, Karachi: The Daily Gazette Press, 1932, p. (g).
90. Hasan, Arif and Mansoor Raza, *Karachi. The Land Issues*, op. cit., p. 9.
91. Hussain, Zahid, 'The war within', *The Herald*, August 1987, p. 66.
92. Ibid., p. 70.
93. Cooley, John K., *Unholy Wars. Afghanistan, America and International Terrorism*, London: Pluto Press, 2002 (1999), p. 94.
94. Hanif, Mohammad, 'The gun-runners of Karachi', *Newsline* (Karachi), October 1989, p. 22.
95. Ibid.

96. Yusufzai, Rahimulla, 'The frontier connection', *Newsline*, October 1989, p. 26.
97. Ibid.
98. In the mid-1980s, most intermediaries between international traffickers and Pashtun heroin wholesalers were Mohajirs; cf. Hasan, Arif, 'Karachi's godfathers', *The Herald*, December 1986, p. 79.
99. Hussain, Akmal, 'The Karachi riots of December 1986: crisis of state and civil society in Pakistan', in Das, Veena (ed.), *Mirrors of Violence. Communities, Riots and Survivors in Souh Asia*, Delhi: Oxford University Press, 1990, p. 188.
100. Hasan, Arif, 'Karachi's godfathers', art. quoted, p. 76.
101. 'Traffic in death', *The Herald*, May 1985, p. 44.
102. Hasan, Arif, 'Karachi's godfathers', art. quoted.
103. The ethnicity of this driver remains a matter of debate, some sources suggesting that he was from Azad Kashmir while others argue that he was Punjabi-speaking; cf. Imtiaz, Saba and Noman Ahmed, 'Bushra Zaidi, the woman who changed Karachi for ever, by dying', *The Express Tribune* (Karachi), 8 March 2012.
104. Feldman, Allen, *Formations of Violence. The Narrative of the Body and Political Terror in Northern Ireland*, Chicago, The University of Chicago Press, 1991, p. 28.
105. Tambiah, Stanley J., *Leveling Crowds*, op. cit., p. 186.
106. 608 rioting cases were registered by the police in 1985, 917 in 1986, 880 in 1987 and 548 in 1988. The number of deaths registered by the police during these incidents rose by 230 per cent between 1985 and 1986, from 80 to 185. In the next two years, 191 people were killed during rioting incidents, according to police statistics. The number of houses destroyed during these incidents also increased significantly between 1987 (62) and 1988 (105); Richards, Julian James, *Mohajir Subnationalism and the Mohajir Qaumi Movement in Sindh Province, Pakistan*, PhD dissertation (Geography), Cambridge: Cambridge University, 1993, pp. 461, 467 and Table 7.1 p. 476.
107. Hasan, Arif, 'Karachi's godfathers', art. quoted, p. 76.
108. Hussain, Akmal, 'The Karachi riots of December 1986', art. quoted, p. 187.
109. Hasan, Arif, 'Profits of doom', *The Herald*, January 1987, p. 46.
110. Hussain, Akmal, 'The Karachi riots of December 1986', art. quoted.
111. Sohrab Goth, the largest of these Afghan 'refugee camps', developed around an old village where seasonal migrants from northern Pakistan and Afghanistan used to stay during the winter months. Both from a geographic and legal point of view, Sohrab Goth (located 25 km from the city centre) was characterised by its marginality well before the beginning of the Afghan war. This unofficial settlement developed illegally on public land and was home to an important market for imported and smuggled goods known as the *Bara* market, which was tolerated by local authorities. On several occasions, Sohrab Goth was at the epicentre of serious 'ethnic' confrontations. On 31 October 1986, for instance, a procession of MQM workers and sympathisers was fired upon while

on its way to Hyderabad. Following this incident, several armed clashes were recorded in localities where Urdu-speaking communities lived alongside Afghans and Pashtuns, leading the residents of these localities to regroup with their ethnic brethren in search for security. Then, on 12 December 1986, the army launched an operation in Sohrab Goth (known as Operation Clean-up, not to be confused with the eponymous military operation that targeted the MQM between 1992 and 1994). Afghan illegal settlements were dismantled and the Bara market was closed. However, following a tip-off, only 150 kilos of heroin, five pistols and two rifles were recovered from what was supposed to be Karachi's major arms and drug den. The following day, Pashtun gunmen attacked Qasba and Aligarh colonies.

112. Khan, Nichola, *Mohajir Militancy in Pakistan*, op. cit., pp. 3–4.
113. A part of wedding festivities, the *mehndi ki rat* is organised a few days before the wedding itself by the parents of the bride for their friends and relatives. Women paint their hands with *mehndi* (henna), before the guests dance to the latest Bollywood hits.
114. Farrukhi, Asif, 'Is shehr mein rahnā' (Urdu) (To live in this city), in Kamal, Ajmal (ed.), *Karāchī kī Kahānī*, op. cit., vol. 2, p. 603.
115. I am here indebted to Jean and John Comaroff, who in a recent review of the transformations of state power and 'dis/order' in postcolonial countries, talk of the transformations of the political landscape and the emergence of 'a palimpsest of contested sovereignties, codes, and jurisdictions'; 'Law and disorder in the postcolony: an introduction', in Comaroff, Jean and John L. Comaroff (eds), *Law and Disorder in the Postcolony*, Chicago: University of Chicago Press, 2006, p. 9.
116. Migdal, Joel S., *Strong Societies and Weak States. State-Society Relations and State Capabilities in the Thirld World*, Princeton: Princeton University Press, 1988, p. 255.
117. On the pathological streak of the literature on 'state failure' and its aporias, see Hagmann, Tobias and Markus V. Hoehne, 'Failures of the state failure debate: evidence from the Somali territories', *Journal of International Development*, 21 (2009), pp. 42–57.
118. I draw this definition of the art of government from Foucault, Michel, *Dits et écrits: 1954–1988*, Paris: Gallimard, 1994, vol. 4, p. 237.
119. Debos, Marielle, *Le Métier des Armes au Tchad*, op. cit., p. 218.
120. Lund, Christian, 'Twilight institutions', art. quoted.
121. Hansen, Thomas Blom, 'Sovereigns beyond the state', art. quoted, p. 170.
122. Hansen, Thomas Blom and Finn Stepputat, 'Introduction', in Hansen, Thomas Blom and Finn Stepputat (eds), *Sovereign Bodies*, op. cit., p. 27.
123. SMC 2011, op. cit., p. 109.
124. Verkaaik, Oskar, *Migrants and Militants. Fun and Urban Violence in Pakistan*, Princeton: Princeton University Press, 2004, p. 65.
125. Richards, Julian James, *Mohajir Subnationalism…*, op. cit.

126. 'Abbasi Shaheed Hospital—den of MQM terrorists', *The Frontier Post* (Peshawar), 8 July 1992, p. 1.
127. Park, Robert, 'The city: suggestions for the investigation of human behavior in the city environment', *The American Journal of Sociology*, 20, 5 (1915), p. 578.

2. FROM STUDENT BRAWLS TO CAMPUS WARS

1. Jalib, Habib, *Harf-e-Haq* (Urdu) (Words of truth), Karachi: Danyal, 2001, p. 26. This poem became an anthem of the anti-Ayub Khan student movement of 1968–1969.
2. This organisation was launched in India in the 1930s to rally Muslim students' support to the Pakistan movement. Although it was under the authority of the Muslim League's leadership, it retained some autonomy and challenged the alliance of the party with landowners and other conservative elements; on the trajectory of this organisation, see Zaman, Mukhtar *Students' Role in the Pakistan Movement*, Karachi: Quaid-e-Azam University, 1978.
3. Paracha, Nadeem F., 'Students politics in Pakistan: a history of lament and celebration'; http://nadeemfparacha.wordpress.com/student-politics-in-pakistan-a-celebration-lament-history/
4. Nasr, Vali Reza, 'Islam and politics: Islami Jami'at-i-Tulaba in Pakistan', *Middle East Journal*, 46, 1 Winter (1992), p. 61.
5. Interview with Munawar Hassan, Karachi, June 2008.
6. I will not deal, here, with the development of student politics in East Pakistan. Suffice it to say, for the purpose of this study, that whereas West Pakistan students found a rallying cry in international causes, East Pakistan students were keener on mobilising around the issue of language and ethnicity. In the early 1950s, they demonstrated against the decision to make Urdu the sole official language of Pakistan, and managed to get Bengali (the language of the majority of Pakistanis, at the time) recognised on an equal footing with Urdu.
7. Siddiqi, Anwar Ehsan, 'Parwarish-e-Loh-o-Qalam (Khud Nawisht)', art. quoted, p. 247.
8. Ibid., p. 248.
9. Naqi, Hussain, 'Students' struggle in historical perspective', *The Daily Times* (Lahore), 8 January 2011.
10. Interview with Sabihuddin Ghausi, senior editorialist for the daily *Dawn*, Karachi (Saddar), 2008.
11. Siddiqi, Anwar Ehsan, 'Parwarish-e-Loh-o-Qalam', art. quoted, p. 268.
12. Interview with Mairaj Muhammad Khan, Karachi (Defence), 2008.
13. Other members of the political elite provided financial support to the students, such as Mirza Abol Hassan Ispahani, a close friend of Muhammad Ali Jinnah and former Ambassador of Pakistan in the United States; Interview with Mairaj Muhammad Khan, Karachi (Defence), 2008.
14. Interview with Mairaj Muhammad Khan, Karachi (Defence), 2008.

15. Mairaj was close to underground leaders of the CPP and generally followed their directives; interview with Akram Qaim Khani, London, 2009.
16. I am grateful to Nadeem F. Paracha for this information.
17. This case involved around fifty political personalities (most of whom belonged to the leftist National Awami Party), who were accused of 'anti-state activities', and in particular of conspiring with outside powers (Iraq and the Soviet Union) to obtain the independence of Balochistan.
18. Interview with Karamat Ali, former NSF activist and executive director, Pakistan Institute of Labour Education and Research (PILER), Karachi (Gulshan-e-Maymar), 2006.
19. Naqi, Hussain, 'Students' struggle in historical perspective', art. quoted.
20. Paracha, Nadeem F., 'Students politics in Pakistan', art. quoted.
21. Hasan, Arif, 'Growth of a metropolis', art. quoted, p. 177.
22. This factionalisation took place along ideological cleavages (the Mairaj group supported the independence of Bangladesh and was the most profoundly influenced by Maoist ideas, whereas the Kazmi faction was pro-Moscow), but also along sectarian lines (the members of the Kazmi faction were predominantly Shia whereas the members of the Mairaj group were generally Sunni); interview with Akram Qaim Khani, London, 2009.
23. Esposito, John L., 'Islam and civil society', in Burgat, François and John Esposito (eds), *Modernizing Islam. Religion and the Public Sphere in Europe and the Middle East*, New Brunswick: Rutgers University Press, 2003, p. 73.
24. Nasr, Vali Reza, 'Islam and politics', art. quoted, p. 62.
25. Interview with Fahim Khan, Karachi (Saddar), 2009.
26. Butt, Iqbal Haider, *Revisiting Student Politics in Pakistan*, Gujranwallah: Bargad, 2009, p. 15; http://www.bargad.org.pk/downloads/Revisiting%20Student%20Politics%20in%20Pakistan.pdf, p. 74.
27. 'Student violence: the rising graph', *The Herald*, October 1988, p. 66.
28. Interview with Fahim Khan, Karachi (Saddar), 2009.
29. Chenoy, Anurada M., *Militarism and Women in South Asia*, Delhi: Kali for Women, 2002, p. 18.
30. 'Student violence: the rising graph', art. quoted.
31. The USM included the PSF, the Baloch Student Organisation (BSO), the Pakhtun Students Federation (PkSF), the Punjabi Students Association (PSA) and the newly formed All Pakistan Mohajir Students Organisation (APMSO).
32. Interview with Akram Qaim Khani, London, 2009.
33. Interview with Akram Qaim Khani, London, 2009.
34. On 'Schmittian' vs. 'Hobbesian' ontologies of conflict, see Kalyvas, Stathis N., 'The ontology of "political violence"', art. quoted.
35. Hussain, Zahid, 'The campus mafias', *The Herald*, October 1988, p. 65.
36. Quoted by Frotscher, Ann, *Claiming Pakistan*, op. cit., p. 116.
37. Butt, Iqbal Haider, *Revisiting Student Politics in Pakistan*, op. cit, p. 15.
38. Ibid.

39. Interview with Fahim Khan, Karachi (Saddar), 2009.
40. Collins, Randall, *Violence. A Micro-Sociological Theory*, Princeton/Oxford: Princeton University Press, 2008, pp. 404–5.
41. Ibid, p. 404.
42. Interview with Akram Qaim Khani, London, 2009.
43. Anwar, Raja, *The Terrorist Prince. The Life and Death of Murtaza Bhutto*, London: Verso, 1997, p. 151.
44. Paracha, Nadeem F., 'The deviant Che', *Dawn.com*, 26 July 2009; http://archives.dawn.com/archives/152158
45. Anwar, Raja, *The Terrorist Prince*, op. cit., p. 91. This version of the events remains controversial and was recently contradicted by Murtaza's daughter, Fatima Bhutto, who claims that the hijacking was Tipu's brainchild and that Murtaza had, in fact, turned down the project; see Bhutto, Fatima, *Songs of Blood and Sword. A Daughter's Memoir*, Delhi: Penguin, 2010, p. 223.
46. These three attributes of political contingency are borrowed from Schedler, Andreas, 'Mapping contingency', in Shapiro, Ian and Sonu Bedi (eds), *Political Contingency. Studying the Unexpected, the Accidental and the Unforeseen*, New York: New York University Press, 2007, pp. 54–78.
47. Kalyvas, Stathis N., *The Logic of Violence in Civil War*, op. cit.
48. Geffray, Christian, *La Cause des Armes au Mozambique. Anthropologie d'une Guerre Civile*, Paris: Karthala, 1990.
49. Although the hijacking would have been planned earlier in Kabul, it was directly linked to the February 1981 incidents at KU: two of the hijackers were on the run after being charged with the murder of Hafiz Aslam, and the first list of political prisoners the hijackers demanded be released were all student activists involved in this incident; see Anwar, Raja, *The Terrorist Prince*, op. cit., p. 99.
50. Interview with Fahim Khan and Nabu Patel, Karachi (Saddar), 2008.
51. Interview with a former PSF activist, Karachi, 2009.
52. Paracha, Nadeem F., 'An election', *Dawn.com*, 25 July 2013; http://dawn.com/news/1031819/an-election/?view=print
53. Paracha, Nadeem F., 'Student politics in Pakistan', art. quoted.
54. Hussain, Zahid, 'The campus mafias', art. quoted, pp. 62, 66. This figure is given for all Karachi campuses (which includes the city's numerous colleges).
55. Ibid.
56. See, for instance, the testimony of 'Arshad', in Khan, Nichola, *Mohajir Militancy in Pakistan*, op. cit., Chapter 1, where this former MQM militant justifies his killings by the 'war situation' which prevailed in Karachi in the late 1980s.
57. Hussain Altaf and Khalid Athar, *Safar-e-Zindagī. MQM kī Kahānī, Altāf Hussain kī Zabānī mein* (Urdu) (My Life's Journey. The Story of the MQM in the Words of Altaf Hussain), Karachi: Jang Publishers, 1988, p. 45.
58. Paracha, Nadeem, 'Student politics in Pakistan', art. quoted.
59. Interviews with students and lecturers, Karachi University, 2008 and 2009.
60. All three elements identified by Hanspeter Kriesi in his definition of the politi-

cal opportunities structure of social movements were relevant here: the formal structure of the state, the informal procedures and the strategies of political authorities towards political challengers, and internal dynamics within political parties; cf. Kriesi, Hanspeter, Ruud Koopmans, Jan Willem Duyvendak and Marco Giugni, *New Social Movements in Western Europe*, London: UCL, 1995. But since these political opportunities are dynamic, co-produced as they are by dominants and challengers, the use of the term 'structure' is problematic here; cf. Fillieule, Olivier and Lilian Mathieu, 'Structure des opportunités politiques', in Fillieule, Olivier, Lilian Mathieu and Cécile Péchu (eds), *Dictionnaires des Mouvements Sociaux*, Paris: Presses de Sciences Po, 2009, pp. 530–40.

3. 'THE MOHAJIRS HAVE ARRIVED!'

1. Nishat, Raqiah, 'Nazr ke sāmne hai aj sāhil merā' (Urdu) (Today, my seashore is in sight), *Naqīb*, June 2000, p. 48.
2. See for instance the writings of the journalist, cultural critic and former student activist Nadeem F. Paracha for *Dawn.com* (http://x.dawn.com/author/nfparacha/), as well as Frotscher, Ann, *Claiming Pakistan*, op. cit., Chapter 5 and Siddiqi, Farhan Hanif, 'Intra-ethnic fissures in ethnic movements: the rise of Mohajir identity politics in post-1971 Pakistan', *Asian Ethnicity*, 11, 1 February (2010), pp. 25–41.
3. Rather than to Tariq Ali's eponymous memoir, which only makes a passing allusion to Pakistani student politics, I am here referring to the excellent TV series produced by Dawn News in 2009 on the history of Pakistan's student politics.
4. Shahzad, Saleem, *Sha'ur kā Safar* (Urdu) (A Journey of the Mind), London: MQM International Secretariat, 2006 (2005), p. 30.
5. Altaf Hussain was born on 17 September 1953 in Karachi, in a middle-class Urdu-speaking family from Agra, where his two grandfathers were religious figures (his *dada* was no less than the city Mufti, whereas his *nana* was a religious personality of lower rank). His father worked as a railway station chief in India and became a clerk in Pakistan, before opening a grocery store in Azizabad after his retirement. The family settled in a modest house of the neighbourhood in the early 1970s.
6. Interview with a former colleague of Altaf Hussain at KU, Karachi, 2009.
7. Jamil, Tahrir Amir, 'Inquelāb parwār quāid-e-tehrīk Altāf Hussain kī jed-o-jehed: tarīkhī ke aine mein' (Urdu) (The struggle of the patron of the revolution and leader of the movement, Altaf Hussain: in the mirror of history), *Naqīb*, September (2006), p. 22; Saleem Shahzad, *Sha'ur kā Safr*, op. cit., pp. 96–7.
8. With the death of Jinnah (1948) and the assassination of Liaquat Ali Khan (1951), the *muhajirin* lost major political patrons, and they failed to place their candidates at the helm of the state in the following years. The delocalisation of the capital to Rawalpindi and later on to Islamabad dealt a further blow to the *muhajirin*'s grip over the affairs of the state. Beyond the symbolism of this decision, which attested

of the increasing domination of the Punjabis over the central state, the physical estrangement of civil servants and politicians from *muhajir* businessmen—which was one of the motives invoked by Ayub Khan to justify the transfer of the capital to the Punjab—deprived the latter from the leverage which compensated for their absence of a strong social base in Pakistan. These early signs of 'decline' should not be overestimated, though. In the 1960s, the Urdu-speaking *muhajirin*, who accounted for 3.5 per cent of the country's total population, still occupied 21 per cent of the positions in the Pakistan Civil Service. At the same time, Karachi-based firms still controlled 96 per cent of Pakistan's private industries, over 80 per cent of the assets of private banks and nearly 80 per cent of insurance companies. Out of Pakistan's forty-two largest industrial groups, thirty-six were in the hands of Karachi-based businessmen—generally members of Gujarati/Kutchi/Kathiawari trading castes/sects, both Sunni (Memons) and Shia (Khojas, Bohras, etc.). Whereas they accounted for 0.4 per cent of Pakistan's total population, Gujarati trading castes (which were subsumed under the *muhajir* label although many of their members were already settled in Karachi long before Partition) controlled 43 per cent of the country's industrial capital. Halai Memons alone (0.3 per cent of the national population) owned 27 per cent of these industries. And while he patronised Pashtun entrepreneurs in Karachi, Ayub Khan also relied upon Gujarati businessmen to finance his electoral campaign in 1964, while facilitating the entry into politics of some *muhajir* entrepreneurs, such as Sadiq Dawood, a Memon industrialist who became an MNA and the Treasurer of Ayub's Convention Muslim League. With the Punjabi-dominated military arriving at the helm of power, the *muhajirin* were downgraded from senior to junior partners of the emerging hegemon. Unlike what has sometimes been suggested, though, they were not deprived of their positions of influence in the bureaucracy, in politics or in the economy in any spectacular way by Ayub's regime. It is only with the secession of East Pakistan and the rise to power of the PPP that the decline of the *muhajirin* became more pronounced and more encompassing, threatening *muhajir* elites but also the burgeoning Urdu-speaking middle class. The creation of Bangladesh deprived the *muhajirin* from their position of arbiter between Pakistan's two largest linguistic communities, the Bengalis and the Punjabis. The indigenous revival of the 1970s, for its part, resulted from the vernacularisation of the Pakistani state—which was originally imagined by the Urdu-speaking elites of North India—through its appropriation by indigenous 'nationalities'. Both in Islamabad and Sindh, these changes brought to power a new kind of Sindhi leadership in the shape of the PPP, whose pro-Sindhi policies constituted the first challenge of its kind to *muhajir* economic and political power. A good proxy, to measure this late but significant decline of the position of the *muhajirin* in the bureaucracy, is the share of Urdu-speakers among the employees of the central government, which went down from 30.39 to 22.3 per cent between 1973 and 1981. Bhutto's nationalisation programme also dealt a severe blow to the *muhajirin*'s interests, not only by targeting the economic assets of the big industrial houses but, more generally, because recruitment to the newly nationalised banks and insurance companies started being regulated by a quota system that disadvantaged them, to the benefit of other nationalities; sources: Samad, Yunas 'In and out of power but not down and out: Mohajir identity politics', in Jaffrelot, Christophe (ed.), *Pakistan. Nationalism without a Nation*, Delhi: Manohar, p. 66; Khan, Adeel, *Politics of Identity. Ethnic Nationalism and the State in Pakistan*, Delhi: Sage, 2005, pp. 168, 171; Kochanek, Stanley, *Interest Groups and Development. Business and Politics in Pakistan*, Karachi: Oxford University Press, 1983, p. 25; Waseem, Mohammad, 'Mohajirs in Pakistan: a case of nativization of migrants', in Bates, Crispin (ed.), *Community, Empire and Migration. South Asians in Diaspora*, Delhi: Orient Longman, 2001, p. 250; Tahir, Tanvir Ahmad, *Political Dynamics of Sindh*, op. cit., p. 667.

9. Korejo, M.S., *G.M. Syed. An Analysis of his Political Perspectives*, Karachi: Oxford University Press, 2000, p. 42.
10. 'Merī awāz sūno' (Urdu) (Listen to my voice), reproduced in Shahzad, Saleem, *Sha'ur kā Safar*, op. cit., pp. 40–2.
11. On this Mohajir trope of sacrifice, see Zamindar, Vazira Fazila-Yacoobali, *The Long Partition and the Making of Modern South Asia*, op. cit.
12. Hussain Altaf and Khalid Athar, *Safar-e-Zindagī*, op. cit., p. 90.
13. Saigol, Rubina, 'The partition of self: Mohajir women's sense of identity and nationhood', in Ahmad, Sadaf (ed.), *Pakistani Women. Multiple Locations and Competing Narratives*, Karachi: Oxford University Press, 2010, p. 196.
14. Reproduced in Shahzad, Saleem, *Sha'ur kā Safar*, op. cit., p. 38.
15. Saleem Shahzad won his first seat in the 1987 municipal election. He was elected at the National Assembly in 1988 and 1990. A long time member of the MQM's Coordination Committee, he was temporarily suspended from the MQM in 2009 for his 'mysterious activities', but rapidly reintegrated.
16. Shahzad, Saleem, *Sha'ur kā Safar*, op. cit., p. 29.
17. Coser, Lewis, *Greedy Institutions. Patterns of Undivided Commitment*, New York: Free Press, 1974.
18. Quoted and discussed by Verkaaik, Oskar, *Migrants and Militants*, op. cit., p. 72 sq.
19. Tahir, Tanvir Ahmad, *Political Dynamics of Sindh, 1947–1977*, op. cit., pp. 535, 697. This demand of a Karachi *suba* had already been put forward by another member of the Karachi-based *muhajir* elite, Mahmud ul Haq Usmani, in 1954. When the NSF (Kazmi) reiterated this demand, though, Usmani opposed it, arguing that Karachi was an integral part of Sindh.
20. Tahir, Tanvir Ahmad, *Political Dynamics of Sindh*, op. cit., p. 611.
21. 'Behind the language riots', *Pakistan Forum*, September (1972), pp. 18–9, 5.
22. Rahman, Tariq, *Language and Politics in Pakistan*, Karachi: Oxford University Press, 2000 (1996), p. 123.
23. Tahir, Tanvir Ahmad, *Political Dynamics of Sindh*, op. cit., pp. 696–7.
24. Quoted in Puri, Balraj, 'Autonomy and participation: dimensions of Indian Muslim identity', *Economic & Political Weekly* (Delhi), 7 October 1978, p. 1707.

25. Tahir, Tanvir Ahmad, *Political Dynamics of Sindh*, op. cit., p. 698.
26. Siddiqi, Farhan Hanif, 'Intra-ethnic fissures in ethnic movements', art. quoted, p. 39.
27. Hussain, Altaf and Khalid Athar, *Safar-e-Zindagī*, op. cit., pp. 38–9.
28. Siddiqi, Farhan Hanif, *The Politics of Ethnicity in Pakistan. The Baloch, Sindhi and Mohajir Ethnic Movements*, London: Routledge, 2012, p. 103.
29. Altaf Hussain's 'autobiography' is in fact the transcript of a long interview he gave to journalist Khalid Akhtar in 1988; it therefore reflects the early phase of the MQM, when the party promoted a resolutely ethnic agenda. Saleem Shahzad's political memoirs were published much later (2005) and reflects the attempt by the MQM to de-ethnicise its rhetoric and join the political mainstream.
30. Shortly after establishing itself at KU, the APMSO set up units in NED University, Urdu Science College, Dawood Engineering College, National College, Jinnah College and Ship Owner's College; Hussain, Altaf and Khalid Athar, *Safar-e-Zindagī*, op. cit.
31. Shahzad, Saleem, *Sha'ur kā Safar*, op. cit., p. 47.
32. Hussain Altaf and Khalid Athar, *Safar-e-Zindagī*, op. cit., pp. 37–8.
33. Shahzad, Saleem, *Sha'ur kā Safar*, op. cit., p. 95.
34. See for instance Altaf Hussain's plea for a merit-based admission policy at the University of Karachi; Hussain Altaf and Khalid Athar, *Safar-e-Zindagī*, op. cit., p. 22.
35. Shahzad, Saleem, *Sha'ur kā Safar*, op. cit.
36. Ibid., p. 32.
37. Hussain, Altaf and Khalid Athar *Safar-e-Zindagī*, op. cit., p. 40.
38. Ibid., pp. 34, 42, 44.
39. Shahzad, Saleem, *Sha'ur kā Safar*, op. cit., pp. 68–9; Hussain, Altaf and Khalid Athar, *Safar-e-Zindagī*, op. cit., pp. 96–7.
40. Ibid., p. 85.
41. Ibid., p. 96.
42. For a recent study of this transition, see Baig, Noman, *From Mohalla to Mainstream*, op. cit.
43. Imran Farooq was the second in command within the MQM. He remained underground in Pakistan for a decade after the launch of Operation Clean-up and was rumoured to be in charge of the MQM's militant wing. He reappeared in London in 1999 and remained there until his murder in September 2010. The circumstances of this murder are yet to be elucidated.
44. Coser, Lewis, *Greedy Institutions*, op. cit.
45. Farooq, Imran, *Nazm-o-Zābat ke Taqāze* (Urdu), London: MQM International Secretariat, 1998 (1986), pp. 10–3.
46. Alberoni, Francesco, *Movement and Institution*, New York: Columbia University Press, 1984, pp. 216, 217.
47. Ibid., p. 217.
48. Ibid., p. 142.

49. Ibid. pp. 172–5.
50. Ibid., p. 215.
51. Baig, Noman, *From Mohalla to Mainstream*, op. cit., p. 130.
52. Muttahida Qaumi Movement (Pakistan), *Guiding Principles*, n.d. (post-1997), p. 11.
53. Daechsel, Markus, *The Politics of Self-Expression. The Urdu Middleclass Milieu in Mid-Twentieth Century India and Pakistan*, London/New York: Routledge, 2006.
54. Ibid.
55. Farooq, Imran, *Nazm-o-Zābat ke Taqāze*, op. cit., pp. 20–1.
56. On these characteristics of the politics of 'self-expression', cf. Daechsel, Markus, *The Politics of Self-Expression*, op. cit.
57. Kazmi, an MQM party worker from Landhi, was implicated in one of the most controversial episodes of the MQM's history: the abduction and torture of Major Kalim, in 1991.
58. Kazmi, Javed, 'Nazm' (Urdu) (Poem), *Naqīb*, September 2006, p. 21.
59. Baig, Noman, *From Mohalla to Mainstream*, op. cit., p. iii.
60. Hussain, Altaf and Khalid Athar, *Safar-e-Zindagī*, op. cit., p. 69.
61. Ibid., p. 104.
62. Tilly, Charles, *The Politics of Collective Violence*, Cambridge: Cambridge University Press, 2003, p. 44.
63. Gazdar, Haris, 'Karachi's violence: duality and negotiation', SPO Discussion Paper Series No. 10, Karachi, 2011, p. 5.
64. Ibid., p. 6.
65. The MQM is known to intimidate voters at their residence and at polling stations and is widely believed to be involved in incidents of ballot box stuffing. During the 2008 elections, for instance, Farooq Sattar was elected with more than 100,000 votes in NA-249, whereas previous candidates of the MQM in that constituency had never registered more than 35,000 votes. The MQM was also suspected of massive rigging in Landhi and Korangi and its activists abducted polling agents in NA-250; cf. Khan, Iffat Humayun, *Electoral Malpractices During the 2008 Elections in Pakistan*, Karachi: Oxford University Press, 2011, pp. 156, 159, 162, 163. The MQM was also accused of malpractices during the 2013 elections (mass rigging, abductions and intimidation of electoral staff,...), leading to a public outcry, especially on the part of PTI supporters.
66. Shah, Mehtab Ali, *The Foreign Policy of Pakistan. Ethnic Impacts on Diplomacy, 1971–1994*, Karachi: Oxford University Press, 1997, p. 75.
67. Extract from the 'History' of the MQM on the website of the Zone H of the MQM Hyderabad; http://ali-h-35.wix.com/sec_h#!about-us
68. Hansen, Thomas Blom, 'Sovereigns beyond the state', art. quoted, p. 191.
69. Frotscher, Ann, *Claiming Pakistan*, op. cit., p. 161.
70. Richards, Julian James, *Mohajir Subnationalism...*, op. cit.
71. Hansen, Thomas Blom, 'Sovereigns beyond the state', art. quoted, p. 171.
72. Frotscher, Ann, *Claiming Pakistan*, op. cit., p. 173.

73. Hasnain, Ghulam, 'MQM's biggest chamber of torture', *Dawn*, 24 June 1992, p. 14.
74. To date, Mirza is the only militant of the MQM ever convicted for target killings. He was arrested in 1998 and sentenced to death by an anti-terrorism court in 1999. His appeals were rejected by the Sindh High Court and the Supreme Court in 2000 and 2001 respectively, but his execution was stayed following the intervention of top leaders of the MQM. Since 2008, the file for Shaukat Mirza's mercy petition has been gathering dust at the Interior Ministry. Police sources confirm that Mirza continued to run the network of MQM target killers from his jail, and a jail official, Amanullah Niazi, was murdered in 2006 after he tried to interfere with Mirza's activities. cf. Noorani, Ahmad, 'Sindh police depressed as Saulat Mirza still alive', *The News* (Karachi), 11 September 2011.
75. The definition of these 'unpleasant individuals' by the MQM is rather blurry and the term seems to encompass any troublemaker disturbing the local order of things, such as petty criminals (bootleggers, drug dealers, pimps,...), religious militants, etc. In 2008–2009, this label was used to chase away Pashtun restaurant owners from Mohajir-dominated localities (see Chapter 7).
76. 'City wardens control traffic at 111 spots in Karachi', *Daily Times*, 30 July 2012; http://www.dailytimes.com.pk/default.asp?page=2012\07\30\story_30–7–2012_pg12_5
77. 'Karachi: city wardens occupy playground: JI', *Dawn.com*, 13 January 2010; http://archives.dawn.com/archives/164638
78. Hansen, Thomas Blom, *Violence in Urban India. Identity Politics, 'Mumbai', and the Postcolonial City*, Delhi: Permanent Black, 2005 (2001), p. 116.
79. Altaf Hussain on 31 January 1987 in Liaquatabad, quoted by Frotscher, Ann, *Claiming Pakistan*, op. cit., p. 175.
80. 'Altaf stresses self-defence, karate classes', *Daily Times*, 11 October 2008.
81. G.M. Syed (1904–1995) was a strong supporter of the movement for Pakistan in Sindh, but became a staunch Sindhi nationalist in the decades that followed the creation of the country. In 1971 he demanded that the province be given the right of self-determination, and the following year he formed the Jiye Sindh Mahaz (Front for the Protection of Sindh), which advocated the autonomy/independence of Sindh. The first meeting between this protector of the 'old Sindhis' and Altaf Hussain, who projected himself as the leader of the 'new Sindhis', occurred in 1985.
82. Hasnain, Ghulam, '"For us, Altaf Hussain was like a God". The diary of a former MQM militant...', *Newsline*, May 1997, p. 33.
83. Hanif, 'Mohammad, The gun-runners of Karachi', art. quoted, p. 23.
84. Ibid.
85. Paracha, Nadeem F., 'Born to run: the rise and levelling of the APMSO', *Dawn.com*, 23 August 2012; http://dawn.com/2012/08/23/born-to-run-the-rise-and-leveling-of-the-apmso/
86. Hussain, Altaf and Khalid Athar, *Safar-e-Zindagī*, op. cit., pp. 15–8.

87. One of the most influential political movements in Pashtun history, the Khudai Khidmatgar of Khan Abdul Ghaffar Khan (1890–1988), subscribed to Gandhian principles and remained non-violent; cf. Banerjee, Mukulika, *The Pathan Unarmed. Opposition and Memory in the North-West Frontier*, Oxford: James Currey, 2000.
88. Khan, Nichola, *Mohajir Militancy in Pakistan*, op. cit.
89. Ibid.
90. Browning, Christopher, *Ordinary Men. Reserve Battalion Police 101 and the Final Solution in Poland*, London: HarperCollins, 1993.
91. This hypothesis is freely derived from the testimonies of MQM killers gathered by Nichola Khan, whose anthropological perspective focuses on the 'political subjectivities', 'desires' and 'fantasies' of these killers, rather than on their violent performances per se. For a discussion of Khan's work, in the perspective of the sociology of dirty work, see Gayer, Laurent, 'Profession: killer', *Books & Ideas*, 25 February 2011; http://www.booksandideas.net/Profession-killer.html
92. See Frotscher, Ann, *Claiming Pakistan*, op. cit., p. 175.
93. Mariot, Nicolas, 'Faut-il être motivé pour tuer? Sur quelques explications aux violences de guerre', *Genèses*, 53 (2003/2004), pp. 154–77.
94. On the relation between 'fun' and violence in the MQM, see Verkaaik, Oskar, *Migrants and Militants*, op. cit.
95. On this 'ethics of illegality', which results from the often incoherent conflation of various 'codes' challenging the ontological status of more transcendental forms of morality (although occasionally and selectively drawing self-justificatory elements from them), see Roitman, Janet, 'The ethics of illegality in the Chad Basin', in Comaroff, Jean and John L. Comaroff (eds), *Law and Disorder in the Postcolony*, op. cit., pp. 247–72.
96. Rehman, Zia ur, *Karachi in Turmoil*, Islamabad: Narratives, 2013, p. 27.
97. Gazdar, Haris, 'Karachi's violence', art. quoted, p. 5.
98. See for instance Ahmed, Feroz, *Ethnicity and Politics in Pakistan*, Karachi: Oxford University Press, 1998; Ahmar, Moonis, 'Ethnicity and state power in Pakistan: the Karachi crisis', *Asian Survey*, 36, 10 October (1996), pp. 1031–48; Kennedy, Charles H., 'The politics of ethnicity in Sindh', *Asian Survey*, 31, 10 October (1991), pp. 938–55; Khan, Adeel, *Politics of Identity*, op. cit.; Samad, Yunas, 'In and out of power but not down and out', art. quoted; Tahir, Tanvir Ahmad, *Political Dynamics of Sindh*, op. cit.
99. Comaroff, Jean and John L. Comaroff, 'Law and disorder in the postcolony', art. quoted, p. 35.
100. Taussig, Michael, *The Magic of the State*, New York: Routledge, 1997, p. 5.
101. See for instance the reference to Max Weber in the Supreme Court 2011 judgment on the deterioration of the 'law and order situation' in Karachi; SMC 2011, op. cit., p. 126.
102. Comaroff, Jean and John L. Comaroff, 'Law and disorder in the postcolony', art. quoted, p. 35.

4. THE BANDITS WHO WOULD BE KINGS

1. Ashura, the tenth day of the month of Muharram, marks the culmination of the celebrations of this month of mourning. On this day, (some) Sunnis and (all) Shias celebrate the martyrdom of Imam Hussein in the battle of Karbala in 680 A.D.
2. The first suicide-attack against a Shia procession in Pakistan only took place in 2004. However, the Shias of Karachi have been the target of sectarian violence since the early 1990s.
3. Uzair Baloch is frequently referred to as Lyari's 'Don' in the local media, as he is suspected of heading Lyari's most powerful crime syndicate. The term 'Don' gained wide usage in the 1970s in the Indian subcontinent, following a series of Indian films that became hits in India as well as in Pakistan, the most notorious of which remains the 1978 film, 'Don', with Bollywood superstar Amitabh Bachchan in the lead role.
4. Interview with Zafar Baloch, Karachi (Lyari), August 2012.
5. Slimbach, Richard A., 'Ethnic binds and pedagogies of resistance: Baloch nationalism and educational innovation in Karachi', in Titus, Paul (ed.), *Marginality and Modernity. Ethnicity and Change in Postcolonial Balochistan*, Karachi: Oxford University Press, 1996, p. 139.
6. Nazir, Hamid, *Wadī Lyārī* (Urdu) (The Lyari River), Karachi: Akasi, 1992, p. 150.
7. Slimbach, Richard A., 'Ethnic binds and pedagogies of resistance', art. quoted, p. 139.
8. Shaheed, Zafar, *The Labour Movement in Pakistan*, op. cit., p. 16.
9. Mujtaba, Hasan, 'Lyari: land of magic', *Newsline*, July 1997. Zikris belong to a heterodox Sunni community based in Makran, whose members look at their founder, Syed Mohammad (1443–1505), as the Mahdi. This community, which is currently going back to the fold of Hannafism, played a leading role in the emergence of the Baloch nationalist movement in the course of the twentieth century; see Khan, Inayatullah, 'Islam, the state and identity: the Zikris of Balochistan', in Titus, Paul (ed.), *Marginality and Modernity*, op. cit., pp. 223–49.
10. Memons (from *momin*, Arabic for 'believers') are descendants of Hindu mercantile castes from Sindh (such as the Lohanas) who converted to Islam before migrating to Gujarat. In Kutch and other trade centres of Gujarat, they specialised in the oceanic trade. Fleeing religious persecutions by local Hindu rulers, Memons fled Gujarat en masse in the late eighteenth century and some of them (re)settled in Sindh. In Karachi, the Memons became an essential component of the colonial economy and they established more than a hundred charitable trusts.
11. Lari, Yasmeen and Mihail S. Lari, *The Dual City*, op. cit., p. 67.
12. Nazir, Hamid, *Wadī Lyārī*, op. cit., p. 169.
13. The Movement of the Silken Kerchiefs was an anti-colonial armed movement which used silken pieces of cloth to circulate its secret messages.

14. Mujtaba, Hasan, 'Lyari: land of magic', art. quoted.
15. Baloch, Sanaullah, 'The battle for the soul of Lyari', *The Express Tribune*, 8 May 2012. Sanaullah Baloch was a member of the Pakistan Senate from 2003 to 2008 and of the National Assembly from 1997 to 1999.
16. Slimbach, Richard A., 'Ethnic binds and pedagogies of resistance', art. quoted.
17. Interview, Karachi (Lyari), December 2011.
18. Sahito, Imhad, *Decade of the Dacoits*, Karachi: Oxford University Press, 2006.
19. Ahmad, Sohail, 'Lyārī ke gang aur gang wār' (Urdu) (Lyari's gangs and the gang war), *BBCUrdu.com*, 17 March 2013; http://www.bbc.co.uk/urdu/pakistan/2013/03/130317_karachi_liyari_gangs_zs.shtml
20. Interview, Lyari, December 2011.
21. Paracha, Nadeem F., 'The good, the bad and the Lyari', *Dawn.com*, 29 March 2012; http://dawn.com/2012/03/29/the-good-the-bad-the-lyari/
22. Ahmad, Sohail, 'Lyārī ke gang aur gang wār', art. quoted.
23. Ali, Shazad, 'Lyari footballers turn to life of crime', *Dawn.com*, 15 June 2009; http://archives.dawn.com/archives/87295
24. 'Clueless police seek Rangers help in Lyari operation', *The Herald*, August 2004, pp. 47–8.
25. Mujtaba, Hasan, 'Lyari, land of magic', art. quoted.
26. Ibid.
27. Slimbach, Richard A., 'Ethnic binds and pedagogies of resistance', art. quoted., p. 145.
28. Paracha, Nadeem F., 'The good, the bad and the Lyari', art. quoted.
29. Auyero, Javier, *Routine Politics and Violence in Argentina. The Gray Zone of State Power*, Cambridge: Cambridge University Press, 2007.
30. Khan, Lal, *Pakistan's Other Story. The 1968–9 Revolution*, Delhi: Aakar Books, 2009, p. 139.
31. Damohi, Muhammad Usman, *Karāchī. Tārīkh ke Aīne mein* (Urdu) (Karachi. In the Mirror of History), Karachi: Indus Publications, 1996, p. 504.
32. Interview with Mairaj Muhammad Khan, Karachi (Defence), June 2008.
33. Brass, Paul R., *Theft of an Idol. Text and Context in the Representation of Collective Violence*, Calcutta: Seagul, 1998 (1997), p. 9; Brass, Paul R., 'The development of an institutionalized riot system in Meerut city, 1961 to 1982', in Talbot, Ian (ed), *The Deadly Embrace. Religion, Politics and Violence in India and Pakistan 1947–2002*, Karachi: Oxford University Press, 2007, pp. 81–107.
34. Arias, Enrique Desmond, *Drugs and Democracy in Rio de Janeiro. Trafficking, Social Networks and Public*, Chapel Hill: University of North Carolina Press, 2006, p. 5.
35. Helmke, Gretchn and Steven Levitsky, 'Informal institutions and comparative politics', *Perspectives in Politics*, 2, (2004), pp. 725–40.
36. Brass, Paul R., 'The development of an institutionalized riot system in Meerut city', art. quoted, p. 81.
37. For an example of such typologies, see Helmke, Gretchn and Steven Levitsky, 'Informal institutions and comparative politics', art. quoted.

38. Briquet, Jean-Louis and Gilles Favarel-Garrigues, 'Introduction: violence, crime and political power', in Briquet, Jean-Louis and Gilles Favarel-Garrigues (eds), *Organized Crime and States*, New York: Palgrave, 2010, p. 4.
39. Geffray, Christian, 'Etat, richesse et criminels', *Mondes en Développement*, 110 (2000), p. 22.
40. Quoted by Roy, Olivier, 'Groupes de solidarité au Moyen-Orient et en Asie centrale: etats, territoires et réseaux', *Cahiers du CERI*, 16 (1996), p. 3.
41. Interview with relatives of Rehman Dakait, Karachi (Lyari), December 2011.
42. Interview with a cousin of Rehman Dakait, Karachi (Lyari), December 2011.
43. Khan, Faraz, 'Rehman Dakait's slain aides served as PPP leaders' security guards', *Daily Times*, 13 August 2009.
44. Dharejo, Salam, 'The godfather of Lyari', *Newsline*, September 2009, p. 67–8.
45. Imtiaz, Huma, 'Kingdom of fear', *The Express Tribune*, 18 July 2010.
46. Dharejo, Salam, 'The godfather of Lyari', art. quoted, p. 68.
47. 'Snapshots of Arshad Pappu through the years', *The Express Tribune*, 18 March 2013.
48. Khan, Uzair, 'Proxy wars continue in Lyari', *Dawn*, 14 February 2012.
49. Akhtar, Syed Nabil, 'Lyārī bārūd ke dher par' (Urdu) (Lyari on a powder keg), *Jasārat*, 3 July 2011.
50. Dharejo, Salam, 'The Godfather of Lyari', *Newsline*, September 2009, p. 68.
51. Interviews with relative of Rehman Dakait, Karachi (Lyari), December 2011.
52. These posters are 'signed' with the formula '*munjanib*' (on behalf of), followed by the alias/nom de guerre (*urf*) of local bandits—'Baba Ladla' (the dear one), Nadeem 'Japan', Shiraz 'Kamred' (Comrade), etc. (cf. photographs in Appendix).
53. Personal observation, Karachi (Lyari), December 2011.
54. Hasan, Arif and Mansoor Raza, *Karachi. The Land Issues*, op. cit., p. 70.
55. Mujtaba, Hasan, 'Lyari: land of magic', art. quoted.
56. Leeds, Elizabeth, 'Cocaine and parallel politics in the Brazilian urban periphery: constraints to local-level democratization', *Latin American Research Review*, 31, 3 (1996), p. 49.
57. Goirand, Camille, '"Philanthropes" en concurrence dans les *favelas* de Rio', *Critique internationale*, 4, Summer (1999), p. 156.
58. Leeds, Elizabeth, 'Cocaine and parallel politics', art. quoted, p. 61.
59. Comment by Jean-François Bayart at the study day 'Violence criminelle, pratiques illicites et pouvoir politique', CERI, Paris, June 2004.
60. Interview, Karachi (Lyari), December 2011.
61. Dharejo, Salam, 'The godfather of Lyari', art. quoted, p. 68; Imtiaz, Huma, 'Kingdom of fear', art. quoted.
62. See for instance the comments by Rahim Baloch, a former leader of the BSO, quoted in Rehman, Zia ur, 'Lyari's Baloch community rethinks support for PPP', *The Friday Times*, 13–19 April 2012.
63. Kaleem, Moosa, 'Inside Lyari', *The Herald*, June 2012, p. 31.
64. Ahmed, Akbar S., 'Trial by ordeal among Bugtis: ritual as a diacritical factor in Baloch ethnicity', in Titus, Paul (ed.), *Marginality and Modernity*, op. cit., p. 54.

65. Fabietti, Ugo, 'Equality versus hierarchy: conceptualizing change in southern Balochistan', in ibid., pp. 3–27.
66. Slimbach, Richard A., 'Ethnic binds and pedagogies of resistance', art. quoted, p. 142.
67. On the emergence of the ethnonym 'Baloch' as an indicator of detribalisation, in the context of southern Afghanistan, see Orywal, Erwin, 'Periphery and identity: processes of detribalization among the Baloch of Afghanistan', in ibid., p. 97.
68. Kaleem, Moosa, 'Inside Lyari', *The Herald*, June 2012, p. 34.
69. Barth, Fredrik, *Ethnic Groups and Boundaries. The Social Organization of Cultural Difference*, Boston: Little, Brown & Co, 1969, pp. 117–34.
70. Fabietti, Ugo, 'Equality versus hierarchy', art. quoted, p. 7.
71. On tribalism as an ideology characterised by its 'rhetoric of appeal', see Caton, Steven C., *'Peaks of Yemen I Summon'. Poetry as Cultural Practice in a North Yemeni Tribe*, Berkeley/Los Angeles: University of California Press, 1990, p. 26.
72. I am here referring to the two major categories structuring the moral landscape of Afro-American ghettos; Anderson, Elijah, *Code of the Streets. Decency, Violence, and the Moral Life of the Inner City*, New York/London: W.W. Norton & Company, 1999.
73. Dharejo, Salam, 'The godfather of Lyari', art. quoted, p. 68.
74. 'Twin bombs strike at Benazir Bhutto's parade', *The Telegraph*, 18 October 2007; http://www.telegraph.co.uk/news/worldnews/1566627/Twin-bombs-strike-at-Benazir-Bhuttos-parade.html
75. On these '*pax traficana*', in the context of Brazil, see Geffray, Christian, 'Etat, richesse et criminels', art. quoted, p. 22.
76. Zia, Amir, 'From beyond the grave', *Newsline*, 28 February 2010.
77. Kaleem, Moosa, 'Enemies forever', *The Herald*, June 2012, p. 33.
78. Quoted in Ayub, Imran, 'Karachi: Lyari wonders how Rehman Dakait lost politicians' love', *Dawn.com*, 12 October 2009; http://archives.dawn.com/archives/161776
79. A local bandit claiming to succeed Rehman at the head of the PAC, Akram Baloch, posed some resistance to Uzair's group. He was, however, militarily defeated by Uzair's stronger faction.
80. '"Rehmān Dakait ko marwākar ghaltī kī, thīk kam kar rahā thā"—Zulfikar Mirzā kā pachhtāwā' (Urdu) ('I made a mistake by getting Rehman Dakait killed, he was doing a great job'—Zulfikar Mirza's repentance), *Jasārat*, 4 September 2011.
81. Zulfikar Mirza, a medical practitioner by training, is the scion of a well known Sindhi family of *jagirdar*s (landlords). He started his career in the Pakistan Navy, before joining Pakistan International Airlines (PIA), from which he was sacked after taking part in the PPP-led movement against the dictatorship of Zia-ul-Haq. A rabid opponent of the MQM, Mirza made a name for himself in 2011 for taking a strong stance against Karachi's dominant party and his leader, which he accused of being responsible for most 'target killings' in Karachi and of using strong-arm tactics to influence the votes of Urdu-speakers.

82. "Rehmān Dakait ko marwākar ghaltī kī", art. quoted.
83. Interview, Karachi (Lyari), December 2011.
84. Ali, Naziha Syed, 'Lyari's recuring nightmare', *The Herald*, February 2010, p. 40.
85. Personal communication by a friend whose fiancée's father owns a clinic in Burns Road and was asked for one million rupees as 'protection money' by the PAC in October 2012.
86. Interview with the leaders of the KRC, Karachi (Lyari), August 2012.
87. PS-108 is a Provincial Assembly constituency covering the neighbourhoods of Agra Taj Colony, Bihar Colony, Hingorabad, Khadda Market, Daryabad and Moosa Lane, where the Kutchi population of Lyari is concentrated.
88. Interview with the leaders of the KRC, Karachi (Lyari), August 2012.
89. Khan, Ansoor and Ramzan Chandio, 'Lyari gangland war hots up', *The Nation* (Karachi), 6 July 2013.
90. Ali, Rabia, 'War strategies: Lyari residents use holes in the walls to escape, gangsters use them to occupy', *The Express Tribune*, 10 July 2013.
91. Interview with a party worker of the MQM living near Chakra Goth, Karachi, December 2011.
92. Frotscher, Ann, *Claiming Pakistan*, op. cit., p. 243.
93. Zia, Amir, 'La cosa nostra', *Newsline*, 30 April 2011.
94. Interview with Nabeel Gabol, Karachi (Defence), August 2012.
95. On 2 March 2012, leaders of the PAC invited representatives from all the parties of Karachi to attend the festivities accompanying Baloch Culture Day in Lyari. Among the chief guests was Ghaus Ali Shah, the leader of the PML-(N) in Sindh; cf. Mandhro, Sameer, 'Lyari spins the wheel for its fortunes', *The Express Tribune*, 7 March 2012.
96. Baloch, Sanaullah, 'The battle for the soul of Lyari', art. quoted.
97. NA-249, which covers parts of Lyari (Kalakot, Chakiwara, Miran Naka, Usmanabad) as well as sections of the Old City (Kharadar, Jodia Bazaar,...), has been a stronghold of the MQM since the late 1980s.
98. Boone, Jon, 'Pakistan's rulers accused of turning to underworld in battle to stay in power', *The Guardian*, 2 May 2013.
99. Barkey, Karen, *Bandits and Bureaucrats. The Ottoman Route to State Centralization*, Ithaca/London: Cornell University Press, 1994, p. 19.
100. According to MPA Javed Nagori, another raid conducted by the police on Uzair Baloch's house, in July 2013, failed to nab the leader of the PAC after a police officer warned him of the operation; 'Arshad Pappu murder case: Uzair Baloch escapes police raid at residence in Lyari', *The Express Tribune*, 27 July 2013.
101. Comaroff, Jean and John L. Comaroff, 'Law and disorder in the postcolony', art. quoted, p. 34.
102. Ibid., p. 171.
103. I am grateful to Nida Kirmani for relating the reactions of her respondents in Lyari, a few weeks after the events.

5. JIHAD COMES TO TOWN

1. Quoted in Agha, Ambreen, 'Battleground Karachi', *Outlookonline* (Delhi), 11 July 2011; http://www.outlookindia.com/article.aspx?277604 (Accessed 3 October 2013)
2. Mansoor, Hasan, 'Islamicizing Pakistan's secular centre', *The Friday Times*, 17–23 January, 2003, p. 3.
3. Zahab, Mariam Abou and Olivier Roy, *Islamist Networks. The Afghan-Pakistan Connection*, London: Hurst, 2004 (2002), p. 27.
4. Marsden, Magnus, 'Introduction: anthropology, Islam and Pakistan', in Marsden, Magnus (ed.), *Islam and Society in Pakistan. Anthropological Perspectives*, Karachi: Oxford University Press, 2010, p. xii.
5. Boivin, Michel, 'Violence, défragmentation et intégration urbaine: Karachi dans la perspective de la courte durée', in *Purusarta*, 26 (2007), p. 217.
6. My understanding of historicism and its hold over scholars of South Asia is heavily indebted to Chakrabarty, Dipesh, *Provincializing Europe. Postcolonial Thought and Historical Difference*, Princeton: Princeton University Press, 2007.
7. Hasan, Amtul, *Impact of Partition. Refugees in Pakistan. Struggle for Empowerment and State Responses*, Delhi: Manohar, 2006, p. 68.
8. Ansari, Sarah, *Life After Partition*, op. cit., p. 108.
9. The Ahmadis belong to a Muslim sect founded at the end of the nineteenth century in Punjab by Mirza Ghulam Ahmad (1835–1908). Ahmad claimed to be the Mahdi, a claim that for orthodox Muslims questions the dogma of the 'closure of the Prophecy' with Muhammad (*khatm-e-nabuwat*).
10. Ansari, Sarah, *Life After Partition*, op. cit., p. 109.
11. Ibid., p. 110.
12. The Majlis-e-Ahrar was founded in 1929 by some Punjabi *ulama* who opposed British rule as well as 'feudals' and Ahmadis. In the late 1930s, its activists were involved in anti-Shia violence in Lucknow. Although the movement declined after Partition, some of its members remained involved in anti-Ahmadi and anti-Shia activities. Several members of the Sipah-e-Sahaba Pakistan (SSP), who would be at the forefront of Pakistan's sectarian war in the late 1980s/early 1990s, hailed from families with an Ahrar background; cf. Zahab, Mariam Abou, 'The SSP, herald of militant Sunni Islam in Pakistan', in Gayer, Laurent and Christophe Jaffrelot (eds), *Armed Militias of South Asia. Fundamentalists, Maoists and Separatists*, London: Hurst, 2009, p. 161.
13. Even in the Punjab, the leadership of the JI was mainly composed of refugees from the eastern part of Punjab; I am grateful to Mariam Abou Zahab for this information.
14. Ansari, Sarah, *Life After Partition*, op. cit., p. 111.
15. Gilani, Sayyid Asad, *Jamā'at-e-Islāmī* (Urdu), Lahore: Feroz Sons Ltd., 1992, pp. 251, 254.
16. Khan, Yasmin, *The Great Partition. The Making of India and Pakistan*, Delhi: Penguin Books, 2007, p. 176.

17. Nasr, Seyyed Vali Reza, *The Vanguard of the Islamic Revolution. The Jama'at-i-Islami of Pakistan*, London/New York: IB Tauris, p. 88.
18. Ansari, Sarah, *Life After Partition*, op. cit., p. 177.
19. Ibid.
20. Ibid., p. 178.
21. Tahir, Tanvir Ahmad, *Political Dynamics of Sindh*, op. cit., pp. 598, 600.
22. Quoted in Mansoor, Hasan, 'Islamicising Pakistan's secular centre', art. quoted, p. 3.
23. Interview with Professor Ghaffoor Ahmad, Karachi, 2006.
24. I am grateful to Mariam Abou Zahab for this information.
25. The SSP is a Sunni sectarian party renamed Ahl-e-Sunnat wal Jama'at (ASWJ) after its ban in 2002. To avoid any confusion and because everyone in Pakistan continues to refer to the ASWJ as the SSP, I only use the original name of the party, although it is officially defunct.
26. See Baig, Noman, *From Mohalla to Mainstream*, op. cit.
27. Ibid., p. 123.
28. I am grateful to Mariam Abou Zahab for this information.
29. Zahab, 'Mariam Abou, The SSP', art. quoted, p. 161.
30. Ahmar, Moonis, 'Sectarian conflicts in Pakistan', *Pakistan Vision*, 9, 1 (2005), p. 8.
31. See for instance Hussain, Zahid, 'Profile of a terrorist', *Newsline*, March 1995, p. 36.
32. Shah, Zulfikar, *Sectarian Violence in Karachi, 1994–2002*, Lahore: Human Rights Commission of Pakistan, 2003, p. 18; these figures are contested and, for 1995, Zahid Hussain advances a much higher number of casualties (250); cf. 'Profile of a terrorist', art. quoted, p. 35.
33. Baloch, Saher, 'Surgical strikes', *Newsline*, 31 July 2010.
34. Ahmed, Khaled, *Sectarian Wars. Pakistan's Sunni-Shia Violence and its Links to the Middle East*, Karachi: Oxford University Press, 2011, pp. 170–1.
35. Shahzad, Syed Saleem, *Inside al-Qaeda and the Taliban. Beyond Bin Laden and 09/11*, London: Pluto Press, 2011, p. 9.
36. Ahmed, Khaled, *Sectarian Wars*, op. cit., p. 150.
37. International Crisis Group, 'The state of sectarianism in Pakistan', *Crisis Group Asia Report* no. 95, 18 April 2005, p. 21.
38. International Crisis Group, 'Pakistan: Karachi's madrasas and violent extremism', *Crisis Group Asia Report* no,130, 29 March 2007, p. 5.
39. Andrabi, Tahir, Jishnu Das, Asim Ijaz Khwaja and Tristan Zajonc, 'Madrasa metrics: the statistics and rhetoric of religious enrolment in Pakistan', in Khan, Naveeda (ed.), *Beyond Crisis. Re-evaluating Pakistan*, Delhi: Routledge, 2010, pp. 430–51.
40. I am grateful to Mariam Abou Zahab for this information.
41. I am grateful to Ahmed Wali Mujeeb for this information.
42. Ahmed, Khaled, *Sectarian Wars*, op. cit., p. 132.
43. The Deobandi *ulama* divided themselves during the 1940s around the issue of

Pakistan. While the dominant Madani faction supported the Congress and opposed Pakistan, the Thanvi group supported it.

44. Source: Jamia-ul-Uloom Islamia; http://www.banuri.edu.pk/en/Number-of-Students
45. Ahmed, Khaled, *Sectarian Wars*, op. cit., p. 129.
46. Zahab, Mariam Abou, 'The SSP', art. quoted.
47. Ahmed, Khaled, *Sectarian Wars*, op. cit., p. 88.
48. Ibid., p. 97.
49. Zaman, Muhammad Qasim, *The Ulama in Contemporary Islam. Custodians of Change*, Karachi: Oxford University Press, 2004 (2002), pp. 132–3.
50. Quoted in Shah, Zulfikar, *Sectarian Violence in Karachi*, op. cit., p. 15.
51. Zaman, Muhammad Qasim, *The Ulama in Contemporary Islam*, op. cit., p. 133.
52. Ahmed, Khaled, *Sectarian Wars*, op. cit., p. 131.
53. Zahab, Mariam Abou and Olivier Roy, *Islamist Networks*, op. cit., p. 60.
54. Ahmed, Khaled, *Sectarian Wars*, op. cit., p. 98.
55. Ansari, Massoud, 'Moving target', *Newsline*, 15 February 2002.
56. Ibid.
57. Abou-Zahab, Mariam, 'The SSP', art. quoted, p. 163.
58. Ibid.
59. Hussain, Zahid, 'Profile of a terrorist', art. quoted, p. 35.
60. Ibid., p. 36.
61. Siddiqi, Farhan Hanif, *The Politics of Ethnicity in Pakistan*, op. cit., pp. 107–8.
62. Zulfikar Shah, *Sectarian Violence in Karachi*, op. cit., pp. 11–2.
63. Hussein, Salman and Fariha Razzak Haroon, 'Sectarian killings in Karachi promise more violence', *The Friday Times*, 3–9 August, 2001, p. 2.
64. On the relations between the SSP and the LeJ, see Abou-Zahab, Mariam, 'The SSP', art. quoted.
65. Shahzad, Syed Saleem, *Inside al-Qaeda and the Taliban*, op. cit., p. 57. Other sources claim that Rigi studied at Binory Town, though, which would suggest that his association with the Sunni sectarian movement was much more ancient; cf. Syed, Baqqir Sajjad, 'Rigi's arrest a godsend for Pakistan', *Dawn.com*, 24 February 2010; http://archives.dawn.com/archives/44508 (Accessed 3 October 2013)
66. On the similitude between Dawat-e-Islami and the Tablighi Jama'at, see Gugler, Thomas K., 'Making Muslims fit for faiz (God's Grace): spiritual and not-so-spiritual transactions inside the Islamic missionary movement Dawat-e-Islami', *Social Compass*, 58, 3 (2011), pp. 339–45.
67. Conversation with a foreign academic with extensive knowledge of Pakistan's sectarian wars; New Haven (Conn.), October 2012.
68. Jamal, Arif, 'Sufi militants struggle with Deobandi jihadists in Pakistan', *New Age Islam*, 24 February, 2011; http://www.newageislam.com/radical-islamism-and-jihad/sufi-militants-struggle-with-deobandi-jihadists-in-pakistan/d/9485 (Accessed 5 October 2013)
69. Rana, Muhammad Amir, *A to Z of Jihadi Organizations in Pakistan*, Lahore: Mashal, 2004, p. 373.

70. Interview with Shahid Ghauri, Karachi (Markaz Ahl-e-Sunnat), June 2006.
71. Rana, Muhammad Amir, *A to Z of Jihadi Organizations in Pakistan*, op. cit., p. 375.
72. Shah, Zulfikar, *Sectarian Violence in Karachi*, op. cit., p. 12.
73. Interview with Shahid Ghauri, Karachi (Markaz Ahl-e-Sunnat), June 2006.
74. Interviews with Zafar Baloch and Uzair Baloch, Karachi (Lyari), December 2011 and August 2012. Whereas the Valika Hospital and the Civil Hospital are administered by the Sindh government, the Abbasi Shaheed Hospital and Lyari General Hospital are administered by the KMC.
75. Human Rights Commission of Pakistan, *Karachi. Unholy Alliances for Mayhem*, Lahore: HRCP, 2011, pp. 32, 39.
76. On the transformation of the mandate of the Rangers in the context of Karachi's conflicts, see Gayer, Laurent, 'The Pakistan Rangers: from border defence to internal "protection"', in Briquet, Jean-Louis and Gilles Favarel-Garrigues (eds), *Organized Crime and States*, op. cit., pp. 15–39.
77. Khan, Faraz, 'Drastic measures: Sunni Tehreek, ASWJ offices in New Karachi demolished', *The Express Tribune*, 15 October 2011.
78. Khan, Faraz, 'New players in NA-244: sectarian parties may give past winners a run for their money', *The Express Tribune*, 6 May 2013.
79. According to journalist Syed Saleem Shahzad, Khaled Sheikh Muhammad (who was related to the Baloch Ramzi tribe) found shelter in the Kalakot area of Lyari and in the fishermen's locality of Ibrahim Hyderi before travelling to Rawalpindi, where he was arrested in 2003; 'Where Pakistan militants go to ground', *AsiaTimesonline*, 23 October 2009; http://www.atimes.com/atimes/South_Asia/KJ23Df03.html (Accessed 3 October 2013)
80. Fouda, Yosri and Nick Fielding, *Masterminds of Terror*, Edinburgh: Mainstream Publishing, 2003.
81. The first suicide-bombing in the city was perpetrated in 2000 by a woman militant and targeted the office of a newspaper on M.A. Jinnah Road. Three people were killed in the blast; cf. Raza, Atif, 'Karachi witnessed 15 suicide attacks after 09/11', *The Daily Times*, 6 April 2012.
82. See in particular Shahzad, Syed Saleem, *Inside al-Qaeda and the Taliban*, op. cit.
83. Siddiqi, Dr. Mehmood, 'Pakistānī Tālibān Karāchī mein?' (Urdu) (The Pakistani Taliban in Karachi?), *Naqīb*, June 2000, pp. 52–4.
84. Hasan, S. Raza, 'Killing of 11 policemen blamed on Taliban', *Dawn*, 30 October 2012.
85. Rehman, Ziar ur, 'The Pakistani Taliban's Karachi network', *CTC Sentinel*, 6, 5 May (2013), p. 3 and *Karachi in Turmoil*, op. cit., p. 49.
86. This offensive started on 5 January 2012 with the killing of Saeed Ahmed Khan, District president of the ANP, in his house in Metroville (SITE Town).
87. 'Taliban spend vacations in Karachi', *The News* (web edition), 1 September 2012; http://www.thenews.com.pk/article-65866-Taliban-spend-vacations-in-Karachi
88. The Dawoodi Bohra community of Karachi has its centre in the Hyderi Market area of north Nazimabad, which was the site of twin blasts that killed eight people in September 2012.

89. Temple-Raston, Dina, 'Multiple feuds bring a record year of violence to Karachi', *NPR.org*, 1 January 2013; http://www.npr.org/2013/01/01/168349318/multiple-feuds-bring-a-record-year-of-violence-to-karachi (Accessed 3 October 2013)
90. Zaman, Fahim and Naziha Syed Ali, 'Taliban in Karachi: the real story', *Dawn*, 31 March 2013.
91. Ibid.
92. Walsh, Declan and Zia ur Rehman, 'Taliban spread terror in Karachi as the new gang in town', *The New York Times*, 29 March 2013.
93. I am grateful to Zia ur Rehman for this information.
94. Mujeeb, Ahmed Wali, 'How the Taliban gripped Karachi', *BBC News*, 21 March 2013; http://www.bbc.co.uk/news/world-asia-21343397 (Accessed 3 October 2013)
95. I am grateful to Zia ur Rehman for this information.
96. I am grateful to Zia ur Rehman for this information.
97. Rehman, Ziar ur, 'The Pakistani Taliban's Karachi network', art. quoted, p. 3.
98. Ibid.
99. Ousat, Ali, 'With Pir Mangho watching over, NA-243 prays for peaceful elections', *The Express Tribune*, 3 May 2013.
100. Khan, Zafar, 'Occupation 101: Manghopir—how it became a no-go area', *The Express Tribune*, 4 April 2013.
101. I am grateful to Frédéric Bobin, South Asia correspondent for *Le Monde*, for this information.
102. Rehman, Ziar ur, 'The Pakistani Taliban's Karachi network', art. quoted, p. 4.
103. 'Awami National Party shuts down offices across Karachi following attacks', *The Express Tribune*, 23 July 2013.
104. Zaman, Fahim and Naziha Syed Ali, 'Taliban in Karachi', art. quoted.
105. Rehman, Ziar ur, 'The Pakistani Taliban's Karachi network', art. quoted, p. 3.
106. Comaroff, Jean and John L. Comaroff, 'Law and disorder in the postcolony', art. quoted, p. 30.
107. Goffman, Erving, *Asylum. Essays on the Social Situation of Mental Patients and Other Inmates*, New York: Anchor Books/Doubleday, 1961, pp. 133–4.
108. The *dars-e-nizami* is the curriculum taught in most south Asian madrasas; it was formalised (and named after) Mullah Nizamuddin Sehalvi, an *alim* of Firangi Mahal, in Lucknow, in the eighteenth century.
109. Khan, Nichola, 'Between spectacle and banality: trajectories of Islamic radicalism in a Karachi neighbourhood', *International Journal of Urban and Regional Research*, 36, 3 (2011), pp. 568–84.
110. Interview with a professor in the science department of KU and Rehman, Zia ur, 'Karachi's new terrorist groups', *The Friday Times*, 6–12 January 2012.
111. In 2006, the Dawat-e-Islami claims to have collected 44.5 million rupees in *zakat* on Eid-ul-Fitr, while the philanthropic branch of the MQM, the KKF, claims to have collected 35.6 million rupees on the same occasion; cf. 'Dawat-e-Islami beats KKF in zakat collection', *The Daily Times*, 30 October 2006.

112. Comaroff, Jean and John L. Comaroff, 'Law and disorder in the postcolony', art. quoted, p. 35.

6. A CITY ON THE EDGE

1. Tilly, Charles, *The Politics of Collective Violence*, op. cit.
2. Frotscher, Ann, *Claiming Pakistan*, op. cit., p. 253.
3. Elias, Norbert, *What is Sociology*, op. cit., p. 15.
4. Elias, Norbert, *The Society of Individuals*, op. cit., p. 62.
5. Frotscher, Ann, *Claiming Pakistan*, op. cit., p. 249.
6. Yusuf, Huma, *Conflict Dynamics in Karachi*, op. cit., p. 4.
7. Abbott, Andrew, 'Status and status strain in the professions', *American Journal of Sociology*, 86, 4 (1981), p. 829.
8. Quoted in Human Rights Commission of Pakistan, *Karachi*, op. cit., p. 14.
9. The only publications to dare criticise openly the *bhatta* system enforced by the MQM are Urdu newspapers affiliated with the Jama'at-e-Islami; see for instance 'Muttahida ki eidī mohim: London qayādat ne 7 kror rupe kā hadf de dīyā' (Urdu) (The MQM's mission to collect donations for Eid: the London-based leadership has fixed a target of 70 million rupees), *Ummat*, 3 October 2007.
10. Frotscher, Ann, *Claiming Pakistan*, op. cit., p. 177.
11. Tran, Mark, 'Pakistan needs to recoup more in taxes before any aid boost, say MPs', *The Guardian*, 4 April 2013.
12. Mbembe, Achille, 'Du gouvernement privé indirect', art. quoted, p. 116 sq.
13. O'Donnell, Guillermo, 'Illusions about consolidation', *Journal of Democracy*, 7, 2 (1996), pp. 34–51.
14. Linz, Juan J., 'Transitions to democracy', *Washington Quarterly*, 13 (1990), p. 156.
15. Tilly, Charles, *The Politics of Collective Violence*, op. cit., chap. 9.
16. Yusuf, Huma, *Conflict Dynamics in Karachi*, op. cit., p. 7.
17. 'Fate of CDGK staff hangs in the balance', *Dawn.com*, 11 July 2011; http://dawn.com/2011/07/11/fate-of-cdgk-departments-staff-hangs-in-the-balance/
18. Ibid.
19. Although this decision to quit the coalition government was officially motivated by the alleged rigging of elections in Azad Kashmir, it took place in an emotionally charged context, a few days before the Sindh government nullified the SLGO 2001.
20. Gazdar, Haris, 'Karachi battles', *Economic & Political Weekly*, 17 September 2011, p. 19.
21. Human Rights Commission of Pakistan, *Karachi*, op. cit., p. 1.
22. Yusuf, Huma, *Conflict Dynamics in Karachi*, op. cit., p. 8.
23. Debos, Marielle, *Le Métier des Armes au Tchad*, op. cit., p. 232.
24. Hansen, Thomas Blom and Finn Stepputat, 'Introduction', art. quoted, p. 29.
25. Hansen, Thomas Blom, 'Governance and state mythologies in Mumbai', in Hansen, Thomas Blom and Finn Stepputat (eds), *States of Imagination*, op. cit., pp. 221–54.

26. Human Rights Watch, *Human Rights Watch World Report 1997: Events of 1996*, New York, p. 176.
27. On the extra-professional activities of the Rangers in Karachi, see Gayer, Laurent, 'The Pakistan Rangers', art. quoted.
28. On this colonial military revolution, see Roy, Kaushik (ed), *War and Society in Colonial India*, Delhi: Oxford University Press, 2010.
29. Bayart, Jean-François and Romain Bertrand, 'De quel «legs colonial» parle-t-on?', *Esprit*, December 2006, pp. 134–60. For an application of this analytical toolbox to the study of military auxiliaries in the course of time, see Debos, Marielle, *Le Métier des Armes au Tchad*, op. cit., Part 1.
30. Roy, Kaushik, *The Oxford Companion to Modern Warfare in India*, Delhi: Oxford University Press, 2009, p. 233.
31. Pinch, William R., 'The slave guru: masters, commanders, and disciples in early modern south Asia', in Copeman, Jacob and Aya Ikegame (eds), *The Guru in South Asia. New Interdisciplinary Perspectives*, London/New York: Routledge, 2012, p. 75.
32. Ahmed, Akbar S., 'Pukhtun tribes in the great game', in *Pakistan Society. Islam, Ethnicity and Leadership in South Asia*, Delhi: Oxford University Press, 1988, pp. 133–57.
33. Hussain, Rizwan, *Pakistan and the Emergence of Islamic Militancy in Afghanistan*, Aldershot: Ashgate, 2005, pp. 39–40.
34. Talbot, Ian, *Pakistan. A Modern History*, London: Hurst, 1998, pp. 94, 113.
35. On the formation of this repertoire of 'tribal warfare' and its transmission to Indian officers, see Moreman, Tim, '"Passing it On": the army in India and frontier warfare, 1914–39', in Roy, Kaushik (ed.), *War and Society in Colonial India*, op. cit., pp. 275–304. Regrettably, Tim Moreman's work deals exclusively with regular operations and does not cover the more occult techniques of warfare of the Raj in Afghanistan, whose history remains to be written.
36. Praval, K.C., *Indian Army after Independence*, Delhi: Lancer, 1995, p. 45.
37. Verkaaik, Oskar, 'The captive state: corruption, intelligence agencies, and ethnicity in Pakistan', in Hansen, Thomas Blom and Finn Stepputat (eds), *States of Imagination*, op. cit., p. 362.
38. Hellinger, Daniel, 'Paranoia, conspiracy and hegemony in American politics', in Sanders, Todd and Harry G. West (eds), *Transparency and Conspiracy. Ethnographies of Suspicion in the New World Order*, Durham, NC: Duke University Press, 2003, p. 210.
39. Sanders, Todd and Harry G. West, 'Power revealed and concealed in the new world order', in ibid., p. 6.
40. For a different interpretation of Altaf Hussain's charisma and another explanation for the title 'Pir Altaf', see Verkaaik, Oskar, *Migrants and Militants*, op. cit., p. 71.
41. Interview with Hydder Abbas Rizvi, Karachi (Defence), November 2006.
42. Khan, Mansoor, 'Karachi: the fire within', art. quoted, p. 32.

43. Gambetta, Diego, *The Sicilian Mafia. The Business of Private Protection*, Cambridge: Harvard University Press, 1993.
44. Khan, Mansoor, 'Karachi: the fire within', art. quoted, p. 33.
45. On the distinction between 'orderly' and 'disordered' markets of protection, see Gambetta, Diego, *The Sicilian Mafia*, op. cit., chap. 8, 9.
46. 'Growing extortion menace haunts Karachi', *Dawn.com*, 9 July 2013; http://dawn.com/news/1022242/growing-extortion-menace-haunts-karachi (Accessed 3 October 2013)
47. Interview, Karachi (Hawke's Bay), August 2011.
48. Gambetta, Diego, *The Sicilian Mafia*, op. cit., p. 176.
49. I am grateful to Hidayat Hussain for bringing this trend to my attention.
50. SMC 2011, op. cit., p. 42.
51. Pécaut, Daniel, 'From the banality of violence to real terror', art. quoted, p. 152.
52. See the testimony of target killer Kaleem Siddiqui, in Houreld, Katharine, 'Politics mix with violent crime in Pakistan's Karachi', *Reuters*, 22 June 2011; http://in.reuters.com/article/2012/06/22/pakistan-karachi-violence-idINDEE85K05B20120622 (Accessed 3 October 2013)
53. Human Rights Commission of Pakistan, *Karachi*, op. cit., pp. 32, 39.
54. Baloch, Saher, 'In Karachi, hospitals are as dangerous as its streets', *Dawn.com*, 1 June 2013; http://beta.dawn.com/news/1015399/in-karachi-hospitals-are-as-dangerous-as-its-streets
55. Khan, Nichola, *Mohajir Militancy in Pakistan*, op. cit., pp. 3–4.
56. Parwaiz, Salis ben, '14 more killed in Karachi violence', *The News*, 30 December 2007.
57. 'Karachi: long term impact of riots on city's economy', *Dawn.com*, 10 January 2008; http://beta.dawn.com/news/283996/karachi-long-term-impact-of-riots-on-city-s-economy
58. Interview, Karachi (Lyari), August 2012.
59. Khan, Mansoor, 'Street surgery', *The Herald*, January 2009, p. 32.
60. Khan, Faraz, 'City swept in "new" terror: videos reveal assault and mutilation by target killers', *The Express Tribune*, 25 August 2011.
61. I am grateful to Zia ur Rehman for this information.
62. Karachi's police force consists of 32,524 personnel, 5,000 to 8,000 of whom are currently allocated to the security of VIPs (political representatives, bureaucrats and members of the judiciary but also businessmen; the relatives of these VIPs are also eligible to police protection, without any legal basis). The 18,000 policemen who make up the operational wing work in day and night shifts, leaving 10,000 police personnel to patrol the streets of the city during the day and only 8,000 during the night; cf. Khan, Faraz, 'To protect and [under]serve: Karachi has 1 policeman to protect every 2,000 people', *The Express Tribune*, 23 May 2011; SMC 2011, op. cit., p. 38.
63. Quoted in Rahman, Perween et al, 'Goths become abadis—Karachi', final draft, Karachi: Orangi Pilot Project, 2012, case study 1, p. 2.

64. Hasan, Arif and Mansoor Raza, *Karachi. The Land Issues*, op. cit., p. 68.
65. Mehmood, Asif, 'Report sees external militant groups behind recent Lyari violence', *Dawn.com*, 17 July 2013; http://dawn.com/news/1029473/report-sees-external-militant-groups-behind-recent-lyari-violence
66. On this persisting reification of the Pakistani state as the neutral promoter of a just society, see Verkaaik, Oskar, 'The captive state', art. quoted.
67. On 6 March 2013, for instance, the CJP warned the Advocate General Sindh in the following terms: 'Do not play with emotions of the people, they have more rights than us'; quoted in Khurshid, Jamal, 'Operation clean-up inevitable in Karachi: SC', *The News*, 7 March 2013.
68. This definition was proposed by one of the judges sitting on the bench of the Supreme Court Karachi registry, Justice Jawwad S. Khawaja; quoted in Shehzad, Rizwan, 'Karachi violence case: police tells SC it cannot lie about no-go areas', *The Express Tribune*, 22 March 2013.
69. Mbembe, Achille, 'Du gouvernement privé indirect', art. quoted.
70. Comaroff, Jean and John L. Comaroff, 'Law and disorder in the postcolony', art. quoted, p. 26.

7. GEOGRAPHIES OF FEAR

1. Khalique, Harris, *Ishq kī Taqwīm mein…*, op. cit., p. 164.
2. Feldman, Allen, *Formations of Violence. The Narrative of the Body and Political Terror in Northern Ireland*, Chicago: Chicago University Press, 1991, chap. 2.
3. Green, Linda, *Fear as a Way of Life. Mayan Widows in Rural Guatemala*, New York: Columbia University Press, 1999, p. 69.
4. Wacquant, Loïc, *Urban Outcasts. A Comparative Sociology of Advanced Urban Marginality*, Cambridge: Polity Press, 2008, p. 205.
5. Henrik Vigh, *Navigating Terrains of War*, op. cit., p. 151.
6. Ahmad, Tania, 'Bystander tactics', art. quoted.
7. de Certeau, Michel, *L'invention du Quotidien, vol. 1, Arts de Faire*, Paris: Gallimard, 1990 (1980) [Eng. tr.: *The Practice of Everyday Life*, Berkeley/Los Angeles: University of California Press, 1984].
8. Adamjee, Maheen Bashir, 'The art of survival', *Newsline*, 30 September 2011.
9. Farrukhi, Asif, 'Is shehr mein rahnā', art. quoted, p. 603.
10. Vigh, Henrik, *Navigating Terrains of War*, op. cit., pp. 154–5.
11. 'Into the abyss', *The Economist*, 27 August 2011.
13. Interview, Karachi, August 2012.
14. Imtiaz, Saba, 'Lyari stunned as 6 funerals emerge from one lane', *The Express Tribune*, 19 August 2011.
15. Spyer, Patricia, 'Some notes on disorder in the Indonesian postcolony', in Comaroff, Jean and John L. Comaroff (eds), *Law and Disorder in the Postcolony*, op. cit., p. 206.
16. Green, Linda, *Fear as a Way of Life*, op. cit.

17. Ahmad, Tania 'Bystander tactics', art. quoted.
18. Shah, Alpa, 'In search of certainty in revolutionary India', *Dialectical Anthropology*, 33, 3/4, December (2009), pp. 271–86.
19. Hasan, Syed Shoaib, 'Pakistan foils "ashura attacks"', *BBC News*, 19 January 2008; http://news.bbc.co.uk/2/hi/south_asia/7197781.stm
20. On the 'carnivalesque' dimension of Muharram celebrations, in the context of colonial Bombay, see Green, Nile, *Bombay Islam. The Religious Economy of the West Indian Ocean, 1840–1915*, Delhi: Cambridge University Press, 2011, pp. 53–6.
21. Hansen, Thomas Blom, *Violence in Urban India*, op. cit., p. 186.
22. England, Marcia and Stephanie Simon, 'Scary cities: urban geographies of fear, difference and belonging', *Social & Cultural Geography*, 11, 3 May (2010), pp. 202–3.
23. Interview, Karachi (Clifton), August 2012.
24. Feldman, Allen, *Formations of Violence*, op. cit., pp. 35–6.
25. Ibid., p. 41.
26. Ibid., p. 37.
27. Verkaaik, Oskar, *Migrants and Militants*, op. cit., p. 13.
28. Hasan, Arif, 'A generation comes of age', *The Herald*, October 1987, pp. 52–3.
29. Interview, Karachi (Lyari), August 2012.
30. Interview, Karachi (Lyari), August 2012.
31. The largest Hindu ghetto of contemporary Karachi is Narainpura, in Ranchore Lines, followed by Rangiwal, in Lyari. Almost all the residents of these neighbourhoods belong to the 'untouchable' 'scheduled castes'; cf. Boivin, Michel, 'Les Hindous de Karachi dans la perspective historique', art. quoted, p. 83.
32. Hasan, Arif, 'The growth of a metropolis', art. quoted, p. 174.
33. Shaheed, Zafar, *The Labour Movement in Pakistan*, op. cit., p. 40
34. Ibid.
35. Ahmad, Nizat, 'Choice of neighbourhoods by mover households in Karachi', *Urban Studies*, 30, 7 (1993), pp. 1261, 1263.
36. Hasan, Arif, 'Politics of ethnicity', *Dawn.com*, 25 June 2010; http://archives.dawn.com/archives/27766
37. See for instance the case of the 'Shipyard' studied by Laura Ring in *Zenana*, op. cit.
38. These unofficial settlements sprung up through the illegal occupation of government land in the outskirts of the city centre in the aftermath of Partition. From the 1960s onwards, these practices of unorganised invasion became less common in the formation of the *basti*s and ceded the way to illegal subdivisions of public land (see Chapter 1).
39. Verkaaik, Oskar, 'At home in Karachi', art. quoted, p. 72.
40. On the enthusiasm surrounding the national project of state- and nation-building in Pakistan's early days, see the testimony of W.C. Smith, who visited the country in 1948, in Smith, Wilfred Cantwell, *Islam in Modern History*, New York: Mentor Books, 1957; quoted and discussed in Khan, Naveeda, *Muslim Becoming. Aspiration and Skepticism in Pakistan*, Delhi: Orient BlackSwan, 2012, pp. 8–9.

41. Verkaaik, Oskar, 'At home in Karachi', art. quoted, p. 72.
42. Ibid., p. 73.
43. Ibid.
44. Ibid., pp. 74–5.
45. Shah, Fawad and Mahim Maher, 'In the shadow of a mountain, shades of grey for the small folk', *The Express Tribune*, 6 August 2011.
46. Hashim, Asad, 'Q&A: ethnicity, land and violence in Karachi', *AlJazeera.com*, 19 June 2012; http://www.aljazeera.com/indepth/features/2012/06/2012661021 53136450.html (Accessed 3 October 2013)
48. Quoted in Mustafa, Zubeida, 'A city with two souls', *Dawn.com*, 12 June 2010; http://archives.dawn.com/archives/31976 (Accessed 3 October 2013)
48. Hasan, Arif and Mansoor Raza, *Karachi. The Land Issues*, op. cit., p. 11.
49. Ibid., fig.1, p. 15.
50. Cowasjee, Ardeshir, 'I own Karachi… and can sell it! 2', *Dawn.com*, 17 May 2009; http://archives.dawn.com/archives/152173 (Accessed 3 October 2013)
51. Frotscher, Ann, *Claiming Pakistan*, op. cit., p. 73.
52. Ibid.
53. Ibid.
54. Hasan, Arif and Mansoor Raza, *Karachi. The Land Issues*, op. cit. p. 19.
55. The residents settled in Altaf Nagar from 2006 onwards were provided with land documents showing the date of settlement as 1983 and the area (though in Gadap Town) as part of Gulshan-e-Zia, in Orangi Town. These documents had the letter heading of the CDGK but no date or signature of any government official; cf. Rahman, Perween et al, 'Goths become abadis—Karachi', art. quoted, p. 3, fn. 6.
56. Frotscher, Ann, *Claiming Pakistan*, op. cit., p. 72.
57. Rahman, Perween et al, 'Goths become abadis', art. quoted, p. 5.
58. Ibid., p. 7.
59. Ibid.
60. Interview with Perween Rahman, Karachi (Qasba Colony), February 2013.
61. Hashim, Asad, 'Q&A: ethnicity, land and violence in Karachi', art. quoted.
62. Interview with a resident of the Sindh Baloch Cooperative Housing Society, Karachi, August 2012.
63. Zaman, Fahim, 'Dying to live', *Dawn.com*, 14 November 2012; http://dawn.com/2012/11/14/dying-to-live/
64. E-mail interview, 19 November 2012.
65. Interview with a resident of the Sindh Baloch Cooperative Housing Society, Karachi, August 2012.
66. I am grateful to the late Amin Khattak for providing me with this letter.
67. Appadurai, Arjun, 'Spectral housing and urban cleansing', art. quoted, p. 644.
68. Ibid.
69. Ibid., p. 649.
70. Naqvi, Maniza, *Mass Transit*, Karachi: Oxford University Press, 1998, pp. 146–7
71. Gazdar, Haris, 'Karachi battles', art. quoted.

72. City District Government of Karachi, *Karachi Rising*, 2009, p. 18.
73. Maher, Mahim, 'Made in China flyover could work wonders for Karachi's "dead" spaces', *The Express Tribune*, 29 July 2012.
74. In September 2007, the Shershah bridge collapsed barely a month after it was opened to traffic, killing five people. The nine accused were acquitted in 2012 over a lack of evidence. The contract to build the bridge had been awarded without bidding to the Army's National Logistic Cell (NLC) and the National Highway Authority (NHA); cf. Husain, Shahid, 'Army to blame for Karachi bridge collapse', *Down To Earth*, 31 October 2007.
75. Maher, Mahim, 'Karachi should bypass the flyover to be truly modern', *The Express Tribune*, 31 July 2012.
76. Channa, Aftab, 'Governor re-baptises bridge to Afza Altaf flyover at inauguration', *Pakistan Today*, 21 April 2011.

CONCLUSION

1. This trade boomed after the American troops' surge in Afghanistan in the first six months of 2010, following which there was a 50 per cent increase in the number of containers unloaded in Karachi (Farooq, Umer, 'Truckloads of money', *The Herald*, December 2010, p. 59). Until the suspension of the overland supply route following an attack by NATO forces on a Pakistani military checkpoint in 2011, 1,300 containers of sustainment cargo and 1,000 fuel tankers were arriving at Karachi Port every month; cf. Yusuf, Huma, *Conflict Dynamics in Karachi*, op. cit., p. 5. Other sources put this figure much higher and suggest that up to 20,000 NATO containers arrived at Karachi Port every month around 2010 (Farooq, Umer, 'Truckloads of money', art. quoted, p. 59).
2. Khan, Mohammad Ali, 'Crime and encouragement', *The Herald*, December 2010, pp. 62–5.
3. Butt, Qaiser, 'Nato supply resumption a boon for Taliban', *The Express Tribune*, 5 July 2012.
4. Conversation with a Canadian public official privy to the discussions around the future of NATO's presence in Afghanistan, Paris, July 2013.
5. Khalaf, Samir, *Civil and Uncivil Violence in Lebanon. A History of the Internationalization of Communal Conflict*, New York: Columbia University Press, 2002.
6. Rozema, Ralph, 'Medellin', art. quoted, p. 65.
7. After interviewing more than 3,000 persons, Scotland Yard made its first arrest in June 2013 (this suspect turned out to be Altaf Hussain's nephew, who was then bailed). A few days earlier, a raid was conducted on Altaf Hussain's residence in Mill Hill. On these developments, see Bennett-Jones, Owen, 'Altaf Hussain, the notorious MQM leader who swapped Pakistan for London', *The Guardian*, 29 July 2013 and Khan, Nichola, '"Remote control" politics of Karachi', *The Friday Times*, 07–13 June 2013.
8. Bennett-Jones, Owen, 'Altaf Hussain…', art. quoted.

9. Khan, Nichola, '"Remote control" politics of Karachi', art. quoted.
10. On these game models, see Elias, Norbert, *What is Sociology?*, op. cit., chap. 3.
11. Ibid., p. 83.
12. Ibid., p. 90.
13. After months of conflict between the MQM and the PPP over the future of local government institutions in Sindh, the Sindh Provincial Assembly repealed the Sindh Peoples Local Government Ordinance Act 2012 in February 2013, shortly after the MQM quit the coalition for the third time, and restored instead the commissionerate system. This has deprived the MQM of one of its major sources of influence and patronage in urban Sindh.
14. Gazdar, Haris, 'Karachi: violence, duality and negotiation', art. quoted, p. 8.
15. Elias, Norbert, *What is Sociology?*, op. cit., p. 85.
16. Hasan, Arif and Mansoor Raza, *Karachi. The Land Issues*, op. cit., p. 48.
17. Elias, Norbert, *What is Sociology?*, op. cit., p. 85.
18. Interview with Perween Rahman, Karachi (Qasba Colony), February 2013.
19. Elias, Norbert, *What is Sociology?*, op. cit., p. 130.
20. Interview with Perween Rahman, Karachi (Qasba Colony), February 2013.
21. Aftab, Safiya, 'Saving Karachi, saving Pakistan', *The Friday Times*, 15–21 July 2011.
22. Quoted by Naqvi, Maniza, *Mass Transit*, op. cit., p. 13.

SELECTIVE BIBLIOGRAPHY

Literary and historical accounts (prose and poetry)

Amrohvi, Rais, 'Pagrī' (Urdu) (Honour), *Jang*, 9 May 1948, reproduced in *Qat'āt Raīs Amrohvī*, Karachi: Rais Academy, 1987, vol. 1, p. 16.

Baillie, Alexander F., *Kurrachee. Past, Present and Future*, Karachi: OUP, 1997 [1890].

Bhopali, Mohsin, *Shehr-e-Ashob* (Urdu) (Lament for the City), Karachi: Aiwan-e-adab, 1997.

Damohi, Muhammad Usman, *Karāchī. Tārīkh ke Aīne mein* (Urdu) (Karachi. In the Mirror of History), Karachi: Indus Publications, 1996.

Farrukhi, Asif, 'Is shehr mein rahnā' (Urdu) (To live in this city), in Kamal, Ajmal (ed.), *Karachī kī Kahanī* (Urdu) (The Story of Karachi), Karachi: Aaj, 2007 [1996], vol. 2, pp. 577–610.

Hasam, Zinat, 'Guzre dīn, guzarte dīn' (Urdu) (Past days, passing days), ibid., pp. 617–53.

Hotchand, Naomul, *The Memoirs of Seth Naomul Hotchand*, Karachi: Pakistan Herald Publications, 2006, p. 3. The autobiography of Seth Naomul Hotchand was originally published as *A Forgotten Chapter of Indian History, as told by Seth Naomal Hotchand, CSI, of Karachi (1804–1878), Written by Himself and Translated by His Grandson Rao Bahadur Alumal Trikamdas Bhojwani, BA, Edited with an Introduction by Sir H. Evan M. James, KCIE, CSI, Commissioner of Sindh, 1891–1899, Printed for Private Circulation Only*, Surat, 1915.

Khalique, Harris, *Ishq kī Taqwīm mein. Harris Khaliq kī Nazmen, 1985–2005* (Urdu) (In the Calendar of Love. Poems by Haris Khalique, 1985–2005), Karachi: Danyal, 2006.

Nazir, Hamid, *Wadī Lyārī* (Urdu) (The Lyari River), Karachi: Akasi, 1992.

Riaz, Fahmida, *Karāchī* (Urdu), Karachi: Aaj, 1996.

Sahil, Zeeshan, *Karāchī aur Dūsrī Nazmen* (Urdu) (Karachi and Other Poems), Karachi: Aaj, 1995.

Shakir, Parveen, *Khud Kalāmī* (Urdu) (Monologue), Lahore: al-Tehrir, 1988.

Siddiqi, Ahmad Hussein, *Karāchī. Gohar-e-Buhīrah 'Arb* (Urdu) (Karachi. The Pearl of the Arabian Sea), Karachi: Fazli Sons, 1995.

Siddiqi, Anwar Ehsan, 'Parwarish-e-loh-o-qalam (khud nawisht)' (Urdu) (Literary upbringing: an autobiography), in Farrukhi, Asif (ed.), *Dunyā Zād*, 32, 2011, pp. 231–76.

Primary sources in Urdu on the MQM (prose and poetry)

Hussain, Altaf and Khalid Athar, *Safar-e-Zindagī. MQM kī Kahānī, Altāf Hussain kī Zabānī mein* (Urdu) (My Life's Journey. The Story of the MQM in the Words of Altaf Hussain), Karachi: Jang Publishers, 1988.

Farooq, Imran, *Nazm-o-Zābat ke Taqāze* (Urdu), London: MQM International Secretariat, 1998 (1986).

Jamil, Tahrir Amir, 'Inquelāb parwār quāid-e-tehrīk Altāf Hussain kī jed-o-jehed: tarīkhī ke aine mein' (Urdu) (The struggle of the patron of the revolution and leader of the movement, Altaf Hussain: in the mirror of history), *Naqīb*, September 2006, pp. 22–25.

Kazmi, Javed, 'Nazm' (Urdu) (Poem), *Naqīb*, 36, September 2006, p. 21.

Nishat, Raqiah, 'Nazr ke sāmne hai aj sāhil merā' (Urdu) (Today, my seashore is in sight), *Naqīb*, June 2000, pp. 48–49.

Shahzad, Saleem, *Sha'ur kā Safar* (Urdu) (A Journey of the Mind), London: MQM International Secretariat, 2006 (2005).

Siddiqi, Mehmood, 'Pakistānī Tālibān Karāchī mein?' (Urdu) (The Pakistani Taliban in Karachi?), *Naqīb*, June 2000, pp. 52–54.

Secondary sources/Social sciences works

Ahmad, Tania, 'Bystander tactics: life on turf in Karachi', *South Asia Multidisciplinary Academic Journal* (*SAMAJ*), 5, 2011; http://samaj.revues.org/3537 (accessed on 7 October 2013).

Ahmar, Moonis, 'Ethnicity and state power in Pakistan: the Karachi crisis', *Asian Survey*, 36, 10, October (1996), pp. 1031–48.

Ahmed, Khaled, *Sectarian Wars. Pakistan's Sunni-Shia Violence and its Links to the Middle East*, Karachi: Oxford University Press, 2011.

Ali, Kamran Asdar, 'Men and their "Problems": Notes on Contemporary Karachi', in Ali, Kamran Asdar and Martina Rieker (eds.), *Comparing Cities. The Middle East and South Asia*, Delhi: Oxford University Press, 2009, pp. 46–64.

Ali, Kamran Asdar, 'Strength of the state meets strength of the street: the 1972 labour struggle in Karachi', in Khan, Naveeda (ed.), *Beyond Crisis. Re-Evaluating Pakistan*, Delhi: Routledge, 2010, pp. 210–44.

Ansari, Sarah, *Life after Partition. Migration, Community and Strife in Sindh, 1947–1962*, Karachi: Oxford University Press, 2005.

Anwar, Raja, *The Terrorist Prince. The Life and Death of Murtaza Bhutto*, London: Verso, 1997.

Arias, Enrique Desmond, *Drugs and Democracy in Rio de Janeiro. Trafficking,*

Social Networks and Public, Chapel Hill: University of North Carolina Press, 2006.

Auyero, Javier, *Routine Politics and Violence in Argentina. The Gray Zone of State Power*, Cambridge: Cambridge University Press, 2007.

Baig, Noman, *From Mohalla to Mainstream. The MQM's Transformation from an Ethnic to a Catch-All Party*, BA Thesis (Political Science), University of Oklahoma, 2005.

Blom Hansen, Thomas *Violence in Urban India. Identity Politics, 'Mumbai', and the Postcolonial City*, Delhi: Permanent Black, 2005 (2001).

Blom Hansen, Thomas, 'Sovereigns beyond the state: on legality and authority in urban India', in Blom Hansen, Thomas and Finn Stepputat (eds.), *Sovereign Bodies. Citizens, Migrants, and States in the Postcolonial World*, Princeton/Oxford: Princeton University Press, 2005, pp. 169–91.

Blom Hansen, Thomas, 'Governance and state mythologies in Mumbai', in Blom Hansen, Thomas and Finn Stepputat (eds.), *States of Imagination. Ethnographic Explorations of the Postcolonial State*, Durham: Duke University Press, pp. 221–56.

Boivin, Michel, 'Karachi et ses territoires en conflit: pour une relecture de la question communautaire', *Hérodote*, 101, (2001/2002), pp. 180–200.

Boivin, Michel, 'Les hindous de Karachi dans la perspective historique: de la domination socio-économique à la marginalisation minoritaire', *Revue des mondes musulmans et de la Méditerranée*, 107–110, September (2005), pp. 61–96.

Boivin, Michel, 'Karachi, "mère des immigrés": business, violence et politique identitaire', *Hérodote*, 139, (2010), pp. 123–42.

Browning, Christopher, *Ordinary Men. Reserve Battalion Police 101 and the Final Solution in Poland*, London: Harper Collins, 1993.

Budhani, Azmat Ali, Haris Gazdar, Sobia Ahmad Kaker, and Hussain Bux Mallah, *The Open City. Social Networks and Violence in Karachi*, Crisis States Research Centre working papers series 2, 70, Crisis States Research Centre, London: London School of Economics and Political Science, 2010.

Chaudhry, Lubna Nazir, 'Reconstituting selves in the Karachi conflict: Mohajir women survivors and structural violence', *Cultural Dynamics*, 16, 2/3, (2004), pp. 259–90.

Collins, Randall, *Violence. A Micro-Sociological Theory*, Princeton/Oxford: Princeton University Press, 2008.

Comaroff, Jean and John L. Comaroff (eds.), *Law and Disorder in the Postcolony*, Chicago: University of Chicago Press, 2006.

Coronil, Fernando and Julie Skurski (eds.), *States of Violence*, Ann Harbor: University of Michigan Press, 2006.

Coser, Lewis, *Greedy Institutions. Patterns of Undivided Commitment*, New York: The Free Press, 1974.

Daechsel, Markus, *The Politics of Self Expression. The Urdu Middle-Class Milieu in Mid-Twentieth Century India and Pakistan*, London/New York: Routledge, 2006.

Daechsel, Markus, 'Sovereignty, governmentality and development in Ayub's Pakistan: the case of Korangi township', *Modern Asian Studies*, 45, 1, (2011), pp. 131–57.

Debos, Marielle, *Le Métier des Armes au Tchad. Le Gouvernement de l'Entre-guerres*, Paris: Karthala, 2013.

Elias, Norbert, *The Civilizing Process*, Oxford: Blackwell, 1994 (1939).

Elias, Norbert, *What is Sociology?*, New York: Columbia University Press, 1978.

Elias, Norbert, 'Figuration', in Schäfers, Bernard (ed.), *Grundbegriffe der Soziologie*, Opladen, Leske en Budrich, 1986, pp. 88–91.

Elias, Norbert, *The Society of Individuals*, Oxford: Blackwell, 1991 (1987).

England, Marcia, and Stephanie Simon, 'Scary cities: urban geographies of fear, difference and belonging', *Social & Cultural Geography*, 11, 3, May (2010), pp. 201–07.

Feldman, Allen, *Formations of Violence. The Narrative of the Body and Political Terror in Northern Ireland*, Chicago: The University of Chicago Press, 1991.

Frotscher, Ann, *Claiming Pakistan. The MQM and the Fight for Belonging*, Nomos: Baden Baden, 2008.

Gambetta, Diego, *The Sicilian Mafia. The Business of Private Protection*, Cambridge: Harvard University Press, 1993.

Gayer, Laurent, 'The Rangers of Pakistan: from border defense to internal "Protection"', in Briquet, Jean-Louis and Gilles Favarel-Garrigues (eds.), *Organized Crime and States. The Hidden Face of Politics*, New York: Palgrave Macmillan, pp. 15-39.

Gazdar, Haris, 'Karachi battles', *Economic & Political Weekly*, 17 September 2011, pp. 19–21.

Geffray, Christian, 'Etat, richesse et criminels', *Mondes en développement*, 110, 2000, pp. 15–30.

Green, Linda, *Fear as a Way of Life. Mayan Widows in Rural Guatemala*, New York: Columbia University Press, 1999.

Hagmann, Tobias and Markus V. Hoehne, 'Failures of the state failure debate: evidence from the Somali territories', *Journal of International Development*, 21, 2009, pp. 42–57.

Hasan, Arif, *Understanding Karachi. Planning and Reform for the Future*, Karachi: City Press, 1999.

Hasan, Arif and Mansoor Raza, *Karachi. The Land Issues* (first draft), Karachi: NED University, Urban Research and Development Cell, 27 June 2012.

Husain, Akmal, 'The Karachi riots of December 1986: crisis of state and civil society in Pakistan', in Das, Veena (ed.), *Mirrors of Violence. Communities, Riots and Survivors in Souh Asia*, Delhi: Oxford University Press, 1990, pp. 185–93.

Inskeep, Steve, *Instant City. Life and Death in Karachi*, Penguin: New York, 2011.

Kalyvas, Stathis N., 'The ontology of "political violence": action and identity in civil wars', *Perspectives on Politics*, 1, 3, September (2003), pp. 475–494.

Kalyvas, Stathis N., *The Logic of Violence in Civil War*, Cambridge: Cambridge University Press, 2006.

Kennedy, Charles H., 'The politics of ethnicity in Sindh', *Asian Survey*, 31, 10, October (1991).

Khan, Adeel, *Politics of Identity. Ethnic Nationalism and the State in Pakistan*, Delhi: Sage, 2005.

Khan, Lal, *Pakistan's Other Story. The 1968–9 Revolution*, Delhi: Aakar Books, 2009.

Khan, Nichola, *Mohajir Militancy in Pakistan. Violence and Practices of Transformation in the Karachi Conflict*, London: Routledge, 2010.

Khan, Yasmin, *The Great Partition. The Making of India and Pakistan*, Delhi: Penguin Books, 2007.

Khuhro, Hamida and Anwer Mooraj (eds.), *Karachi. Megacity of Our Times*, Karachi: OUP, 1997.

Kochanek, Stanley, *Interest Groups and Development. Business and Politics in Pakistan*, Karachi: Oxford University Press, 1983.

Lari, Yasmin and Mihail Lari, *The Dual City. Karachi During the Raj*, Karachi: Oxford University Press, 1996

Leeds, Elizabeth, 'Cocaine and parallel politics in the Brazilian urban periphery: constraints to local-level democratization', *Latin American Research Review*, 31, 3, 1996, pp. 47–83.

Lund, Christian, 'Twilight Institutions: An Introduction', *Development and Change*, 37 (4), 2006, pp. 673–84.

Naqvi, Maniza, *Mass Transit*, Karachi: Oxford University Press, 1998.

Nasr, Seyyed Vali Reza, 'Islam and politics: Islami Jami'at-i-Tulaba in Pakistan', *Middle East Journal*, 46, 1, Winter (1992), pp. 59–76.

Nasr, Seyyed Vali Reza, *The Vanguard of the Islamic Revolution. The Jama'at-i-Islami of Pakistan*, London/New York: IB Tauris, 1994.

Pécaut, Daniel, 'From the banality of violence to real terror', *in* Koonings, Kees and Dirk Kruijt (eds.), *Societies of Fear. The Legacy of Civil War, Violence and Terror in Latin America*, London/New York: Zed Books, 1999, pp. 141–67.

Raeymaekers, Timothy, Ken Menkhaus, Koen Vlassenroot, 'State and non-state regulation in African protracted crises: governance without government', *Afrika Focus*, 21 (2), 2008, pp. 7–21.

Rahman, Tariq, *Language and Politics in Pakistan*, Karachi: Oxford University Press, 2000 (1996).

Rehman, Zia ur, *Karachi in Turmoil*, Islamabad: Narratives, 2013.

Richards, Julian James, *Mohajir Subnationalism and the Mohajir Qaumi Movement in Sindh Province, Pakistan*, Ph.D dissertation (Geography), Cambridge: Cambridge University, 1993.

Richards, Paul (ed.), *No Peace, No War. An Anthropology of Contemporary Armed Conflicts*, Athens/Oxford: Ohio University Press/James Currey, 2005.

Ring, Laura, *Zenana. Everyday Peace in a Karachi Apartment Building*, Bloomington and Indianapolis: University of Indiana Press, 2006.

Roitman, Janet, 'The politics of informal markets in sub-Saharan Africa', *The Journal of Modern African Studies*, 28, 4, December (1990), pp. 671–96.

Saigol, Rubina 'The partition of self: Mohajir women's sense of identity and nationhood', in Ahmad, Sadaf (ed.), *Pakistani Women. Multiple Locations and Competing Narratives*, Karachi: Oxford University Press, 2010, pp. 194–232.

Samad, Yunas, 'In and out of power but not down and out: Mohajir identity politics', in Jaffrelot, Christophe (ed.), *Pakistan. Nationalism without a Nation?*, Delhi: Manohar, 2002, pp. 51–62.

Sanders, Todd and Harry G. West (eds.), *Transparency and Conspiracy. Ethnographies of Suspicion in the New World Order*, Durham: Duke University Press, 2003.

Shah, Zulfiqar, *Sectarian Violence in Karachi, 1994–2002*, Lahore: Human Rights Commission of Pakistan, 2003.

Shaheed, Zafar, *The Labour Movement in Pakistan. Organization and Leadership in Karachi in the 1970s*, Karachi: Oxford University Press, 2007.

Shapiro, Ian and Sonu Bedi (eds.), *Political Contingency. Studying the Unexpected, the Accidental and the Unforeseen*, New York: New York University Press, 2007, pp. 54–78.

Siddiqi, Farhan Hanif, 'Intra-ethnic fissures in ethnic movements: the rise of Mohajir identity politics in post-1971 Pakistan', *Asian Ethnicity*, 11, 1, February (2010), pp. 25–41.

Siddiqi, Farhan Hanif, *The Politics of Ethnicity in Pakistan. The Baloch, Sindhi and Mohajir Ethnic Movements*, London: Routledge, 2012.

Slimbach, Richard A., 'Ethnic binds and pedagogies of resistance: Baloch nationalism and educational innovation in Karachi', in Titus, Paul (ed.), *Marginality and Modernity. Ethnicity and Change in Post-Colonial Balochistan*, Karachi: Oxford University Press, 1996, pp. 138–67.

Tahir, Tanvir Ahmad, *Political Dynamics of Sindh, 1947–1977*, Karachi: Pakistan Study Centre, 2010.

Talbot, Ian, *Pakistan. A Modern History*, London: Palgrave/Macmillan, 1998.

Tambiah, Stanley J., *Leveling Crowds. Ethnonationalist Conflicts and Collective Violence in South Asia*, Delhi: Vistaar, 1997.

Tan, Tai Yong and Gyanesh Kudaisya, *The Aftermath of Partition in South Asia*, London/New York: Routledge, 2000.

Taussig, Michael, 'Terror as usual: Walter Benjamin's theory of history as a state of siege', *Social Text*, 23, Autumn-Winter (1989), pp. 3–20.

Taussig, Michael, *Law in a Lawless Land. Diary of a Limpieza in Colombia*, Chicago/London: Chicago University Press, 2003.

Tilly, Charles, *The Politics of Collective Violence*, Cambridge: Cambridge University Press, 2003.

Verkaaik, Oskar, *Migrants and Militants. Fun and Urban Violence in Pakistan*, Princeton: Princeton University Press, 2004.

Verkaaik, Oskar, 'At home in Karachi: quasi-domesticity as a way to know the city', *Critique of Anthropology*, 29, 1, (2009), pp. 65–80.

Verkaaik, Oskar, 'The captive state: corruption, intelligence agencies, and ethnicity in Pakistan', in Blom Hansen, Thomas and Finn Stepputat (eds.), *States of Imagination*, op. cit., pp. 345–64.

Vigh, Henrik, *Navigating Terrains of War. Youth and Soldiering in Guinea Bissau*, Oxford/New York: Berghahn, 2007.

Volkvov, Vadim, *Violent Entrepreneurs. The Use of Force in the Making of Russian Capitalism*, Ithaca/London: Cornell University Press, 2002.

Wacquant, Loic, *Urban Outcasts. A Comparative Sociology of Advanced Urban Marginality*, Cambridge: Polity Press, 2008.

Waseem, Mohammad, 'Mohajirs in Pakistan: a case of nativization of migrants', in Bates, Crispin (ed.), *Community, Empire and Migration. South Asians in Diaspora*, Delhi, Orient Longman, 2001, pp. 245–60.

Yusuf, Huma, 'City of lights: violence and Karachi's competing imaginaries', in Anjaria, Jonathan Shapiro and Colin McFarlane (eds.), *Urban Navigations. Politics, Space and the City in South Asia*, Delhi: Routledge, 2011, pp. 298–318.

Yusuf, Huma, *Conflict Dynamics in Karachi*, Washington: United States Institute for Peace, 2012.

Zaidi, Akbar S., 'Politics, institutions, poverty: the case of Karachi', *Economic & Political Weekly*, 20 December (1997), pp. 3282–93.

Zaman, Muhammad Qasim, 'Sectarianism in Pakistan: the radicalization of Shi'i and Sunni identities', *Modern Asian Studies*, 32, 3, July (1998), pp. 689–716.

Zaman, Muhammad Qasim, *The Ulama in Contemporary Islam. Custodians of Change*, Karachi: Oxford University Press, 2004 (2002).

Zaman, Mukhtar, *Students' Role in the Pakistan Movement*, Karachi: Quaid-e-Azam University, 1978.

Zamindar, Vazira Fazila-Yacoobali, *The Long Partition and the Making of Modern South Asia. Refugees, Boundaries, Histories*, Delhi: Penguin, 2008 [2007].

INDEX

Ahmad, Afaq 86
Akhtar, Maulana Hakim 267
Ali, Jam Sadiq 75, 103, 104, 108, 262
Aligarh Colony 36, 47, 49, 225, 295
Altaf Nagar 264, 266, 278, 321
Amrohvi, Rais 35, 85
ANP 26, 29, 30, 33, 103, 104, 114, 115, 118, 119, 164, 179, 180–182, 184–187, 189, 190, 203, 205, 211, 224, 226–229, 233, 244, 246, 257, 263, 269, 273, 277, 278, 314
APMSO 60, 70, 73–76, 79–83, 86–90, 93, 95, 97, 98, 107, 110, 119, 120, 169, 178, 185, 297, 302
Aslam, Hafiz 68, 70, 205, 298
Azhar, Masood 172, 175, 199
Azizabad 90, 102, 155, 299

Badayuni, Maulana Hamid 167
Baig, Mirza Jawwad 85
Baloch, Shah Jahan 158
Baloch, Uzair 124, 125, 139, 140, 143, 146–148, 150, 151, 155–161, 229, 231, 243, 245, 255, 306, 309, 310
Baloch, Zafar 29, 125, 126, 146, 148, 157, 161, 291, 306
Banaras Chowk 7, 45–47, 154, 226, 242, 271
Bashir, M.A. 83
Bhojoomal, Seth 33
Bhutto, Asadullah 107
Bhutto, Benazir 30–32, 74, 131, 139, 143, 144, 149, 150, 184, 215, 226, 254, 262, 282
Bhutto, Bilawal 158
Bhutto, Murtaza 32, 67, 69, 267, 298
Bhutto, Zulfikar 18, 28, 57, 67
Bilawal House 139, 243
Binori, Muhammad Yusuf 174, 175, 185
'Binori Town' (Jamia-ul-Ulum Islamia) 164, 172–176, 183,185, 198, 199, 201
BSO 62, 63, 69, 131, 297, 308

Chaudhry, Iftikhar Muhammad 104, 224, 232
CPLC 6, 8, 9, 10, 33, 206

'Dadal' 131, 132, 134, 136, 140
'Dakait', Rehman 123, 131, 132, 134, 135, 138–140, 142, 143, 146–152, 155, 158, 159, 243

Edhi, Abdul Sattar 142
Engineer, Rafiq 151

Faiz, Faiz Ahmed 130

Farooq, Imran 86, 90, 92, 94, 106, 276, 302
Farrukhi, Asif 47, 241
Fazlullah, Maulana 187, 189, 192, 193, 228
Future Colony 170, 177, 187, 228, 229

Gabol, Allah Bakhsh 131
Gabol, Nabeel 102, 131, 149, 151, 155, 156
Gabol, Nadia 149
Ghalib, Mirza 2, 47, 283
Ghauri, Shahid 179, 182, 203, 247, 248

Haider, Salim 85
Haq, Zia-ul 19, 43, 59, 64, 71, 171, 174, 176, 212, 219, 220, 261, 309
Haroon, Abdullah 130
Haroon, Mahmud 130, 136
Haroon, Yusuf 130
Hasan, Mehdi 18
Hassan, Munawar 55
Hekmatyar, Gulbuddin 61
Hotchand, Seth Naomul 33
Hussain, Altaf 74, 80, 82, 83, 86, 87, 89, 90, 92, 93, 95, 97, 100, 102, 105, 106, 109, 110, 143, 163, 169, 171, 208, 220, 264, 272, 276, 299, 304, 317, 322

IJT 19, 45, 54, 55, 58–66, 68–75, 80, 89, 90, 109, 110, 113, 120, 169, 170, 202, 205
Insha, Ibn-e- 55

Jalib, Habib 53, 57
Jalil, Nasreen 123, 124
Jhangvi, Haq Nawaz 171, 176, 177, 228
JI 19, 55, 61, 64, 68, 71–73, 84, 107, 120, 167–170, 202, 210, 311
JuD 178, 180

Kalim, Major 31, 75, 104, 303
Khaliquzzaman, Chaudhry 135
Kamal, Mustafa 107, 124, 270, 321
Kati Pahari 246, 260, 273
Kazmi, Amir Haider 83
Kazmi, Javed 95
Khan, Ayub 28, 36, 44, 56–58, 71, 129, 132, 134–137, 168, 289, 292, 296, 300, 334
Khan, Amir 86, 177
Khan, Chaudhry Aslam 155
Khan, Fahim 65, 69
Khan, Fatehyab Ali 60
Khan, Imran Ahmed 250
Khan, Mairaj Muhammad 56–58, 60, 136, 297
Khan, Muhammad 264, 265, 278
Khan, Muhammad Bahadur 95
Khan, Naimatullah 169, 185
Khan, Nawab Muzaffar 84
Khan, Saleemullah 171
Khan, Sir Syed Ahmed 81, 95
Khani, Akram Qaim 62, 63, 65–68, 297
Korangi 5, 7, 36, 37, 40, 90, 104, 154, 156, 173, 177, 228, 229, 256, 261, 292, 303
KU 59–61, 66, 68–77, 80, 83, 84, 87, 90, 97, 109, 199, 201, 205, 247, 298, 299

Ladla, Baba 152, 161, 308
Lal Masjid 200
Langra, Javed 109
Lalu, Haji 133–135, 138, 140, 152
Landhi 37, 40, 75, 90, 95, 104, 106, 118, 156, 177, 180–182, 187, 217,

220, 226, 228, 229, 250, 252, 256, 303
Liaquatabad 7, 29, 30, 41, 45, 46, 58, 84, 109, 111, 242, 244, 252, 286, 289, 304
Lyari 7, 14, 15, 29, 30, 33, 35–39, 123–161, 163, 176–178, 180, 181, 186, 203, 213, 214, 223, 225, 226, 229–232, 240, 243–245, 249, 251–257, 261, 262, 271, 272, 278, 306
Ludhianvi, Maulana Yusuf 174, 175, 185

Malik, Rehman 187, 198
Maududi, Abul Ala 55, 167
Mehsud, Hakimullah 186, 190
Mirza, Zulfikar 139, 149, 155, 231, 309
MQM 3, 7, 11, 13, 15, 19, 21, 29–33, 43, 44, 47, 50–52, 66, 70, 73, 75, 76, 79–83, 86, 89–127, 134, 140, 141, 144, 149, 150, 152–159, 163, 164, 168–171, 177, 178, 180–186, 189, 190, 201–233, 236, 244–248, 250, 252, 254, 257, 259, 263–278, 281, 289, 294, 295, 301, 302, 305, 309, 310, 315, 316, 322, 323, 326
Muhammad, Khaled Sheikh 183, 314
Mukhtar, Habibullah 175, 185
Musharraf, Pervez 32, 103, 104, 108, 118, 139, 172, 200, 209, 210, 214, 231–233, 280

Nadeem, Abdul Ghafoor 176
Naqi, Hussain 60
Nasir, Hasan 56
NATO 152, 275, 276, 322
Nawaz, Asif 31
New Karachi 5, 7, 37, 41, 180, 182, 227
North Karachi 7, 177, 261
NSF 56, 57, 59–63, 66, 67, 71, 74, 76, 81, 83, 110, 130, 135–137, 301

Operation Clean-up 36, 75, 106, 107, 155, 215, 216, 217, 219, 295, 302
OPP 263, 266, 280, 292
Orangi 4, 5, 7, 45–47, 108, 155, 187, 226, 242, 249, 257, 264, 265, 271

PAC 7, 29, 105, 118, 119, 125, 126, 139, 146, 148, 150–161,163, 180, 186, 205, 227, 229, 231, 243, 249, 251, 254, 275, 278, 310
Pappu, Arshad 134, 135, 140, 150, 152, 153, 155, 160
Patel, Abdul Qadir 151
PPP 29, 30, 31, 33, 58, 60, 62, 64–66, 72, 75, 84, 100, 102, 103, 108, 110, 118, 119, 127, 131, 134, 139, 140, 142–145, 147, 149–159, 168, 169, 181, 184, 189, 208, 210, 211–213, 221, 226, 231, 232, 261, 262, 264, 266, 267, 269, 272, 277, 278, 280, 300, 309, 323
PTI 102, 103, 154, 158

Qadri, Mumtaz Hussein 179
Qadri, Saleem 178–180
Qasba Colony 7, 47, 49, 154, 225, 242, 295

Rahman, Perween 39, 266, 280, 282
Rehman, Wali ur 187
Rizvi, Akhtar 85
Rizvi, Hyder Abbas 220

Saddar 18, 34, 36, 37, 123, 138, 152, 166, 180, 245, 247, 256
Saeed, Qari 176

Sahil, Zeeshan 1, 2
Shahzad, Saleem 83, 86–90, 97, 99, 302
Shakir, Parveen 21–23
Shamzai, Nizamuddin 174, 175
Sharif, Nawaz 31, 32, 279
Shiv Sena 104, 269
Siddiqi, Anwar Ehsan 17, 55
Sohrab Goth 30, 44, 46, 47, 242, 294, 295
SSP 170, 171, 175, 176–183, 203, 227, 228, 248, 290, 311, 312
ST 165, 178, 179, 182, 183
Syed, G.M. 86, 109, 304
Syed, Shahi 26, 29, 81

'Tapi', Owais Muzaffar 156
Taqi, Syed Muhammad 85
Talpur, Faryal 157
Tariq, Azam 172, 176, 177
Tariq, Azim 169
Thanvi, Maulana Ehteshamul Haq 167
Tonki, Mufti Wali Hasan 174
Tipu, Salamullah 54, 62, 65, 67–69, 298
TTP 104, 164, 184–188, 190, 192–195, 200, 228

Usmani, Maulana Shabbir Ahmad 166, 171, 174

Wahab, Fauzia 150

Zaidi, Bushra 45, 270, 275
Zardari, Asif Ali 131, 139, 140, 153, 156, 158
Zikri, Ghaffar 141, 142, 150, 152, 161
Zubair, Ilyas 176